THE
Catholicism
Answer Book

The 300 Most Frequently Asked Questions

REV. JOHN TRIGILIO JR., PhD, ThD AND
REVEREND KENNETH BRIGHENTI, PhD

SOURCEBOOKS, INC.
NAPERVILLE, ILLINOIS

Published by Sourcebooks, Inc.
P.O. Box 4410, Naperville, Illinois 60567-4410
(630) 961-3900
Fax: (630) 961-2168
www.sourcebooks.com

Library of Congress Cataloging-in-Publication Data

Brighenti, Kenneth.
  The Catholicism answer book : the 300 most frequently asked questions / Kenneth D. Brighenti and John Trigilio, Jr.
      p. cm.
  Includes index.
  1. Catholic Church--Doctrines--Miscellanea. 2. Theology, Doctrinal--Popular works. I. Trigilio, John. II. Title.

BX1754.3.B75 2007
282--dc22
                                                    2006038963

Printed and bound in the United States of America.
VP 10 9 8 7 6 5

Nihil Obstat: Rev. Msgnr. James M. Cafone, M.A., S.T.D.
                Censor Librorum
                December 20, 2007

Imprimatur: Most Rev. John J. Myers, D.D., J.C.D.
                Archbishop of Newark
                December 26, 2007
                Feast of Saint Stephen, Protomartyr

Dedication

This book is dedicated to the former Josef Cardinal Ratzinger, now His Holiness **Pope Benedict XVI**, the Vicar of Christ, Successor of Saint Peter, Bishop of Rome and Servant of the Servants of God. He and Pope John Paul the Great were our heroes during our seminary training and throughout our priesthood; to His Eminence **Francis Cardinal Arinze**, Prefect of Divine Worship and the Discipline of the Sacraments; to the **Most Rev. Kevin C. Rhoades** (Bishop of Harrisburg) and **Reverend Mother Angelica** (Abbess and founder of EWTN), **Mother Vicar Catherine** and all the **Poor Clare Nuns of Perpetual Adoration** at Our Lady of the Angels Monastery, Hanceville, AL ; to **Rev. Fr. Robert Levis, PhD**, for all his wisdom, knowledge, inspiration, counsel, advice, and most of all his holy example of priestly piety and staunch orthodoxy; and to all the faithful members of the **Confraternity of Catholic Clergy**.

In loving memory of His Holiness Pope John Paul II the Great, Doctor of Light, and of John Trigilio, Sr. (father), Mary Jo Trigilio (sister), Michael Trigilio (brother) and Joseph Trigilio (brother)

Acknowledgments

We would like to thank the following for their prayers and support throughout this project: our **mothers** (Norma Brighenti and Elizabeth Trigilio); **father** (Percy Brighenti); our **friends** (Lou & Sandy Falconeri, Drs. Keith & Christina Burkhart, MD, Thomas & Bridgette McKenna, Michael Drake, Doug Keck, Colin Donnovan, Stephen Beaumont, Noah Lett, Michael Warsaw, Ned & Lee South, Sam Ranelli) and especially the **religious sisters and friars** (Missionary Franciscans of the Eternal Word; Franciscan Friars of the Renewal; Fathers of Mercy; Religious Teachers Filippini, Villa Walsh, NJ; Discalced Carmelites Nuns of Erie, PA and Flemington, NJ; Dominican Nuns of the Perpetual Rosary, Lancaster, PA)

Contents

CREED—CATHOLIC DOCTRINE

THIS SECTION HANDLES QUESTIONS ABOUT CATHOLIC TEACHINGS (DOGMAS AND DOCTRINE).

Chapter 1

WHO IS GOD?

This chapter looks at questions about God, the Trinity, and Creation.

- Question 1. How do we know there is a God?
- Question 2. Is God male, female, or neither?
- Question 3. Why is the Holy Trinity not actually three gods?
- Question 4. Creation or evolution: which is it?
- Question 5. If God is all good, then why is there evil in the world?
- Question 6. Did God make the devil? And if he did, why?
- Question 7. What color (race) is God?
- Question 8. Did Creation actually take six days?
- Question 9. Do angels earn their wings?
- Question 10. If God created Eve from Adam's rib, then why do men have the same number of ribs as women?
- Question 11. What was the original sin?
- Question 12. Did God create alien life on other planets?

Question 1. How do we know there is a God?

The most obvious question anyone asks a believer is "How do you know God exists?" It's a simple question that has both a simple and a complicated answer. First, the easy part: faith is believing in something or someone you cannot see or believing in what cannot be proven. In other words, faith depends on not having any evidence; otherwise, it would not be faith. So those who believe in God or in a supreme being are taking the word of others or just trusting their own instincts that such an almighty divinity does exist. Many people, whether they are Jewish, Christian, or Islamic, whether Roman Catholic, Eastern Orthodox, or Protestant, believe in God because they believe in the revealed Word of God, called Sacred Scripture or the Bible.

A more complicated answer is that Catholic Christianity does believe you can prove the existence of God. Reason can conclude that a supreme being exists and is necessary, but only faith (believing what cannot or is not known) tells us that there is but one God (monotheism). Judaism, Christianity, and Islam believe in only one God, and Christianity is the only of the three to believe that there are three Divine Persons in that one God. Human reason could never figure out the mystery of how there can be three persons but not three gods. Faith is needed to believe that doctrine, and some people never embrace that faith.

The fact that God exists can be known by reason alone, or it can be believed by faith. The ancient Greeks and Romans used philosophy (logic and reason) centuries before Christ to prove the existence of God or a supreme being. Saint Thomas Aquinas was a Catholic philosopher and theologian in the thirteenth century AD who used that same ancient reasoning to demonstrate the reasonableness of anyone "knowing" that God exists, regardless of whether or not they have faith. He showed that the existence of God can be proved by reason, but after that, one needed supernatural faith to believe the supernatural revelation about the nature of God (for example, the Trinity).

Aquinas used five proofs to demonstrate that, using human reason alone, any human being could know that there is a God. The first method is called motion. This is not physical movement from point A to point B on a map or on a road. It means moving from being purely potential to being actual. Philosophers call this motion "potency into act." So, for example, the sculpture of the Pieta done by Michelangelo was potential until it moved into actuality once the artist began chiseling the stone. The finished product was first potential and then made actual, but not by itself. The artist was the "mover," that is, the one who moved the "potential Pieta" to become the "actual Pieta." He did this by hammering away at the marble until he finished. Were there no artist, then the potential sculpture would remain potential forever. Only something already actual can move something else from being potential to being actual. You and I were potential human beings until our parents moved us into being actual once we were conceived.

Aquinas reasoned that the entire universe was potential (before the Big Bang) until something or someone moved it from potency to act (from being a potential universe to being an actual universe). Since everything has a beginning, then that must mean everything was potential at one time. Only a "prime mover" or something always actual and never potential, could be considered a supreme being. If God had a beginning, then there would have been a time when there was no God; if that were the case, then who or what would have moved Him from being a potential God to being an actual God? Aquinas said reason compels us to discover there must have always been something which always existed, the Prime Mover, who moves everything from being possible to being real.

If your head does not hurt yet, hold on. The second proof is called causality. Every crime sleuth from Sherlock Holmes to Lord Peter Whimsey to Miss Marple solves the murder mystery based on the principle of cause and effect. A dead body is found in the room with five bullet holes and a knife in the back. That is the effect. Something and someone (the murderer) caused a living person to become a corpse. Bullets and knives do not kill people; people kill people. Causality is the underpinning of science, logic, and most of our experiential knowledge. We see a burnt piece of paper (the effect) and automatically reason that something or someone was the source (the cause) of the burning. It is nothing more than connecting the dots, so to speak. Aquinas reasoned, therefore, that every effect has a cause; otherwise, it would not exist. You and I are effects, and our parents are the causes. He also reasoned that every cause was in turn an effect of a previous cause. Grandma and Grandpa had something to do with us, too, since without them (cause) they would have had no children (effect) and without those children growing up to become our parents (cause), there would have been no us (effect).

Therefore, if we reason backwards, like we did with motion, and deduce that every cause must have had a previous cause, there must be a first cause like there was the prime mover. This first cause is the cause of all causes. It had no cause since it has always existed. The Uncaused Cause, the Cause of All Causes and the Prime

Mover, can be called God or the Supreme Being, if you like. Aquinas never claimed this was as theatrical as the burning bush that Moses encountered, but it makes sense.

The third proof is called necessity. As important as your boss thinks he is, in reality, the universe would not cease to exist if he ceased to exist—he is not necessary. But don't tell him that unless you don't want that raise you've been asking for! No matter how important, nothing in the world or in the universe is absolutely necessary. Everything is *contingent*; that means it does not have to exist in order for reality to exist. Only one being is necessary, and that is the Source of being itself, the Being that keeps everything in existence. Causality and motion merely explain how something got here, namely, everything is created and has an origin. Necessity and contingency, on the other hand, show us that something or someone is needed to keep things going even after they are made. Edison may have invented the light bulb, but he died, and we still use electric lights well after his death. Electricity is needed, however, to keep any and all light bulbs working. Think of the Necessary Being, the Being itself, or the Existence itself (you can even call it God or the Supreme Being), as the electricity which *keeps* everything in existence. That which keeps in existence everything there is, is a necessary being. Everything which depends on that necessary being is contingent. Head hurt yet?

The fourth proof is called gradation. There is a hierarchy of being in the universe. First, at the most fundamental level, even at the subatomic, there is inanimate matter and energy. It exists, but it is not alive. Then you move up into the food chain and we have the second level of being: plant life (vegetative). Basic, simple, uncomplicated, plant life carries on three activities: nutrition, growth, and reproduction. The third level of being, however, is more complicated. While it has the same three principles, it also has sensation. Animal life is higher than plant life because these creatures have bodies which transmit information (data) from their senses to their brains. Though these brains act on instinct, when a sound is heard through their ears or images are seen by their eyes, animals react as instinct dictates. This fourth level of being incorporates the first two but goes into a much more sophisticated mechanism. Human life not only consists of nutrition, growth, and reproduction (as does plant life), and has sense knowledge from the physical body (as does animal life), but it also involves the ability to reason. Human beings have rational intellects and free will. While animals act out of instinct, only men and women can make free choices and base them on reason. When was the last time you saw a hungry dog or cat turn away food just because they were on a diet and needed to lose weight? Pooch or Kitty will eat out of instinct whenever they are hungry. Human beings can resist hunger and freely choose to diet. The beings above humans are angels. These are beings which, unlike us, are not body and soul. They are pure spirit. They have intellect and will, like we do, but they are not limited by physical bodies which can feel hunger, pain, cold, heat, sickness, and death. Angels cannot die since they are spiritual beings with no mortal bodies to hinder them. The last and highest level of being, however, is not angelic but divine. Angels may not die, but they were created. They are limited and finite, while the fullness of being is God. He is the highest, the Supreme Being. God has no beginning and no end. God always existed. Since He is everywhere (omnipresent) and knows everything (omniscient) and can do anything (omnipotent), He is the pinnacle and zenith of being itself.

The fifth and last proof is called governance. This has nothing to do with city hall, Parliament, Congress, or the White House. Something or someone with intelligence created a world and a universe which operates on intelligent and rational laws and principles. Whether you believe in Creationism or subscribe to a form of evolution, you recognize that there is a systematic plan upon which reality operates. The laws of physics and chemistry were not created by scientists; they were discovered by them. Those laws apply equally in any country and on any planet. Governance merely means an intelligent Being created the intelligent laws and systems that maintain order and prevent chaos. That Governor can be called God.

Need an aspirin now? No one ever claimed these five proofs would convert an atheist overnight. They do show, however, that the existence of God can be known by reason. The pagan Romans and ancient Greeks, for example, among many other peoples, figured out there was a supreme being even without having that deity reveal himself. Yet that is the limit of human reason. We can only know that there *is* a God. To *know* God and not just know *about* Him involves faith. Faith allows you to believe in the truths revealed by God. Reason helps make some sense of that, but much of the mystery of religion does not contradict reason; rather, it goes beyond the limitations of human reason. Then you just have to believe.

Question 2. Is God male, female, or neither?

God is a pure spirit, which means that He has no physical body. God is neither male nor female, neither masculine nor feminine. God has no gender. Human beings and animals have gender since we do not reproduce asexually. Males and females need their counterpart in order to reproduce. Men and women complement one another since neither gender possesses the fullness of humanity. We are incomplete on our own. We need others. God does not need anyone. God is perfect and is the fullness of being.

So why do we use the masculine pronoun "He" and say God is a "He"? The answer goes beyond mere cultural or patriarchal tradition. Catholic Christianity, like all other Christian religions (Protestant or Eastern Orthodox), firmly believes in the doctrine of the Triune God. Divine revelation, which comes from God, revealed that there is but one God (monotheism) but that one God is also Triune: three persons in one God (trinitarianism). It is God who revealed Himself as God the Father, God the Son, and God the Holy Spirit. The Bible is considered the inspired and revealed written word of God. It uses the pronoun "He" since God also reveals His "fatherhood" in the Old Testament. Jesus Christ, the Son of God, revealed His "sonship" in the New Testament. The Holy Spirit is portrayed as the spouse of the Virgin Mary by which she miraculously conceives and gives birth to Jesus, the Son of God. The Holy Spirit is also referred to with the male pronoun "He," as Mary, the mother, is "she."

Since Christianity staunchly believes that God is Father, Son, and Holy Spirit, then the use of the masculine or male pronoun is not considered anthropomorphic. It is revealed. Yet only the Second Person of the Trinity (Jesus) took on a human nature and had an actual human (male) body. God the Father and God the Holy Spirit have no physical bodies. The mystery of the Triune God, though, is that these three persons are distinct but not separate. Hence, what affects one person affects all three persons, and vice versa.

Male human beings, however, cannot misinterpret this to mean that they have an edge over women. Genesis (the first book of the Bible) tells us, "God created man in his own image, in the image of God created he him; male and female created he them" (1:27). This means that men and women are equal in the eyes of God. While there are physiological and emotional differences between the genders, spiritually men and women are alike. Using the masculine pronoun "He" when referring to the Almighty is nothing more than acknowledging the revealed relationship of God as Father, Son, and Holy Spirit. Those who try to be politically correct and use novel terms like "God our mother" or who refer to the Holy Spirit as "She" are guilty of perpetrating anthropomorphism.

The spousal relationship of husband and wife as also being male and female is seen in the Bible as well. God is portrayed as the faithful spouse, and Israel is His often unfaithful bride. Whenever the Hebrew people dabbled in idolatry and pagan worship, it was seen as violating the covenant between God and the chosen people. It is no coincidence that marriage between a man and woman whereby they become husband and wife is also called a covenant. God even tells the prophet Hosea to marry a harlot, Gomer, to symbolize the relationship between the faithful Lord and the unfaithful Israelites. No matter how many times she is unfaithful, the prophet takes her back. He never stops loving or forgiving her. Likewise, the faithful Lord never abandons or gives up on His unfaithful spouse, the children of Abraham. That spousal relationship of God as bridegroom and the chosen people as bride requires pronouns like "he" and "she" just to keep things sensible.

Jesus himself in the Gospel of the New Testament is portrayed as the new bridegroom and the Church as his bride. Biologically male in his humanity, Jesus in his divinity (because He is true God and true Man) has no gender per se. Yet, the pronoun "He" is also used not just because of His human masculinity but spiritually because Jesus Christ loves the Church as a groom loves his bride, says Saint Paul (Ephesians 5:25).

Question 3. Why is the Holy Trinity not actually three gods?

Christianity, like Judaism and Islam, is monotheistic. That means Christians espouse a belief in only one god. Polytheism is the belief in many gods. Unlike Jews and Muslims, however, Christians believe in a Triune god. This is not three gods, which would be polytheism. It is a belief that there is one God but there are three Persons in that one God. That concept is known as the Trinity. Common sense tells us that 1+1+1=3, so why is this not considered three gods? Well, that same math teaches us that 1x1x1=1. The three Persons of the Holy Trinity are distinct but not separate. Each has Its own name because each one is a distinct Person: God the Father, God the Son, and God the Holy Spirit. While three Persons, there is only one divine intellect and one divine will, which all three Persons share equally. This means that what the Father knows, the Son and the Spirit know. What one Person wills, all three will.

The Holy Trinity is the greatest mystery of the Christian religion. The monotheistic dogma of one God must be kept intact but so, too, must the revealed truth of three Persons in one God. Some may confuse the Trinity with multiple personalities or with different manifestations or expressions of the same deity. Neither is true.

The Trinity is one God, three Persons: Father, Son, and Holy Spirit. This is why Christians invoke the Holy Trinity every time they bless themselves. Jesus said to baptize *"in the name of the Father, and of the Son, and of the Holy Spirit"* (Matthew 28:19).

While the human intellect can never fully understand the mystery of the Trinity, for to do so would be to know God as God knows Himself (and then you would *be* God), our human reason can appreciate some elements of this revealed truth. The term Father implies an offspring. If God the Father was always God the Father from all eternity and there was never a time when He was not God the Father, then this implies that God the Son always existed from all eternity as well. My dad was a father only after I, his eldest child, was born. While my father preexisted before me, he was not a "father" until he had a son. Likewise, if there was even a second when there was no God the Son, then that would mean there was an instant where there was no God the Father. Fatherhood depends on having children (as does motherhood). So God the Father is eternally Father, therefore the Son is eternally Son. Sonship also implies parenthood. It is a word which defines a relationship. Father and son is a relationship. There is no father without a son and no son without a father.

These two persons, Father and Son, are distinct (hence the different names) but they are never separate as they share the same divine nature and essence. Both are equally divine; both are God. The two of them loving each other perfectly and eternally and infinitely, "spirates" the third person, the Holy Spirit. He is the fruit of the love of God the Father and God the Son. Since both exist from all eternity, both love each other from all eternity. The mutual love of these two persons is personified in the Holy Spirit. The Catholic Mass begins and ends with the sign of the cross, where the priest and people bless themselves with their right hands, touching their foreheads, their chest, and their left and then their right breast. While doing so, they say, "In the name of the Father, and of the Son, and of the Holy Spirit." The priest continues the opening of the Mass with "The grace of Our Lord Jesus Christ, the love of God the Father, and the fellowship of the Holy Spirit be with you all" (2 Corinthians 13:14). This phrase, from Saint Paul, shows that the early Church believed in the Holy Trinity. The Apostles Creed, which goes back to the time of the Apostles (first century AD), and the Nicene Creed of 325 AD, profess a belief in God the Father, Son, and Holy Spirit.

Question 4. Creation or evolution: which is it?

Catholicism staunchly believes in Creation, that God created the world, the universe, and especially the human soul. It believes that God created man and woman in the image and likeness of God, as told to us in Genesis. Creation is to make something out of nothing. It is not changing one substance into another; it is making something which did not previously exist. Genesis 1:1 tells us, "In the beginning, God created the heavens and the earth." Verse 27 of that same chapter says "God created man in his own image, in the image of God he created him; male and female he created them." The Apostles Creed and Nicene Creed also profess a belief "*in God, the Father almighty, creator of heaven and earth.*"

That said, what about evolution? Does the Catholic Church condemn or embrace evolution? Atheistic evolution, which denies the existence and the necessity of a Supreme Being and Creator, is very much condemned. However, a modified theory of evolution that retains the existence and the necessity of a divine creator is allowed. God could use evolutionary processes to change aspects of His creation. This would imply that God created evolution just as He created the laws of physics, the laws of chemistry and mathematics, and the laws of gravity. If evolution does exist and operate, it must be part of divine will since nothing can or does exist or happen outside the will of God.

What Pope Pius XII (1939–1958) taught in his encyclical letter *Humani Generis* (1950) was that Catholic faith demanded a belief in *monogenism*—that the human race originated from one set of human parents (named Adam and Eve in the Bible). *Polygenism* is the theory that the human race came from several sets of parents. Thirty-three years later, a group of biochemists in California, avowed agnostics, discovered that mitochondrial DNA showed that every human being on the earth who ever lived or will live is related, since all men and women can genetically be traced back to one original biological woman. She is the genetic mother of the human race.

When proponents of evolution leave God out of the equation, it is considered antithetical to the Catholic Christian faith. Any scientific theory proposing that human life is nothing more than a chance mixture of amino acids under favorable conditions independently evolving into higher forms of life is not acceptable to Catholicism. If a theory maintains that natural forces were underway, but does not deny the intelligent design behind these physical and biological operations, that is acceptable. Claiming that humans evolved from apes is one thing, but to deny that at some point the Divine Creator endowed human beings with a rational and immortal soul is considered heresy. Genesis 2 says God took the dirt of the earth and breathed into it the breath of life, and man was thus created. Dirt by itself will never evolve into an immortal soul. Nature may or may not change entire species of animals, but the spiritual dimension of mankind that makes men and women the image and likeness of God lies in the immortal soul created by God. Apes and all other animals do not have immortal souls. Only human beings do.

Some Christians maintain God created the world in exactly six days of twenty-four hours each. Others maintain that the word "day" used by Genesis in the Bible is a figure of speech—an analogy or metaphor. Catholicism teaches that it is for the scientists to discover how Creation took place. Religion explains *who* did and *why*. Science merely discovers *how* and *when*. A day could represent a period or epoch, or it could mean a day as we experience it. Before Creation, there was no time and no space, so it is difficult to explain and describe where and when before there was a where and a when. God existed from all eternity, and He exists outside of time and space, so He is not limited to nor constrained by the same spatiotemporal reality you and I are stuck in.

Question 5. If God is all good, then why is there evil in the world?

God did not create evil, rather, good beings (angels and men) chose to become evil, and their evil deeds (sins) caused a rupture in the peace and harmony of the universe. The first book of the Bible tells us that God created the world in six days and saw that it was good. Lucifer and the other bad angels were originally created good, but they made a freewill decision to rebel against God. Their sin resulted in the creation of hell. Once there, the fallen angels became known as devils and demons. Lucifer then became Satan.

Adam and Eve, the first humans and the parents of the human race, were also created good. Creation existed in peace (tranquility of order) until the sin of Adam and Eve came along. Their sin was not just disobedience to the divine law of God, but was also an act of rebellion and an infection to their souls. The entire created universe was tainted by original sin. Human nature was wounded, and the cosmos was shaken up and disturbed. No more perfect harmony, and hence there exist some occasional catastrophes like floods, earthquakes, fires, drought, blizzards, avalanches, tornadoes, hurricanes, tsunamis, and meteor collisions. These are sometimes known as physical or earthly evils. War, crime, violence, terrorism, hatred, bigotry, racism, and abuse are moral evils caused by man.

Had there been no sin, Adam and Eve would have never been expelled from the Garden of Paradise. There would have been no pain, no suffering, and no physical evils whatsoever. The blame for their existence is not on the Creator who made the world good, but on the creatures that freely chose to do and to become evil.

Question 6. Did God make the devil? And if He did, why?

God did not make the devil; He created the angel, Lucifer, who later of his own free will made himself into the devil by opposing the will of God. Just as Genesis tells us that God created everything inherently good ("and God saw that it was good"), it was only after sin that humans and some angels became evil of their own free choice. Other religions contend that there has always been an eternal struggle between good and evil, between God and the devil. That is called dualism and it is not Christian teaching. Revelation (Apocalypse) 12:3–9 speaks of a great heavenly battle between the Archangel Michael and the other angels (Lucifer and the third of the angelic host who followed him). The fallen angels were cast into hell and, once there, became known as devils or demons, whereas the two-thirds of the good angels went to heaven and are still called angels.

God originally created the devil and the devil's demonic followers as angels. Angels, unlike human beings, have no physical bodies. You and I know things by using our bodies, primarily the five senses; the human intellect then abstracts ideas from this sense data. Angels do not see, hear, taste, smell, or feel. Therefore, all the knowledge they have was given to them (infused) at the moment God created their intellect. Angels knew everything they will ever know at the moment they were created. Their choices or decisions are irrevocable and forever. Angels cannot change their minds. They had one chance and one chance only, but they knew that before they made their choice. Human beings can have incomplete information due to imperfect senses or due to imperfect judgment of their rational intellect on the information given. An optical illusion, for example, is not a case where our eyes are lying to us. Instead, it is an improper judgment of the mind. When someone concludes that a pencil in a glass of water is bent—when in actuality the light rays are bent through the water—it is our eyes that lead us to make that conclusion.

Lucifer and the other angels were given a test. What test we do not know. None of the angels were actually *in* heaven during or before the test. Once in heaven you can never leave, nor do you ever want to leave. The angels had to prove themselves to God, so God gave them a test. Theologians have speculated for ages what it could have been. Some contest it was that God revealed to them that He would create human beings next and that He would give them a test; those that passed would also be given the reward of heaven. Lucifer was one of the most intelligent of angels, and it is speculated his pride could not stomach sharing heaven with an inferior creature like man. Angels are as far above us in beauty, intelligence, and power as you and I are above ants, or even microbes.

Other theologians propose that God disclosed the fact He would create man, man would sin, and God would later forgive men and women since our human intellect and will is not like the angelic. We can change our minds and we can repent of evil or we can go bad after a life of goodness. Our capacity to change for the better or worse makes us different from the angels, who only have one chance to do good or evil. The scholars who promote this theory believe that Lucifer was outraged that man would be given a chance to repent or that he would be redeemed by a Savior while the fallen angels would have to spend eternity in punishment and damnation.

Some hypothesize that God showed a vision of Adam and said that, one day, an offspring of Adam would have to be worshipped as God, and the pride of Lucifer turned his heart full of anger and hatred. How dare an angel be asked to bow before a descendant of man, an inferior creature? This offspring, of course, refers to Jesus Christ, Who in His divinity is the Son of God, but in His humanity is the Son of Man, or a Son of Adam. That God would one day take on a human nature and would become one of us, but would never take an angelic nature and became one of them, would have further infuriated Lucifer.

Whatever the test was (this is all speculative), the Bible does tell us that Lucifer and his third were defeated by Michael and the other (good) two-thirds of the angels. Once in hell, he was forever known as the devil, Satan, or the Evil One. He made himself what he is today. God gave him a chance, as God gave Adam and Eve a chance. God gave Judas a chance; he could have freely chosen not to betray Christ for thirty pieces of silver, *or*, after he committed his sin, he could have repented—as did Peter and the other disciples who let Jesus down when He needed them most. Even evil tyrants like Adolf Hitler or Josef Stalin were originally created good. Each freely chose to become and to commit evil. Mother Teresa of Calcutta freely chose to do and be good while she lived on Earth. She could have chosen the path to darkness, evil, and sin, but she chose the path to goodness and holiness.

If God knew beforehand that Lucifer would go bad, why create him at all? Why not just spare the universe the devil in the long run? Fair question. Again, remember that God creates good. Only creatures with a free will can choose evil and sin, and then face the consequences of their choice. If God prevented the devil from being created merely because later, after being created, Lucifer would freely choose to go bad, then it is the same as not having a free will after all. If only those who choose good are allowed to exist, what freedom is that? That we can choose to do good or to do evil (although not choose what *is* good or evil) means there is a consequence to our decisions. Were the evil people and angels not allowed to exist before they even made their choice, it would not be just. It would be condemning a person *before* they commit the crime. Punishment must come after the fact, not in anticipation of it. For instance, imagine a parent disciplining a two-year-old child for bad behavior she will commit as a teenager.

Question 7. What color (race) is God?

God, being a pure spirit, has no physical body; therefore He has no race. Only creatures with a physical body have race. So God is neither white, black, European, African, American, nor Asian. Jesus Christ, the second Person of the Holy Trinity, did assume a human nature when He was conceived in the womb of His mother, the Virgin Mary. He had a male body, but he was a divine Person. His human nature came from his mother, who was of the Jewish (Hebrew) race and religion. We have no idea the color of His complexion, the color of His eyes or hair, his height or weight. He probably would have been darker in skin tone than those in Northern Europe two thousand years ago. At the time of Christ, racial labels like white or black did not exist. People were more known by the language they spoke, the land where they lived, the religion they practiced, and the culture they came from. Most obvious of all, He looked like any other adult male Jew living in that region at the time. Artistic representations of Jesus as being Asian, Northern European, Latin American, or African are just that: artistic symbols, not historical or theological tenets. Though Jesus was of Jewish ancestry, God as pure spirit, especially before the Incarnation (when Jesus was conceived in His mother's womb) two millennia ago, has no ethnic or racial configuration.

Question 8. Did Creation actually take six days?

The first chapter of Genesis (which is the first book of the Bible) tells the story of God creating the world in six days. On the seventh day, He rested. Some people believe that Creation literally took six calendar days, of twenty-four hours each.

Some creationist scientists go so far as to say that this is plausible due to Einstein's Theory of Relativity. Many people know—from high school science class or from watching *Star Trek*—that time slows down near a black hole. Since the gravitational pull is so enormous, not only is light unable to escape its clutch, but time itself is affected. If that is true, imagine how slow time would be at the epicenter of the Big Bang. At one moment in the early history and birth of the universe, all known matter was compacted into one very small and tight space. The density was enormous yet the size was small. Time near the center of the Big Bang would pass by more slowly than in the outer regions farther away from the center. So it is theoretically feasible that a literal day near or at the center of the Big Bang would appear to someone galaxies away as millions of years.

Another (and more plausible) explanation is that Genesis is not a science book. It is the revealed, inspired, and inerrant written word of God, yes; but it was not written by scientists or historians. God inspired human beings to write, but He did not choose scientists or historians. He chose men of faith to explain things of faith. The purpose of Genesis is to teach the truth that God is the Creator. The details of telling that truth are meant to be taken in context. As we will see in another question on how to interpret the Bible, Catholic Christianity warns its members never to take a Scripture text out of context, lest they get a pretext.

Figures of speech are not considered lies or deception, but neither can they be interpreted literally. If I say someone is pulling my leg, I mean he is joking with me—not that he is yanking on one of my limbs. Similarly, the Bible uses many forms of literature and literary genre, and some of those are metaphor, analogy, hyperbole, and other figures of speech. So when the Bible says God created the earth in one day, it may just be a figure of speech; the intended meaning and faithful interpretation is that God created in a sequential order, or that He works systematically, not chaotically.

Question 9. Do angels earn their wings?

Hollywood often portrays angels as either naked cherubs floating in the air or as bumbling esoteric creatures trying to protect human beings from themselves. A popular storyline consists of an angel trying to earn his wings by doing good deeds for a human being on Earth. If the angel succeeds in his mission, God gives him his wings. Some movies even depict angels as deceased humans who, before entering the pearly gates, must earn their eternal reward.

Catholicism repudiates all of that. First of all, human beings are not angels and they can never become angels, just as animals never become human and plants never become animals. When human beings die and go to heaven, they are then called saints. Angels are good spirits who already live in heaven. They were never human in a previous life. Their test took place before God created the earth or Adam and Eve.

No one earns their way to heaven, either. Pelagianism is the heresy that anyone can work their way to salvation. Saint Augustine vehemently opposed this idea in the fifth century AD. He taught that any good work, corporal or spiritual works of mercy, could only be done efficaciously by the power of divine grace. Whereas Martin Luther proposed the notion of faith alone (*sola fide*), St. Augustine would have preferred the idea of grace alone (*sola gratia*). Grace is needed to accept and persevere in faith and to perform meritorious good works.

It is euphemism and anthropomorphism to speak of angels earning their wings. As spirits with no bodies, they actually neither need nor have wings. Religious art depicts angels with wings and saints with halos. Both are devices used to symbolize something invisible to the human eye. In the movie *It's A Wonderful Life*, Clarence the angel needs to save George Bailey in order to earn his wings. If Clarence had really been a guardian angel, he would have already had his "wings." As an angel, he would have already gone to heaven, and there is no. need to prove anything once there.

Question 10. If God created Eve from Adam's rib, then why do men have the same number of ribs as women?

The creation of Eve as told in Genesis 2:21–22, where God puts Adam to sleep and takes one of his ribs to fashion a woman (Eve), is not a feat of genetic engineering. Neither is it to be understood literally as if it were a scene from *The Island of Dr. Moreau*. When we speak of heartache, we do not mean a literal coronary arrest but a figurative emotional distress. Likewise, the use of Adam's rib is a poignant way to describe the union of husband and wife in marriage because, after God creates Eve, Adam takes her as his wife and says, "This one, at last, is bone of my bones and flesh of my flesh; This one shall be called 'woman,' for out of 'her man' this one has been taken" (2:23).

Unlike the animals and plants that God created in the first chapter of Genesis just by speaking (and God said, let there be…), Adam is formed from the dust of earth and God blows the breath of life into him. Eve is created from Adam's rib. This is a way of saying that human beings are different from the rest of creation. Made in the image and likeness of God, man is profoundly different from the rest of creation.

Question 11. What was the original sin?

First of all, the Bible never says that Adam and Eve took a bite out of an apple. The fruit they ate from the tree of knowledge of good and evil is never identified in Sacred Scripture. Artists over the centuries have used the apple merely out of habit and tradition. What kind of fruit they ate is irrelevant. The point is that Adam and Eve disobeyed God.

Original sin is the term used to describe the first sin of our first parents. As prototypes of the human race, their sin had consequences—not just for them, but for their descendants. It is called "original" since it was the first sin committed by any human. It was a sin since it was a deliberate and voluntary act against the will of God.

The effects of original sin are significant. If Adam and Eve had been exposed to radioactive material, they would have passed the effects on genetically to subsequent generations. Spiritually, their sin was transmitted in the same way. We inherit their sin as much as we inherit our genes. For us, original sin is not that we committed a sin while in the womb of our mother. Rather, it means we inherit a proclivity to sin; we are born with a tendency to sin. When you were born, you did not have childhood diseases like measles or chicken pox, but you were born with a vulnerability and susceptibility to these nasty illnesses. When your parents took you to the pediatrician, who inoculated you with vaccines, those vaccines helped your body to fight off these diseases should you ever be exposed to them.

Original sin is like being born without a resistance to temptation. When God created the first man and woman, He endowed them with sanctifying grace, which makes a person holy. Though sanctifying grace does not make you sinless, it makes you spiritually strong so you can better fight temptations to commit sin and evil.

Original sin wounded human nature like a viral or bacterial infection can wound a physical body. Disobeying God is more than just breaking divine law—it is dangerous to the health of your soul. Sin is as much a spiritual disease as it is an act of defiance against the law of God.

The parents of the human race infected their spiritual health with sin, and that first sin wounded their human nature and, by inheritance, ours. First, there was the loss of sanctifying grace, which meant their descendants would be born vulnerable to the temptation to sin. Second, their souls were wounded, which resulted in a darkened intellect, a weakened will, and a disordering of the lower passions (emotions like happiness, sadness, etc.). This is why everyone at some time, regardless of intelligence, can have trouble thinking clearly when it comes to moral dilemmas presented while under great stress and strain. Then there are times when we know what we should do, but we just lack the resolve or perseverance to see it through. (Ask anyone who has been on a diet or has tried to give up smoking.) Even the Bible tells us that "the spirit is willing but the flesh is weak" (Matthew 26:41).

The next consequence of original sin is the disordering of the lower passions. God did not create robots, androids, or Vulcans; He created humans who experience emotions as part of their human nature. Jesus Christ, who was a divine person (second Person of the Holy Trinity) had a fully human nature (with emotions) and a fully divine nature. The only difference is that His human nature was not wounded since He was not conceived or born in original sin like the rest of us. His emotions were always under the control of his intellect and will. Thanks to original sin, the rest of us often have to wage a battle with our own passions and emotions to keep them in line.

Death and the loss of heaven were the final consequences of original sin. God had given mankind the preternatural gift of immortality, and the disease of sin killed that. The gravity of the offense is measured by the dignity of the person. If I slap my brother, it is wrong. If I slap my mother, it is worse because she is my mother and deserves more respect and honor. Disobeying God is a slap in His face, and since His dignity as the Almighty Lord of Heaven and Earth is infinite, the offense against Him is equally infinite. Original sin meant humanity *needed* a savior and a redeemer.

Question 12. Did God create alien life on other planets?

If scientists ever discover any alien life on other planets or here on earth (after traveling from their home world or galaxy), it would necessarily mean that God did in fact create other forms of life, and we would know this by using the same logic we employed to deduce that the human race had a Creator. Aside from the characters portrayed on *Star Trek* or *Doctor Who*, we have no idea what intelligent alien life would look like. It could be humanoid, or it may not be. The big question is whether or not extraterrestrial aliens would have immortal souls.

Human beings have souls because the Bible tells us that we are made in the image and likeness of God. God is a pure spirit and has no body. Jesus took on a human nature and a human body when He became our Savior. The human body in and of itself is distinct from the soul. Human persons are a union of a body and a soul. Intelligent or rational alien life could be in the form of physical bodies which do not resemble mankind in any way, shape, or form, but if the creatures have intellect and free will, it would be a safe guess that such beings might also possess immortal souls. If intelligent life is ever found out in the recesses of the universe, evangelization (sharing faith) would not be an alien concept since many have done it before with alien cultures though not yet with alien species. God has a divine intellect and a divine will, and mankind has a human intellect and a human will. While people are made in the image and likeness of God, it is not their human bodies but their immortal souls that are in the image of God. The body is not incidental, however, since Christianity firmly believes and teaches the resurrection of all the dead at the end of time.

Chapter 2

WHERE IN THE BIBLE?

This chapter examines the questions about divine revelation and Sacred Scripture, Bible versions, translations, and interpretations.

Question 13. What is the difference between a Catholic Bible and a Protestant Bible?

A Catholic Bible has seventy-three books in it while a typical Protestant Bible has sixty-six books. Both of them have the same number of books in the New Testament (twenty-seven); it is in the Old Testament that the two differ. Catholic Bibles have seven more books (Judith, Ecclesiasticus or Sirach, Wisdom, Baruch, Maccabees 1 and 2, and Tobit) because they are using the older Greek (Alexandrian) list of authorized books, called a canon, going back to the year 250 BC. At that time, seventy scholars were commissioned to translate the thirty-nine already existing Old Testament books from Hebrew into Greek. They then included the seven other (called *deuterocanonical*) books which were originally written in Greek by Jews in Exile. By the third century BC, two-thirds of the Jews were no longer in their homeland. The Babylonians and Assyrians had exiled a good portion of the Jewish people, and only a third were left behind. That small portion lived in what was then called Palestine (modern-day Israel), and they spoke and wrote in Hebrew. The majority of Jews who were in exile, however, were forbidden to teach their young the Hebrew language, so they grew up knowing Greek since it was the language of the Empire (of Alexander the Great), commerce, and academia.

Because those seventy scholars were alleged to have taken seventy days to translate the Hebrew scriptures into Greek, the Latin word for seventy (*septuaginta*) or the Roman numeral LXX was given to designate this collection of forty-six books (thirty-nine translated from Hebrew into Greek, plus seven originally written in Greek). Judaism and then Christianity accepted and used all forty-six books of the Septuagint until the year 90 AD, when the Jewish religious leaders decided to revise the list of authorized books. After the Temple of Jerusalem was destroyed by the Romans in 70 AD, the Christians and Jews parted from each other and established separate religions. Twenty years later, as Jewish scholars became concerned that the Greek Christian influence had to be removed, the seven books of the Old Testament, which were never originally written in Hebrew but only in Greek, were dropped from the list. This newer Hebrew list is sometimes called the Palestinian Canon because of the name of the Holy Land at that time. Christians, however, now independent, retained their older Greek (Alexandrian) list of forty-six books, while the Jews kept only thirty-nine.

Saint Jerome was commissioned by Pope Damasus I in 400 AD to translate all the Hebrew and Greek texts of the Old and New Testaments into one language and one volume. At that time, Latin was the official language of the Empire. He used the Septuagint Greek version and retained all forty-six Old Testament books with the twenty-seven New Testament books to formulate the first single-volume edition of the Christian Bible, totaling seventy-three books.

Things didn't change for fifteen centuries, until the Protestant Reformation. Martin Luther, an Augustinian monk, Catholic priest, and scripture scholar, knew the Jews had a shorter list of books (thirty-nine) compared to the longer list (forty-six), and he knew that some of the abuses and scandals in the late medieval church originated in a doctrine based on one of those deuterocanonical books (Maccabees, which is used to explain the Catholic doctrine of purgatory). The sin of selling indulgences was too much for Luther to stomach, and he responded with a rejection not only of the abuse but also of the doctrine that the dead needed prayers to get to heaven. He embraced the Hebrew (Palestinian) canon of thirty-nine books in the Old Testament, and the newly translated German Bible that contained sixty-six books with no deuterocanonical books included at all. With Maccabees gone, Luther hoped the abuse would go as well.

Catholics, on the other hand, since the Council of Trent, decided to keep the Greek (Alexandrian) canon of forty-six books in the Old Testament, because that was what the Christians knew and used at the time of Christ and the apostles. It was also the same list used by Saint Jerome for his Vulgate Bible and has been consistently used ever since. So since the time of the Reformation in the sixteenth century, there have been two kinds of the Bible: the Protestant and the Catholic, which are 99 percent identical in order and text except for those seven books written in the third century BC. Some Protestant Bibles now include them in a section called the Apocrypha, which comes at the end of the Old Testament before the Gospels of the New Testament. Catholic Bibles have always had these books, which they call deuterocanonical.

Both Bibles begin with Genesis and end with Revelation and have four Gospels. The only difference is the inclusion or exclusion of seven additional books in the Hebrew Scriptures (Christian Old Testament).

Question 14. What are the "lost" or "missing" books of the Bible?

The so-called "missing," "lost," or "forbidden" books of the Bible are the many writings which no Jewish or Christian group has ever considered inspired text. Only books considered divinely inspired have the guarantee of inerrancy (freedom from error).

Most of these "lost" texts were written two to three centuries after the apostles were long dead and buried, and their authorship and authenticity are greatly disputed.

The Protestant tradition calls these books in the Old Testament *Pseudepigrapha*, from the Greek meaning "false" writings, in contrast to what they label *Apocrypha*, meaning "hidden" writings. The Catholic Bible calls these lost books d*euterocanonical*.

Some examples of Pseudepigrapha (Protestant)/Apocrypha (Catholic) would be the books of Adam and Eve, Apocalypse of Moses, book of Enoch, Apocalypse of Adam, Apocalypse of Abraham, Martyrdom of Isaiah, Testaments of the Twelve Patriarchs, and the book of Jubilees.

What Protestants call Old Testament Apocrypha, Catholic and Eastern Orthodox call deuterocanonical: Baruch, Maccabees 1 and 2, Tobit, Judith, Ecclesiasticus (Sirach), and Wisdom. These seven books, plus some chapters in Daniel and Esther, are always in the Old Testament of Catholic Bibles and usually found in Protestant Bibles listed as Apocrypha.

In the New Testament, both Catholic and Protestant traditions merely use the term Apocrypha for the books left out which were never considered divinely inspired, like the Gospel of Thomas, Gospel of Philip, Gospel of James, Gospel of Nicodemus, Gospel of Peter, Death of Pilate, Acts of Andrew, Acts of Barnabas, Passing of Mary, History of Joseph the Carpenter, Apocalypse of Peter, the Revelation of Paul, and the infamous Gnostic Gospel of Mary Magdalene. These texts were never included in any Bible. Rather than classifying them as lost, missing, or even forbidden, most Christians simply call them Apocryphal.

Question 15. Is the Bible to be taken literally?

When you pick up a telephone book and read it, the author intends you to understand or interpret it literally. That means there is only one meaning for each word and phrase. The name and the phone number have but one meaning and if you get the wrong one, you will dial the wrong number and not reach the right person.

Other books and forms of literature which are considered nonfiction (which are to be taken as true), have a literal sense or meaning but can also have either a literal interpretation or a figurative interpretation. The literal sense is the immediate understanding of what each printed word means. When you read the word "salt" in the Bible, you know that it is an English noun that refers to a chemical compound known as sodium chloride. That is the literal sense of the word "salt." If you were reading a German Bible, you would have to know that the word "salt" is "salz," or "sale" in Italian; "sal" in Latin; "melah" in Hebrew; and "halas" in Greek. If you could not read the Greek or Hebrew alphabet, it would be impossible for you to recognize the literal sense of the word.

Knowing what the letters spell and what the words mean is the literal sense. The Bible and every written book depend upon it; they would be totally useless if no one could read and understand them. A literal interpretation is the opposite of a figurative or symbolic interpretation. In Matthew 5:13, Jesus says, "You are the *salt* of the earth." The literal sense is that the word "salt" refers to the substance chemists call sodium chloride. Does Jesus or the sacred author, however, intend a literal interpretation of that text? If so, it would mean that you and I are table salt. If all Scripture must be interpreted literally, then there is only one way of understanding the text. If, on the other hand, Jesus and the Gospel writer (in this case, Saint Matthew) intend a figurative interpretation, we call it a metaphor.

Jesus speaks metaphorically when He says, "You are the salt of the earth," since He is not asking us to place ourselves in salt shakers and sit on kitchen tables. He wants us to use the qualities of salt as a preservative and flavoring. Likewise, when Jesus says "I am the vine, you are the branches" (John 15:5), you must first be able to read and understand the words "vine" and "branches" to get the literal sense. The literal interpretation, however, would be that we are plants, whereas the metaphorical or figurative interpretation is that we must be connected to Christ like branches are to a vine.

Sometimes the text itself does not explicitly tell you or indicate whether or not the phrase is to be interpreted literally. Knowing when to interpret the Bible literally or figuratively is therefore important. Mark 9:47 says, "If your eye causes you to sin, pluck it out." Matthew 5:30 says, "And if your right hand causes you to sin, cut it off and throw it away." Why does no Christian denomination require sinners who have stolen something to amputate their arm? What about looking at indecent images with your eyes? Thankfully, no one interprets these passages literally.

Roman Catholic and Eastern Orthodox Christians literally interpret John 6:52–56 and Mark 14:22, in which Jesus speaks of eating His flesh and drinking His blood. At the Last Supper, He says over the bread, "This is my body," and over the cup of wine, "This is my blood." Many Protestant Christians interpret those passages figuratively, not literally. Catholicism and Orthodoxy rely on the principles of interpreting any text *in context* of what came before and after that passage, and depending on the teaching authority of the Church (called the *Magisterium*, from the Latin word "magister," meaning teacher).

Question 16. Are there any mistakes in the Bible?

Saint Augustine once said if he ever ran across an apparent error in the Bible, he would conclude that a) the translator of the sacred text made a mistake when he translated the original Hebrew or Greek into the vernacular or common language; b) the person who copied the manuscript from the original made a mistake; c) he as the reader is misinterpreting a text and is not using the author's intended meaning. He could never accept the premise that the Bible has any mistakes. This idea is known as inerrancy.

No one denies that there are some difficulties in the biblical texts. Originally written in Hebrew and Greek, the Old and New Testaments were copied by hand. Most inconsistencies or irregularities in the Bible are human error and not from the original sacred author, but from human translators who hand-copied from the original or from another copy. Misspelled words, wrong numbers (plural nouns with singular verbs and vice versa), improper gender (feminine-ending adjectives with masculine- or neutral-ending nouns and vice versa), etc., can be found in many manuscripts. Today, computers run spell checks. Back then, you had to use a human editor. These copied texts were then translated into Latin, German, French, Spanish, English, Polish, Russian, Slovenian, Czech, Vietnamese, Korean, Japanese, Chinese, Portuguese, Arabic, etc.

Only the original manuscript written by the sacred author (called the "autograph" by scripture scholars) is guaranteed inerrant, infallible, and inspired. Unfortunately, there are no surviving originals. Papyrus was used back then and it was more vulnerable to climate changes than today's paper. Historians and theologians are convinced, however, that our modern translations and versions of the Bible are pretty close to the original.

Difficulties in the Bible arise when a literal interpretation is given to a Biblical passage which should be taken figuratively. When Jonah was sent by God to Ninevah, the Bible says it was such a large city that it took three days to go through it (Jonah 3:3). Literally interpreted, if the average person at that time could walk twenty miles in one day, it would mean the city was sixty miles in diameter. Ever see a traffic jam in downtown Manhattan or Center City Philadelphia? When there are wall-to-wall people and streets crowded with merchants, vendors, animals, carts, etc., it is not like walking on the Appian Way to Rome. Your walking time and distance will be much different in a large city than in a rural town. If taken figuratively, three days does not mean seventy-two hours of nonstop walking.

Ancient Hebrew had no comparative or superlative as we do in English (good, better, best). So they used hyperbole to make a point. It was not intended to be interpreted literally. Jesus said in the Gospel, "If any one comes to me and does not *hate* his own father and mother and wife and children and brothers and sisters, yes, and even his own life, he cannot be my disciple" (Luke 14:26). Literally interpreted, a Christian would have to hate his mother and father, yet the commandments say we must honor them. Without a comparative, ancient Hebrew could not say what we can say in English, that is, to "love more than," so it had to make an almost absurd exaggeration. Matthew 10:37 uses the Greek concept when it says, "He who loves father or mother more than me is not worthy of me." When you compare both these passages, you see that the proper way to understand "hate" in Luke 14:26 is as to "love less than" rather than to harbor animosity.

Question 17. When was the Bible written?

Most of the Old Testament (forty-six books) was written in Hebrew (which had no vowels back then) and several books were written in Greek during the Babylonian Captivity and Diaspora (587–100 BC), the period of Jewish history during the pre-Christian era when three quarters of the Hebrews were forcibly exiled from their homeland and into foreign kingdoms. Over time, many of their descendants spoke and understood more Greek than Hebrew because Alexander the Great, King of Macedonia, had made the Greek language and culture the dominant force until the Romans came on the scene.

The New Testament (twenty-seven books) was written in Greek. By the fourth century AD, the Roman Emperor Constantine had legalized Christianity and it became the official state religion in 391 AD. Pope Damasus contracted Saint Jerome to translate both the Old and New Testaments from the original languages of Hebrew and Greek into the common (vulgate) tongue, which at that time was Latin.

No one person or group sat down and intended to write a complete Bible as we have it today. Each book of the Bible was written by an individual person who was inspired by God, the Holy Spirit. It is therefore often called the "Word of God written by man under divine inspiration." God is the ultimate author, but He chose human beings we call "sacred authors" (because they wrote the sacred text of Scripture) to physically write the inspired words onto paper (or more accurately, onto papyrus).

Each human author wrote the text of the books of the Bible as if they were separate writings. None of them had a vision or intention of one day combining all the books into one volume as we have today.

Before any one word was ever written, however, came the oral tradition phase. This means that for centuries, from Abraham to Moses (approximately six hundred years), the only way the Hebrew people knew about the creation of the world and the beginning of the human race was by word of mouth (oral tradition). Parents verbally told their children, who in turn told their children, and so on. Nothing was actually written since the people were basically nomads, wandering and shepherding, and did not yet have a distinct and recognizable nation.

Moses is traditionally identified as the first one to write down the oral tradition of the Hebrew religion. The forty years during which the people wandered in the desert gave him ample time, and since he had been a prince of Egypt schooled in the court of the Pharaoh, he alone could read and write while the rest of his people had been poor slaves to the Egyptians.

Many biblical scholars believe that sometime in the thirteenth century BC, Moses penned the first five books of the Hebrew Bible (which Christian Bibles list as the Old Testament), named Genesis, Exodus, Leviticus, Numbers, and Deuteronomy. Called *Torah* (law) in Hebrew or *Pentateuch* (five books) in Greek, these five books tell of the origins of the world and of the patriarchs (Abraham, Isaac, Jacob, and Joseph) of the Israelites. Some modern scripture scholars maintain that four distinct groups—not just one man (Moses)—wrote the Torah. They allege that Yahwist (Jahwist), Elohimist, Deuteronomist, and Priestly (JEDP) "sources" actually wrote parts of the first five books of the Bible and later on, someone edited them into one entity. Each source comes from a distinct group of Hebrew scholars and usually from different time periods. The Yahwist gets its name from the fact that the word Yahweh (the sacred name of God) is used in those manuscripts. Elohimist sources used the word Elohim (generic word for God) instead of the sacred name. Deuteronomist sources allegedly wrote most of the book of Deuteronomy. Priestly sources supposedly wrote most of the book of Leviticus, which contains the rituals for the priests to perform. This documentary source theory is not shared by all biblical experts. Most scholars believe that Moses wrote—or at least edited—some, if not all, of the text and constructed the five books as they exist today.

The Torah (law) was written around 1250 BC, but the *Ne'vi-im* (Prophets) were written from 1200–500 BC and the *Ke'tuvim* (Writings) were written from 500–100 BC. Thirty-nine of these Old Testament books were originally written in Hebrew, while the last seven were originally written in Greek. Here is the breakdown of the three divisions of the Old Testament:

    Torah (Law)

    Genesis

    Exodus

    Leviticus

    Numbers

    Deuteronomy

    Ne'vi-im (Prophets)

    Joshua

    Judges

    1 Samuel

    2 Samuel

    1 Kings

    2 Kings

    Isaiah

    Jeremiah

    Baruch *

    Ezekiel

    Hosea

    Joel

    Amos

    Obadiah

    Jonah

    Micah

    Nahum

    Habakkuk

    Zephaniah

    Haggai

    Zechariah

    Malachi

    Ke'tuvim (Writings)

    Psalms

    Proverbs

Wisdom *
Job
Song of Songs
Ruth
Lamentations
Ecclesiastes
Esther
Daniel
Ezra
Nehemiah
1 Chronicles
2 Chronicles
Tobit *
Judith *
Ecclesiasticus (Sirach) *
1 Maccabees *
2 Maccabees *
* *deuterocanon/apocrypha*

The New Testament was written between 49–100 AD. Matthew (49 AD), Mark (54 AD), Luke (60 AD), and John (99 AD) wrote the four gospels, which were preceded (48–64 AD) by the letters (epistles) of Paul, James, Peter, John, and Jude. Luke also wrote the book of Acts, and John wrote the book of Revelation (or Apocalypse).

Gospels
Matthew
Mark
Luke
John
Acts
Epistles
Romans
1 Corinthians
2 Corinthians
Galatians

Ephesians
Philipians
Colossians
1 Thessalonians
2 Thessalonians
1 Timothy
2 Timothy
Titus
Philemon
Hebrews
James
1 Peter
2 Peter
1 John
2 John
3 John
Jude
Revelation (Apocalypse)

Here are some important dates for the compilation of the entire Bible as one single volume of the seventy-three individual books. (Also see Question 18.) The word "canon" means authorized list and comes from the Greek word *kanon* meaning a reed. Reeds were often used to measure the depth of water, and so the word "kanon" in Greek came to mean a measuring rod or authorized list of books.

1250 BC: earliest date for writings from the Torah or Pentateuch.
250–150 BC: translation by seventy scholars (at request of Greek King of Egypt Ptolemy II Philadelphus) of all Hebrew manuscripts into *Greek* Septuagint (LXX); Alexandrian Canon established; forty-six books in Old Testament.
100 AD: Jewish Council of Jamnia determined the Palestinian Canon (in *Hebrew*): thirty-nine books in Hebrew Bible (Christian equivalent of Old Testament).
400 AD: Saint Jerome translates and compiles first complete Bible in *Latin* with seventy-three books total, based on Septuagint Version.
1455 AD: Gutenberg invents printing press with movable type. First printed and

complete Bible, Latin Vulgate version.

1536 AD: Martin Luther translates Bible from Latin into German and adopts the shorter but younger (Hebrew) Canon of the Old Testament (thirty-nine books).

1609 AD: Douay-Rheims, first complete English translation of Catholic Bible.

1611 AD: King James (Authorized) Version with Apocrypha (Deuterocanon).

1885 AD: King James Version officially removes Apocrypha; Revised Version is written.

1946 AD: Revised Standard Version (RSV)

1966 AD: Jerusalem Bible (Catholic)

1970 AD: New American Bible (Catholic) (NAB)

1973 AD: New International Version (NIV)

Question 18. Who put the Bible together?

If Matthew, Mark, Luke, and John wrote the four gospels and Paul wrote most of the Epistles, who edited the final version of what we today call the Bible? As mentioned in Question 17, the Old Testament took final shape in the third to second centuries (250–100 BC) when the Septuagint was commissioned. King Ptolemy II Philadelphus of Egypt (309–246 BC) built an exquisite library in Alexandria and decided to crown his collection with a Greek translation of the Hebrew Scriptures. At that time, two-thirds to three-quarters of the world's Jews had been dispersed (called the Diaspora) during the Babylonian Captivity (586 BC). Most Jews no longer used the Hebrew language since the common tongue at that time was Greek. King Ptolemy asked over seventy scholars to begin the task of translating from Hebrew into Greek, which took more than seventy days. Their one-volume edition contained forty-six books, thirty-nine of which had been originally written in Hebrew and seven of which had been originally written in Greek, since the sacred authors lived during the captivity and were only fluent in the Hellenistic (Greek) language.

The complete Bible, with Old and New Testaments, did not appear in one single volume and language until 400 AD, when Saint Jerome did the monumental task of translating the Hebrew and Greek into Latin (the common tongue at that time). Before that, the Councils of Laodicea (363 AD) and Carthage (397 AD) had declared the number of books for the New Testament to be twenty-seven. There was some scholarly disagreement about the authorized list (canon) of books for the Old Testament—Saint Athanasius (296–373 AD) and Saint Gregory Nazianzus (325–389 AD) opted for the shorter and more recent Palestinian-Hebrew canon of thirty-nine books—but the final word came in 400 AD, when the Latin Vulgate of Saint Jerome included all forty-six books of the longer and older Alexandrian-Greek canon at the request of Pope Damasus I. In 405 AD, his successor, Pope Innocent I, reaffirmed the authenticity of those seven additional books. Just eight years before (397 AD), Saint Augustine and the Third Council of Carthage gave their seal of approval on the Septuagint listing—the longer canon containing forty-six instead of only thirty-nine books.

Christianity would therefore have forty-six books in the Old Testament and twenty-seven in the New Testament for over a thousand years, from 400–1517 AD, until Martin Luther and the Protestant Reformation chose to remove from the Old Testament what they considered to be apocryphal books (Baruch, Maccabees 1 and 2, Tobit, Judith, Ecclesiasticus, and Wisdom) and to adopt the Palestinian-Hebrew canon of 100 AD. The Roman Catholic and the Greek Orthodox Churches kept those seven deuterocanonical books, since they retained the Alexandrian-Greek canon of 250 BC. It was further maintained that Jesus and the early Christians knew, used, and regarded those books as being part of Scripture. Christians had been seen as a sect or branch of Judaism from 33–70 AD until the Temple of Jerusalem was destroyed by the Romans. Christianity was repudiated by Jewish religious leaders, and it became an independent and separate religion thirty years before the Jewish scholars at Jamnia (100 AD) formally rejected the Alexandrian canon and opted for the Palestinian one instead.

The Council of Trent (1545–1563 AD) solemnly defined that Catholics were to accept—as inspired and part of revelation—all forty-six books of the Old Testament, in addition to the twenty-seven books of the New Testament. The Lutheran, Anglican, Calvinist, Presbyterian, Methodist, Baptist, etc., denominations would only accept the thirty-nine books, but you will often find those seven deuterocanonical books listed in the back of the Protestant Bible under the classification of "apocrypha" (see Question 14).

Question 19. What is inspiration?

Inspiration comes from the Latin *inspirare*, meaning "to breathe upon." The Greek word for inspiration is *theopneustos*, meaning literally "God-breathed"; in Hebrew, one can use either *neshamah* or *ruwach*. Divine Inspiration is understood to mean that God directly influenced each and every sacred author to write without interfering with his individual free will. Pope Leo XIII gave the best definition when he said, "Inspiration consists in that supernatural influence by which God so arouses and directs the sacred authors to write, [and] assists them in writing, so that all and only what He Himself wills do they correctly formulate in their minds, determine to write faithfully, and express aptly in an infallibly truthful manner" (*Providentissimus Deus*, #20, 1893).

What inspiration is *not* is *verbal dictation* (the Holy Spirit did not give an interview); nor is it *subsequent approbation*, where the author submits written material for divine approval (God is not an editor, either); nor is it only an *ideological inspiration* on just moral or spiritual matters. Unlike infallibility, which is a negative charism (spiritual gift) that prevents the source from teaching error, inspiration is a positive charism whereby the sacred author writes only what God wants and how He wants it, while still retaining his free will.

Inspiration, since it comes directly from God, is also infallible (free of moral or doctrinal error) and inerrant (free of mistakes) to protect the integrity and sanctity of the revealed message. The human authors, however, are free to convey the inspired word using vocabulary and idioms known by the person.

Only inspired text is allowed to be in the Bible and only divinely inspired text can contain divine revelation. Books which did not get into the Bible, like the Gospel of Mary Magdalene or the Apocalypse of Moses, are not considered inspired. One mistake some people make is to conclude that only inspired text is true. Being that they originate from God, all inspired books are true and inerrant. Yet, other human texts can be and are true but are not considered inspired. A phone book is true in that the numbers and names are accurate. A chemistry book is true in that water is two parts hydrogen and one part oxygen. However, neither of these is inspired text.

It is not the author, the subject, nor the date of the document which makes it inspired. If Saint Joseph, the husband of the Virgin Mary and foster father of Jesus, had written something and archeologists found it tomorrow, it would not be considered inspired just because of who wrote it, when it was written, or even what it contained. The commentaries of the Gallic Wars by the Roman Emperor Julius Caesar in which he says *"Gallia est omnis divisa in partes tres"* (All Gaul is divided into three parts) was written in 58 BC, which predates the New Testament, and is considered truthful but not inspired.

Only an authority can decide whether or not a book is inspired. The recognized authentic authority is the Church—especially the "teaching authority" of the Church, which is called the magisterium. The Bible itself never says which books belong in it or are considered inspired. The word Bible is not even in the Bible. Modern editors and publishers print a table of contents, but the original sacred authors never had such a list. The Church did not create the Bible but was the one to determine which books belonged in it and in what order, and is the one authorized to faithfully interpret the Bible as well.

Question 20. Who put the numbers (chapters and verses) in the Bible?

The next time you go to a baseball or football game, look for someone in the crowd holding a sign that simply reads: John 3:16. What does it mean? It is a reference to the Gospel of John, chapter three, verse sixteen, which says, "For God so loved the world, that he gave his only begotten Son, that whosoever believeth in him should not perish, but have everlasting life." It is a nice, public demonstration of Christian faith. If you and I, however, were at a chariot race in the Coliseum in Rome in the year 200 AD, and saw that sign (it would probably be in Latin: Ioannes III:XVI) we would have no idea what it meant even if we were devout Christians at the time.

What most people take for granted today when they pick up their Bibles is that they can find any passage merely by knowing the book, the chapter, and the verse. Ironically, the original sacred authors never used these tools. When Matthew, Mark, Luke, and John wrote their respective versions of the Gospel, none of them included chapters and verses. Even translators like Saint Jerome, who was the first person to translate the entire Old Testament from Hebrew and Greek into Latin and to translate the entire New Testament from Greek into Latin, and then combine both in a one volume book (circa 400 AD), never used chapter and verse. No Bible had this until 1205 AD, when the Archbishop of Canterbury Stephan Langton assigned chapter numbers to make reading the Bible easier. It took another three and half centuries before the verses were added by Robert Stephanus in 1550 AD. That means there was no 3:16 until 1550. People had to memorize entire passages in their entirety before they could simply say "Matthew 16:18" or any other citation. Another interesting tidbit is that the original sacred authors did not use any punctuation marks, either. Commas, periods, apostrophes, question marks, exclamation marks, and the rest did not exist at the time the books of the Bible were being written. Later on, translators added those to conform to their native tongues and the rules of grammar for languages.

Question 21. What is revelation?

The word "revelation" comes from the Latin *revelare*, meaning "to unveil." Greek uses the word *apokalupto*, (where we get the word "apocalypse") and Hebrew uses the word *galah* which also means "to uncover" or "to unveil." Pulling back a veil to reveal what's behind it is the key to understanding biblical revelation. The Ark of the Covenant containing the ten words of God (*Debarim*) or, as they are more commonly known, the Ten Commandments, was kept in the Temple of Jerusalem. The room where it was located was called the Holy of Holies and was separated from the rest of the Temple by a veil. No one could go behind the veil into the Holy of Holies and stand before the Ark except the High Priest, and he was only allowed to do so once a year on the Day of Atonement (Yom Kippur). Revelation was the "unveiling" of the Word of God.

Natural revelation is the process by which ordinary human beings can ascertain certain truths by their own power. Everyone knows fire is hot because everybody has at least felt the heat of a flame. That knowledge is natural revelation. Empirical truth is what can be observed by scientists through observation and experimentation. Philosophical truth is what can be deduced by reason. $2 + 2 = 4$ is a self-evident truth. That $2 + 2 = 5$ is logical and is philosophically true. The same applies to the reality that if $A = B$ and $B = C$, then $A = C$ must be true. Likewise, the philosophical principle of noncontradiction means something cannot be its opposite at the same time; for example, you cannot be simultaneously alive and dead, since these terms are mutually exclusive. You're either dead or alive, but you cannot be both at the same time.

Theological truth, however, is not known by reason or observation, even though it is not necessarily in conflict with philosophy or science. Theological truth is known by divine revelation and is accepted on faith. Faith is believing what cannot be known by human reason alone. Faith is taking the word of someone else without having empirical evidence. The revealed truth that there is one God, but also Three Persons in one God, is a theological and divinely revealed truth. That Jesus Christ is the second Person of that Trinity or that He is one divine Person with two natures, human and divine, is also communicated through divine revelation. It is through faith that we believe in the truth of these divine revelations.

Theologians therefore define revelation as the disclosure by God of those supernatural truths necessary for our salvation. Divine revelation comes from God and can be transmitted through either Sacred Scripture or Sacred Tradition. (For more on Sacred Scripture and Sacred Tradition see Question #22.)

Question 22. What is the difference between Sacred Tradition and Sacred Scripture?

Sacred Scripture is just another way of saying "the Bible." Sacred Tradition refers to what is not written but is as much divinely revealed as Sacred Scripture. The best way to understand the Catholic concept of revelation is to see it as being the revealed Word of God. Sacred Scripture is the written Word and Sacred Tradition is the unwritten or spoken Word. Both the written and the unwritten Word make up the totality of divine revelation.

This does not mean that scripture and tradition are in competition with one another. In fact, since they both come from the same source (God), neither can contradict the other. Sacred Tradition predates Sacred Scripture, since the unwritten Word was spoken for centuries and generations before it was ever written down. Hebrew children were verbally told about Adam and Eve, Cain and Abel, Noah and the Ark, Abraham and Isaac, etc., from their parents and grandparents. There were no books or bibles in antiquity. Moses may have been the first person to write the book of Genesis, but its content was known centuries before he was ever born. People spoke the revealed words of the Old Testament; only later were they written by the sacred author.

Even in the New Testament, Sacred Tradition predates the written Gospel. Jesus first said and did what He did in time, then His apostles told people (preached). Only later did the Evangelist (Gospel writer) write down the text of the Gospel. Matthew, Mark, Luke, and John did not take notes while Jesus preached or performed miracles. The unwritten word came first and was followed by the written word; both contain the same message.

Even the Gospel of John ends with, "There are also many other things that Jesus did, but if these were to be described individually, I do not think the whole world would contain the books that would be written" (21:25). Those other things are part of Sacred Tradition. That Jesus never married is not explicitly stated in Sacred Scripture, but wherever the Bible is silent or ambiguous, Sacred Tradition fills in the gap. Sacred Tradition is that Jesus never married nor had any children. Sacred Tradition is that the Virgin Mary remained a virgin her entire life and had no other children other than her son Jesus. (For more on this, see Question 31.) Sacred Tradition determined what books belong in the Bible and which ones do not.

Rather than a dichotomy between Sacred Scripture (Bible) and Sacred Tradition, both are like two lungs in one body, or two sides of one coin. Both originate from

God and both are authentically interpreted by the Church.

Sacred Tradition is equal to Sacred Scripture since both originate with God Himself. Divine revelation comes from both vehicles of the one source (God). If there appears to be a contradiction between the two, then the mistake is in the copy, translation, or interpretation of the written text. Since the Bible in and of itself never gives an exhaustive list of which books should or should not be considered part of the Bible, only Sacred Tradition can tell infallibly which books are inspired and which are not. No inspired book says "I'm inspired," and no sacred author was aware that he was being inspired since none ever say so.

Sacred Tradition is different from human tradition. Tradition comes from the Latin word *artumon*, meaning "to hand down." Human traditions are imperfect, flawed, fallible, and open to change. Many of the religious customs of both Jews and Christians were human tradition, that is, man-made. Sacred Tradition originates from God and is divinely made. It cannot change. That is why there will never be any more books added to the Bible. Sacred tradition says that revelation ended with the death of Saint John the Beloved (around 100 AD). Any manuscript discovered afterward will never be included in future versions of the Bible. Apocryphal Gnostic writings like the Gospel of Mary Magdalene, for example, were written in the third or fourth century AD.

There is a distinction between what the Church considers Sacred Tradition and what are merely human traditions. Saint Paul says in 2 Thessalonians 2:15 (from the King James Version), "Therefore, brethren, stand fast, and hold the traditions which ye have been taught, whether by word, or our epistle." The original Greek word used by Paul, *paradoseis*, means "traditions." This does not contradict what he says in 2 Timothy 3:16: "All scripture is given by inspiration of God, and is profitable for doctrine, for reproof, for correction, for instruction in righteousness," since he never says Scripture alone (*sola scriptura*) or only in Scripture is found inspiration, as was held by Martin Luther. It is the same Paul who authored 2 Thessalonians 2:15 and 2 Timothy 3:16, and both epistles are in the Bible and considered inspired text. He also says in 1 Corinthians 11:2, "I commend you because you remember me in everything and maintain the traditions even as I have delivered them to you."

Saint Paul, from what is quoted in the previous paragraph, has no problems or issues with Sacred Tradition. He is concerned about human traditions and customs which have been taken out of context or given more attention and priority than those of divine origin. Matthew 15:3 has Jesus rebuke the Pharisees: "And why do you transgress the commandment of God for the sake of your tradition?" The key here is the word "your." When Jesus speaks of "your tradition," it is distinct and separate from "divine" or "sacred" tradition. The man-made, human traditions the Pharisees scrupulously maintained were not superior or even equal to the traditions which originated from God.

Question 23. Which version of the Bible should I read?

Someone of the Protestant Christian faith will want a Protestant Bible, whereas a Catholic Christian will want a Catholic Bible.

"*Traduttorre traditore*," says the Italian proverb—"the translator is a traitor." This simply means that the further away you get from the original language of the text, the more susceptible it is to error. Only the original text written by the sacred author is guaranteed inerrancy, infallibility, and inspiration, but unless you speak and can read Greek, Hebrew, or Latin, it is best to get a Bible translated into your native language. Translations and versions can help or hinder in some ways.

Dynamic equivalence and formal correspondence are two methods of translating biblical text from the original language into the vernacular (common tongue). The first emphasizes what the author meant and intended and uses contemporary idioms rather than the original so the modern reader can understand better. Ancient Greek used a phrase *"en gastri echousa"* (*in utero habens* in Latin) which is found in Matthew 1:18. Literally, it translates to "having in the belly," but few people today, if anyone, would understand that phrase. So, dynamic equivalence uses an idiom to convey the same message, hence the phrase "to be with child" is used and makes more sense to us. Ancient Hebrew also had no comparatives or superlatives. Modern English can say "love less or "love more," but ancient Hebrew could only use a Semitic linguistic technique that uses hyperbole.

"If any one comes to me and does not hate his own father and mother and wife and children and brothers and sisters, yes, and even his own life, he cannot be my disciple" (Luke 14:26). Does Jesus mean we must literally "hate" our father and mother? Would that not violate the commandments? A dynamic equivalence translation would read that same passage as "If anyone comes to me but loves his father, mother, wife, children, brothers, or sisters—or even life—more than me, he cannot be my follower." Here the idiomatic meaning is that the believer must love Jesus more than he loves his father or mother, but not that he must hate his family. The Jerusalem Bible is a dynamic equivalence translation as is the New English Bible (NEB).

Formal Correspondence translations do not put the emphasis on using idioms, as they seek to translate word for word, from the original language to the modern. Luke 21:2 is the passage where Jesus sees "a poor widow put in two mites" into the donation box. The word "mite" is *leptos* in Greek and a word-for-word translation retains that. An idiomatic translation changes it to "penny" or "copper coin." The Revised Standard Version, Catholic Edition (RSVCE) is a formal correspondence translation, and so are the Douay-Rheims, New American Bible (NAB), and the King James Version (KJV).

Question 24. Who has the final word: the Bible or the Church?

Martin Luther began the Protestant Reformation (sixteenth century AD) with the concept of *sola scriptura* (scripture alone) as the final authority in doctrinal matters. The Council of Trent convened that same century and solemnly defined that the Church, or more precisely, the teaching authority (Magisterium) of the Catholic Church had the ultimate and last word—not because it is superior to the Bible, but because the whole of divine revelation, from Sacred Scripture (Bible) to Sacred Tradition, was entrusted to the Church for protection and for proper interpretation.

Nowhere in the Bible does Jesus say to *read*, but He does often command that we *listen*. The written word did not come immediately, but the spoken and unwritten word did follow after Jesus performed His many miracles. Matthew 16:18–19 is the famous passage where Jesus says to Simon, "And I tell you, you are Peter, and on this rock I will build my *church*, and the powers of death shall not prevail against it. I will give you the keys of the kingdom of heaven, and whatever you bind on earth shall be bound in heaven, and whatever you loose on earth shall be loosed in heaven." The Greek word *ekklesia* is translated as "church." The passage makes it clear that the Church is built *by* Christ, it is His Church, and it has the power to bind and to "loose" in heaven and on earth. How can the Word of God go against the will of God? If it is Jesus who built the Church and He gave it full authority to teach in His name, then there is no competition between the Bible and the Church any more than there can be opposition between Sacred Scripture and Sacred Tradition.

Chapter 3

WHO IS JESUS?

This chapter answers the questions about Jesus: His origins, family, nature, person, divinity, and humanity.

Question 25. Was Jesus really born on December 25?

While Christians in the West (Catholic and Protestant) celebrate the birthday of Christ every year on the twenty-fifth of December, no one knows for sure what exact day the birth occurred. There is no birth certificate. We have no references or citations in the Bible about the Apostles having birthday parties for Jesus, and the calendar day of His birth is never mentioned. That He was born is accepted as fact. What day of what month is not specified in any biblical or historical record. The Bible tells us Jesus was born of Mary in the town of Bethlehem. Later, the holy family (Jesus, Mary, and Joseph) fled into Egypt to escape the slaughter of male infants imposed by King Herod. After Herod's death, the family settled in Nazareth, where Joseph worked as a carpenter.

After Jesus' death and resurrection came three hundred years of Roman persecution (54–305 AD) by Emperors Nero, Domitian, Trajan, Marcus Aurelius, Septimius Severus, Maximus, Decius, Valerian, Aurelian, and Diocletian, which made Christianity an outlawed and ghettoized religion. Only after the Emperor Constantine issued the Edict of Milan in 315 AD, granting legal protection for Christians and their religion, did people begin to ask when they could celebrate the birthday of the Savior.

Without knowing the actual day, there are two ways to determine a day on the calendar for the annual birthday of Christ. One school of thought maintains that the Annunciation (when the Archangel Gabriel appeared to the Virgin Mary and announced that she was to be the mother of the Savior), already established in antiquity as March 25, would also have been the day Jesus was conceived in the womb of His mother. Luke 1:36 tells us that the same day of the Annunciation is also the six-month anniversary of the conception of Saint John the Baptist in the womb of his mother, Saint Elizabeth. Luke 1:56–57 tells us that after three months, Mary returns home when her cousin gives birth. If the Annunciation took place on March 25, then the birth of John the Baptist must be three months later, and the Church does in fact celebrate the birth of John on June 24. Mary would have been with child since March 25, and nine months from that date brings us to December 25.

If the actual day of the Annunciation or the Visitation (when Mary visited Elizabeth) is not known, someone like Saint Augustine would propose that it was based on the solar calendar of the Roman Empire. Rather than adapting a pagan feast day of the sun god as is often suggested, other scholars use the following line of reasoning: without a firm date to use, Scripture helps by using analogies. Jesus said in John 8:12 "I am the Light of the World." John the Baptist, the cousin of Jesus and son of Elizabeth, said in John 3:30 "I must decrease, He must increase." Using those two biblical passages, Christians then looked at when the shortest and the longest days of the year occurred—the summer and winter solstices.

The longest day occurs in mid-June and the shortest day occurs in mid-December. On the day after the summer solstice, the amount of daylight decreases every day until we reach the shortest day of the year. The day after the winter solstice, the amount of daylight increases until we return to the longest day. The day when the hours of light begin to increase would be designated as the birthday of Christ ("I am the Light of the World") and the day when the hours of light began to decrease would be the designated as the birthday of John the Baptist ("I must decrease, He must increase"). There are exactly six months between the birth of John the Baptist and the birth of Christ as told in Luke's Gospel, and there are exactly six months between the summer and winter solstices. Hence, the day when light decreases becomes the birth of John on June 24, and the day when the light increases becomes the birth of Jesus on December 25. It may not be as precise and as accurate as astronomers and chronologists might prefer, but it works.

Question 26. Was Jesus a god or a man?

The question of the divinity and humanity of Jesus Christ has been one of the most important questions for Christianity. Judaism and Islam may affirm his humanity but only Christianity professes his divinity. If only a man, then how could he have performed miracles and, after being dead for three days himself, rise from the grave? If God alone, how could He have suffered and died, since Divinity is immortal and feels no pain?

Catholic Christianity, as well as Eastern Orthodox and Protestant Christianity, firmly believe that Jesus Christ is "true God and true Man" as stated in the Nicene Creed of 325 AD. What is not taught is that Jesus is only half human and half divine. He is not a hybrid and, unlike Mr. Spock of *Star Trek*, He is not the offspring of two species. While His mother is very much human, He has no biological human father since it was by the power of the Holy Spirit that He was conceived in the womb (Luke 1:35). Nine months after His conception, Jesus was born and "He grew and became strong, filled with grace and wisdom" (Luke 2:40).

The Church believes that in His human nature, Jesus had a fully human body with five senses. He got hungry, ate, slept, laughed, cried, felt pain, and could die like any man or woman. Jesus was not like Superman from another planet who had a super body. His human nature not only had a human body but also a human soul which possessed a human intellect and a human will.

Docetism was a heresy of the early church that denied the humanity and human nature of Christ. It maintained that Jesus only pretended to be human—that His divinity was real but His humanity was a phantasm or appearance. Arianism (promoted by a priest named Arius) was a heresy of the same period that denied the divinity and divine nature of Christ. It maintained that Jesus was the "adopted" Son of God but that He only had a similar substance to God the Father, and not the same substance.

The Council of Nicea (325 AD) condemned Arianism and solemnly defined that Christ was consubstantial to God the Father in his divine nature as God the Son. The term the council used was *homoousios* (same substance) as opposed to the one used by Arianism, *homoiousios* (similar substance). Homoousios explained how Jesus could perform miracles by using His divine nature and how He was able to suffer and die for our sins by using His human nature.

Jesus had human emotions the same way He had human DNA, genes, chromosomes, flesh and blood, hormones, organs, etc. Only in His divine nature did He enjoy divine powers, such as the ability to walk on water; change water into wine; give sight to the blind; cure the deaf, the mute, and lame; expel demons; and raise the dead.

Since Adam and Eve committed the first sin, human nature had been wounded but not destroyed. What is wounded can be healed and is redeemable and salvageable. What is corrupt and dead is beyond repair. Human nature alone could not atone for the sin since the offense against God was measured by the dignity of the one who was offended. Only divinity could save and redeem mankind, but only humanity could suffer, die, and make the sacrifice. A God-Man, someone true God and true Man, could be the only one to both offer the sacrifice (priest) and be the sacrifice itself (victim).

Question 27. Who were Jesus' parents?

Jesus only had one human parent, his mother Mary. Her husband, Joseph, was not the biological father of Jesus as it was God the Holy Spirit who enabled the Virgin Mary to conceive without the cooperation of a human male. This is why Jesus is called the Son of God and the Son of Mary. Mary was human just like the rest of us in that she had two human parents (Saints Joachim and Ann) and she was as much a part of the human race as anyone else. This meant she was neither perfect nor divine. She was not a goddess. Her son, though, was divine; since she gave birth to the Son of God, by way of analogy, we can call her the mother of God because you cannot ever separate the divinity and humanity of Christ.

Jewish custom, tradition, and law made it clear that legal adoption had the same effect as natural birth. So Joseph, the legal spouse of Mary, became the legal (but not biological) father of Jesus. This is why Jesus is sometimes called the "carpenter's son" or the "son of Joseph." Even the Greeks and Romans had the same practice of showing equal privilege and rank to an adopted son as to a son from natural birth.

No one knows when Joseph died, but it was before Jesus began his public ministry in 30 AD. Present at His birth and circumcision, His foster father also taught Him the art of carpentry, as indicated in Mark 6:1: "Is this not the carpenter?" referring to Jesus as a carpenter Himself. Joseph is only mentioned in the Bible at the time of Jesus' birth and when Jesus was twelve. Nothing more is known about him beyond that time, but it is speculated that Jesus grew up in Nazareth and learned carpentry from His foster father.

If Joseph died when Jesus was thirty, it would explain why Jesus only began his official public ministry as a rabbi at the age of thirty, just three years before his death. Until then, he was merely known as the carpenter's son or as a carpenter himself. Mary survived to see her only son crucified, killed, and buried, but then to reunite with Him after the Resurrection on Easter. She lives beyond the Ascension of Jesus into heaven forty days after Easter, and she is recorded as present in the upper room on the day of Pentecost, when the Holy Spirit came upon her and the twelve apostles.

We do not know when the mother of Jesus left this earth. The Bible is silent about her departure. Catholicism does believe that when her time came, she was taken up body and soul (called the Assumption) by her divine Son into heaven. Though it is celebrated liturgically each year on August 15, no one knows for sure if that is the exact date.

Question 28. Was Jesus a prophet or a messiah?

He was both. Many non-Christian religions consider Jesus of Nazareth to be a holy or revered prophet. Christians, however, believe he was indeed a prophet but much more than that. Prophets are not fortune tellers who gaze into crystal balls, read tea leaves, or use tarot cards. Prophets rarely, but occasionally, predict the future. The main function and job of a prophet is to teach; that is, to speak to the people in the name of the Lord.

Catholic Christianity sees Jesus simultaneously as a priest, a prophet, and a king. Others before Him were and could only be one of those at a time. Priests sanctified, prophets taught, and kings ruled. Priests offered sacrifice in the temple. Jesus offered the supreme sacrifice of His very self on the altar of the cross. He became both priest (the one who makes the sacrifice) and victim (the one who is sacrificed) by willingly laying down His life to save sinners.

Kings have authority; they govern their subjects and their territory. Jesus spoke of the reign of God and the kingdom of heaven. He had authority over unclean spirits and over physical disabilities. He commanded the dead to rise, and they did. He said his kingdom was not of this world.

Prophets teach and speak on behalf of God. Jesus taught in the synagogues, in the temple, in the towns and cities. He preached a message of mercy and forgiveness. He spoke what the Father sent him to speak just as all the prophets before him had. The only difference was that Jesus as the Son of God was one with God the Father. The fullness of truth and grace were revealed by Jesus, hence there was no need for any more prophets after Him.

We refer to Jesus as the Messiah, which in Hebrew means "anointed one." Greek uses the word *christos* for the same meaning, hence Christ means "anointed one" or Messiah. Christ was not Jesus' surname but a title, just like Savior or Redeemer.

Question 29. Were those real miracles He performed?

Rudolph Bultmann (1884–1976) was a theologian of the Lutheran denomination who espoused a scholarly ideology known as Liberal Protestantism (which had nothing to do with politics). He is best known for his term *demythologization*, the process of explaining all supernatural events recorded in the Bible through logical and rational explanations. He did not believe the miracles of Jesus as told in the Gospels really happened; however, most Christians, including the Catholic Church, reject this ultimate skepticism. The miracles are pivotal since they prove the divinity of Christ. Bultmann was right on one thing—no mere human being could cure the sick; give sight to the blind, hearing to the deaf, and speech to the mute; or raise the dead. Only a deity could expel demons, command the sea and the wind, multiply five loaves and two fish to feed five thousand, and walk on water.

The fact that miracles are rare and do not happen every day is what makes them miracles. They are essentially exceptional occurrences where God intervenes in the physical world. The laws of nature are not violated or broken, but rather the natural effects or consequences are suspended. When Jesus rose from the dead, He had a glorified body that enabled Him to walk through doors and walls, yet He was no ghost since His apostles, especially Doubting Thomas, were allowed to touch His hands and side.

If only one person witnessed a miracle, not many people would believe it since anyone can be mistaken or make an erroneous judgment. When hundreds and thousands witness a miracle, it cannot be easily dismissed. Jesus miraculously fed five thousand men (not counting the women and children who were there) and the crowd wanted to carry Him off and make Him king.

Bultmann and other skeptics claimed that in this particular miracle, Jesus did not really multiply five loaves and two fish to feed thousands; rather, he took the little they had and inspired the mob to share the food. Again, if that had been true, then why would the crowd react to Him as they did? Only if He actually fed a multitude by miraculous power would people flock to Him, as we see in John 6.

Because people truly believed Jesus raised Lazarus from the dead after being in the tomb for three days, the enemies of Christ plotted His death. They feared His growing popularity among the people for being a miracle worker. The bottom line, however, is that someone today in the twenty-first century either believes the miracles of Jesus as told in the Gospel or does not. There is no empirical evidence to prove these supernatural events took place, but the New Testament does provide witness testimony. Faith allows a person to believe in what cannot be seen or proved. Physical evidence leads to knowledge, whereas the lack of it leaves only two choices: belief or disbelief. The fact that an entire religion is based on the believed miracle that one man was crucified, died, and on the third day rose from the dead by his own power, and that this religion has endured two millennia and comprises over a billion members speaks for itself.

Question 30. Did Jesus know who He was and where He came from?

Those same liberal theologians who casually dismiss the miracles of Jesus also claim that He did not know of His divine origins or divine nature until after the Resurrection. Jesus had no identity crisis. The Councils of Nicea (325) and

Chalcedon (451) defined that Christ was one divine person with two natures: human and divine. The Creed, professed every Sunday and holy day, states Jesus was true God and true Man. His humanity included His human body and His human soul, which possessed a rational human intellect and a human free will. His divinity consisted of His divine soul that shared the same divine intellect and divine will of God the Father and God the Holy Spirit. Christ's divinity resided in His divine personhood as He was the Second Person of the Holy Trinity, i.e., He is God the Son.

The reason Jesus had to know who He was at all times is that the "who" refers to the person. When you look in the mirror and see your reflection, the "me" that you recognize is your person. Though Christ had a fully human nature (body and soul) and a fully divine nature, there was only one *divine person* in Christ. So whenever Jesus said "I," it was the divine person speaking, acting, curing, etc. Only if Jesus had a human person either in addition to or instead of the divine person could there be confusion or ignorance of His self-identity. The early councils of the Church defined that Jesus was in fact one divine person with a fully human nature and a fully divine nature. Any other configuration was deemed heresy.

Even the Bible attests to His self-knowledge of His divine origins in Luke 2:41–52. When Jesus was twelve years old, His mother Mary and her husband Joseph thought He was lost for three days, but they eventually found Him in the Temple teaching the teachers. When asked by His parents why He was missing for three days, Jesus the adolescent replies, "Did you not know that I must be in my Father's house?" When brought before the High Priest Caiaphas, He was asked, "Are you the Christ, the Son of the Blessed?" And Jesus said, "I am" (Mark 14:62). Before His crucifixion and death, Jesus told Pontius Pilate, "My kingdom is not of this world" (John 18:36). Doesn't appear to be an identity crisis, does it?

Question 31. What about the brothers and sisters of Jesus?

Many people ask about the alleged siblings of Jesus mentioned in the New Testament (Matthew 12:46, 13:55; Mark 3:31–32, 6:3; Luke 8:19–20; John 2:12, 7:3–5; Acts 1:14; 1 Corinthians 9:5). These passages refer to Mary and the "brethren" or the "brothers and sisters" of Jesus. First, we go to the original Greek text of these citations.

The word used to describe these siblings, as some describe them, is *adelphoi*. This is the plural form of *adelphos*, which can mean "brother," but it is also used to describe more distant relations, like cousins, uncles, and nephews. Any relative or relation, from brother to cousin, can be called an adelphos since ancient Hebrew had no precise distinctions as we do today. Proof of this is in the Bible itself.

Genesis 11:27 ("Terah begat Abram, Nahor, and Haran; and Haran begat Lot.") and 11:31 ("and Lot the son of Haran") and 14:12 ("and they took Lot, Abram's brother's son") make it clear that Abram and Haran are brothers and Lot is the son of Haran, which makes Abram his uncle. Lot is therefore the nephew of Abram. Yet the only way ancient Hebrew could describe the relationship between Abram and Lot was to either say it in a very complicated way, as in Genesis 12:5 where it says "and Lot [Abram's] brother's son" or it can use an inclusive word like adelphos in Greek or (*ach*) in Hebrew. This is done in Genesis 14:16: "his brother Lot." If Lot was the son of Haran, the brother of Abram, then how can Abram call Lot his brother in 14:16? This only makes sense if the words used in Hebrew and Greek are not exclusively restricted to one form of relationship. Adelphos is the Greek word used in the Septuagint, the Greek translation of the Old Testament, and "brother" is used in the English King James Version of the Bible in Genesis 14:14, 16. Obviously, without having a word like "uncle" or "nephew," the same word used for "brother" is also used for these extended relationships. Hence, when we read in the New Testament about the adelphoi of Jesus, they can be the same kind of relatives Abram and Lot were to each other. Jesus did have one cousin for certain, John the Baptist.

Joseph could have had siblings with children, who would have been his nieces and nephews and legal cousins to Jesus. Mary could have had siblings or cousins with children the same age as Jesus, too. If a brother of Joseph died leaving children to be raised, Joseph would have taken them into his home and Jesus would have been raised with his cousins, who would have been called adelphoi in Greek and, in English, that particular word is translated as "brethren."

Further proof of the nonexistence of other children of Mary and Joseph: where are they at the Crucifixion? John 19:26–27 has Jesus giving His mother Mary to John and vice versa. Had there been any actual siblings, they would have been there with Mary at Calvary and there would have been no need to entrust his blessed mother to the care of John the Beloved Disciple.

Question 32. Was Mary Magdalene Jesus' girlfriend?

No. Jesus had no wife and no girlfriend. Mary Magdalene was a disciple of the Lord from whom Jesus cast out seven demons. She was also at the foot of the cross with Mary, His mother. Finally, Mary Magdalene is mentioned as the first one Jesus appeared to on Easter morning after His Resurrection. Other than that, there is nothing in the Bible or in Sacred Tradition to infer, imply, or insinuate any romance or nuptials between the two. There is no credible evidence of any offspring, either.

Conspiracy fans may believe fictional accounts found in novels such as *The DaVinci Code* alleging that a family was started by Jesus and Magdalene, but it is based on ludicrous sources such as the Gnostic Gospel of Mary and the Apocryphal Gospels of Philip and Thomas. Not only are these nonbiblical and therefore noninspired, but they were also contrived and manufactured some one to three hundred years after the life, death, and resurrection of Jesus Christ and well after the death of Mary Magdalene, too. Furthermore, the alleged references are taken out of context.

Even these sources themselves do not clearly indicate such a relationship between Mary Magdalene and Jesus: "And the companion of the [?] Mary Magdalene [?] her more than [?] the disciples [?] kiss her [?] on her [?]" (Apocryphal Gospel of Philip). The only surviving manuscript has holes in it or has places where the text is illegible, as indicated here with the bracketed question mark. The Greek word for "companion" is *koinonos*, while the word for wife is *gyne* (which is not used in this passage). Saint Paul uses the same term (koinonos) in 2 Corinthians 8:23 when he calls Titus his "partner" or "companion." Luke uses the same word in his Gospel to refer to James and John as the "partners" or "companions" of Simon. Obviously, there is a more benign interpretation to that Greek word than the suggested romantic or spousal relationship.

There are other theories for Mary Magdalene's role as well. "Simon Peter said to them (the disciples), 'Let Mary leave us, for women are not worthy of Life.' Jesus said, 'I myself shall lead her, in order to make her male, so that she too may become a living spirit, resembling you males. For every woman who will make herself male will enter the Kingdom of Heaven" (Apocryphal Gospel of Thomas). The Gnostics had a bizarre idea that only males could get to heaven, so even Mary Magdalene had to become a man in order to be saved, according to the passage from the Gnostic Gospel of Thomas, which is certainly not a credible source by any means.

The Gnostic Gospel of Mary Magdalene does not even mention a romance or marriage between her and Jesus. It does speak of a confrontation between Peter and the Magdalene over who will be the authority in the Church. It also refers to secret knowledge (the hallmark of Gnosticism) which Jesus allegedly told Mary Magdalene but withheld from Simon Peter. The secret is that the flesh is evil and only the spirit is good. Pure Gnosticism and pure heresy. If the flesh were truly evil, then Jesus took on evil in the Incarnation when He assumed a human nature that included a human body. This would contradict two thousand years of Christian belief and would make no sense.

Question 33. Who killed Jesus: the Romans or the Jews?

Throughout the centuries of Christianity, the Jews have often been unjustly accused and vilified as the killers of Christ. Neither the Bible nor the Church has ever made such a statement, but individuals on their own have promoted this horrible lie. Historically, the Roman soldiers were the ones who scourged and crucified Jesus until He died on Good Friday. While it is true that Jewish religious leaders from the Sanhedrin conspired with Judas for thirty pieces of silver to betray Christ so as to easily arrest him, they did not by any means represent the entire Jewish population nor the Hebrew faith.

While Jews in general cannot be blamed, neither can Romans or their descendants (the Italians). Specific persons of the Jewish religious leadership sought the demise of Jesus and falsely accused him in court so as to ensure a death penalty. The real culprits, those who are guilty of the horrible death of Jesus, are every single human being who ever lived or will live. All of us have blood on our hands. We are all guilty. He died because of our sins. It does not matter who was there two thousand years ago. Humanity sinned against God and humanity had to be redeemed and saved through the Crucifixion of Jesus.

Question 34. Why did Jesus die?

Jesus died to save us from our sins. Were He only a man and not also divine, then His death would have been tragic but not salvific. The human race could only be saved by a Savior and only redeemed by a Redeemer. Original sin wounded human nature so that everyone born after Adam and Eve was incapable of saving even themselves, let alone the rest of humanity. Mankind needed a Savior. That Savior would have to make the ultimate and supreme sacrifice. Jesus Himself said there is no greater love than to lay down one's life for a friend (John 15:13).

Saint Paul says in his epistle to the Corinthians, "Christ died for our sins" (1 Cor. 15:3). Matthew tells us in his Gospel, "The Son of man came not to be served but to serve, and to give his life as a ransom for many" (20:28). Even the prophet Isaiah foretold in the Old Testament before Christ was born, "he was wounded for our transgressions, he was bruised for our iniquities; upon him was the chastisement that made us whole, and with his stripes we are healed…and the Lord has laid on him the iniquity of us all. He was oppressed, and he was afflicted, yet he opened not his mouth; like a lamb that is led to the slaughter" (53:5–7).

Greek has three words for love: *eros, philia,* and *agape.* Pope Benedict XVI points out in his recent papal encyclical *Deus Caritas Est* (*God is Love*) that despite the sinful distortion and perversion by pornography, eros (possessive love) is still intrinsically good when kept in perspective and proportion. It is not just sexual or physical love. Eros is the love that wants to have—to be with the beloved, to have time and memories, to say this is *my* beloved. It is also the reality that we all need to *be* loved. Philia is a love between friends (as with Philadelphia, the City of Brotherly Love). It is one of affection and loyalty. Agape (*caritas* in Latin) is what Pope Benedict calls oblate love. It is sacrificial. Whereas eros wants to have and possess the beloved, agape is willing to make sacrifice (oblation) for the other.

God's love for us is perfect and is truly agape, as He willingly sacrificed His only Son and the Son willingly sacrificed His own life for our salvation. The death of Jesus was not forced upon Him; He willingly embraced it as painful and horrible because of His love for each one of us. This supreme act of sacrificial love atoned for the sin of pride of our first parents (Adam and Eve) and for all our own individual sins which in essence are acts of rebellion against the dominion of God. Jesus' death opened the gates of heaven which were previously shut when man and woman arrogantly placed their will above God's will.

Question 35. What was Jesus' mission on Earth?

Jesus primarily came to save us from our sins, so we call Him Savior and Redeemer. As priest, He offered Himself on the cross in an act of sacrificial love. He was also a prophet, so he taught for three years before He went to his Passion and Death on Good Friday. The message of Christ was one of mercy and forgiveness. Most of the parables Jesus told had a message about the importance of being merciful and forgiving to one another.

He also commanded His apostles and disciples to preach the Good News (i.e., "the Kingdom of Heaven is at hand"). From that time on, sanctity and holiness became available to anyone and everyone who freely accepted and cooperated with divine grace; this is still true today. Christ's death redeemed human nature and made it possible for human beings to receive sanctifying grace which comes from the sacraments. He told His disciples in Matthew 28:19 to go and make disciples of all nations and baptize them "in the name of the Father, and of the Son, and of the Holy Spirit."

The bottom line is that Jesus not only opened the gates of heaven and made paradise once again possible to humankind, He also provided the means to become holy and therefore get to heaven. He also said in Luke 9:23, "If anyone wishes to come after me, he must deny himself and take up his cross daily and follow me." Christianity is not a religion of taking advantage of what was done in the past, but an opportunity to imitate Christ and follow Him on earth and up into heaven.

The mission of Christ to sanctify (as priest), to teach (as prophet) and to lead and rule (as king) is continued in the mission of the Church via the seven sacraments (that make us holy), her Magisterium (the Church's teaching authority), and the hierarchy (the pope and bishops who are successors to Saint Peter and the Apostles, respectively).

Question 36. Could Jesus sin?

No, Jesus could not sin because He was a divine person. It is metaphysically impossible for Him to sin because to sin is to oppose the Will of God. While there is only one God, He is one God in three persons (Father, Son, and Holy Spirit). Each person of the Trinity is God but there are not three Gods, only one. This means each divine person shares the same divine intellect and divine will. What one person knows, all three know. What one wills, all three will. As the Second Person of the Holy Trinity (God the Son), Jesus is God. Therefore, it is impossible for Him to oppose His own will. Were any of the divine persons able to oppose the divine will, it would mean He would be negating Himself, which is impossible to do. Since God cannot sin (meaning He cannot go against His own will), then none of the three divine persons can sin, either.

While acknowledging that in His divinity or divine nature Jesus could not sin, some may ask whether he could sin in His humanity and human nature. The Council of Chalcedon (451) did define that Jesus had two natures (human and divine), which meant He also had two intellects and two wills. Could His human will oppose the divine will? Wasn't His human will free? Free, yes, but so is the divine will. Free does not mean being able to deny or defy reality. You and I have a free will but we are not free to become something we are not. We are not free to become divine. We are not free to turn what is good into evil nor are we free to turn what is evil into good. We are free to choose to do good or evil, and suffer the consequences of our choices.

Jesus' human free will, like His human rational intellect, are faculties of His human soul, united to His human body but *hypostatically* united to His one divine person. That means his human will and divine will are always in sync, always united and working harmoniously. This does not mean He was not tempted. The devil tempted Jesus in the desert (Matthew 4:1–11; Mark 1:9–13; Luke 4:1–14), but that was an external temptation. Jesus was not born with original sin like we were. Even though baptism washed away original sin in us, we still have the effects of it, namely concupiscence, which is the darkening of the intellect, weakening of the will, and disordering of human emotions (passions)—like the desire for pleasure, comfort, happiness, etc. Since Jesus was born without original sin, He had no concupiscence. Before the Fall, Adam and Eve had no concupiscence, either. The devil could only tempt them externally as he did in the garden (Genesis 3). The devil tried to tempt Jesus externally in the desert as well. We are tempted through our wounded human nature.

What makes us human? Is it our weaknesses? Our sins? No. Our immortal souls that have a rational intellect and a free will are what make us human and what make us created in the image and likeness of God. Those who claim that the sinlessness (also called impeccability) of Christ makes Him less human are incorrect because it is not the ability to sin that constitutes human nature. The ability to reason and to make freewill decisions is human. Animals act out of instinct and computers operate on programming. Only human beings can reason and make moral choices that are either good or evil. Jesus' inability to sin does not diminish or negate His humanity or human nature or even His human free will. As Pope John Paul the Great once said, "Freedom is not license." It is not the ability to do anything you want, but the opportunity to do what you ought to do—the power to do the right thing for the right reason.

Chapter 4

WHAT ABOUT MARY, THE MOTHER OF JESUS?

This chapter looks at the questions about the mother of Jesus: her role in salvation, her background, her virginity, and her motherhood.

■ Question 37. Who were Mary's parents?

■ Question 38. How many children did Mary have?

■ Question 39. Why does it seem like Catholics worship Mary?

■ Question 40. Was Mary perfect?

■ Question 41. What is the Immaculate Conception?

■ Question 42. Was Mary saved? Did she need to be?

■ Question 43. How is she a virgin mother?

■ Question 44. Why pray to Mary when you can go to Jesus?

■ Question 45. Did Mary die?

■ Question 46. What is the Assumption of Mary?

■ Question 47. Why does Mary have so many titles?

■ Question 48. What are Marian apparitions?

Question 37. Who were Mary's parents?

There is not much we know about Mary's parents since their names do not even appear in Sacred Scripture. Tradition has placed their names as Saint Ann and Saint Joachim. What information we can retrieve is from an apocryphal source. Apocryphal sources are numerous, and they fill in much detail that is not in the four Gospels. However, since they are not part of the Sacred Canon of Scripture, they are considered only legends. Nevertheless, the Proto-evangelium of Saint James which was written in 165 AD states that Mary's birth was miraculous because her parents were sterile, and that an angel predicted her birth to Mary's father Joachim after he had fasted for forty days in the desert.

Often, statues that depict Saint Ann show her as an elderly woman, which would fit the legend of them being in advanced years. Statues also depict Mary as a little girl with a book open, standing next to her mother. Ann is always pointing to the book to show that she was a teacher to her daughter in religious and secular studies. Joachim is portrayed by himself and is also elderly.

What we can glean from the Gospels about Ann and Joachim is from their daughter, Mary. As the old axiom says, "The apple does not fall far from the tree." Mary was extremely devout in her beliefs. Though she did not understand how she would become pregnant without the assistance of a human father ("How can this be since I know not man?"), nevertheless, Mary trusted in God ("Be it done unto me according to your word") and the Angel Gabriel then reassured her that she would conceive by the power of the Holy Spirit. She, along with her chaste husband, Saint Joseph, brought Jesus to the temple in Jerusalem as was customary. She was family-oriented. She went to help her cousin Elizabeth, who was pregnant with Saint John the Baptist. Based on all these things, we can say that Saint Ann and Saint Joachim must have been deeply religious and a close-knit family.

In French Canada there is a famous shrine to Saint Ann in Beaupre. The Shrine of Saint Ann de Beaupre attracts thousands of visitors annually. They come on pilgrimage to pray and to be renewed in the Lord. Often, people come with a request or seeking a miracle from Almighty God through the intercession of Saint Ann. Those whose prayers are granted often leave an article, such as crutches or wheelchairs that they no longer need because God has worked through Saint Ann and performed a miracle to cure them from their maladies.

On her feast day, July 26, over one hundred thousand people attend the special Mass in honor of Saint Ann. The day usually concludes with a candlelight procession and recitation of the Holy Rosary.

Question 38. How many children did Mary have?

It is Catholic doctrine that Mary was a virgin before, during, and after the birth (*ante partum, in partu, post partum*) of our Savior; therefore, Jesus is the only child of Mary conceived by the power of the Holy Spirit. The feast in the Catholic liturgical calendar through which we celebrate this miraculous event is the Annunciation; the Archangel Gabriel announced to Mary that she would be the Mother of God and the Holy Spirit would overshadow her, denoting miraculous conception. The Feast is celebrated on March 25. When you add nine months you reach December 25, which of course is the Feast of Christmas, or Christ's birth.

Often, non-Catholics ask about the phrase "her firstborn son," since it implies that there were more children afterwards. Today we use the phrase "only son" if there are no other offspring but use "firstborn" to indicate chronological order of more than one child. Ancient Hebrew, however, used the phrase "firstborn" (*bekor* in Hebrew; *prototokos* in Greek) to indicate primogeniture (i.e., the custom that the firstborn male would inherit the birthright and all property and authority from the father, regardless of how many children were born). An only child would still have the legal title of "firstborn," even if there were no second or third child.

Many theologians throughout the centuries wrote beautiful dissertations on the perpetual virginity of Mary. They argued that if you had divinity, Christ, within you, then you would desire nothing else. So as a woman and mother, Mary was totally fulfilled in being the Mother of God. She had attained the highest vocation she could want or ask for. She was a tabernacle of the Lord; our Blessed Savior, the Second Person of the Blessed Trinity, resided in her womb for nine months.

Scripture scholars have also delved into the question of the brothers and sisters of Jesus. It all centers in on the Greek word *adelphoi*. This word can be translated to mean brothers, cousins, or relatives, such as nephews and uncles. Therefore when we read in Matthew's Gospel chapter 13:55 concerning the brothers of Jesus, it is ambiguous whether the word adelphos is referring to brothers, cousins, nephews, or uncles. (See Question 31 for more on this point.)

At the foot of the cross, Jesus gave His beloved Mother to the custody of His disciple, John. If Jesus had had a blood brother or sister, He certainly would have given His Mother over to his or her care. Yet, the Scriptures are clear it was to His beloved disciple that Mary was entrusted. With the doctrine of the perpetual virginity of Mary, the lack of scripture to back up the idea that Jesus had siblings, and no part of Church tradition making any references to these relationships, we can conclude Mary had only one child.

Question 39. Why does it seem like Catholics worship Mary?

Catholics do not worship Mary; rather, we venerate her as the mother of God, giving her first honors. Catholics, like all Christians, worship God alone. The first three commandments focus on our worship of the one true God, his name, and his day. In Latin, the term for the worship of God is *latria*. In addition to the Commandments, both professions of faith, the Apostles and Nicene Creeds, speak of the belief in one God. Catholic Liturgy, the Holy Sacrifice of the Mass, Benediction, the Liturgy of the Hours, and the celebration of the other six sacraments all give worship, glory, and honor to the Triune God. In our doctrine, liturgy, church law, belief and worship of the one God is tantamount to what it means to be Catholic and Christian.

The Church uses the Latin word *hyperdulia* to indicate the relationship we have with the mother of God. It means that we give first honors after Almighty God to Mary because of her role in salvation history. Hyperdulia is not worship; rather, it is respect we give to an important figure. In American history we give honor and respect to the founding fathers of our country, and we give especially high regard to George Washington, our first president. Similarly, we give first admiration to Mary above all the saints. First, because she said "yes," or in Latin "fiat," which means, "thy will be done." By her affirmative acclamation, she became the mother of God. All of Mary's titles, attributes, and privileges center on this theological fact. Second, she is a model for all Christians to follow on how to attain heaven and be close to her Son. Third, as Mother of the Redeemer and saint in heaven, she is a powerful advocate and intercessor for us on earth. Think of the first public miracle of Jesus, the wedding feast of Cana. The family went to Mary with the problem of wine. She instructed, "Do whatever He tells you to do." She began her prayers for us at that wedding.

In American history, after we honor George Washington, then we pay tribute to the other signers of the Constitution for how they witnessed to our rights to liberty, life, and the pursuit of happiness. Similarly, *dulia* is the affection we give to all other saints besides Mary. In our Catholic faith, Saint Joseph is the first to receive dulia. As with hyper-dulia, it is not worship but acclamation of the fact that this person in her life lived the quality of the Gospel to the fullest and is a living testimony of how we can follow Jesus by his living examples and testimony. A Catholic worships only God, and reveres Mary and the saints.

Question 40. Was Mary perfect?

The quality of perfection in Mary centers on the theological fact that she is the mother of God. The doctrine of the Immaculate Conception of Mary teaches that she was preserved from original sin from the first moment of her conception in the womb of Saint Ann. This preservation is an attribute of perfection. Think of a stained glass window. There are many pieces of colored glass that come together to form a magnificent picture. Salvation is like a stained glass window. There are many pieces of doctrine that come together to form our salvific history. Mary is the daughter of God, our heavenly Father, mother of Jesus, and spouse of the Holy Spirit. She is central in the plan of salvation. Therefore, God had perfected her like no other in His creation.

Being preserved from original sin means she did not have to suffer the consequences of sin—namely death. However, the perfections of Mary in no way obliterated her free will. Throughout her life, Mary always made a free will act of love and obedience to God. In the Annunciation, the Archangel Gabriel announced God's plan for Mary to become the Mother of God. Mary questioned the Archangel, "How can this be since I do not know Man?" Then the Archangel responded by saying that the conception of Jesus would be of divine origin; in other words, the Holy Spirit would overshadow her. Mary responded, "Yes, Thy will be done."

This simple response is a powerful testimony to the perfection of Mary's spiritual life. Indeed, God endowed Mary with many special privileges, graces, and attributes because she was to be the mother of God; however, it was her humility and obedience to the Father that is the hallmark testimony of her faith. She could have said no. She could have decided not to participate in God's divine plan and done her own thing. Yet she did the opposite; she united her will to God's will: "Not my will, but Thy will be done." In her humble obedience, not only did she exalt women and motherhood, but she also expounded by her example what it means to be a follower of Jesus.

Disobedience of Adam and Eve brought us into the mess of sin, and it was the obedience of the new Eve (Mary) and the new Adam (Jesus) that brought about redemption and salvation. This perfection of Mary is an example for any faithful follower of her Son to practice, "Not my will, but Thy will be done."

Question 41. What is the Immaculate Conception?

Ask many Catholics, and they often get confused on the topic. Commonly, Immaculate Conception is taken to mean the miraculous event of the birth of Jesus.

However, Immaculate Conception refers to Mary, the mother of Jesus. It was about her own conception within her mother's womb and not when Jesus was conceived. The Immaculate Conception was a gift from God to Mary that enabled her to be able to give Jesus a sinless human nature as His mother. It was always believed as an article of faith by the Church, and only formerly defined as a dogma on December 8, 1854, by Pope Pius IX. Mary was preserved from original sin from the first moment of her conception.

Original sin is a condition inherited through our first parents, Adam and Eve. Their disobedience to God brought about a fallen world, a darkened intellect, a weakened will, and a disordering of the passions. No longer did they have the preternatural gifts of agility, ease of work, health, and continual life. There was an imbalance in nature, and the human race became sick and died. Through ignorance, weakened will, and passions personal sin was introduced. People consciously disobeyed God.

It was the merit of Jesus Christ on the cross that brought about redemption. Through redemption, the soul is elevated by grace, first received in baptism. The world, though saved by Christ, still suffers from concupiscence. However, through grace, humanity can rise above the darkness of sin to the loftiness of God.

Because of the Immaculate Conception, Mary never suffered under the contagion of sin. In God there is no time, but since we exist in time, He prefigured His Son's redemption and applied it to the womb of Mary's mother, Ann. Think of an old telephone switch board. The switch operator takes a wire from a call and applies it to an outlet. God anticipates His Son's salvific work and applies it to Mary. Why is this so important? Because Mary is to give the sacred humanity to the second Person of the Blessed Trinity to redeem us from sin. Therefore, at no time could that humanity be under the contagion of sin itself.

Mary's sinlessness began from the first moment of her conception. Mary never committed any personal sin from the time she reached the age of reason to the time she died. Since she did not have original sin, she did not deserve to suffer the consequences of it; at the end of her life she was assumed by her son into paradise. The Eastern Church calls this the dormition of Mary. December 8 was chosen for the Feast because nine months later we celebrate Mary's birthday on September 8.

Question 42. Was Mary saved? Did she need to be?

Mary was saved by her Immaculate Conception in the womb of her mother. All of humanity was saved on Good Friday. It is part of the universal salvific will of God. How it is applied to each individual soul depends on the way that soul cooperates with the will of God and His graces that He bestows upon it.

Mary, who is part of the human race, would have been born with original sin. She would have suffered the consequences of original sin had it not been for the miraculous event of God in which He prefigured His Son's redemption and applied it to the soul of Mary at the very moment of her conception. This is how Mary was saved.

Catholics and non-Catholic Christians alike are saved in the waters of baptism. Baptism removes the stain of original sin. The outward sign of baptism is water, the physical vehicle that transmits the blood of Christ shed on the cross to the soul. Once the negative is removed, there is room for the positive—grace. Supernatural grace is God's life within the soul, also known as sanctifying grace. The only way sanctifying grace is lost is by personal sin that is mortal. It is restored by the Sacrament of Penance, which applies the blood of Christ through the words of absolution.

For Mary, all this took place immediately upon conception, hence the title Immaculate Conception. It is a doctrine of the Church that when Mary reached the age of reason, she never committed personal sin. So attuned to the life of grace, so close to Almighty God was she, that she never wanted to lose sanctifying grace. As the Archangel Gabriel greeted her when he announced that she would be the mother of God, "Hail Mary *full of grace*." Saint Therese of Liseux once explained this miraculous event by stating,   "Mary's soul was like a full glass of water that has no room for anything else." Filled with God's grace, there was no room for sin, original or actual. She could then give her son, Jesus, an untainted and spotless human nature.

Saint John the Baptist was possibly the only other human born without original sin; however, he was conceived in the normal fashion every human is. This means that by being human, he inherited original sin upon conception. Scripture tells us that when Mary, who was pregnant with Jesus, visited Saint Elizabeth, who was pregnant with Saint John the Baptist, the baby in Saint Elizabeth's womb leapt for joy. Many theologians contend that this is when Saint John was, in effect, "baptized." God the Father took the saving events of His Son who was in the womb of Mary and applied it to Saint John the Baptist.

Question 43. How is she a virgin mother?

Mary was a virgin before, during, and after the birth of Jesus. This is known as the doctrine of the perpetual virginity of Mary. By the miraculous event of the Annunciation, the Holy Spirit overshadowed Mary and she conceived and bore a Son, named Jesus. Though this is a mystery, it is totally logical to conclude this theological point. A mystery is a divine truth that is revealed but not fully explainable. The chief reason it is not fully explainable is because of language. When we speak of divine truths, which are infinite, we have only finite language to explain them. The very fact that it is finite indicates a limit. We can explain divine truths at times only by analogy because of this limitation.

Our limitations do not mitigate the theological fact of the Virgin Birth. For one thing, the Nicene Creed is specific regarding Christ's origin. We profess in the creed, "I believe in Jesus Christ His only Son, our Lord who proceeds from the Father." Mary became the vehicle in which the Holy Spirit brought about Incarnation. The Second Person of the Blessed Trinity, Who exists at all times with the First and Third Person, takes flesh from the Virgin Mary. The fusion of the two natures in one divine person is called the hypostatic union. Since this did not occur by man, the virginity of Mary remained intact.

St. Joseph was the chaste foster father of Jesus. He was the guardian of the holy family and spouse of Mary. It is the doctrine of the church that the marriage between St. Joseph and Mary was true but was not consummated in the carnal sense. In the scriptures, the only reference to the relations of Jesus is by way of the term *adelphoi*. "Adelphoi," besides meaning brother, can also be translated to mean uncle, nephew, or cousin. Genesis 11:27 tells us that Abraham was the brother of the father of Lot, which made him his uncle. Ancient Hebrew and Greek did not have a word for "uncle" or "nephew" or "cousin." The word "brother" was used in the same way we use the word "relative" today. Genesis 14:12, 16 (in the King James Version) refers to Lot as Abraham's "brother" (*ach* in Hebrew or *adelphos* in Greek). When reading the modern English translation of the Bible, James is referred to as "brother of Jesus," but not "son of Mary." You can only conclude then that the second meaning of the word, which is "cousin," is the appropriate translation.

There is no reference to any sibling of Jesus at the foot of the cross with His mother Mary. Since Mary's cousins were mentioned, it would have also been appropriate for the evangelists to mention Jesus' siblings by name. Since they are mute on this, it is determined he had no other brother or sister. Hence, Mary was a virgin before, through, and after the birth of her only Son, Jesus Christ.

Question 44. Why pray to Mary when you can go to Jesus?

This question has a limiting atmosphere. That one may pray to Jesus through Mary in no way lessens the direct mediation of our Blessed Savior. We have only one mediator and that is Jesus. Catholics do not substitute Jesus for someone less. Jesus brings our prayers to the Father and brings the Father's response to us. Chiefly, this is done through the holy sacrifice of the Mass.

Let's consider the role of "intercessor." A mediator bridges two sides or two parties. Jesus is both God and man, divine and human. Therefore, He alone is mediator between heaven and Earth, between God and humanity. An intercessor, however, is merely someone who makes a request on behalf of another. Many people in the Gospel interceded for their loved ones to Christ. They asked Him to cure someone else. Intercession does not violate nor dilute mediation. At Mass, through the ministry of the priesthood, the priest is an intercessor on behalf of his people to Jesus. He brings to Jesus the people's offerings, prayers, and needs. In return, the priest brings to the faithful Jesus' blessings, gifts, and response. It is in this same way that we understand the intercession of Mary and of all the other saints as well.

In the Nicene Creed, we profess belief in the communion of saints. Community connotes interaction. In heaven, the blessed are in communion around the Godhead in constant adoration, love, and praise. When Catholics pray to a saint, they are not replacing the one Intercessor with the blessed, but rather are praying to the one Intercessor through the blessed. Again, love is not limiting but ever-expanding. It is the love that Jesus has for humanity that allows prayers to come to Him through the blessed.

At Mass, or when someone asks us to pray for them, don't we offer a prayer or do a good work for their intention? If we can do this, why can't the saints in heaven do the same for us? Their intercessions in no way reduce the power of God, but ever increase it. Church militant (the faithful on earth) and Church triumphant (the blessed in heaven) are united along with Church suffering (the holy souls in purgatory waiting to enter eternal life). At death, life is changed rather than ended, so there is a wonderful community in the afterlife. The unity of all three churches is most superbly expressed at Mass, when all are united at the altar of praise.

When we love the coheirs and friends of Jesus, we honor God who is their Creator, Redeemer, and Sanctifier; we do this by invoking their prayers. Mary, who is the first of all saints and has a special honor and place in the church, is also our spiritual mother. How fitting it is to go to the mother of God, the mother of the Church, for she is the closest to her Son. Saint Louis de Montfort said beautifully, "To Jesus through Mary." Mary doesn't replace Jesus, she augments His importance by uniting us to Him in prayer.

Question 45. Did Mary die?

There are two important theological opinions on this question. Many church fathers in the West tend to believe the Virgin Mary experienced a real physical death, whereas many Church fathers in the East propose that she "fell asleep" (called the holy dormition) but did not actually die before leaving this earth. Though preserved from original sin in the womb of her mother, Saint Ann, through the Immaculate Conception, Mary nonetheless died because of the world's loss of the preternatural gifts at the Fall. When Adam and Eve sinned, they lost certain gifts bestowed freely upon humanity. These gifts consisted of the following: intelligence (people did not have to learn by their mistakes), health (no one ever got sick or became old), agility (there was no pain in working or in childbirth), perfect balance in nature, and never-ending life. These gifts were not due to our nature. Our bodies are prone to sickness and disease, so when these gifts were lost, they were lost for good.

Mary belongs to the human race. Though she was preserved, in the most perfect way, from original sin, she still experienced a world with the consequences of original sin—for instance, an imbalance in nature; storms, cold, and heat; bodies becoming sick; darkened intellects; and a need to study. So it is conceivable to believe that at the end of her life she died and then experienced the resurrection of the body and was assumed into paradise by her Son, Jesus Christ. In the Nicene Creed, we profess belief in the resurrection of the body, which means that after we die and the world comes to an end, our bodies will rise in their glorified states modeled after our Blessed Savior and His mother, Mary, and will be reunited with our souls. The doctrine of the Assumption meant that resurrection took place for Mary instantly; she did not have to wait until the end of the world, which would have been a punishment from original sin that Mary was preserved from.

The Eastern Church, such as Byzantine Catholic (in union with Rome) and Orthodox (Greek, Russian, etc.—not in union with Rome), professes belief in the "dormition (meaning 'falling asleep') of Mary," which simply states that because Mary was preserved from original sin, she did not even have to die. Rather, at the end of her life on Earth, she simply fell asleep and then was assumed into paradise by the power of her Son. In Jerusalem there is the beautiful shrine and basilica of the dormition of Mary.

Both views are perfectly acceptable to believe. What is theologically important is the fact that she did not have to suffer the consequences of original sin since she was preserved from it at the moment of her conception, and therefore reigns in heaven as queen of heaven and earth.

Question 46. What is the Assumption of Mary?

In the past 150 years, there have been only two dogmas regarding this issue that have been formally defined by the pope in an *excathedral* statement of papal infallibility. The first is the dogma of the Immaculate Conception in 1854, and the second is the dogma of the Assumption of Mary in 1950. An article of faith is usually defined in a solemn fashion in an excathedra statement because it is being denied, falsely represented, or attacked. Excathedra refers to the pope's power of infallibility in matters of faith and morals given to him by the Holy Spirit upon his elevation to the chair of St. Peter. *Cathedra* means "seat," hence the expression "from the chair of St. Peter."

In these two instances, the belief in Mary's Immaculate Conception and her Assumption into paradise were not attacked, but were commonly believed and taught since the time of the apostles. When Pope Pius IX defined Mary's Immaculate Conception, however, it naturally flowed that her Assumption should also be defined.

In Revelation 12:1 we read, "A great sign appeared in the sky, a woman clothed with the sun, with the moon under her feet, and on her head a crown of twelve stars." With these words, Pope Pius XII solemnly defined Mary's Assumption for all generations. In this document the pope states that because Mary did not have original sin due to her Immaculate Conception, she did not have to suffer decay on earth. Instead, her divine Son, Jesus, assumed her body and soul into heaven. Ascension is different from Assumption. Ascension refers to Jesus ascending into heaven by His own power, because He is the Second Person of the Most Blessed Trinity. Assumption refers to the fact that someone had taken Mary into heaven; in other words, she could not do this herself. Of course, that someone is her Son, Jesus Christ.

The Assumption of Mary is also a feast of hope for members of Church militant—the faithful keeping up the fight of good against evil. Her Assumption prefigures our Resurrection of the body on the last day and subsequent Assumption into heaven when the world ends. The reward for Mary's fidelity, humility, and obedience to God was her Assumption. Remember, it was original sin that brought death and separation about. It is therefore consoling for members of the Church to remain steadfast in belief and untiring in service to the Lord, like Mary did, so that we, too, may enjoy eternal bliss in heaven.

Question 47. Why does Mary have so many titles?

After the worship of the one true God, we honor His chief creation, Mary. She has many titles because she is the Mother of God. All her attributes, perfections, and privileges result in this most important of all her titles (mother of God) because she was chosen to bring forth the Savior of the world. The Ecumenical Council of

Ephesus in 434 AD solemnly defined her as *Theotokos*, or the Mother of God. She is the mother of God not because she gave Jesus his divinity but because she gave him his sacred humanity. Another doctrine, the hypostatic Union, defines this miracle concisely: "one divine Person with two natures, divine and human." Because it is a *union* of natures in the divine Person, Mary is considered the Mother of God.

Mary's second most important title is Mother of the Church. During the Second Vatican Council, which took place in the mid-1960s, Pope Paul VI inserted Mary in the middle of Lumen Gentium (the dogmatic constitution on the Church) by calling her our Spiritual Mother; however, she became the Mother of the Church at the foot of the cross. Jesus gave his last and most prized possession before He died, His Mother. He turned to Saint John the Beloved Disciple and said, "Son, behold thy Mother." Then He turned to His Mother and said, "Mother, behold thy Son." From that moment on, Mary became the Mother of the Church. It is important to note that blood and water flowed from the side of Christ that day when the Church was born. Through baptism, we are all adopted children of God, adopted brothers and sisters of the Lord Jesus, and therefore Mary is also our adopted mother.

There are countless other titles which have been given to Mary over the two thousand years of the Church. Many are contained in a beautiful prayer entitled "The Litany of Our Lady of Loreto." This litany is often prayed at the end of the rosary during the months of May and October, which are devoted to her, and is said on her feast days. Loreto is a little town in Italy on the Adriatic Coast where it is believed the holy house of Nazareth remains. Miraculously, this house was transported from Nazareth to Slovenia and finally to Italy by angels. The following are some of her titles that are prayed: Mother of Divine Grace, Most Pure, Chaste, Good Counsel, Prudent, Mirror of Justice, Seat of Wisdom, Cause of Our Joy, Queen of Angels, Queen of Saints, and Queen of the Most Holy Rosary. Other titles of Mary refer to special places where she has appeared, such as Our Lady of Lourdes, Our Lady of Fatima, and Our Lady of Mount Carmel.

Question 48. What are Marian apparitions?

An apparition can be an appearance of Jesus, Mary, or the saints. Apparitions are quite different from public divine revelation. Public divine revelation is about God and His plan of salvation. The last public revelation took place with the last apostle, Saint John the Beloved. After his death, public revelation ended. Subsequently, only further definition or clarification made by the teaching office of the Church, known as the magisterium, took place. Public revelation is part of the sacred deposit of faith contained in Sacred Tradition and in sacred word. They are known as doctrines and dogmas, and affirmations in faith are to be our only response to them.

Apparitions belong to private revelations, and one can choose either to believe or to reject them. Even when the Church affirms a certain apparition of Jesus, Mary, or the saints as being authentic, one does not have to accept it. When the church declares an apparition as being authentic, it does so in order to differentiate from false prophesy and, consequently, to aid Christians on their journeys of faith.

Apparitions are different from locutions. Apparitions are images imprinted on the senses of the visionary; locutions are speeches received from the visionaries. Not everyone can see or hear apparitions or locutions. In most of the Marian apparitions (apparitions in which Mary appears), there is a message of the Blessed Virgin to pray to her Son and to do penance. Apparitions also take place over the course of the centuries to encourage the faithful to remain close to her Son and to the Church. Sometimes this is achieved by commencing a new devotion.

For example, Our Lady (an affectionate way Catholics refer to the Virgin Mary) appeared to Saint Catherine Laboure, a nineteenth-century sister of charity in Paris. She instructed this nun to create a new medal, the miraculous medal with the words, "O Mary conceived without sin." In Fatima, Our Lady appeared to three little children—Jacinta, Francesco, and Lucia. She asked for total consecration to her Immaculate Heart, for prayer for conversion of sinners to avert war, and for an end to communism. The devotion that began was the five first Saturdays in honor of Mary Immaculate.

It is important to note that there are relatively few apparitions or locutions that are authentic. (Many who have made claims are either misguided at best or deceivers at worst.) The Church declares an apparition only after conducting a rigorous investigation. Ultimately, though, all we need to know in order to attain heaven has already been publicly revealed to the apostles and further defined by the Church.

Chapter 5

DEATH, JUDGMENT, HEAVEN, HELL

This chapter considers questions about life after death, the soul, and where we spend eternity.

Question 49. What are the Last Things?

Eschatology (from the Greek *ta eschata*) literally means "the study of the last things." It is a branch of theology that focuses on what has traditionally been called the Four Last Things, individually (death, judgment, heaven, hell) and universally (Second Coming of Christ, the resurrection of the dead, general judgment, the end of the world). (See Question #64.)

Human beings will experience, individually, the *end* of their own earthly life, and then, at a time known to God alone, the entire world (and physical universe) will meet its own *end* as well. The first 'four last things' occur when the person dies and the second 'four last things' happen at the end of the world. Each man and woman on earth, since the time of Adam and Eve, has or will experience death. Genesis 2:17 states that death is the penalty for sin, and since we have all sinned in one way or another, then all of us must die someday (Romans 5:12).

What happens after death? Particular judgment occurs immediately after the person dies. Philosophically and theologically, once the immortal soul leaves the mortal body, there is death. The dead body begins to incur rigor mortis and finally putrefaction (decay and decomposition). The soul, however, since it is immortal, cannot stay on a physical place like Earth without a physical body. Particular judgment happens instantaneously when death occurs. Jesus Christ appears, but not as Savior and Redeemer as He did on earth on Good Friday; rather, He appears as Judge of the living and the dead. The dead person is judged by the life he or she lived on earth.

Avoiding sin (keeping the commandments) is only half the mission every human person is given by God. The other half is doing good. What did the person do in life? It is not enough to say, "I did not kill," or "I did not steal," or "I did not commit adultery," even though avoiding those things and any sin for that matter is a good thing. Matthew 25:31–46 tells the parable in which Jesus is compared to a shepherd with a flock of sheep and goats. The sheep are placed on the right, and the goats on the left. Those on the right go to heaven, those on the left are sent to hell. What determines if you are a goat or a sheep? That same passage explicitly shows that the sheep are those who took care of others (friends, neighbors, and strangers), while the goats are those who ignored the needs of others. Jesus says to the goats in this section of Matthew's Gospel, "'I was hungry and you gave me nothing to eat, I was thirsty and you gave me nothing to drink, I was a stranger and you did not invite me in, naked and you did not clothe me, sick and in prison and you did not visit me.' They also will answer, 'Lord, when did we see you hungry or thirsty or a stranger or naked or sick or in prison, and did not help you?' He will reply, 'I tell you the truth, whatever you did not do for one of the least of these, you did not do for me.' Then they will go away to eternal punishment, but the righteous to eternal life."

Sins of omission, such as neglecting the corporal and spiritual works of mercy (see Question # 148) are incriminating evidence that you are a goat and will be placed on the left to be cast into hell. People often think their salvation is assured, so there's no need to "do good" as long as they have faith and, at most, avoid committing sin. Matthew 25, however, mentions no quiz on what people believe; rather, they are judged on whether or not they have put faith into practice.

Catholicism teaches that at particular judgment, one of three verdicts occurs. One is the worst-case scenario: an evil and immoral person who has not only committed a mortal sin and is unrepentant, but has also neglected to help others. That person is condemned to hell. The other alternative is the best-case scenario; a good and holy person who has kept the commandments; lived a moral, virtuous, and holy life; and has consistently helped stranger and friend alike is rewarded with the joy of heaven.

A third or middle possibility is that the person is not bad enough to go to hell but also not good enough to go directly to heaven. Their sins have been forgiven on earth but there is still some attachment to sin (they have fond memories of some of their sins). They need some cleansing (purgation); hence, they go to purgatory before going to heaven. (See Question # 67.) Everyone in purgatory is absolutely guaranteed to go to heaven, but they must first remove any and all attachment to sin before walking through the pearly gates.

Question 50. Is hell a place?

Where is hell? If you dig deep enough into the earth and permeate the mantle and magma to reach the iron core of the planet, you will not find the Devil and his minions. Hell does not have a location in space, and there is no longitude or latitude. No GPS can find it, and it has no ZIP code, area code, or URL.

Hell is very real, however. The Catholic Encyclopedia quotes Saint Chrysostom (347–407 AD), who reminds us, "We must not ask *where* hell is, but *how* we are to escape it." Jesus warned about the fires of hell (called *Gehenna* in Hebrew) at least fifteen times in the Gospels. Greek uses two words for hell, *hádés* and *géenna*. Hebrew does the same thing, using *Sheol* and *Gehenna*, respectively. The first is a temporary place of the dead, and the second is a perpetual one. English, however, uses one word to describe both: hell. Our only way of differentiation, then, is to speak of the "hell of the dead" and the "hell of the damned."

After the sin of Adam and Eve, no human soul could go to heaven until the human race was redeemed by the Savior (Jesus Christ). Only the evil deserve the eternal punishment of hell, but if they could not go to heaven, and were not bad enough to go to hell, where did they go? What happened to Adam and Eve, Abraham and Sarah, Isaac, Jacob, Joseph, Rachel, Ruth, Esther, Judith, and so on? Theologians used the term "hell of the dead" to describe where these good and virtuous Old Testament heroes went and where they waited century upon century for the arrival of the Messiah.

The evil people, however, went to the "hell of the damned." This was a place originally created for the Devil and his demons. God created only good angels, but one third of them went bad by their own free will. One of those angels, the most intelligent of them all, was Lucifer. Michael, Gabriel, and Raphael (the archangels and no relation to any Ninja Turtles) were part of the two-thirds of the angels who chose to remain good. The bad angels, like Lucifer, Beelzebub, Asmodeus, and Leviathan, became "fallen" angels, and hell was created for them as their eternal residence, a very nasty place characterized by an eternity of suffering and pain and by the absolute absence of any love whatsoever.

The "pains of hell" (*poenae inferni*) are two types. The pain of loss (*poena damni*) is the suffering of being separated forever from God, who is love. God is the perfect fulfillment of what the human soul needs and wants—essentially, truth and goodness—which are the objects of the human intellect and will, respectively. Our intellect seeks to know the truth, and our will seeks to possess the good; both are completely and perfectly satisfied only in God, who is Truth and the Supreme Good (*summum bonum*). Never having that which is the one and only reality that can make you happy for eternity is the pain of loss. The pain of sense (*poena sensus*) is the physical pain which accompanies the pain of loss. This is the "fire" and "wailing and grinding of teeth," the torture and pain experienced in hell—especially after the body is reunited with the soul after the resurrection.

Fire is used metaphorically in that souls cannot burn since they are immaterial, but resurrected bodies can feel the pain of intense heat and still remain immortal. That means that those in hell will be tormented forever; there will be no end to their punishment—which is one good reason to avoid hell at all costs. It's a good idea to obey the stop sign and the speed limit to avoid accident or death, but another incentive is the cop hiding somewhere ready to give you a speeding ticket. The fear of hell may not be the most sublime reason to avoid sin (hence, it is called imperfect contrition), but it will suffice. The best reason to avoid sin or to be repentant when we do sin is the pure love of God (called perfect contrition).

Heaven, on the other hand, is the exact opposite. Hell is lonely—not because no one is there, but because everyone there hates everyone else. Everyone in hell wants to be alone; everyone in heaven is happy that everyone else is there. Heaven is basically having the beatific vision defined in the Catechism #1028: "Because of his transcendence, God cannot be seen as he is, unless he himself opens up his mystery to man's immediate contemplation and gives him the capacity for it. The Church calls this contemplation of God in his heavenly glory 'the beatific vision.'" In other words, the beatific vision is knowing God directly and immediately, seeing him face-to-face, and being in his presence at all times. The effects of this vision are eternal happiness and unending joy.

Question 51. Who can go to heaven? Who can't?

No one is owed heaven, and no one earns their way to heaven. Heaven is a purely and totally free gift from God that he lovingly offers to humankind. It is the individual human person who freely and knowingly either accepts the gift or rejects it. While no one deserves heaven, every human being, thanks to Christ's death and resurrection, now has the possibility and the opportunity of going to heaven.

Theologically speaking, since the sin of Adam and Eve (original sin), human nature has been wounded and has fallen. It needs sanctifying grace from God, which is a supernatural divine assistance that justifies and redeems by the merits and sacrifice of Jesus Christ's death on the cross. Only baptism confers this special grace; without this grace, the soul cannot enter heaven. Jesus died for all men and women (sufficient grace, as Saint Augustine would call it), but it only affects those who freely accept and cooperate with it (efficacious grace). Jesus redeemed human nature by making salvation possible, but salvation occurs at the moment the person enters heaven. That is why Catholics do not refer to any of the living as "saved," since only the saints in heaven are actually saved (that is, they are now in heaven and will be there forever). Catholics do say they are "redeemed" since all men and women were redeemed by the sacrifice of Christ on the cross.

Think of it this way. A drowning man is thrown a life preserver on a rope. That is redemption. He is now capable of being saved. Without it, he would be lost. Getting him safely out of the water and onto the ship is salvation. Only those in heaven have been saved and we on Earth, though redeemed, still wait for our salvation—which comes only through Christ at the time of our death.

If baptism is necessary and Christ is the only way to salvation, then does that mean only Christians go to heaven? No. Anyone who through no fault of his own has not consciously or willingly rejected Christ and His church is not culpable (guilty), and God does not punish us for things for which we are not responsible. Besides the baptism of water, there are also the baptism of blood and the baptism of desire. (See Question #81.) If it is not their fault that they do not know and believe that Jesus Christ is the only means of salvation, or that he founded the Catholic Church to accomplish that salvation of souls, then their ignorance of the truth will excuse them from being deprived of the joys of heaven. They will be judged according to the morality of the life they lived on earth. Whatever faith they had, they will be judged as to what they did or did not do with that faith.

The Catholic Church condemned and excommunicated those who said only formal (baptized and registered in a parish) members of the Catholic Church are saved. The proper understanding of the axiom *extra ecclesia nulla salus* (outside the church there is no salvation) is explained in Question #243. Since the Church believes in the universal salvific will of God—that He offers everyone sufficient grace to be saved even though it is only efficacious to those who accept and cooperate with it—there is also the teaching that many non-Catholics and non-Christians are saved implicitly. They are considered "anonymous" Catholic Christians. God-fearing Jews, Muslims, Hindus, Taoists, Buddhists, and those of all faiths who do not know that Christ and His Catholic Church are necessary for salvation, and as a result have not *deliberately* rejected Christ or His Church, are not penalized for what they do not know. So the Catholic Church does not teach that Protestants and Jews and Muslims and other non-Catholics go to hell simply because they are not Catholic. The reason someone is not Catholic is crucial. Most people are not Catholic because that is not the religion they were born into or because no one taught them properly. Most non-Catholics who choose not to become Catholic base their decision on what they think, presume, or have been told Catholicism teaches and does. The real doctrines and disciplines have not been fully and adequately explained to them. Some base their decision on emotion or experience. Hence, bad examples of Catholic Christianity from clergy to laity alike—whether a neighbor, relative, classmate, or coworker, or a distorted caricature of what Catholicism is about (like accusations of Catholics worshipping Mary or attempting to buy souls out of purgatory)—all color the perception.

What is perceived is what is rejected, but our salvation depends on believing what is real and true. If our perception is not clear, or if it has been tainted, discolored, or even blinded, then it is not our fault. We cannot be held liable for what is not within our control. Therefore, anyone and everyone has the possibility and potential for heaven as long as they sincerely seek to know and do the will of God. Obviously, part of God's will was to send His Son, Jesus Christ, and His will was to found a Church and institute seven sacraments which would be administered by that Church.

Question 52. What happens at the end of the world?

Doomsday, Day of Reckoning, and Armageddon are various names for the end of the world. The four last things at a universal level are: the second coming of Christ, the resurrection of the dead, general judgment, and the end of the world. Jesus said he would return in John 14:3: "I will come back again and take you to myself, so that where I am you also may be"; in Luke 17:26, He says, "When the Son of Man returns…."

The first coming of Christ was the time when He was born in Bethlehem, two millennia ago. The Second Coming of Christ will be at the end of time. Early Christians thought the *Parousia* (Greek word for the Second Coming) was immanent soon after the Ascension and Pentecost. After the Apostles died off and the Church continued with no Second Coming, they realized Jesus truly meant what he said, "You know neither the day nor the hour" (Matthew 25:13).

The Second Coming is followed by the resurrection of the dead. Christianity firmly believes in the resurrection of all the dead. Jesus rose by his own divine power, but human beings will be reunited body and soul, no matter how many centuries, millennia, or eons have gone by since death separated bodies and souls.

The Catechism teaches the doctrine of the resurrection of the dead in #1038: "The resurrection of all the dead, 'of both the just and the unjust,' will precede the Last Judgment. This will be 'the hour when all who are in the tombs will hear [the Son of man's] voice and come forth.'" This is based on Acts 24:15 ("That there shall be a resurrection of the dead, both of the just and unjust") and John 5:28 ("The hour is coming in which all who are in the tombs will hear his voice and will come out").

The resurrection of the dead makes sense since we are created as a union of body and soul. The pagan Greek philosopher, Plato, held that the soul was a prisoner of the body, and only in death are we free to return to a world of immaterial ideas. Aristotle, his pupil, however, maintained that man was an essential union of body and soul. Without a body there are no senses, and without sight, hearing, or touch, how would we know anything? He held that the fullness of human existence depends on both body and soul.

Since the creation of Adam and Eve in Genesis, and especially since the Incarnation (when divinity and humanity, God and man, were united in the person of Jesus Christ), the union of body and soul are seen as important and part of God's will.

Forty days after Jesus rose from the dead on Easter, He ascended into heaven, body and soul. If the body were useless or redundant after death, then why take His to heaven, unless that is where it is meant to be, always united to the soul?

General judgment occurs after the dead are raised. Many ask what the need is for a General Judgment if there were a particular judgment at death. General judgment is not an appeal or retrial, nor is it a parole hearing. Those in hell will stay in hell; those in heaven will stay in heaven. General judgment does not change any previous decree—it merely reveals and ratifies it to the whole of Creation. Everyone will know who got into heaven and why, and who ended up in hell and why. Every sin and evil deed will be revealed, and every good, kind, merciful, and compassionate deed will also be made known. Those in heaven will not be embarrassed by their forgiven sins since they are forgiven. Think of general judgment as watching a previously recorded trial on Court TV. The judgment already took place and the sentence has been given, and this is merely the reporting of what transpired at that trial.

After the good and the bad have been exposed, then comes the *end of the world*. Revelation (Apocalypse) 20:11 says, "Next I saw a large white throne and the one who was sitting on it. The earth and the sky fled from his presence and there was no place for them." Matthew 24:29 is more explicit: "The sun shall be darkened and the moon shall not give her light and the stars shall fall from heaven and the powers of heaven shall be moved."

The earth, the moon, the sun, the solar system, and indeed the entire physical universe will one day end. They are all material, and material things break down and decay. Even physics has a law of thermodynamics called entropy where energy (heat) is constantly decreasing and seeking equilibrium. The universe will eventually "run out of gas," so to speak. There was a moment in which it was created, and there will be a moment when it will cease to exist. We simply do not know when.

Question 53. What about the rapture?

Since the popularity of the *Left Behind* books and movies, many Catholics ask why they were never taught about the word "rapture." Truth be told, the word is not in the Bible. It is interesting that those Christians who staunchly maintain that the Scripture alone (*sola scriptura*) is the only authority would use a term and idea that comes from outside the Bible.

"Rapture" actually comes from the Latin translation of the Bible completed by Saint Jerome in 400 AD at the direction of Pope Damasus I. This was the first one-volume, one-language edition of the Bible. Both Old and New Testaments were translated from their original Hebrew and Greek into the common (vulgar) tongue of that time and place (which, thanks to the Roman Empire, was Latin).

The Greek word *harpagésometha* is used in Saint Paul's epistle, 1 Thessalonians 4:17, which Saint Jerome translated into Latin as *rapiemur* in the text of the Vulgate Latin Bible. Both words mean "we will be seized" or "we will be caught up" or "we will be snatched up."

The King James Version of this passage reads: "For the Lord himself shall descend from heaven with a shout, with the voice of the archangel, and with the trump of God: and the dead in Christ shall rise first: Then we which are alive and remain shall be caught up together with them in the clouds, to meet the Lord in the air: and so shall we ever be with the Lord." No English Bible uses the word "rapture," and it was not taught as Christian doctrine by the Catholic, Eastern Orthodox, or even Protestant Reformed churches. The notion comes from the nineteenth-century Evangelicals, so even the reformers like Luther, Calvin, Zwingli, Hus, and Cramner (three hundred years beforehand) never used the word or taught the doctrine of the rapture. Most Christians had merely believed that when the end of the world occurred, there would obviously be some living human beings still around; those who were good would be "taken up" while the evil ones would be left behind, yet there was no specific doctrine of "rapture." The "taking up" was considered incidental, like the other phenomena predicted in the book of Revelation (Apocalypse) such as the four horsemen and the seven seals. Only in recent times have Christians of various denominations put emphasis on particular apocalyptic events, like the "rapture." Medieval and Reformation era Christians did not focus as much attention on these peripheral details since none of them directly affect a person's ultimate destiny of heaven or hell.

Question 54. Who is the Antichrist?

It is not Damian Thorn (the fictional character from the movie *The Omen*, which was about the Antichrist), and he does not have a tattoo of the numbers 666 on his scalp. Only four explicit references to the Antichrist occur in Scripture: 1 John 2:18, 1 John 22, 1 John 4:3, and 2 John 7. The Greek word *antichristos* is not the evil twin of Jesus Christ, nor is he the exact opposite. The Antichrist is the enemy and adversary of Christ, but his power and influence are extremely limited despite what Hollywood portrays in film.

Jesus is definitely the Son of God, and he also reserved to himself the title the Son of Man. This does not mean, however, that the Antichrist must necessarily be the Son of Satan or the Son of the devil. The evil one likes to mock God and blaspheme what is sacred and holy by making cheap imitations or parodies (like the Black Mass in devil worship, the recitation of the Lord's Prayer backwards, the inverted crucifix, or the antibeatitudes). So he could very well try to insult God by having his own offspring of sorts. All we know is that there will be an Antichrist, and he will oppose Christ.

The Bible is ambiguous about the identity of the Antichrist. Revelation (Apocalypse) 13:18 tells us, "Let him who has understanding reckon the number of the beast, for it is a human number, its number is six hundred and sixty-six." Many scholars point out that in Hebrew, every letter (except vowels, which do not exist in the Hebrew alphabet) has a numerical value so that a name written in Hebrew would have a sum total of the letters. This is called *gematria* (Hebrew numerology). Early Christians thought the Roman Emperor Nero was the Antichrist. His name (Nero Caesar) transliterated in Hebrew has the numerical equivalence of 666 (50 + 200 + 6 + 50 + 100 + 60 + 200). Yet the world did not end at that time. Nero, however, did meet his end.

During the Reformation, some Protestant-printed pamphlets (thanks to the printing press) called the pope the Antichrist and called the Roman Catholic Church the Whore of Babylon This was merely rhetoric meant to stir up the crowd and attack the other side. Today, there are a few who claim the Internet is evil because the letters "WWW" used to begin an Internet web page (from the "world wide web") also add up to 666 through *gematria*.

Someone will rise to become a world leader and will attempt to lead many souls astray by renouncing Christ (apostasy). That person is the Antichrist. What many spiritual writers remind people, however, is that no one knows the day nor the hour nor even the month, day, year, or century. We do not know who the Antichrist will be. What is more important, urgent, and fruitful is to not worry about the Antichrist but to worry more about the Devil who tempts us every day to sin. When and how the world ends does not affect where we spend eternity. How we live today will determine where we spend the ultimate tomorrow.

Question 55. What is purgatory and where is it in the Bible?

The word "purgatory" is not in the Bible, but neither is the word "bible." Catholicism is not based on the premise of *sola scriptura* (only the Bible), but it does find seeds of doctrine in many scriptural passages as well as in Sacred Tradition, which is as valid a vehicle for divine revelation as is Sacred Scripture. What is in the book of 2 Maccabees 12:42–46 (one of the Deuterocanonical books which Protestant Bibles often include but list as Apocrypha; see Question #17) are these key passages: "He then took up a collection among all his soldiers, amounting to two thousand silver drachmas, which he sent to Jerusalem to provide for an expiatory sacrifice. In doing this he acted in a very excellent and noble way, inasmuch as he had the resurrection of the dead in view; for if he were not expecting the fallen to rise again, it would have been useless and foolish to pray for them in death. But if he did this with a view to the splendid reward that awaits those who had gone to rest in godliness, it was a holy and pious thought. Thus he made atonement for the dead that they might be freed from this sin."

What is happening here is that Judas Maccabeus (a Jew) had just led a successful revolt against the Syrian King Antiochus IV Epiphanes from 167–160 BC. Some of his soldiers died, though, and it was discovered that a few of them wore amulets around their necks as good luck charms. These were strictly forbidden under Mosaic Law, as the commandments forbade any graven image, and these medallions had an image of a pagan god. Hence, the soldiers were guilty of idolatry. They died in sin even though they died fighting for the freedom of their people and their religion.

Instead of leaving it at that, 2 Maccabees 12:42–46 tells how Judas Maccabeus made supplication (prayer of petition) for the dead soldiers. He also made sure that sacrifices were made to ask God to pardon their sins. Here is an example of a doctrine that centers on the praying for the dead. The only way that prayers for the dead can be of any good or can be praiseworthy is if they actually do some spiritual good. If a person is in hell, no prayers can help; if in heaven, no prayers are needed. If there is a third alternative, a place before heaven where sinners are purged (cleansed) and enter heaven once made clean, then why not call it purgatory from the word for cleansing, purge (*purgare* in Latin)?

Purgatory is not hell with parole or hell with a time limit. It is not a suburb of hell, close enough to smell the stench, hear the screaming, and feel the heat, but far enough away to leave when it is time to go. If anything, the analogy that works better is that purgatory is a suburb of heaven, close enough to hear the beautiful music and singing, feel the warm sun and cool breeze, and smell the sweet flowers, but far enough away to long and yearn for the day when you can actually be there.

Purgatory is not a spiritual prison or torture chamber. The souls in purgatory want to be there just as a surgeon wants to scrub up before surgery and just as the patient wants the surgeon to scrub up. Sometimes, the dirt is under the fingernails and takes a little effort and elbow grease to dislodge. Sometimes an old stain takes longer to remove than a fresh one. Purgatory is the temporal punishment due to sin. (See Question #248.)

Sin can merit eternal punishment (hell) or temporal punishment (purgatory). Unforgiven venial sins and already forgiven mortal sins may still have some attachments—the sinner's fond memories of those sins. Purgatory is a state of cleansing where the soul is detached from former sins. The belief that purgatory exists is a dogma. That anyone or everyone has to go to purgatory is not a doctrine of the Church. Some may have their temporal punishment here (often people say of another, "He had his purgatory on Earth"); others may have it in the afterlife.

The discomfort of purgatory is being so close but not quite there. The hope and joy of those in purgatory is the certain knowledge that one day they will in fact go to heaven. That is guaranteed.

Question 56. What about reincarnation?

Reincarnation, or metempsychosis, is the transmigration of souls. It is a pagan concept, alien to Judaism, Christianity, and Islam. Basically it contends that after death, a human soul can return to earth in another human body or, if the person was evil, into the body of an animal. The notion of "previous lives" is a variation of this belief that souls are somehow recycled after death.

Christians—Catholic, Orthodox, and Protestant—strongly repudiate this idea. Genesis tells us that God created Adam and Eve with a body and soul, and both were good. Jesus Christ took on a human nature which meant in addition to his divine nature, he also had a human body and soul, both uniquely his own. He suffered and died for each and every one of us, body and soul.

If an evil life can be atoned merely by coming back in another form or by using another body, then there is no need for redemption or salvation. Christianity says otherwise. One person, one body, and one soul. The doctrine of the resurrection of the dead clearly conflicts with reincarnation. If multiple bodies could be used by one soul, which resurrected body gets the soul at the end of the world? Despite the hallucinations of some Hollywood celebrities, mainline Christians, Muslims, and Jews place no credence in reincarnation.

Question 57. What is limbo?

The word "limbo" is not in Scripture, and it is not in the Catechism, either. It was never a dogma or doctrine of the Catholic Church. If anything, it was a theory or hypothesis of theology, technically called a theological conclusion or construct. Since baptism is necessary for salvation, the question arose as to what happens when good people die before ever being able to be baptized: are they damned to hell?

The Church fathers (See Question #229) spoke of two limbos, *limbus patrum* (limbo of the fathers) and *limbus parvulorum* (limbo of infants). Both were places of natural happiness where souls went after death. Unbaptized adults who lived virtuous lives but died before the coming of Christ and the redemption of the human race would go to this limbo and await Good Friday to be saved. Adam and Eve, Abraham, Isaac, Jacob, David, Solomon, etc., would have gone to this place (sometimes called the hell of the dead).

Unbaptized infants who died in the Christian era would end up in limbo, a place of eternal natural happiness, but not heaven since baptism was necessary to enter there. This proposition maintained the doctrine of the necessity of baptism and the divine mercy and justice of God to reward, not punish, infants who died before being baptized.

The notion of baptism by desire was not well formulated until a little later. (See Question 81 and Question 256.) The current Catechism omits the word and the concept of limbo and prefers to talk about the universal salvific will of God, the doctrine of sufficient and efficacious grace, and the truth that God's mercy and justice are never in conflict. If the unbaptized child would have been baptized had she lived long enough or would have wanted to have been baptized, for example, in the case of abortion or miscarriage, then many theologians propose that would be a baptism of desire either on the part of the parents or implicitly on the part of the child.

WHY SEVEN SACRAMENTS? —CATHOLIC WORSHIP

THIS SECTION HANDLES QUESTIONS ABOUT CATHOLIC WORSHIP, LITURGY, RITUALS, SACRAMENTS, ETC.

| Chapter 6 | # DIVINE GRACE |

This chapter answers the questions about divine grace, its purpose and necessity and how it works.

- Question 58. What is a sacrament?
- Question 59. What is grace, and why do we need it?
- Question 60. What kinds of grace are there?
- Question 61. Can I get grace only from the sacraments?
- Question 62. Why bother with all the symbolism and ritual?
- Question 63. Why does the Catholic Church have seven sacraments while most Protestant churches only have two?
- Question 64. Can sacraments ever be denied to someone?
- Question 65. How can ordinary people become holy?
- Question 66. What determines whether someone is named a saint?

Question 58. What is a sacrament?

A sacrament is an outward sign (something tangible to the senses) instituted by Jesus Christ to confer grace. Sacraments are the chief way that He communicates His life with us. For example, in Baptism the outward sign is water, which is poured over the head in threefold action in the name of the Trinity. In the Holy Eucharist the outward sign is bread and wine which become the body, blood, soul, and divinity of Jesus by the sacred words of Institution. In Confirmation, the outward sign is oil; when oil is placed on the forehead with the special prayer of consecration, the Holy Spirit is conferred. In Holy Orders, it is the laying on of hands along with chrism oil to ordain a man to the priesthood. In Holy Matrimony, it is the verbal exchange of vows between the man and woman, which marries the couple. In Anointing of the Sick, it is the oil of the infirmed placed on the forehead and palms of the sick person. Finally, in Penance, the penitent confesses her sins, and the words of absolution of the priest bring about forgiveness.

In order for the sacraments to be validly celebrated, there must be a union of matter, form and intention. The minister must intend to do what the Church does. The matter of the sacrament is an external action by the minister. The form of the sacrament are the sacred words that have to be used. Finally, a delegated minister must celebrate the sacrament. For example, for Eucharist, Confirmation, Penance, and Anointing of the Sick to be validly celebrated, the minister must be a priest who has faculties by the bishop to celebrate these sacraments. In marriage it is the couple who marries each other, but it must be done in front of a validly ordained deacon, priest, or bishop. The deacon and priest must have proper delegation from the pastor or bishop of the diocese. In case of ordination, only the bishop has the faculty to do so. Finally, in Baptism the ordinary minister is deacon, priest, or bishop. However, in cases of emergency anyone can perform a baptism if they do what the church intends by using water, baptizing in the Trinitarian formula, and pouring water on the head at the same time. The bishop has authority to celebrate all seven sacraments since he is the ordinary minister of all the sacraments.

The purpose of the sacraments is to sanctify the faithful in life. Life is considered a pilgrimage, which has a specific beginning and end. For a Catholic, spiritual life begins at Baptism and ideally culminates in heaven around the Primordial Sacrament, Christ Himself. The sacraments nourish the faithful along the way so that they do not lose their way.

Question 59. What is grace, and why do we need it?

Grace is a gift from God that does not belong to our nature as human beings and, therefore, is called supernatural, or above our nature. It belongs to the realm of God. Quite simply, grace is God's very life within you. The origin of grace is God—most specifically, the merits of Jesus Christ on the wood of the cross—and grace is absolutely necessary to attain life. Grace helps us to achieve this ultimate goal in our lives. Grace is available to everyone because of the universal salvific will of God: the doctrine that God offers every human being the chance or possibility of being saved. Whether or not any individual goes to heaven or hell depends totally on his personal decisions and actions in life. God offers everyone "sufficient grace" to be saved, but it only becomes "efficacious grace" for those who freely accept and cooperate with that grace. No one is predestined to hell or damnation. God would like everybody to go to heaven, but because we have free will, He respects our decisions even to reject Him, His grace, and heaven, if in our sinfulness we choose to do so.

We depend upon God for everything. Our very next breath is a gift from God. It goes without saying that even the higher faculties, such as knowledge, depend upon God. As children in catechism class, we learned early on that we were created to know, love, and serve God, and to prepare ourselves in this life to be with Him for all eternity. This ability requires the supernatural gift of grace in order for us to grasp eternal truths about God and His plan for our salvation. Because of original sin and our fallen and wounded human nature, we are not as loving as we were created to be, hence, the ability to love God beyond all things is the supernatural gift of grace. Original sin wounded our human nature in that it darkened the intellect, weakened the will, and disordered our passions and emotions. This makes us vulnerable to sin and temptation. Divine Grace compensates for the Fall of Adam and Eve, and it is grace which actually heals our wounded human nature by enlightening our intellect, strengthening our will, and keeping our human emotions and passions under control. In fact, even the ability to do good and works of charity depends upon the gift of divine grace. Finally, the abilities to pick ourselves up from sin, to be forgiven, to follow the commandments, and even to avoid sin depend upon grace.

St. Thomas Aquinas, a thirteenth-century Catholic theologian, said that grace builds upon nature and perfects it. To be sustained in the presence of God, to avoid sin, and to persevere requires grace, but because of our free will we can always lose grace. Through grace we become the adopted children of God, members of His mystical body, the Church, and heirs to the heavenly throne. Grace elevates our nature. It brings us to share intimately in the life of God. Chiefly through the sacrament of baptism we become the temples of the Most Holy Trinity, and our humanity is raised.

Grace is absolutely important at the end of our life. It prepares the soul for God. In order for us to be saved, we must have the grace of final perseverance. Jesus tells us in the Gospels, "Those who persevere to the end shall have eternal life." In Catholic devotions, St. Joseph is the patron saint of a blessed death because he intercedes with God for us to persevere in the final transition from this life.

Question 60. What kinds of grace are there?

There are two kinds of grace—actual and sanctifying. Sanctifying grace makes a person holy by the indwelling of the Blessed Trinity, that is, the three Divine Persons of God the Father, God the Son, and God the Holy Spirit that reside in the human soul. It is obtained through the sacrament of baptism. By pouring or immersing the person in water and saying the Trinitarian formula ("I baptize you in the name of the Father, and of the Son, and of the Holy Spirit"), the person is redeemed through the blood of Christ which was shed on the cross. "Sanctifying grace is a habitual gift, a stable and supernatural disposition that perfects the soul itself to enable it to live with God, to act by his love. Habitual grace, the permanent disposition to live and act in keeping with God's will" (Catechism #2,000). Through this grace, we share in the Divine Life; this is why the baptized are called adopted children of God.

Sanctifying grace can be increased through good actions, prayer, practicing the virtues, and worthy reception of the sacraments. The chief manifestations of sanctifying grace are the practice of virtue and the seven gifts of the Holy Spirit: wisdom, understanding, counsel, fortitude, knowledge, piety, and fear of the Lord with its corresponding twelve fruits: charity, joy, peace, patience, kindness, goodness, long-suffering, humility, fidelity, modesty, continence, and chastity.

On the contrary, sanctifying grace can be lost through mortal sin. Mortal sin is that bad thought, word, or deed that kills the soul. For a sin to be mortal, three requisites must be present. First, it has to be serious—a *grave matter*—which means the thought, word, or action has to be gravely wrong. Second, the sinner must know the sin is serious, that is, he or she must have *full knowledge*. Finally, the sinner must have *deliberate consent*—he must freely choose to commit the sin anyway—in order for the sin to meet the criteria. If a person dies with mortal sin on his soul, he loses eternal life. Mortal sin kills the life of grace in a soul, and grace restores that life. Through the sacrament of Penance, God's mercy, love, and compassion heal the soul, and sanctifying grace is restored.

Actual grace is supernatural help or assistance from God. There are two types. The first informs the mind of the difference between good and evil; the second motivates our will to do decent and upright things. Unlike sanctifying grace, which can be lost, actual grace is always being offered to a person, prodding the soul back to God. It is the gentle inspiration, holy thought, or desire. A soul in the state of grace (meaning someone not conscious of being in mortal sin), however, is more inclined to see the promptings of actual grace and then respond in the affirmative. In times of temptation, suffering, and illness, actual grace helps the person to persevere. Finally, actual grace can be medicinal in that it aids the soul's healing process from sin and helps the person to observe the natural moral law.

Question 61. Can I get grace only from the sacraments?

The seven sacraments are the primary vehicle through which God conveys grace. However, being almighty and powerful, He is not limited to the sacraments. For example, those without the light of faith receive grace in different ways. This is part of the universal salvific will of Christ—when Christ died for humanity it was not limited to specific time. Rather, He died for all: past, present, and future. God, who exists outside of time, knows all. Therefore, when our Blessed Savior hung upon the cross and shed His precious blood for humanity, He consciously did so for all those in the future as well.

There is a theological concept known as the "anonymous Christian." This means that if a person through no fault of his own did not consciously and deliberately reject Jesus Christ and His one true Church, and if that same person follows his faith to the best of his ability according to held beliefs, then by the merits of Christ on the cross, he can still be saved. He is only accountable for that which he knows. The old axiom, "The more you know the more you are held accountable," is different from American law in which you are accountable for every law known or unknown to you. God is more merciful. However, once you receive the light of faith in Christianity and do not do anything about it, then all things change. Conversion is absolutely necessary once you receive the grace of enlightenment.

Missionaries are important because the Church is not satisfied with "anonymous Christians." The Church wants everyone to have a conscious relationship with the Lord who saves and continues to bless them through the sacraments. While it is true

God comes to us in many ways, inspirations, thoughts, and kindnesses from people, He primarily comes to us in the sacraments. Jesus Christ and His Church (the mystical body of Christ) is the primordial sacrament. In other words, He is the way in which grace is conferred. Second, the Church is the sacrament of Jesus Christ, or the continual living vehicle for the transfer of grace. The seven sacraments are the final way that Christ bestows grace upon the Church. While a person can spiritually survive with a minimum of grace, it is like living on life support. Living a full, robust, and healthy spiritual life means accepting and cooperating with as much divine grace as God offers, day in and day out.

Sacramentals bestow actual grace (as opposed to sacraments which confer sanctifying grace), but their effect chiefly depends upon disposition of the recipient (*ex opere operantis* in Latin). This means a very good or holy person receives more spiritual benefit than someone who is merely just okay. Sacramentals can be objects, such as rosaries, medals, holy water, and scapulars, and they can be actions, like blessings and exorcisms. The blessing of a priest, at the end of Mass or over a person, is a prime example of a sacramental. Sacramentals differ from sacraments since they were not instituted by Christ and they do not confer sanctifying grace.

Question 62. Why bother with all the symbolism and ritual?

Human beings are created with a physical, mortal body and a spiritual, immortal soul. Actual grace comes to us in many ways, one being sacramentals. One of the forms of sacramentals is ceremony or ritual. The way the sacraments are celebrated, their cultural and ritual practices, are of great importance. Time, energy, and care should be executed when sacraments are being administered, since they are encounters with divinity. Sacred ceremonies and rituals, like the holy sacrifice of the Mass, exposition and benediction of the Blessed Sacrament, etc., help believers transcend this earthly existence and contemplate heaven. Devotion and novenas to saints and their corresponding rituals are also important to the Christian on the pilgrimage of faith to heaven.

Rituals and their symbolisms are also important since human beings are tangible people. We are a body and soul composite. The soul needs the body to bring information to the intellect via the five senses. Your mind would not know what hot or cold meant unless you first experienced these sensations in your body. We worship the Almighty God not only with our minds, but also with our bodies. In fact, our bodies are the temples of the Holy Spirit. Therefore, the rituals in the ceremonies convey our deepest sentiments to God through words, actions, and gestures. During religious ceremonies, Catholics make the sign of the cross and bless themselves with holy water; they genuflect before the real presence of Jesus in the Tabernacle; they are inspired by a holy image; they light candles to communicate their prayers. Symbols and rituals are important in Catholic worship, devotion, and spiritual life.

We praise God through the five senses. Sight—a beautiful church with stained glass windows, frescoes, paintings, and statues—tells a story of faith to the person. Touch—the sign of peace, kneeling, genuflecting, the striking of the breast at the confiteor, and sprinkling of holy water—conveys the sacred actions of prayer. Smell—incense and candles burning—transports the person to another world: the sphere of the divine. Incense has long been associated with our prayers rising to God; the fragrant smell is a pleasing symbol of our offering to God. Through taste, in the reception of the Holy Communion, we have the foretaste of the heavenly banquet that Christ has prepared for us. Finally there is sound, not only from the preaching of the Word and recitation of prayers, but also in the singing of liturgical music. Good Saint Augustine, a fourth-century bishop and theologian, once said, "Singing is praying twice."

Jesus Christ is the Word that existed for all eternity and then took on flesh. His sacred humanity elevated ours. Hence, when we worship God through the senses of our human bodies, we give credence to the Incarnation.

Question 63. Why does the Catholic Church have seven sacraments while most Protestants Churches only have two?

Basically, it is historical. Many of the Protestant denominations had their origins in earlier, previous Protestant sects that originally broke from Roman Catholicism at the time of the Reformation. The Anglican (and Episcopalian) Church, the Lutheran Church, and the Calvinist or Reformed Church are the four major breaks in the sixteenth century. Later centuries experienced further subdivision of those churches (like the Methodist, Presbyterian, Congregational, and Baptist churches). The further anything gets away from its roots the more different the forms it takes. Different Protestant churches emphasize different things. For example, Baptists highlight the baptism of adults (rather than infants or children) so that those receiving the sacrament are conscious of having already been saved. Evangelicals and Pentecostals stress the Holy Spirit and being slain in the Holy Spirit. Presbyterians, Calvinists, and Congregationalists consider preaching most important. Every Protestant denomination agrees on the importance of baptism and sees it as a sacrament. Holy Communion or Holy Eucharist (sometimes called "The Lord's Supper") is also considered a sacrament by mainline Protestant denominations even though they differ greatly on the substance and effect of this sacrament. Christian marriage or matrimony is not technically called a sacrament in most non-Catholic or non-Eastern Orthodox traditions, but it is considered a holy estate and ordinance not to be ignored or disrespected. The other "Catholic" sacraments—for example, confirmation, Holy Orders, anointing of the sick, and penance (Confession)—take on just a ritual effect in the Protestant perspective. Eastern Orthodox have all seven valid sacraments."

Many Protestant denominations have rituals that point toward, imply, or symbolize the sacraments, such as the ceremony of the Last Supper and confirmation. But their understanding of these rituals is that they are no more than symbolic or allegorical reenactments. The closer the division is to the root of Catholicism, the greater the preservation of the seven sacraments. For example, many high church Anglicans (some of whom call themselves Anglo-Catholics) claim to celebrate all seven sacraments.

While Anglicans and Catholics agree that Christ instituted seven sacraments, they will disagree on continuity and validity of the celebration of the sacraments. All mainline Christian religions have valid baptism in the eyes of the Catholic Church, hence, Protestant converts are never rebaptized unless there is a serious doubt to the matter (pouring or immersing in water) or form (pronouncing the Trinitarian baptismal formula of words). The Catholic Church also recognizes the valid reception of Christian marriage whenever two baptized persons (a man and a woman) each enter for the first time into holy matrimony of their own free will. Yet the Catholic Church rejects the validity of the other interdenominational sacraments (confirmation, orders, etc.) based on a serious break in apostolic succession in the ordination of bishops and priests and deacons, as well as the use of substantially different words and the intention of the minister in relationship to what the Catholic Church uses and sees as necessary.

This being said, from the time of the apostles, Catholics have always believed and celebrated the seven sacraments as instituted by Jesus Christ to confer grace. All seven are rooted in Sacred Tradition and are mentioned in the Bible (Sacred Scripture): baptism (Matthew 28:18–20), confirmation (Acts 8:14–17, 9:17–19, 10:5), Eucharist (Matthew 26:26–28, Mark 14:22–25, Luke 22:7–20, John 6:25–71), penance (John 16:1–8, Matthew 16:13–19), anointing of the sick (James 5:13–16), marriage (Matthew 19:3–12), and Holy Orders (Acts 14:22–23, Hebrews

5:1–10). They are to be seen as an organic whole which resembles the stages of natural life and spiritual life, such as sacraments of initiation, sacraments of healing, and sacraments of mission and discipleship.

Question 64. Can sacraments ever be denied to someone?

Sacraments can be denied or postponed for different reasons. The most drastic is called excommunication. It is the penal exclusion of a baptized faithful from the community of faith. There are two ways excommunication can occur: *non-declared* (automatically) or *declared* (judicial process or administrative decree). Automatic excommunication is the most common. A famous declared excommunication took place in 1953 when the Vatican punished a Boston priest, Father Leonard Feeney, for his refusal to recant a distorted teaching on the principle of *extra ecclesia nulla salus* (outside the church there is no salvation). He erroneously and publicly maintained that only Catholic Christians could go to heaven and that Protestants would go to hell unless they converted to Catholicism. (For the real and authentic teaching on this doctrine, see Question #256.)

The 1983 Code of Canon Law lists seven reasons for automatic excommunication: apostasy, heresy, schism, desecration of the Holy Eucharist, laying violent hands on the pope, absolution of an accomplice in the sin against the sixth commandment, episcopal consecration without approval and authorization from the pope, violation of the seal of confession by a priest-confessor, and procuring a direct abortion. The excommunicated are barred from receiving the sacraments and sacramentals, and are therefore deprived of receiving sacramental grace.

A person who remains in the state of mortal sin should not receive the sacrament of the Holy Eucharist until he or she receives absolution in the sacrament of penance. Along this line, if the person is in a persistent state such as an invalid marriage, it is the obligation of that person to have his or her marriage rectified in the Church, and until then should also refrain from receiving Holy Communion. A notoriously sinful person, such as a known criminal who is unrepentant or one whose sin is common knowledge and would cause scandal to the faithful, can be barred as well. It was common for members of the Mafia not to be permitted to be buried in a Catholic cemetery.

A person can also be denied the sacraments for a more benign reason. For example, a person who is baptized but not in full communion with the Catholic Church is not permitted to receive the Holy Eucharist. One must be *in* communion in order to *receive* Communion; in other words, they must be united and in agreement with all the doctrines, disciplines and authority of the church or religion which is offering the Communion. Communion implies union of mind and belief as well as union of church. The word itself comes from two Latin words, "cum" (with) + "unio" (united). *Communio* in Latin means to be "united with" or to be in agreement. Catholic understanding of the Holy Eucharist and Protestant understanding is quite different. At this point in time there is no inter-communion between Catholics and Protestants. Often at Catholic weddings the celebrants will invite people to read the guidelines for Holy Communion in the back of the missalette, or in the back of a wedding program, to educate them regarding who can receive the Blessed Sacrament. The sacraments of Penance, Holy Eucharist and Anointing of the Sick can be administered to members of Eastern Orthodox Churches not in full communion with the Catholic Church, if they spontaneously ask for them and are properly disposed. The same applies to members of other Churches which have all seven valid Sacraments, like the Polish National Catholic Church in the USA and Canada. Finally, a Catholic in confession who is not ready to give up the sin, confess, and make amends might be deterred from receiving absolution until a time when the penitent is ready to make the firm purpose of change.

Question 65. How can ordinary people become holy?

A common definition of a saint is an ordinary person who does ordinary things in an extraordinary way. It is the last criterion that determines holiness. By the sacrament of baptism everyone is called to be holy and a saint. How we cooperate with God's graces and practice the virtues is up to us. We are given this life to prove our love for God. We have been created to know, love, and serve God, and to prepare ourselves in this life to be with Him for all eternity.

God helps us in many ways to become holy. First, He sent His only Son to show us the way. Jesus is the Way, the Truth, and the Life. Any person serious about becoming holy needs to allow Jesus to be in the driver's seat; his or her will must be united with God's will. The Lord gave us the Church to be a beacon of holiness. The Church is holy not because of its members, though there are many saints who belong to the Church, but because of Jesus, the Founder. It is holy because Jesus endowed His Church with special gifts—eternal truths contained in sacred tradition and Sacred Scripture and the Sacraments which confer grace—making the Church the vehicle of salvation.

Staying close to the teaching magisterium of the Church, attending the holy sacrifice of the Mass, and receiving the sacrament of penance when needed, are all spiritual tools to aid a person in becoming holy. In addition, there are many role models to aid the person in holiness. The lives of the saints are a fertile ground of holiness; they give examples of how to become perfect as our Heavenly Father is perfect. In addition, the communion of saints prays for us here on earth. The saints bring our prayers to Jesus and want us to share in the same joy that they have in paradise.

The Holy Scriptures, prayers, devotions, sacramentals, and pilgrimages all help the person grow closer to Jesus. In addition, Jesus gives us one another to lend support on our spiritual pilgrimage. Our fellow passengers on the road to heaven can pray for us, encourage us, guide us, and counsel us. In the negative sense, a fellow passenger can also test our holiness when he or she is not loving to us. We should learn to love them as Jesus loved His enemies on the wood of the cross.

By cooperating with the graces that God bestows upon us every day, we have every chance to become holy in this life. Holiness means we are on the right track to salvation. It is not an exclusive club, though few accept it.

Question 66. What determines whether someone is named a saint?

It is important to note that there are many more blessed in heaven than the Church has officially "canonized," or made saints. The solemnity of all saints is the Church's way of saying there are countless faithful in Heaven. On November 1 we celebrate this glorious feast. Anyone who has died in the state of grace (which means as a friend of God) and has been admitted either directly or indirectly (via purgatory) into heaven is a saint. We all know great and holy people in our lives—whether family members, colleagues, neighbors, or church members—who lived exemplary lives. They may not have been formally declared by the church to be saints, but this in no way negates the fact that they are enjoying the bliss of eternal life in heaven.

The official process of determining who is canonized (named a saint) is long and tedious, since the Church must be extremely scrupulous when investigating a candidate for sainthood. The process begins on the local level, where the holy person lived, and it doesn't start until five years after death—though this requirement can be dispensed. It could be introduced to the bishop of the diocese by the pastor of the parish, the people the holy person lived with or, if a member of a religious community like the Dominicans, by the superior. At this local level, if the bishop accepts the known facts of the candidate's holiness, then he or she is declared "venerable" and a formal process of examining the life of this person commences. In many instances, the process stays at this level. Much time, energy, and even money is needed to carry out a lengthy investigation.

Once proof of holiness has been established, a miracle must be attributed to the holy person's intercession to God. This miracle has to be authenticated by doctors, theologians, and, at times, scientists. If it is beyond a doubt that it is a miracle, the next stage is beatification. During this process, as in the previous, the holy person's writings and the people he or she was in contact with are interviewed. Beatification takes place through the pope or at the local level through a bishop. The holy person is called "blessed," can have a statue erected, and a feast can be placed on the liturgical calendar. Yet it is not an infallible statement as further investigation is required. Another miracle of intercession is needed. Scientific research into the miracle has to be performed. Upon a positive conclusion, the pope can canonize the person to be a saint for all times. An exception to this lengthy process is a martyr, one who witnesses to the faith and dies for Christ. Since martyrdom is so rare and such a total sign of one's fidelity to God, lengthy investigations and verifying miracles are not required for canonization. The only requirement is that the martyr is specifically killed because of his Catholic Christian faith and not for any other reason (political, racial, ethnic, etc.). Unlike terrorists, who pervert the concept of martyrdom, Christianity does not consider those who kill innocent victims to be true martyrs. Martyrs must be victims, not perpetrators, and the reason for their death must be their refusal to deny their religion.

Chapter 7

BAPTISM AND CONFIRMATION

This chapter looks at questions about two of the sacraments of Initiation, Baptism and Confirmation, and their origin and purpose.

Question 67. Are Catholics born-again?

Catholics are "born-again" in water and the Holy Spirit. The term "born-again" is a bit strange in Catholic colloquialism. Nevertheless, through Baptism we are spiritually born or "born-again." It is through Baptism that we become adopted children of God, hence the notion of being "born-again." While Catholics believe one does not need to be aware of being "born-again" in order for it to still happen (as in the case of infant Baptism), Evangelical Protestants believe only a mature person who is able to reason and make adult decisions is able to be effectively "baptized." Accepting Jesus Christ as personal Lord and Savior is the moment of rebirth, and the sacrament of Baptism merely ratifies that decision according to their tradition.

Infant Baptism whereby Catholics are "born-again" is followed by another sacrament called Confirmation, when Catholics can and must speak for themselves. As babies, parents and godparents spoke on their behalf. Confirmation, on the other hand, any time from second grade to high school (usually around eighth grade in many places), when young people are asked to confirm the faith they were given at baptism by consciously embracing it. It is the sacrament by which the baptized are more perfectly bound to the Church and are enriched with a special strength of the Holy Spirit. In one sense, Confirmation is the time when Catholics are asked to accept Jesus Christ as Lord and Savior. Evangelicals believe they are saved in the blood of Christ and confirmed in the Holy Spirit at the same time, hence they do not have a separate sacrament of confirmation distinct from baptism, as do many other Christian denominations.

Catholics also believe they are saved through the blood of Christ and receive the gifts of the Holy Spirit in the sacrament of Baptism; however, Catholics receive them in a different sacrament. Western (Latin Rite) Catholics are baptized as infants and usually receive confirmation as an adolescent. Eastern (Byzantine) Catholics get both sacraments as an infant on the same day. In Baptism, Catholics are born-again in water and the Holy Spirit. In Confirmation, the gifts of the Holy Spirit are imparted to the previously baptized.

All Christians baptize by water to confer the saving effects of the blood of Christ that was shed on Good Friday. Water is the outward sign that signifies what is taking place spiritually. Spiritually, the soul is cleansed of original sin (inherited from our first parents, Adam and Eve), then infused with sanctifying grace. Sanctifying grace is the indwelling of the Holy Trinity. The effects of Baptism are phenomenal; we become adopted children of God, heirs to the heavenly kingdom, and members of Christ's mystical body, the Church.

Eastern Orthodox and Byzantine Catholics receive all three sacraments of initiation (Baptism, Confirmation, and Holy Eucharist) at once. So a baby is baptized, is confirmed (called chrismated), and receives Holy Communion upon her baptismal day. This goes back to the ancient rite of early Christianity, when the early Church was receiving many adult converts. After the Peace of Constantine, there was a mass conversion of adults, so all three sacraments were celebrated at once.

Question 68. Is baptism necessary for salvation?

Yes. Jesus states in John 3:5, "I solemnly assure you, no one can enter into God's kingdom without being begotten of water and spirit." Baptism is a supernatural rebirth during which we become adopted into God's family. It removes original sin, the sin we inherited from our first parents. Original Sin is passed from generation to generation like a trait is passed from one family member to the next generation family member.

The Book of Genesis gives us the account of the Fall. Original sin stemmed from the vice of pride; it was because of pride that Adam and Eve were tempted. It was through their pride that we ultimately lost preternatural gifts; we will get sick, die, have to learn because of ignorance, and toil in pain. There will be no balance in nature. The loss of preternatural gifts was symbolized by the banishment from the Garden of Eden, the place where there was a balance of nature and moral certitude.

Though God punished Adam and Eve and their future generations through the inheritance of original sin, He did not abandon the human race. Genesis 3:15 contains a promise of redemption. "I will put enmity between you [the serpent who tempted Eve] and the woman, and between your offspring and hers; He will strike at your head, while you strike at his heel." Scripture scholars agree that this was the promise of the Messiah who would redeem mankind from sin.

Jesus is the new Adam, and Mary, Jesus' mother, is the new Eve. Disobedience brought sin, death, darkness, and destruction into the world, and it was obedience to God that brought in healing, eternal life, and light. In Catholic devotion, a statue of the blessed mother, known as our lady of grace, shows our lady with hands open and feet crushing the serpent. The symbolism is derived from Genesis 3:15. The grace is God, and Mary's obedience to His will. By her obedience she brought about the Fullness of Grace, Jesus Christ, who, by His complete obedience to the Father's will, crushed the head of the ancient serpent. This obedience led Jesus to be crucified, and the shedding of His blood was and is redemptive for all generations. This redemption is applied to our souls in the waters of baptism, which brings about salvation.

Question 69. What kinds of baptism are possible?

The standard type of baptism is by water and the Spirit. In Matthew 28:18–20, Jesus states, "Full authority has been given to me both in heaven and on earth; go therefore, and make disciples of all the nations, baptizing them in the name of the Father, and of the Son, and of the Holy Spirit." This scripture passage comes just before our Lord ascends into heaven. It is the formula that is used in the rite of baptism. Water becomes the vehicle to transmit divine grace, because our Lord was baptized in the River Jordan by Saint John the Baptist. The baptism that Saint John used was different than Christian baptism; it was one of penance and reform. Since our Divine Lord was and is sinless, by submitting to this baptism, Jesus instituted a new type of baptism that would prefigure His redeeming death and resurrection. In the waters of the Jordan, the Holy Spirit (in the form of the dove) hovered over Jesus. This event symbolizes that the Church lives in the age of the Holy Spirit. Christ used water and all its properties of cleansing and restoration to transmit eternal life.

The Church also has taught about two other types of baptism—one of blood and the other of desire. These two types of baptism do not have the moral certitude or prominence of baptism by water or by the Spirit. However, they do give a theological conclusion to what happens to those who receive water and the Spirit. Baptism of blood deals with martyrdom. The word martyrdom derives its meaning from the Greek *martus* which means "witness." A Christian martyr witnesses to Christ through thoughts, words, and actions; sometimes this comes into conflict with the society, and he is killed as a result.

One important distinction must be made between the original and authentic use of the word "martyr" and the distorted and erroneous application used by terrorists and religious fanatics. Martyrdom is a passive activity, that is, one is martyred for his or her faith. People who intentionally kill themselves and others are not real martyrs. The Christians who were slain by the Roman Empire for nearly three hundred years were martyrs. The Jews killed by the Nazis in the Holocaust (Shoah) were martyrs. Anyone of the Islamic faith who is murdered just because of his or her religion is a martyr.

The Judeo-Christian Scriptures and the Koran forbid suicide and the killing of innocent people, yet some radical extremists have distorted the holy notion of true martyrdom. So-called suicide bombers are actually homicide bombers, and they are guilty of murder. Murderers are not and cannot be martyrs. Martyrs are innocent victims themselves; they do not kill innocent victims.

Baptism of blood refers to a person who is studying for entrance into the Catholic faith but is martyred for Christ before it happens. This type of baptism began during the Roman persecution of the Christians after the fire of Nero. Adults who were studying for conversion, known as catechumens, might not make it to be baptized. They might be arrested and then fed to the lions, or fall to gladiators' swords. It was their intention to be baptized and because they were arrested for being presumed to be Christians and then subsequently killed, they received baptism of blood.

Scripturally, there is a reference to this kind of baptism. In Matthew 2:16 we read, "Once Herod realized that he had been deceived by the astrologers, he became furious. He ordered the massacre of all the boys two years old and under in Bethlehem and its environs, making his calculations on the basis of the date he had learned from the astrologers." This was an attempt by Herod to kill the newborn Savior, Jesus. The astrologers are commonly known as the three wise men or the three kings from the East. The holy innocents shed their blood for Christ so that He could live. The Catholic Church celebrates the martyrdom of the holy innocents on December 28, right in the middle of the Christmas season.

Finally, the Catechism of the Catholic Church in section 1258 concurs and states, "The Church has always held the firm conviction that those who suffer death for the sake of the faith without having received baptism are baptized by their death for and with Christ." Not only the holy innocents (those infant boys slaughtered by King Herod in the attempt to kill the Messiah at the time of Jesus' birth), but everyone who dies in this fashion receives baptism of blood.

The third kind of baptism is that of desire. God offers *sufficient* grace to everyone to be saved. Since every human person has a free will, divine grace is not forced or coerced but can only be accepted or rejected. When accepted, and when the person cooperates with that sufficient grace, it then becomes *efficacious* grace— it achieves what it is meant to do (sanctify the person and get him into heaven). By the merits of Jesus Christ on the cross, He died for all people in all generations. Theologians call this the universal salvific will of Christ. The term "anonymous Christian" can be applied. This is not meant to be used in the pejorative sense. Rather, it recognizes that all religions have bits of truths in them, and if a person follows his or her religion to the best of their ability according to the rules of their religion, then it is believed that he intuitively desired baptism. It would be unfair and unjust for a person who did not have the opportunity of faith to know and accept Jesus Christ to be denied heaven. God gives every person the chance to enter paradise; it is up to that person to cooperate with the graces to achieve this end. The Catechism of the Catholic Church in article 1260 states, "Since Christ died for all...we must hold that the Holy Spirit offers to all the possibility...[of] being saved."

It is important to note, however, that the more one knows, the more one is held accountable. In other words, if a person comes to the conclusion that Jesus Christ is Lord and Savior and does not convert, then he is held responsible for this action. In the Catholic Church reside the four marks of the true Church; there is *one* Church, and it is *holy, apostolic,* and *catholic,* or universal. No other Church can claim this possession entirely. The fullness of revelation is contained in the teaching magisterium of the church. The sacraments, which are the vehicles of grace, are dispensed from the church. This is why the Church sends missionaries out into the world to heed the mandate of Christ to baptize all nations in the Trinity. In the new evangelism that Pope John Paul II called for at the beginning of the millennium, the church is to be seen as a beacon of truth and the way to salvation. It is not enough to be satisfied with being an anonymous Christian. Rather, it is better to know the one true Lord and Savior.

Question 70. Can someone be rebaptized?

The sacrament of baptism confers on the soul an indelible character. Therefore, this sacrament can only be received once in your life. In fact, when we die, we speak in an analogous fashion that the soul has the mark of baptism. Confirmation and Holy Orders also leave an indelible mark on the soul and can only be received once in a lifetime. Confession, Holy Eucharist, and anointing of the sick can be received as many times as necessary. Confession must be received at least once during the Easter season (which starts on Ash Wednesday and ends on Corpus Christi Sunday) if the person is in mortal sin. Daily Communion is encouraged. Anointing of the sick is to be given every time a person is in danger of death, for example, if they are going under anesthesia. Marriage can sometimes be received more than once, but only in the cases of the death of a spouse or the annulment of a marriage.

Some Christians may use the term "rebaptize," but it is an oxymoron since a valid baptism by nature cannot be repeated. You can only become a child of God once, and it is never undone or lost. For example, a baby could be born in the hospital and not expected to live. Church law gives anyone the permission to baptize in the case of urgent necessity. As long as real water flows over the skin and the correct Trinitarian formula is spoken, the person is validly baptized. This is called extraordinary baptism. If the baby survives, then she is brought into the Church for what is called "supplying the ceremonies." In other words, a new or second baptism is not celebrated, but the other rituals of anointing and profession of creed by parents and godparents are performed to complete the liturgical dimension of the sacrament. The Church record will indicate that baptism occurred on a specific date in the hospital and the ceremonies were supplied on another date in Church.

A similar procedure exists that is referred to as conditional baptism. The formula is similar to regular baptism but the words "I conditionally baptize you" are used by the minister. Conditional baptism is performed when the candidate for the sacraments cannot prove that he was baptized, or if there is substantial doubt as to the validity of his baptism. No document exists. Without the moral certitude and because of the necessity of baptism, conditional baptism is recommended. This might arise after an accident when a person is dying. Also, some denominations may claim to be Christian but in actuality are not because they do not believe in the doctrine of the Holy Trinity, nor do they use the Trinitarian formula for baptism. In these cases, a candidate to be received into the Catholic Church is to be baptized properly.

Question 71. What do godparents or sponsors do?

Often, it is thought that godparents are just a nice touch added to the baptism ceremony. But the Code of Canon Law puts a much heavier responsibility upon these witnesses. "Godparent" and "sponsor" are synonymous terms used interchangeably. A godparent is entering a spiritual relationship with the one being baptized. The font of the Church is considered the "womb" which brings forth eternal life. Through baptism we become adopted children of God, calling God our Father and the Church our mother. We need a sponsor to guide us by prayer and example in the ways of the faith.

In today's society, while carrying no legal right to custody, the role of the godparent is completely spiritual. Besides praying for the child, the godparent should be actively involved as a Christian role model in the child's life. This is why the term "sponsor" is used for a godparent. The godfather or godmother is to be a spiritual "coach" who teaches by example. Just like the lives of the saints give us examples of how to live our faith, godparents who practice their faith should be living examples.

Godparents assist parents in the Catholic education of the child. They never supplant the role of the parents, who are the primary educators of their children in the Catholic faith. However, at times when the parents are weak in the faith, it is not uncommon for a godparent to step in to make sure the children are being reared properly in the Church.

Question 72. Who can be godfather or godmother?

The new (1983) Code of Canon Law is quite specific about the qualifications of godparents. First, they cannot be the parents of the child since parents already have a unique and special relationship with their son or daughter. Second, godparents have to be sixteen years of age or older. Third, they have to have been confirmed and made their First Communion. Fourth, they have to be practicing Catholics.

What does it mean to be a practicing Catholic? First, you should be a registered parishioner in your local church and attend Mass every week and on Holy Days of Obligation. Second, if married, the marriage has to be recognized by the Catholic Church as being valid. Therefore, divorced and remarried people without the benefits of annulment are not permitted to be sponsors. A person who is married outside the Catholic Church without permission is also in an invalid marriage and cannot be recognized as a godparent. Catholics who do not regularly go to Mass and rarely, if at all, go to confession are not suitable candidates. This is not a question of whose turn it is to be godparent. Johnny or Joey might be the brother of one of the parents, but his relationship as uncle of the baptized is not sufficient in and of itself for him to be godfather. If he does not go to Church, if he lives an immoral lifestyle, if he espouses opinions and values that contradict Christian doctrine (racism, abortion, promiscuity, drunkenness, etc.), then he should not be asked to assume the sacred duties of godparent.

Question 73. How many godfathers or godmothers can someone have?

One godparent is all that is necessary for baptism. The one godparent must be a practicing Catholic in good standing. However, a candidate for baptism is permitted to have two godparents—one female and the other male. Also permitted is the participation of one Catholic godparent and one Christian witness. A Christian witness is a baptized Protestant who was never Catholic but who practices his Christian faith. A Christian witness would not have the same obligations as a Catholic godparent in seeing to it that the child is being properly raised Catholic. In the baptismal registry, a Christian witness would be noted as such and not as a godparent.

Christian witnesses have to bring a certificate of their baptism in a Protestant Church. This is done for two reasons: first, to prove that they are baptized, and second, to prove that they were never Catholic. In the former instance, to be a Christian witness it goes without saying that you have to be baptized. In the latter case, a baptized Catholic who is now a professed Protestant is not permitted to be a Christian witness because he has formally renounced the Catholic religion.

At baptism ceremonies, in addition to a godparent, one may have a proxy. A proxy is one who is standing in for the godparent who could not physically be in attendance (for example, someone in the military who is overseas can still be a godparent by use of proxy). A proxy must also have a sponsor certificate to show that she is a baptized, practicing Catholic in good standing with the Church.

Finally, many ethnic cultures in the Catholic Church have the custom of multiple sponsors for baptism. In this case, only two godparents are placed in the baptismal registry. They are the official godparents and have the official obligations as such. The others in attendance may symbolically participate, but they are never admitted into official status as godparents.

It is always important to remember when choosing godparents that you do so in realms of faith and belief, not just because they are blood relations or others that the family wants to honor. Fifty years ago, it may have been easier to select blood relations that were practicing Catholics, but in our increasingly secular society, this is often not the case. Godparents are entering into a primarily spiritual relationship with the child. It is hoped that by the way they practice their Catholic faith they will influence the child, even if the child lives far away.

Question 74. Is everyone confirmed at the same age?

For the first few centuries, confirmation of the Church in the West (the Roman Catholic Church) was celebrated in the Sacrament of Baptism. In the Eastern Catholic Church (Byzantine and Orthodox), confirmation is still celebrated with Baptism and First Communion as an infant. In the first few years of the Church, the bishop was the primary celebrant of all the sacraments. As the church expanded, it became necessary for priests to be delegated to Celebrate these sacraments. As the number of infant baptisms also began to grow, the Western Church began to separate the two sacraments. The custom arose that the parish priest baptized the babies and the bishop would later visit the parish to celebrate Confirmation. This custom is still practiced today.

The age at which one can be admitted to the Sacrament is left up to each Episcopal Conference (national gathering of Catholic bishops). In the United States, the conference established the age for Confirmation to be anywhere from seven to sixteen. Any time after that, a person can be admitted to the sacrament. In more recent years, the age tends to be older, between eighth and tenth grade.

A person who is to be confirmed must already have been baptized and have received first Penance and first Holy Communion. The Code of Canon Law is quite specific about the preparation for the sacrament. Pastors must provide adequate and ample time in preparation. This occurs either in Catholic School, in a religious education program in the parish or, more recently, as part of a Catholic homeschool program, such as the Mother Seton Program. The prevailing attitude toward the sacrament is one of maturity. Therefore, a candidate must be capable of passing an exam. Often a candidate is called a soldier of Christ. Since Confirmation is usually the culmination of the candidate's religious education, he should have the adequate knowledge to defend his faith in a mature fashion when questioned. Just as a soldier is called upon to defend his country, monarch, or president, so is the soldier of Christ called upon to defend Christ and Christ's Church.

A Confirmation candidate should also possess a maturity of practice. It is not only important to defend one's faith, but also to practice it. This is why there are many projects of service which should continue beyond the reception of the sacrament. The service projects are examples of how to practice the giving of time, talent, and treasure. A mature Catholic is one who practices stewardship; it is hoped that this maturity level has been attained at the age of reception.

Question 75. Who has the authority to confirm candidates?

The ordinary minister for Confirmation is the bishop. The bishop, who is the ordinary of his diocese, is always and everywhere the chief teacher, dispenser of the sacraments, and shepherd. A priest is ordained to be the vicar of the bishop in the local parish. A deacon is ordained to serve the bishop, priest, and the people of Christ. When the bishop celebrates the sacrament of Confirmation with his priests in attendance, usually surrounding him, it expresses unity.

However, for practical purposes, the bishop may delegate the authority to confirm to an auxiliary bishop, an abbot of a monastery, or a priest. For example, if a parish has a special needs program, the priest of the parish writes to the Bishop for faculties (delegated power) to confirm these candidates. Often, these candidates have to receive the sacrament in a limited environment, so for pastoral purposes the bishop then gives permission to the priest to celebrate the sacrament. Second, a Catholic, who has been baptized and has received first Holy Communion but never received Confirmation, may also be confirmed by the parish priest. The requirements of writing in for delegation from the bishop and of proper instruction of the candidate through a continual religious education program are the same. The bishop often delegates adult confirmations to take place at the local parish level.

A priest, according to the diocese, usually has delegation to confirm when a convert is being baptized or being received into full Communion with the Catholic Church, or when a Catholic is also receiving first Holy Communion. At the Easter Vigil, these sacraments, which are also known as the Easter Sacraments, are celebrated in local parishes by the pastor or parochial vicar with permission of the pastor. The program these candidates attend for preparation is called the Rite of Christian Initiation of Adults or Children, depending upon the candidates' age. Usually, the program begins in September and culminates at the Easter Vigil. The program continues afterward in a period known as Mystagogia.

Finally, a priest is given automatic permission to confirm in the case of an emergency. For example, the section in the anointing of the sick ritual, called the continuous rite of celebrating the sacraments of initiation, is used when someone who has never been baptized or confirmed is in danger of death (*in periculo mortis*, in Latin). When the person is dying, he can receive all three sacraments of Initiation (Baptism, Confirmation, and Holy Eucharist) from any priest. Due to the importance of the sacramental life of the dying person, such delegation is automatic.

Question 76. Why be confirmed?

While not absolutely necessary for salvation, it is nonetheless recommended for all Catholics to be confirmed. First, it concludes the sacraments of initiation which are Baptism, Communion, and, of course, confirmation. Second, the sacrament couldn't come at a better time. While it is true that we receive the seven gifts of the Holy Spirit at Baptism, they are strengthened at Confirmation. It is like receiving a Vitamin B12 shot in order to boost one's immune system to fight off disease.

Baptism inoculates us from original sin, but we still deal with the residue of that sin known as concupiscence. Concupiscence is a state of a weakened will, a darkened intellect, and capitulation to the passions. It sometimes takes a lifetime to overcome, or at least subdue, concupiscence. We have to study and learn in order to grow from ignorance and prejudice. We have to constantly conform our wills to God's will, for it is in following God's will that we are most happy. Sometimes it takes a lifetime to realize this. We conform our wills to God's by practicing the virtues; it takes a lot of work to keep our passions and vices in check.

At the age of puberty, everything seems to go all weak in the knees. We sometimes rebel against our parents, God, and the Church. We have to deal with new temptations. Confirmation then strengthens our gifts of the Holy Spirit at Baptism. Like at any sacrament, God gives us grace. Yet we have to cooperate with these graces in order for the sacrament to work in our lives. Think of the gifts of the Holy Spirit as wrapped presents. In order for us to enjoy the gifts and use them, we have to unwrap the box and open it.

Wisdom gives the person common sense in the natural world in order to figure out right from wrong. *Understanding* is a gift that helps us in the supernatural world in areas of faith and morals. *Counsel* creates unity of mind and heart, while *fortitude* gives us courage in times of trial. *Knowledge* in the areas of God and what He wants for us helps us to follow His will. *Piety*, our outlook on life, prepares us to be with God for all eternity. Finally, *fear of the Lord* is a gift of holy reverence to revere God as Creator, Redeemer, and Sanctifier. These gifts all need a special boost during puberty, as well as when we become adults. There are many temptations, false prophets, and misleading voices. The gifts of the Holy Spirit give us a discerning spirit.

Question 77. Is Confirmation the Catholic equivalent of a bar or bat mitzvah?

In the theological sense, a bar mitzvah is not a sacrament; therefore, it is unlike Confirmation because it does not confer grace. However, in the practical sense the two have a lot of similarities. In the Latin Church, the sacrament of Confirmation is given to candidates beginning in their teenage years. It is seen as a sacrament of maturity. Once candidates receive the sacrament of Confirmation, they are supposed to take their rightful place as adult Catholics in the church by practicing stewardship of time, talent, and treasure. The sacrament is often conferred after years of study, service projects, and spiritual preparations. It used to be the custom that candidates at the confirmation ceremony had to be able to know and respond to ninety-nine questions from the bishop. During the homily, the bishop would ask any of the candidates a basic question in the faith and receive a proper answer.

The same questions asked at Baptism ("Do you renounce Satan?" "Do you believe in God, the Father Almighty?") are asked again in confirmation. This time, instead of the priest or deacon, the bishop asks the questions and the response comes from the young person being confirmed rather than his parents or godparents, as was the case when he was baptized as an infant.

Along this line, bar mitzvah (for boys) or bat mitzvah (for girls) is a rite of maturity for Jewish teenagers. They must have general knowledge of their religion and its history, and know the holy days and why they are celebrated. Finally, the teens must be proficient in Hebrew and be able to say certain prayers and readings from Holy Writ in this language. Upon completion of preparation, the teens are tested by the rabbi. When they pass, the congregation celebrates bar mitzvah for boys and bat mitzvah for girls. After the ceremony, they are fully pledged members of synagogue.

Confirmation is more than a rite of passage; it is a vehicle to confer grace. Grace is transmitted through the laying on of hands, the prayer of the Spirit, and the anointing with the chrism oil. Chrism oil is one of three oils used in the celebration of the seven sacraments, the other two being the oil of catechumen, used in Baptism, and the oil of the infirmed, used in the Anointing of the Sick. All three oils are blessed by the bishop at the cathedral during Holy Week known as the Chrism Mass. Chrism oil is special from the other three because it is mixed with a fragrant balsam. Not only is it used in Confirmation, but also in Baptism, in Holy Orders, and when a Church and its sacred objects are blessed as set aside for worship of God.

The effects of Confirmation when cooperating with the graces create the twelve fruits of the Holy Spirit, which are charity, joy, peace, patience, benignity, goodness, perseverance, mildness, faith, modesty, continency, and chastity.

Question 78. Why are Baptism, Confirmation, and Holy Eucharist called sacraments of initiation?

They are called the sacraments of initiation because they are three sacraments to be received by a person whereby their relationship and connection to the Church is fully established. One is fully initiated into the faith community by receiving all three of these sacraments. Membership has its privileges, as well as its duties and obligations. Fully initiated members are expected to come to Mass every weekend and to go to confession.

After the Roman Emperor Constantine issued the Edict of Milan (313 AD), the

Church was able to come above ground from the catacombs and worship freely. It could expand its missionary activities and lead people to conversion. Also, after the Emperor converted, it became fashionable to be a Christian. In fact, the opposite form of persecution took place against the pagans. With this mass entrance into the one holy Catholic and Apostolic Church, a program of preparation had to be developed. Our present-day convert program, known as the Rite of Christian Initiation of Adults, is based on this early time in our Christian history.

Adult converts were not permitted into the church proper—only into the atrium. They would witness the beginning of the Mass, or the liturgy of the Word, from the entrance to the Church. After the homily, the candidates would be dismissed for further instruction while the liturgy of the faithful or Eucharist continued. It was called "faithful" because only the baptized could attend. Today, candidates in RCIA sit in the church proper; after the prayers of the faithful and before the liturgy of the Eucharist, they are dismissed for further instruction.

It is at the Easter Vigil that these candidates are invited to stay for the whole Mass. At this Eucharistic celebration, they will receive the sacraments of Baptism (for those who are not baptized), Confirmation, and first Holy Communion. After reception, they are fully initiated members in the Catholic Church. For those who are baptized as infants or children, the sacraments of initiation are staggered over a ten-year period. After Baptism, children are prepared for first Communion at the age of seven. Part of the preparation is the reception of the sacrament of Penance. After age ten, but usually before age eighteen, children are prepared to receive Confirmation. Upon reception of this sacrament, they are fully initiated and considered full members of the Church. The sacraments of initiation are referred to as such because that is what they were intended to be: initiations of the faithful.

Chapter 8

PENANCE AND ANOINTING

This chapter examines the two sacraments of healing and why they are important.

Question 79. Why confess to a priest when I can go directly to God?

There are many different names for the sacrament of penance, including reconcili-ation, confession, and forgiveness, which all give a clue as to why Catholics go to a priest to confess their sins. A priest acts *In Persona Christi*, or in the Person of Christ. It is not the priest who absolves the penitent from sin; rather, it is Jesus Christ through the sacramental ministry of the priesthood. The words of absolution, or for-giveness, hint at this, since it is said in the first person. If the "I" referred to the priest, then the sacrament would have no effect. Rather, the first person is Christ. "I absolve you from your sins, in the name of the Father and of the Son and of the Holy Spirit."

Second, sacraments are encounters with divinity. Sacraments are the chief way in which God communicates grace, His saving life within us. The sacrament of penance is an encounter with the healing Jesus. It is through the words of absolu-tion that the merits of the blood of Christ are poured over the penitent. Thus, we are healed and forgiven in the blood of Christ.

Third, every sin, no matter how personal, is an offense to Almighty God. Like Adam and Eve, filled with pride through our conscious and free will, we decide what is best for us rather than allowing God to decide for us. Classically, sin is defined as a turning away from God towards a lesser thing. Since all sin ultimately involves pride, the sacrament of penance is a true act of humility which counterat-tacks pride. It is a humbling experience to confess one's deepest faults to another person, even though that person, a priest, is acting in the name of Christ. By this act of humility, we express to Almighty God how truly sorry we are that we offended Him. The penance that is given by the priest helps us to work out our offense and practice the virtue of humility. While it never erases the insult sin commits against Almighty God, it certainly makes our guilt less.

Fourth, it is a sacrament of reconciliation. Sin not only separates us from God, but it also disrupts our relationship in the mystical body, the Church. Mortal sin cuts us off from that relationship. Therefore, the sacrament of reconciliation not only restores our relationship with God, but also restores us to the Church. True forgive-ness begins outside the confessional. Our attitude of true contrition and firm pur-pose of amendment must antecede confession. Yet our Lord instituted this sacrament as the way to communicate His forgiveness.

Question 80. Weren't all sins forgiven on Good Friday?

Absolutely all sins, from the past, present, and future, were forgiven that day on the cross. Our Lord is an eternal now. He exists outside the realm of time, since time is a creation of God, and His actions can apply for all eternity. We have to work out salvation through time. Therefore we need the sacraments, especially confession, which applies the saving balm of the blood of Christ to our wounded souls.

Our divine Lord in His infinite wisdom and knowledge knew that we would deal with the residue of original sin, known as concupiscence. Though we are created good, and through baptism we have been redeemed by the blood of Christ, we still have the use of our free will and can freely reject these gifts from God. We may choose not to cooperate with the abundance of grace God offers to us through the sacraments. Christ, therefore, instituted the sacrament of penance as a vehicle of mercy and healing. In Mark 2:17, Jesus states, "…I have come to call sinners, not the self-righteous."

Knowing that we have a weakened will, a darkened intellect, and passions that become inordinate at times, He understood that we would fall into sin and would need His forgiveness. Classic scriptural reference to the institution of this sacrament of forgiveness is in Matthew 16: 13–19. In this passage, our Lord gives authority to the apostles and their successors, bishops, and priests of the keys of the kingdom. In fact, one of the most ancient symbols to denote the sacrament of Penance is two keys lying over each other. It refers to the binding and loosening. "I will entrust to you the keys of the kingdom of heaven. Whatever you declare bound on earth shall be bound in heaven; whatever you declare loosed on earth shall be loosed in heaven" (Matthew 16:19).

In fact, the priest who acts in the Person of Christ has to use this binding and loosening. Christ loosens with the key of forgiveness but binds in the case when the person is unrepentant and has no intention of changing. The priest, in the sacred tribunal of the sacrament, has to judge the intentions of the penitent. While it is rare that he has to defer the sacrament and withhold absolution, it does happen. If a person confesses the sin of contraception and has no intention of changing their life because it's too hard or they just don't want to, a priest must withhold absolution until he can ascertain that the penitent is sorry and wants to change.

Question 81. How can I trust the priest not to tell anyone my confession?

There is a term in sacramental theology known as the *Seal of Confession*. The priest is bound by virtue of his ordination to absolute privacy of the penitent. This closure assures that the sacramental seal shall not be violated. Because of this, when people go to the sacrament of Penance, they know that their most private of actions will be kept just private. Only God, the priest, and the penitent will ever know.

If a priest violates the seal, he is automatically excommunicated and defrocked. Only the pope himself can rescind this ultimate penalty. If the penitent wants to discuss any sin confessed in the confessional with the priest outside the confessional, the priest must demand that he start from the beginning; the priest cannot bring any knowledge from inside the confessional outside and vice versa.

When a priest needs to seek advice or counsel about a sin (maybe there is a need to remove a censure that is reserved to the bishop of the diocese, for example) he has to ask the penitent for permission. Once permission is granted from the penitent, he is never referred to by name so that no one could ever figure out who confessed the sin.

Information that is gathered inside the confessional can never be used outside the confessional. To do so would violate the seal of confession. For example, if a person confesses to murdering someone, the priest who heard the confession cannot go to the authorities and turn in the penitent. The priest can advise the penitent that going to the police and confessing is a moral duty, but can never demand it or report the penitent.

There was a famous case in the Baltimore Archdiocese about forty years ago in which a known murderer went to Confession. The priest was summoned to trial and put on the stand. In no way could he violate the sacred seal. Ultimately, he was put into prison for not telling the information he received in the sacraments. Finally he was released, and the laws were changed to protect confessors and the rights of penitents to seek confession without a word being released.

A person who sins and goes to Confession should never fear disclosure. Not only is there a severe penalty on the violation, but the Holy Spirit gives a special gift to the priest, in which he forgets what he hears in confession.

Question 82. What sins must I confess?

In order for the sacrament of Penance to be validly celebrated, the penitent must confess all mortal sins. If the penitent knowingly withholds any mortal or serious sin, then the confession is invalid and the penitent incurs another sin: sacrilege. If the penitent has truly and honestly forgotten to mention a mortal sin in Confession, however, then upon absolution all their sins are forgiven. You are only held accountable for that which you know. It is common practice for the penitent to say at the end of confession, "…these and all my sins I have forgotten since my last confession, I ask for absolution and penance."

What is a mortal sin? Objectively, it is grievous matter—something seriously wrong that is or leads to a severe violation of God's commandments. Subjectively, there are two other conditions for a sin to be mortal—knowledge and free will. The person must know that the sin is a grave matter and freely do it anyway. All three conditions have to be present in order for a sin to be mortal. Otherwise, the sin is venial or less serious.

One does not have to go through the sacrament of Penance to confess venial sins. A good act of contrition—the taking of Holy Water with the consciousness of one's venial sins, asking pardon, and finally, Holy Mass itself, with a contrite and penitential spirit—will remove venial sins. Catholics are still encouraged to go to Confession even if only for venial sins, since these sins can wear the soul down and make it vulnerable to mortal sins. Think of a venial sin as if it were a cold. When left untreated, a cold can turn into bronchitis or pneumonia. The grace conferred through the sacrament of Penance is protective and will help the penitent to be more aware of his surroundings, temptations, and things that need to be changed. The grace of the sacrament—God's healing life within—will help the penitent to avoid the near occasion of sin or temptation in the future. In an analogous way, the grace of the sacrament becomes a vitamin to build up the soul in order to help it resist sin in the future.

Sometimes people go to the sacrament of Reconciliation in order to make what is known as a general confession. A general confession is going over one's whole past. It is true that once a sin is forgiven in the sacrament of Penance, it does not have to ever be brought up again. At times, before a major change in one's life, a devotional or general confession is good for the spiritual life. It could take place before one gets married, is ordained, makes a major career change, or after a retreat. Thinking about where one has been, is now, and wants to go, helps the person to reflect upon past mistakes in order not to commit them in the future.

Finally, people go to the sacrament of Penance when they are dealing with a bad habit that they are trying to break. Though the person is not in mortal sin because free will is reduced, he or she still has the obligation to change. The sacrament of Penance, with its healing balm and strengthening grace, will help the penitent to "kick the habit" and replace it with a good one. The priest offers advice and encouragement to the penitent, which also aids in the healing process.

To help the penitent, a series of pamphlets entitled "An Examination of Conscience" takes the Ten Commandments and all their refinements and puts them into modern language. They also reflect on the six commandments of the Church and the seven capital, or deadly, sins which are also listed as vices. The examination of one's conscience must take place prior to the sacrament. It helps penitents to be truly honest with themselves.

The six commandments, or precepts of the Church, are specific duties of Catholics: to keep holy the day of the Lord's resurrection and holy days of obligation; to lead a sacramental life by receiving Holy Communion and Penance regularly; to study Catholic teaching in preparation for the sacrament of Confirmation, then to be confirmed and continue to study and advance the cause of Christ; to observe the marriage laws of the Church and to give religious training to one's children; to strengthen and support the Church by stewardship of time, talent, and treasure; and finally, to do penance, including abstaining from meat and fasting from food on the appointed days.

The seven capital sins are pride, covetousness, lust, anger, gluttony, envy, and sloth. These deadly sins are always at the root of or the motivation behind the violation of God's commandments. They are fodder for confession because in confessing, the penitents becomes aware of what make them sin.

Question 83. How often should I go to Confession?

Canon law tells us that we should go to Confession at least once a year if we have any mortal sins on our souls and to go to Holy Communion at least once during Easter time. In the United States, Easter time is considered from Ash Wednesday to Trinity Sunday, which gives the penitent almost three months to go to Communion; however, as soon as you are aware that you have mortal sin on your soul, you should get to the sacrament of Penance as soon as possible.

Mortal sin cuts off your relationship with God and neighbor. When you die with mortal sin on your soul, you send yourself to damnation. In the rare case that the sacrament is not available—for instance, if one is in danger of death—one can make a perfect act of contrition. This type of contrition expresses the sentiment that one is truly sorry for his sins, not because he fears the pains of hell and the loss of heaven, but because he is truly sorry for offending Almighty God. However, if the emergency passes and the person lives, he must go to the sacrament of Penance as soon as possible.

Spiritually, Confession can be received as often as you need the sacrament. For example, if you are trying to rid yourself of an immoral habit, you might need the sacrament much more frequently. If you want to receive the healing gift of grace, you may make frequent devotional confessions. It used to be the custom to go to Confession every time Holy Communion was received as a way of preparing the soul for the Blessed Sacrament. Today, it is recommended that Catholics go to Confession monthly. A monthly examination of conscience, followed by Confession and absolution, will aid the soul in maintaining its baptismal purity and innocence.

Another devotion that involves Confession is divine mercy. This feast, instituted by Pope John Paul II, takes place the Sunday after Easter. It entails Confession at least one month prior to the celebration of the feast in order to receive all the merits. In cases of receiving a plenary indulgence, the Catholic must either go to Confession seven days prior to or seven days after the spiritual act is performed in order to receive the indulgence.

Question 84. What if my sins are always the same?

If they are the same, then you have to ask yourself, "Am I truly making a firm effort to amend my life?" If we are engaging in an immoral habit that we are truly trying to break, then it is understandable that it will take time, energy, and commitment to change. Replacing bad habits with good ones can be an arduous process. Sometimes you move a step ahead and sometimes you move two steps behind. God sympathizes with the penitent and will offer a plentitude of grace in the sacrament to aid in conversion.

At other times, penitents will utter the same laundry list because they haven't properly examined their conscience. Examination takes place outside the confessional before the sacrament. If my sins are always the same, do I take the time to go over God's commandments and its refinements as delineated by the Church? Sometimes we don't because we are comfortable with our sins and don't want to change. Change is difficult, but not impossible, with God's grace. "Examination of Conscience" booklets are available in almost every Catholic Church. Just pick one up and read.

Question 85. What is a bad or invalid Confession?

A Confession is invalid when the penitent knowingly conceals a mortal sin in his or her life. If you are consciously aware of a mortal sin and for some reason choose not to confess, you make a mockery of the sacrament; this is sacrilege. Article 2120 of the Catechism of the Catholic Church defines sacrilege in this fashion: "…consists in profaning or treating unworthily the sacraments and other liturgical actions, as well as persons, things, or places consecrated to God." Therefore, knowingly withholding a mortal sin from the priest in Confession, the penitent is making a sham of the sacrament. Sacrilege is a grievous sin, and a person shouldn't receive Holy Communion until it is rectified in Confession, otherwise that Communion received would be a further sacrilege.

A Confession is also considered invalid when the penitent has no intention of revising his life and will continue the same sin.

Question 86. What is Extreme Unction?

The term "Extreme Unction" was one commonly used before the Second Vatican Council to indicate one aspect of the sacrament: the last anointing a person received before he or she died. Though never forbidden to be received more than once, it was often put off until the person was near death. Another common term for the sacrament was Last Rites. After the Second Vatican Council, and with improvements in medicine in the twentieth century, the fuller understanding of the sacrament is celebrated. This is not to deny the fact that the fuller meaning of the sacrament of Anointing of the Sick was always believed or taught.

In the past, people often succumbed to death in situations in which modern medical technology can now aid in the treatment of the person. This is not to deny the spiritual power of the sacrament, but the fact that the infirm may receive the sacrament more than once in life. Catholics believe that God gives us knowledge and the ability to use that knowledge for the good of mankind. Therefore, technology, medicine, and medical procedures should be used when they do not violate God's law. Along with technology, the soul is also prepared through the sacrament of Anointing of the Sick to fight against evil and depression, and to ask for bodily and spiritual healing.

We read in Sacred Scripture (James 5:14–15), "Is there anyone sick among you? He should ask for the presbyters (priests) of the church. They in turn are to pray over him, anointing him with oil in the Name of the Lord. The prayer uttered in faith will reclaim the one who is ill, and the Lord will restore him to health. If he has committed any sins, forgiveness will be his." Clearly, the sacrament is to be used for healing. This verse also serves to introduce the rite of Anointing in which the priest or bishop says this prayer by way of preparing the patient for the sacrament.

Though bodily healing is prayed for in the sacrament, forgiveness of sins and therefore spiritual healing is utmost in the mind of the celebration. If the patient is conscious, then Confession often precedes the anointing. If unconscious, then conditional absolution over the person is given. The Catholic is on a pilgrimage in life toward paradise. The Lord Jesus gives us every possible way to achieve that end, and the sacrament of Anointing is a vital step in the journey. One of the beautiful prayers said after the sacrament is administered reminds the patient that he or she is surrounded by God's grace.

Question 87. Who is supposed to be anointed?

A baptized Catholic who reaches the age of reason and is seriously sick can receive the sacrament of Anointing. The Church defines "serious" as life-threatening. Many people have serious medical conditions, as well as the usual aches and pains, in their older age. If a Catholic is going for even a minor operation that will involve anesthesia, the person can be anointed. Anesthesia can be risky business and some people die from it; therefore, it is appropriate to receive the sacrament.

A person who has a serious illness that will likely result in death can be anointed. Even if the expected death is not imminent, it is encouraged that the person receives the anointing. Miracles do happen, and there is always hope in a cure from God through the sacrament. Through the sacrament, the grace of God encourages, supports, and often enlivens people to endure whatever cross they may have. While bodily healing may not occur, spiritual strength will, and it will aid the person against despair. Remember Jesus' words that those who persevere until the end shall have eternal life. Often, long illness can be debilitating and demoralizing. Life is a battleground of good against evil. When life begins to end, the devil certainly steps up his attacks against the soul and tries to rob it of its peace. Anointing of the sick gives souls the grace and courage of Christ Himself, so that the souls may endure their cross faithfully to the end.

Anyone over the age of sixty-five may also be anointed. Even if the senior is not ill or not in immediate danger of death, age itself is considered a good cause for anointing. Who doesn't have serious aches, pains, or even loneliness at an older age? Again, the sacrament is a vehicle of God's encouragement. Often, parishes celebrate Mass of the Anointing. The elderly, those who are seriously ill, or those who are about to go for an operation often attend the Mass. Not only are they strengthened by the sacrament, but they are also encouraged by the support and prayer of the community and fellow travelers on the way to paradise.

Redemptive suffering is an important spiritual experience. This means that the elderly, the sick, and the infirmed offer up their own crosses to Christ crucified. There they receive plenteous grace to endure their crosses, to find meaning for their suffering, and ultimately to move on in life with the virtue of hope.

Question 88. Who can anoint and what do they do?

The ordinary ministers of the sacrament of the Anointing are bishops and priests. Deacons share in the sacrament of Holy Orders but do not have the power to forgive in the sacrament of Penance. We read in James 5:15, "If he has committed any sins, forgiveness will be his." It is intended that the sacrament of Penance be included in any celebration of the sacrament of Anointing of the Sick. Even if it is not included, James's letter is also clear that presbyters (priests) are to be sent for. Bishops have the fullness of the priesthood, so it is implied that they are included with presbyters.

If the person is dying, it is quite important that the priest is present to prepare the soul for her last journey. The common term now used for the Anointing of the Sick, or Last Rites, is Anointing unto Glory. When the sacrament is employed at this stage there are several prayers, blessings, and commendations that only a priest can give. Often, it is an opportunity to hear the last Confession of the departing soul and to impart Christ's absolution.

Another prayer the priest employs at the last Anointing is the apostolic pardon. The priest is given delegation to impart this pardon (which is attributed to the apostolic or Holy See) upon the departing soul. When sins are remitted through the sacrament of Penance, there is true contrition upon the penitent; due to this forgiveness, he can receive pardon from temporal punishment in purgatory. After absolution, a penitent must perform a work of charity, prayer, or spiritual exercise as part of his penance. The penance is spiritually united to divine grace, which eradicates the penalty due for making an offense against Almighty God. If the penance is not finished upon the person's death, the soul goes to purgatory before entering eternal life. In this temporal state, the soul realizes that it still has earthly attachments or unfinished repentance and wants to finish its cleansing. Apostolic pardon is a plenary indulgence that, when worthily received, removes all temporal punishment and time in purgatory.

The priest then commends to God the soul whom God created, redeemed, and continues to sanctify. Only the priest can offer the prayer of commendation, for it is Christ through the sacramental priesthood who is imparting the blessing. Finally, Mass might be celebrated in which, for the last time, the dying person will receive the Holy Eucharist, called *viaticum*—food for the journey.

Question 89. How many times can a person be anointed?

A person can receive the sacrament of Anointing of the Sick many times during the course of his or her life. During old age or whenever there is a surgery, life-threatening illness, or serious condition, the person is a proper candidate to receive the Anointing. Pastorally, for the infirm or shut-ins, the sacrament should be administered every six months. Many Catholics who are confined to their homes have a "sick call" kit. This kit includes a crucifix, a candle, altar linen, and holy water. When the priest comes to visit the person's home, these articles should be placed on a table in preparation for Holy Communion and Anointing, usually on the first Friday of the month.

The tradition of receiving Holy Communion on first Friday derives from the private revelation of the sacred heart of Jesus to Saint Margaret Mary, a seventeenth-century visitation nun. Part of the revelation asked for nine consecutive first Friday receptions. It is quite traditional for the priest to bring the holy oils and the Eucharist for the shut-in. The priest will light the candle because whenever our Eucharistic Lord is present there should be at least one candle lit in celebration. Holy water is sprinkled to remind the person that in Baptism she was called to be a saint. Finally, the linen is used to place the pyx, which contains the Blessed Sacrament. The priest then may hear the person's Confession, administer the sacrament of Anointing of the Sick, and distribute Holy Communion. All in all, the person feels the support of Jesus and the mystical body of Christ the Church through such visits.

Communal celebrations of the sacrament take place in the parish church, usually once or twice a year. These celebrations are important since they may be the only times when shut-ins may come to the Church. Special care is always taken with parish nurses, doctors, and members of a men's group on hand in case of an emergency. Communal celebration of Anointing is a great way to support the elderly and infirm and let them know that not only God but the community, which is the mystical body of Christ, cares for them.

Saint Paul emphasizes this beautiful analogy of the Church as the mystical body.

Christ is the head, and the baptized are the body. When one of the members of the body is sick, the whole body is sick. This is why great care is given to the elderly and infirmed. Anointing of the Sick at Mass in the parish church emphasizes the communal responsibility and spiritual work of mercy to pray for the sick.

Question 90. Can someone be anointed if already dead?

The sacraments are for the living (*sacramenta sunt propter hominem*) and therefore cannot be administered to the dead. They were given to the Church by Jesus to confer grace at the different stages of life. Baptism, Eucharist, and Confirmation are collectively the sacraments of initiation of new beginning. Eucharist is encouraged to be taken throughout life as food for the soul. Just as you need physical food to grow and be strong and healthy, the soul needs the body, blood, soul, and divinity of Jesus to remain spiritually healthy.

The sacraments of healing, Penance, and Anointing of the Sick (collectively, the sacraments of mercy) are also important during the various stages of life. When the soul is sick through sin, reception of the sacrament of Penance is administered to heal it. When the body is infirm, it receives the sacrament of the Anointing to pray for both spiritual and bodily healing.

The sacraments of vocations are Holy Orders and marriage. They go hand in hand. Married couples support priests by the way they witness to Christ in the world through their vows. Priests dispense the mysteries of God through the sacraments to help married couples become holy and bring forth children and to educate them in the Catholic faith.

None of the sacraments can be given to a person who is deceased. But what constitutes death? Is it when the heart stops? When there is no more brainwave activity? Saint Thomas Aquinas, the great thirteenth-century theologian, argued that one can be reasonably certain that the soul remains in the body while the body is still warm. It is Catholic teaching that death is the separation of the soul from the body. Signs that the soul has left the body are rigor mortis (stiffening of the joints) and putrefaction (the decaying of flesh). As long as rigor mortis has not set in, the body is still warm, and there is no odor of decay, then the sacrament of Penance and Anointing of the Sick can be administered conditionally with the words, "If you are alive, I conditionally absolve you of your sins…." On the other hand, if the body is cold to the touch, then in the anointing ritual there are special prayers for the dead that are read aloud, which are comforting to those who are still alive and around the deceased. But once death has taken place, the corpse can only be blessed and prepared for Christian burial; sacraments, like Anointing, can only be given while the soul is in the body, that is, while the person is still alive. Absolution or forgiveness of sin can only take place while there is still life in the body. At the moment of death, particular judgment takes place and the soul goes directly to heaven, hell, or purgatory.

Since the sacraments are for the living, no one should ever wait to call a priest until death is imminent or has already come. Rather, the priest should be informed during the person's illness so that the sacraments can be administered and he can be spiritually prepared to meet his Lord when he is called home in death. How much more comforting, to the sick person who has experienced the Lord throughout the illness, to be called by Him at the end. Death is not so frightening.

Chapter 9

HOLY ORDERS AND MATRIMONY

This chapter deals with the sacraments of community and the impact of marriage and ordained ministry.

- Question 91. What are the roles of priests, deacons, and bishops?
- Question 92. Why are priests called "Father"?
- Question 93. Why are there no female priests?
- Question 94. Is celibacy a doctrine or discipline?
- Question 95. Are priests different from ministers?
- Question 96. What are minor orders?
- Question 97. What makes a valid marriage?
- Question 98. Are children necessary?
- Question 99. Can we get married outdoors?
- Question 100. Why was the word "obey" removed from the marriage vows?
- Question 101. Why can't Catholics divorce and remarry?
- Question 102. What is an annulment?
- Question 103. What about same-sex unions?

Question 91. What are the roles of priests, deacons, and bishops?

Holy Orders is the sacrament through which one is made a priest, deacon, or bishop. The sacrament is one of two that is listed as a sacrament of vocation, the other is marriage. It is a sacrament that confers an indelible mark upon the soul, like baptism and confirmation, and therefore one is only ordained once through the sacrament of Holy Orders to the diaconate, priesthood, or episcopacy.

Jesus Christ instituted the sacrament of Holy Orders at the Last Supper on Holy Thursday when He simultaneously instituted the sacrament of Holy Eucharist. He intended that the holy sacrifice of the Mass be continued for all ages. These two sacraments are intimately connected. Without Holy Orders, there can be no Mass; without the Mass, there is no Holy Eucharist. The primary purpose of the priesthood is to offer the holy sacrifice of the Mass. By the words, "Do this in memory of me," the apostles were ordained in the fullness of the priesthood as bishops, "fullness" indicating that a bishop is the chief shepherd, sanctifier, and teacher in his respective diocese. Bishops are able to celebrate all seven sacraments. The pope is first and foremost a bishop; as the bishop of Rome, he automatically possesses full, supreme, immediate, and universal authority as visible head of the Catholic Church. He is called the supreme Roman pontiff, Vicar of Christ, successor of Saint Peter, and the servant of the servants of God.

Priests share in the bishop's pastoral responsibilities in the diocese. Just as bishops are considered the successors to the apostles, the priests are considered successors to the disciples, especially the seventy-two mentioned in the Gospels, who were distinct and separate from the twelve apostles. As the early Christian Church quickly expanded, the New Testament listed three levels of ordained ministry which were instituted: bishop, deacon, and presbyter (now called priest). It was increasingly important that the sacraments be dispensed not only in the mother church, the cathedral, and by the bishop, but in smaller churches attached to the cathedral known as parishes. Priests, then, were extensions or representatives of the bishop. They exercised their authority to teach, preach, and sanctify in so far as the bishop of the diocese gave them permission. In Acts of the Apostles 14:23, which was written in the first century AD, we read, "In each church they installed presbyters and, with prayer and fasting, commended them to the Lord in whom they had put their faith."

In Saint Paul's epistle to Titus 1:7–9 we read the qualities of a presbyter (bishop or priest): "He may not be self-willed or arrogant, a drunkard, a violent or greedy man. He should, on the contrary, be hospitable and a lover of goodness; steady, just, holy, and self-controlled. In his teaching he must hold fast to the authentic message, so that he will be able both to encourage men to follow sound doctrine and to refute those who contradict it."

The essence of the priestly role in the New Testament comes from the epistle to the Hebrews 5:6: "You are a priest forever, according to the order of Melchizedek." (Melchizedek was a priest, an Old Testament character with no origins, who offered bread to Abraham.) This all prefigured Christ, who is High Priest and has no beginning or end because of His divinity.

A man who is ordained shares in the priesthood of Jesus Christ, so that Christ may continue to work through him, by way of dispensing the grace of the sacraments. Priests hear confessions, offer the holy sacrifice of the Mass, witness marriages, baptize, confirm (with special delegation from the bishop), bury the dead, conduct Eucharistic celebrations, and are extensions of the bishop in teaching the faithful in matters of the faith.

You may see a priest given special recognition from the Holy Father with the title of monsignor. A priest is not ordained a monsignor, but honored with this title for the good work he has accomplished.

Deacons are also ordained, and they are called to serve the bishop, priests, and the people of Christ. Biblically, they were called to work among the poor. Even today, many deacons chair the Saint Vincent de Paul Society of the parish. This society's primary function is helping the destitute. Deacons may also baptize, proclaim, and preach the Gospel, witness marriages, assist at Mass, bury Christians, and conduct Eucharistic celebrations such as benediction. There are two kinds of deacons—permanent and transitional. A permanent deacon is one that will not be ordained any further as a priest or bishop. The permanent diaconate in the Latin Church was reinstituted by Pope Paul VI after the Second Vatican Council. The Byzantine and Eastern Catholic Church always retained a permanent, as well as a transitional, diaconate. A transitional deacon is one who will later be ordained a priest. Yet, both are clergy and have the exact same functions. A married man may be ordained a permanent deacon, but an unmarried deacon cannot marry after his ordination according to ancient custom. Even the Byzantine and Eastern Orthodox priests who have a married clergy maintain the same custom that matrimony must precede Holy Orders. Married men can be ordained deacons or priests in that tradition, but if one is ordained as a single man, he cannot later marry. Only unmarried deacons or priests in the Eastern Church are ordained and consecrated bishops, hence there is no married episcopacy. The Latin church will make exceptions for married permanent deacons whose wives die while there are still minor children to raise; these deacons may petition to remarry, but that request must be sent to the Pope.

Bishops, priests, and deacons can retire from active ministry but in no way do they stop being what they were ordained to be. In his epistle to the Hebrews (5:6), Saint Paul quotes Psalm 110, which states "you are a priest forever," hence the Church considers Holy Orders to be permanent, not only unto death like marriage, but even beyond into the next life. It is an indelible mark on their souls, even if they were laicized or defrocked. The term defrocked refers to the fact that the priest can no longer wear clerical clothes or the habit of his religious community. After a canonical procedure, the Holy Father can laicize members of the clergy. Officially, they cannot officiate in their ordained capacity. They are dispensed from the obligations of praying the divine office and in some cases they can marry. In the late 1960s, there was a mass exodus among the priesthood. Many priests applied to Pope Paul VI to be laicized so that they could marry in the Church. Under the reign of Pope John Paul II, laicization was not often granted. In recent times, dismissal from the clerical state (commonly called "defrocking") is imposed as a punishment for committing a very serious crime or sparking public scandal. These defrocked clergy are stripped of the title "Father" and "Reverend" if priests, the title "Bishop" and "Most Reverend" if bishops, and of the title "Deacon" and "Reverend Mister" if deacons. The sacrament of Holy Orders is still with them, but they are forbidden to licitly function and to celebrate any of the sacraments since they are no longer authorized ministers. They are still ordained, but their ministry is totally restricted. Only when someone is in danger of death can a laicized priest administer the sacraments of penance and anointing of the sick, and only if no authorized priest is available.

Question 92. Why are priests called "Father"?

Priests have been addressed as "Father" since ancient times. The term emphasizes spiritual generation and family relationships. How can we reconcile this with the biblical passage in which Jesus admonishes His followers to never call anyone father? There was also an admonition not to call anyone teacher or rabbi. In reality, these admonitions are more regarding relationship than language. Rightful place must be given to God the Father, and no one can ever replace God's role in our lives. Therefore, when referring to a priest as Father, you are referring to his function as spiritual leader and shepherd, which he exercises in union with Jesus as priest. If the admonition of Jesus referred to any earthly title, why would Jesus Himself have used the term father in referring to his foster father, Saint Joseph? Jesus even used the title to refer to "Father" Abraham, yet he himself said "call no man 'father.'" He still referred to the commandment to honor your father and mother, though. Jesus also said "call no one 'teacher,'" yet what do we call the instructors of our children? Evidently, the prohibition not to call any man on Earth "father" must be understood in context. A principle of Catholic interpretation of Sacred Scripture is to never take a verse of the Bible out of context; otherwise you get a pretext. If the husbands of our mothers can be called "father," then calling priests "father" is no different. There are 144 places in the New Testament when the title of "father" is used for someone other than God.

Saint Paul used the term for himself in 1 Corinthians 4:15 when he said, "Granted that you ten thousand guardians in Christ, you have only one father. It was I who begot you in Christ Jesus through my preaching of the Gospel." Saint Paul was explaining the spiritual relationship a priest has with his flock. He also referred to Timothy as his son: "This charge I commit to you, Timothy, my son, in accordance with the prophetic utterances which pointed to you, that inspired by them you may wage the good warfare" (1 Timothy 1:18). Timothy was not the biological son of Paul; rather, Paul was Timothy's spiritual "father." Clearly, the term "father" that Saint Paul is using in no way takes away from the supreme reverence we owe to God. Rather, it refers to a symbolic function of his office.

What Jesus was forbidding was the improper use of the word "father." At the time of Christ, His fellow Jews had the practice of giving the title "father" to a founder of a school of thought for rabbinical teaching, and rival traditions often fought with each other based on who followed which "father." Christ condemned the misuse of the word "father" in that context, but he did not forbid its analogous use. The Scribes, Pharisees, and Sadducees would enjoy the privileges and the honor of being considered the "fathers" of Israel, but they did not act like spiritual fathers, who loved and cared for their spiritual children, when they misused their authority for personal aggrandizement. That abuse of fatherhood is what was being condemned.

Friar Lacordaire wrote a beautiful poem about the duty, dignity, and role of priests. This poem makes it clear why priests are called "father." "To live in the midst of the world without wishing its pleasures; to be a member of each family, yet belonging to none; to share all sufferings; to penetrate all secrets; to heal all wounds; to go from men to God and offer Him their prayers; to return from God to men to bring pardon and hope; to have a heart of fire for charity and a heart of bronze for chastity; to teach and to pardon, console and bless always—what a glorious life! And it is yours, O Priest of Jesus Christ!" Friar Locordaire points out the fact that a priest's parish is his spiritual family and like a natural father, he must guide, protect, nourish, and raise it up according to the dictates of the faith. It is in this shepherding role that a priest is a father.

When addressing a priest by mail or by another official method, then "Reverend" is used. Father is a familiar phrase usually said when addressing a priest in conversation. Priests may also receive the honorary title of Monsignor from the Pope via the bishop of the diocese.

Finally, if a priest has an important position "Very Reverend" is used.

Question 93. Why are there no female priests?

Jesus instituted an all-male priesthood because each priest is to act *In Persona Christi*—in the Person of Christ. Christ is the high priest, and a man is ordained into His priesthood. Jesus is true God and true man, fully divine and fully human. He has a divine nature and a human nature. His human nature has a gender like any other human nature, and his gender was male. As God, He is pure spirit without gender, but in his humanity, Jesus Christ is a man. The Priest who acts in the person of Christ needs to be male in order to represent the God-Man.

At the Last Supper, our Lord ordained twelve of His apostles in the fullness of the priesthood. If it was our Lord's intention to ordain women, He certainly would have ordained one of the countless women who followed Him when He preached all over Palestine. His mother, Mary, was His most faithful and obedient disciple, yet she was not chosen to be an apostle. Martha and Mary were close to Christ and were loyal followers, but neither of them became apostles, either. For women to be allowed to be instructed, to be preached to, and to be in conversation with our Lord was a radical concept for the first-century Jewish religion. Not only were women faithful followers, but wealthy women often funded the expeditions of our Lord and His apostles, so it wouldn't have been inconceivable for our Lord to ordain women.

We therefore have to look at the theology behind the all-male priesthood. First, no one, male or female, deserves to be a priest. It is a gift freely bestowed by God. When a man is ordained to the priesthood, his dignity does not lie in himself, but in the fact that he shares in the priesthood of Jesus Christ. It is Christ who is the priest, using the sacramental priesthood as the vehicle to confer grace. For example, the holy sacrifice of the Mass is the same sacrifice of Calvary (but in an unbloody manner); it is Jesus who is priest and victim at every Mass.

Second, we need to look at the theology of creation in which God created man and woman as equals but with distinct roles. Pope John Paul II wrote an encyclical letter on women. In this letter, he mentions that woman have a rightful calling that should not be overshadowed by the concept of women clergy. Instead, it is important to develop their role as generative and maternal. Only a woman can bear and bring forth children. Naturally, women possess qualities of nurturing. In his letter to women, he also notes that women who do equal work should also get equal pay and equal opportunities in employment and education. This is where equality of the sexes must be defended. However, man and woman have distinctive roles; one is not better than the other, rather they complement each other. To deny a woman's role in salvation is to deny her femininity.

Third is the theology of the Church. The Church is always noted in the feminine: she, Holy Mother Church, the bride of Christ. Saint Paul refers to Jesus as the bridegroom. Christ loves the Church as a groom loves his bride. The spousal relationship even goes back to Old Testament times, when God ordered the prophet Hosea to marry the prostitute Gomer. She was an unfaithful spouse, and Hosea was the faithful husband who kept taking her back no matter how many times she fell. This marital relationship was to symbolize the relationship between God and His chosen people who had time and time again become unfaithful, engaging in idolatry and false worship of pagan gods. Since a priest shares in the one priesthood of Jesus Christ, then the references of the Church as mother and priests as father connect; thus priests take on the masculine role of fathers.

Question 94. Is celibacy a doctrine or discipline?

Celibacy is a discipline that Holy Mother Church connects with priesthood and bishopric. In the Latin Rite or Roman Catholic Church when a man is called to the priesthood, he is also called to be celibate. They are two distinct callings from God that work hand in hand. In the latter part of the twentieth century, especially after the Second Vatican Council, this discipline was attacked and maligned, so it is important to define what celibacy is. Celibacy is the formal and solemn oath to never enter the married state. Celibate men and women renounce their right to marry in order to dedicate themselves totally to God and Church. The virtue of chastity (refraining from sexual intercourse) is of course implied in celibacy, since sex is reserved for marriage.

In modern colloquialism, the terms have been used in a synonymous way but everyone, whether single, married, ordained, consecrated, religious, or widowed, is called to be chaste according to his or her particular state in life. For example, a married man must refrain from impure thoughts or desires that would tempt him from his vow of matrimony. The virtue is easily applied to everyone. Celibacy, however, is a calling from God to live a particular disciplined way of life. It is not a doctrine of the Church. In the early Church there were married clergy. Indeed, many of the apostles (including Saint Peter) were married.

In the Eastern Church, or according to Byzantine Catholics outside of the United States and the Orthodox Church, the clergy can marry, but only once and before ordination. An Orthodox or Byzantine Catholic man who either has intentions of becoming a bishop or of entering a monastery, however, has to be celibate. Even married Anglican and Lutheran pastors who convert to Catholicism may be ordained and thus become married priests, but only if they are married before their ordination in the Catholic Church. Unmarried clergy from other Christian traditions may be ordained Catholic priests if they convert to Catholicism, but once ordained, they must remain celibate. Celibacy was normative in the Western (Latin) Church since the Council of Elvira (306), and it became mandatory in 1075 by Pope Gregory VII. The Eastern and Byzantine Church always had optional celibacy, except for bishops who came from the ranks of the celibate monks.

Our Blessed Savior Jesus Christ never married. He never married Mary Magdalene or any other woman and there was never a romance between them, either. Contrary to the retelling by *The DaVinci Code*, which is a scurrilous and fictional fantasy, Christ never married except in a mystical way to the Church. Sacred Scripture never mentions a wife, and Sacred Tradition maintains Christ's earthly celibacy. He is the bridegroom and the Church His spiritual bride. In this supernatural way, Jesus, who is Lord and Savior, is for all people, all generations, and all races until the end of time. A priest who observes the discipline of celibacy is imitating the great High Priest, Jesus Christ.

The classic biblical reference for celibacy is the epistle of Saint Paul 1 Corinthians 7:32–33, "I (Paul) should like you to be free of all worries. The unmarried man is busy with the Lord's affairs, concerned with pleasing the Lord; but the married man is busy with this world's demands and occupied with pleasing his wife. This means he is divided." The passage is not meant to downplay marriage; rather, it highlights the importance of the priest's undivided attention to the Lord and His people in the priest's sacred duty. Saint Paul realistically knew that a priest would have to be brother and father to all—not a nine-to-five job but an enduring vocation that has to be lived out all his life.

Celibacy provides the discipline to help the priest give undivided attention to the Lord and His Church. How this regulation is used by the individual priest is another story. We may have all been witness to married clergy who do a superb job. We may also have observed broken vows and commitments, but this tragedy does not downplay the significance of celibacy. The discipline of celibacy implies that the priest, who acts *In Persona Christi*, is married to the Church. A priest is addressed as "Father" because he has many children through the sacraments. He gives spiritual birth through Baptism, feeds his children through the Holy Eucharist, and heals his children through Penance and the Anointing of the Sick.

The requirement of celibacy in the priesthood can be changed by the pope in the future; however, considering the current physical make of living quarters, clerical lifestyles, and the great witness that celibacy expresses to the Kingdom of God, it is a discipline that will be here to stay for many years. It should be noted that a priest does not give up something or deny himself anything without receiving many more great and awesome spiritual gifts in return. Rather, the discipline of celibacy is a gift that enables the priest to shepherd a great family. It also demands sacrifice. But marriage demands sacrifice as well. In marriage, the husband sacrifices his own wants, desires, and will for the sake of his spouse, and a wife does the same. In celibacy, the priest freely gives up wife and children in order to serve God and parishioners, which become his family.

Question 95. Are priests different from ministers?

Protestant ministers do not receive a sacrament, which is an outward sign instituted by Jesus Christ to confer grace. Rather, they are commissioned by their church to preach, teach, and shepherd their flock. Depending upon the denomination, when a minister retires it is like retiring from a company, and he can begin a whole new career. Also, it is not uncommon for a minister to hold down a secular job in order to support his family. Ministers are usually interviewed by the intended congregation they are going to serve. It is up to that congregation to impart salary, benefits, housing, etc. In some higher circles, such as Episcopal or Lutheran churches, a bishop is involved in the assignment of its clergy. Yet the local congregation has much to say regarding the type of clergy it desires.

A Catholic priest, through his ordination, receives a sacrament. The sacrament (Holy Orders) configures an indelible mark on his soul: once a priest, always a priest, even in the afterlife. The sacramental seal makes a priest an *alter Christus*, or another Christ. Consequently, the priest acts *In Persona Christi* or in the Person of Christ. When the priest baptizes, it is Christ who baptizes. When a priest absolves sin, it is Christ who absolves sin. When a priest offers the holy gifts to become the body and blood of Christ, it is Christ who is priest and victim. In all seven sacraments, Jesus Christ is the priest, and priesthood is the instrument through which grace is given to the people of Christ.

A priest is assigned by his bishop to a parish or ministry within the diocese. He is seen as the extension or vicar of the bishop. For that reason, there is unity in the church. A priest has his faculties to serve in direct consequences of the bishop of the diocese. If faculties are removed he cannot serve in public. Benefits, housing, and insurance are all determined by the bishop. This allows certain freedom, since it is not the congregation who approves of the priest's assignment, but the bishop; the priest can teach and preach freely, without worrying about acceptance from parishioners.

Question 96. What are minor orders?

"Minor orders" was a term used in the Church before the Second Vatican Council. Minor orders included various roles within the church such as tonsure, porter, lector, exorcist, and acolyte. *Tonsure* was the symbolic cutting of hair around the crown of the head. Monks and friars often had a large amount of their hair cut off with a single band of hair going horizontally across the back of their head. This was a sign of their consecrated life as religious. Diocesan clergy (parish priests), when tonsured, merely had a small amount of hair cut off from the back of the head, the usual place where many men get their so-called bald spot. Tonsure signified entrance into clerical life, but a man could still leave the seminary or monastery without needing to be dispensed by Rome should he discern he was not meant to go on further. Celibacy was not imposed during minor orders, only at subdiaconate.

Porter was the minor order in which a man was given the symbolic key; the term comes from medieval times—the porter was the guy who locked up at night and made sure visitors were allowed in while unfriendly elements stayed out. *Lector* was the next minor order, which authorized a man to recite the biblical readings at common prayer and at Mass. *Exorcist* was a minor order whereby a man could say prayers of exorcism during the rite of Baptism. He could not perform a formal exorcism ritual in the case of diabolical possession, though. Only a priest could do that, and only with permission of the local bishop. *Acolyte* was the minor order in which a man could light the altar candles, carry them in procession, and assist the deacon and subdeacon. Minor orders were replaced in 1972 with ministries of acolyte and lector. Candidacy replaced tonsure, and denotes that the man is officially studying for the priesthood and is attached to a diocese.

Question 97. What makes a valid marriage?

For a marriage to be a valid sacrament, in the Catholic sense, it must be between two baptized Christians who have never been previously married (validly), except for the death of a spouse. There are variations to the rule in which proper dispensations or permissions can make the marriage valid under other circumstances as well. For example, a Catholic can marry a baptized Protestant and it would be equally valid provided that the couple was prepared by the Catholic Church, the Catholic promises to raise any children from the marriage Catholic, and permission is procured from the chancery office of the diocese. When all these steps are taken, then the marriage can be witnessed in the Catholic Church and is valid.

In Catholic marriage there are always two things to consider: first the civil, or the contract, and second the sacrament, or the covenant. Catholic marriage, when prepared by a valid representative of the church, such as a priest or deacon, has to cover both aspects of marriage. The prenuptial investigation covers the backgrounds of both candidates for marriage. Couples usually have to take an inventory test, known as FOCCUS. This objective test helps the minister to counsel the couple in certain key areas before marriage. It also rates their compatibility. Next the couple attends either an Engaged Encounter Weekend or Pre-Cana. These preparation programs further aid in the couple's communication and self-knowledge.

Finally, the priest or deacon finishes the inventory and collects all the vital documents required by canon law, such as recent baptismal certificates, confirmation certificates, and, if need be, necessary dispensations or permissions from the bishop for a non-Catholic partner or one who was previously married. "Recent" refers to a document less than a year old. The original baptismal certificate your mother has in the attic is no good, at least from the perspective of Canon Law. Every time a Catholic receives a sacrament, the church of baptism is notified. When a person obtains a recent baptismal certificate by contacting the church where they were originally baptized, not only is the information on the front contained as in the original document (name of baptized, name of parents and godparents, date of birth, date of baptism) but on the back would be listed all the sacraments received as of the date that recent certificate was issued. Since most Catholics are baptized as infants, you would not see any notations on the back of their original baptismal certificates mentioning marriage or holy orders. If a man or woman has been previously married, the church of baptism would have been notified, and it would appear on any recent baptismal certificate issued since that time. That is why these documents cannot be older than one year.

Not only is Christian marriage the sacrament of matrimony, it is also a legal contract in civil law. A contract or marriage license is procured from the state or commonwealth in which the bride or groom lives. The bride and groom, along with a witness, simply fill out the proper paperwork at the town hall. At the rehearsal or on the day of the wedding, the best man and maid of honor (or at least two witnesses), and the clergyman, who acts as official witness for the state, sign the legal certificate, which must be mailed in to the town hall within five to ten days. This certificate becomes part of the legal documentation in the county of the marriage.

Question 98. Are children necessary?

Saint Augustine of Hippo, a great theologian and bishop of the fourth century, came up with important aspects of marriage known in Latin as *bona* (goods), the ends or fruits of marriage. First and foremost, Christian marriage is for the good of the couple (both the husband and the wife). This is called the *bonum coniugum* in Latin. It is the very essence of the sacrament of matrimony.

Catholic theology teaches that a valid sacrament of Christian marriage depends totally on the intention of both the bride and the groom on their wedding day, specifically at the moment they exchange consent (by either saying "I do" or by saying the vows together). Both must intend to enter a permanent, a faithful, and, God-willing, a fruitful union, otherwise there will be no bonum coniugum and therefore, no marriage. Saint Augustine referred to these three intentions as *bonum sacramenti* (permanence), *bonum fidei* (faithfulness), and *bonum prolis* (offspring).

Children are not the only purpose of marriage, as some claim Catholicism maintains. However, procreation is one of the three essential aspects. It is crucial to point out here that it is the intention, desire, and willingness to have children that is essential. Married couples who are biologically unable to have children are still very much married and in a valid sacrament. Sterility is not an impediment to the sacrament but a dispensation can be given to individuals who are impotent and thus unable to consummate the marriage. It is only those who purposely frustrate the overall good of the couple by intentionally excluding one or more of the three necessary goods (e.g., by habitual use of contraception or nontherapeutic sterilization) that render the union invalid.

Certainly understandable, but nonetheless still sinful, are immoral ways of procuring children, such as in vitro fertilization, egg and sperm donation and implantations, and surrogate mothers. These scientific processes involve immoral means, such as masturbation, selection of the "best" fertilized egg and abortion of the others, freezing fertilized eggs, and infidelity. Children must be brought forth in a human way between a husband and a wife, not in a laboratory. Fertility can be aided by science, such as in vivo fertilization, which involves no immoral means. When infertility is experienced by the couple, it is a cross that should be carried bravely. Though not required to, the couple is encouraged to consider adoption, a selfless act of love on the part of the married couple.

Being open to the possibility of children does not mean having as many babies as is biologically possible, either. Natural family planning is a moral and ethical way to use morally acceptable means to guide the number and frequency of pregnancies. If one or both spouses intend never to have children, this is as serious a defect as would be the intention not to be faithful or the intention not to enter a permanent relationship. Prenuptial agreements are indications that someone may not be intending a permanent bond, which invalidates the union. Equally invalidating would be those situations when people intend never to have kids lest they ruin their chances for a promising career.

In 1968, Pope Paul VI issued his famous papal encyclical, *Humanae Vitae*, in which he teaches that Christian marriage and especially the marital act of sexual intercourse are sacred and holy symbols of the unitive (love) and the procreative (life) dimensions which make up the foundation of the sacrament of Marriage.

Marriage is seen as one of the two sacraments of vocation, the other being Holy Orders. Through this sacrament, the couple promises to enter a permanent bond that can only be dissolved by death, to be always faithful (in other words, exclude any other sexual partners), and to be fruitful or to be open to the possibility of children if God wills it. The last requirement comes from the Old Testament (Genesis 1:28), when God said to Adam and Eve, "Be fruitful and multiply." In the Catholic sense, marriage is the fertile ground not only to populate the earth, but eventually to populate heaven—our ultimate goal in the road of life.

Question 99. Can we get married outdoors?

Sometimes couples have a soap opera–like vision of getting married on the beach at sunset or in a gazebo in the backyard. It looks beautiful on television and at the movies, but couples fail to realize the essence of the marriage. Marriage is a Catholic sacrament. A sacrament is instituted by Jesus Christ to confer grace. The Catholic Church regulates this sacrament in many ways. First is by delegation of its ministers. The minister performing the ceremony must be a validly ordained bishop, priest, or deacon. In turn, this minister must have proper jurisdiction from the bishop and pastor in whose parish the marriage is going to take place. In other words, Reverend Smith just can't walk into any Catholic Church and perform a marriage. If the priest is the pastor of the church, the bishop of the diocese gives ordinary faculties to witness marriages in his parish. If the priest or deacon is assigned to the parish in which the marriage is going to take place, they usually have faculties from the bishop for that parish as well. If it is an outside clergyman, then the pastor has to give delegation to perform the ceremony in the parish.

Second, the proper place for marriage is in a sacred place, which is usually the parish church. For pastoral reasons, weddings can take place in the chapel of a college that one of the couples attended, in a military chapel, or, if need be, in the hospital. Permissions are obtained by the Catholic minister who is preparing the couple from the chancery office and the Catholic chaplains of these chapels.

Third, a marriage can take place in a sacred space that is not Catholic. When either the bride or the groom is not Catholic and it would cause great problems for the non-Catholic families to celebrate a marriage inside a Catholic Church, the Catholic minister may obtain permission from the chancery for the marriage to take place in another denomination's church.

Fourth, a marriage can take place outside of a sacred space by way of dispensation from the bishop in which the proposed marriage is going to take place. For example, when a Catholic marries a Jewish person, for the sake of peace in the families, a Catholic minister may apply for a dispensation for the marriage to take place in the reception hall. The marriage file is then registered at the Catholic Church closest to the hall. Yet, marriages of this sort are usually never given permission to take place on the beach or in some common space. Even in the reception hall, great care must be taken to set aside a chapel for the proper celebration of the marriage. This permission is never given to two baptized Christians, whether both are Catholic or not.

Question 100. Why was the word *obey* removed from the marriage vows?

In the old texts, one would often hear "obey," which had its origins in the Letter of Saint Paul on the proper attitudes of wives toward their husbands. It was always understood that while wives must obey their husbands, husbands must love their wives as Jesus loves His Church, that is, sacrificially. Pope Benedict XVI calls this oblative love—love which is willing to make any sacrifice for the beloved. Saint Paul also tells husbands they are to love and to respect their wives as they do their own bodies.

In today's society, the word obey connotes many negative feelings. The misuse of the term leads to the notion of "lording over someone," with one spouse becoming subservient to the other and feeling almost like a slave. Abuse can result in the misinterpretation of the word "obey." As Catholics, we have to look at the word's original meaning. It was the pride of our first parents, Adam and Eve, that brought about sin and destruction. Their disobedience had a rippling effect in all generations. To counterbalance this negative effect, the total obedience of Jesus Christ (the new Adam) and His mother, Mary (the new Eve), brought about redemption. Obedience is the hallmark of a good Christian.

First and foremost, obedience must be given to Almighty God. Good Christians strive to follow the divine will of God, not their own wills, in their lives. Secondly, a good Christian tries to follow legitimate authority. All authority comes from God, and when exercised in union with God's laws it is perfectly laudable to follow. In the case of marriage, it is a partnership of equality. No one person is the authority, only God. When husband and wife try to ascertain and ultimately follow the will of God in their lives, then they are doing what God wants. In a paternalistic society, it usually fell to the husband to ascertain the will of God. In our modern society, the responsibility falls to both. At times, one of the members may have to remind his partner about following the will of God. It is understood that Christian marriage is a partnership designed by God in which the partners help each other on the way to heaven. Obedience *to God* is the most basic and important sign that you are on the right way to heaven.

Question 101. Why can't Catholics divorce and remarry?

Christ our Lord taught that marriage is an indissoluble bond. In the Gospel of Mark 10:11–12, Jesus says, "Whoever divorces his wife and marries another, commits adultery against her; and if she divorces her husband and marries another, she commits adultery." It was common for the pagans and Jews alike to divorce and remarry. Christ taught that this was not the original intention of God our Father. From the book of Genesis it was understood that God created man and woman to be one in an unbreakable bond of love. Due to original sin, marriage lost its permanent character. It was through Jesus Christ who elevated the natural state of marriage to a sacrament that permanence was reinstated. The analogy of Christ as the bridegroom and the Church as the bride takes on this special resilient relationship.

Jesus reiterates the original meaning of marriage in Matthew's Gospel 19:6: "so they are no longer two but one flesh." Unity is the essence of the Blessed Trinity—three divine persons in one God. God creates unity among us. Marriage is a unity of two people who become a new family. This unity mirrors the love of the Holy Trinity—the Father loves the Son, the Son loves the Father, and out of the love of Father and Son comes the Holy Spirit. Similarly, husbands love their wives, wives love their husbands, and out of love of husbands and wives, children are born.

Marriage establishes a permanent and exclusive bond through which God blesses the couple with grace. Once the marriage is witnessed in the Church and consummated it can only be dissolved by death. Marriage, unlike Baptism, Confirmation, and Holy Orders, does not continue beyond the grave. Upon death of a spouse, the other is free to marry again.

When a Catholic divorces civilly, she is still married in the eyes of the Church. In other words, divorce does not dissolve the sacrament. For a marriage to be valid, there has to be a valid consent from two baptized Catholics who freely enter the bond of marriage. Outside of death, there are rare instances when the Church can dissolve a marriage. First, if the marriage was never consummated (*ratum et non consummatum*). Consummation occurs when husband and wife become one in the act of sexual intercourse. The second is what is known in Canon Law as Pauline privilege, or privilege of the faith, whereby two unbaptized persons' natural (nonsacramental) marriage is dissolved by the local bishop if one of them gets baptized and the couple divorces, and the baptized spouse now seeks to enter a sacramental marriage (between two baptized persons) with a baptized Catholic. The third is known as Petrine privilege, whereby the pope dissolves a nonsacramental marriage between a baptized person and an unbaptized person which ended in divorce, and either party converts to Catholicism and wants to enter a sacramental marriage with a baptized Catholic.

Question 102.   What is an annulment?

An annulment is often misconstrued as a divorce, Catholic-style. Nothing could be further from the truth. An annulment is a declaration by the Catholic Church that, after careful investigation, flaws were discovered in the relationship that prevented it from becoming a marriage. These flaws have to exist prior to consent in a way that would impede true consent and result in the invalidity of the marriage. An annulment has no bearing in civil law. This is why a civil divorce precedes the commencement of an annulment.

Canon Law dictates the area that would impede a valid marriage. First, some impediments, like a previous bond of marriage, religious vows or holy orders, non-age (not of canonical age) or close blood relationship (consanguinity) prevent the sacrament from occuring. Some can invalidate the consent, like lack of mental competence, grave lack of discretionary judgment, or serious psychological problems. Second, homosexuality, alcohol or drug addiction/abuse, gross immaturity, etc., can also affect the validity. Third would be that at the time of the wedding, the bride or groom held an intention contrary to the essential understanding of Christian marriage, such as refusing to have children.

The annulment is processed through a Church court known as a tribunal. The petitioner is assigned an advocate. Witnesses are required because marriage is a public event. A defender of the bond is employed that defends the bond of marriage. After the witnesses and petitioner are interviewed and an external forum is convened, which determines that there was in fact something that impeded true consent of the marriage, then an annulment is granted. The annulment is automatically sent to the next higher ecclesiastical court to make sure the process was done properly and to hopefully ratify the judicial decision.

A documentary annulment process is different from the formal annulment process. The first kind is a process of paperwork that applies when the marriage was invalid from the start because of a lack of canonical form is a process of paperwork that applies when the marriage was invalid from the start because of a lack of canonical form. To be valid, Catholic marriage must be between two consenting adults who state their intentions before two witnesses and a valid Catholic minister inside the Church. Lack of canonical form means one of these things was missing. If a baptized Catholic marries outside the Church without a dispensation, the marriage is invalid. To obtain the declaration of nullity, a priest or deacon has to obtain baptismal certificates and the marriage certificate, and the petitioner has to fill out a questionnaire along with two witnesses who will testify that the couple never had their marriage convalidated in the Catholic Church. The paperwork is sent into the chancery office, and a decree of nullity is given.

Question 103. What about same-sex unions?

This question has become more common in recent years with the passage of laws in some states that recognize gay unions. The Catholic Church has always taught that the homosexual inclination is disordered. It distinguishes the sexual *orientation* from sexual *activity*. Whether the orientation is biological, psychological, or social, in most cases it is believed to be involuntary; hence, there is no culpability merely for the inclination. The sinfulness comes not in the homosexual orientation, which is, however, disordered, but in the acting out of the orientation—any and all acts of homosexual activity. It is not sinful to have the homosexual orientation, but it is sinful to engage in homosexual behavior. The Church still considers the orientation disordered but recognizes many homosexuals do not choose to have this inclination. Only when they engage in homosexual activity is there culpable sin. Any and all human sexual activity, whether heterosexual or homosexual, which is outside of marriage (between one man and one woman) is considered seriously and gravely sinful. Masturbation, adultery, promiscuity, fornication (sex before and outside of marriage), artificial contraception, pornography, and homosexuality pervert the original intention that God has for marriage, namely love (*unitive dimension*) and life (*procreative dimension*). We learn this from the book of Genesis, in which God creates male and female and tells them to be fruitful and multiply.

It is impossible to see homosexual unions as being in line with God's intentions for marriage since the product of intercourse is not fruitful. Along with masturbation, fornication, and adultery, homosexuality is a selfish act that cannot fulfill the divinely ordained purpose of the reproductive powers. The Church teaches that God instituted the sacrament of Marriage, and only He has the authority to change the nature of marriage. Neither the Church nor the state has the competence to alter the substance of marriage, or the family, for that matter. Any attempts by civil governments to alter the law in favor of same-sex unions distort the true meaning of marriage, which has existed for thousands and thousands of years.

The Church encourages people who suffer from the disorder of a homosexual orientation to live a chaste and celibate life. All unmarried persons, regardless of their sexual orientation, are called to live chaste lives. Chastity is required of all people, no matter what their state in life—single, married, or clerical. It is a virtue in which our thoughts, words, and actions are modest. Celibacy is a discipline by which one does not marry. The grace from frequent reception of the sacrament of Penance will help the homosexual in his or her commitment to be chaste. There are also many good Catholic support groups (for example, Courage) to help people with homosexual tendencies to live good and virtuous lives. Other groups, like Dignity, which promote monogamous relationships, are not considered in conformity with Catholic teaching. Sexual intercourse is a holy and sacred act reserved for husband and wife who are a man and woman married in the eyes of God, and who are committed to living a permanent, faithful, and, God-willing, fruitful union.

Chapter 10

EUCHARIST AND COMMUNION

This chapter answers questions on the third sacrament of initiation and its centrality to Catholic doctrine, morality, and worship.

Question 104. What is Mass?

The term "Mass," used for the weekly Sunday service in Catholic churches as well as services on Holy Days of Obligation, derives its meaning from the Latin term *Missa*. It was used at the end of the Liturgy when the Priest said, *"Ite missa est,"* which translates to "Go, the [congregation] is sent." It was a commissioning. Today, the dismissal is similar: "The Mass is ended. Go in peace." At the end of the Mass, the mind is filled with the Word of God, and the soul is filled with the Body, Blood, Soul, and Divinity of Jesus in Holy Communion. Parishioners are commissioned to go and take Christ into our broken world. In other words, cooperating with the graces received from the sacrament, the communicants, once they are dismissed, have to be the eyes, ears, and hands of Jesus in our world.

The Sacred Liturgy, or Holy Mass, is divided into two main parts, the Liturgy of the Word and the Liturgy of the Eucharist. The first focuses on the written and spoken Word of God, especially and in particular the readings from the Bible. Before that happens, however, there is a Penitential Rite, which is merely a public acknowledgement of guilt that we are all sinners and are all in need of God's forgiveness. It is followed by the Gloria, which praises God. This is followed by an opening prayer, and then the scripture readings are recited aloud. Priests, deacons, or bishops alone are allowed and are obligated to preach a homily immediately after the Gospel is proclaimed by a cleric (bishop, priest, or deacon).

The second half of the Mass focuses on the Word made flesh—the consecration of the bread and wine into the Body and Blood of Christ. The bread (wheat) and wine (grape) are placed on the altar of offering and the priest says the exact and precise words spoken by Jesus at the Last Supper: "This is my body" (over the wafers of unleavened wheat bread) and "This is the cup of my blood" (over the chalice of grape wine). The separate consecration of bread and wine into the Body and Blood of Christ mystically represents the separation of body and blood which occurred at Calvary when Jesus died on Good Friday. This is why Catholicism calls it the Holy Sacrifice of the Mass. It is not a second or other sacrifice, it is the one and same sacrifice of the Cross reenacted in an unbloody fashion. Once this holiest part of the Mass is complete, the Lord's Prayer (Our Father) is prayed and Holy Communion is soon to be given to those who are in full communion with the Catholic Church. A closing prayer ends the Mass and the people are dismissed.

Biblically, the apostles were commissioned before our Lord's ascension into paradise. Our Lord said, "Go and teach all nations baptizing them in the name of the

Father, the Son, and of the Holy Spirit." This order is very much part of our spiritual lives. We have a sacred duty as disciples of the Lord to go and bring the Good News of Salvation to everyone we meet, from our homes to the workplace to the marketplace. The Holy Eucharist is what enables us to be the Lord's present day apostles.

Also, the Mass is seen as the source and summit of Christian living. The first part of our week after Sunday celebration of Mass is to be seen as a thanksgiving for the holy gifts received. The second part of the week is the preparation for next awesome celebration of the Holy Eucharist. When our week is viewed in this way, time becomes sanctified, and Sunday becomes central.

Other names for the Mass are the Holy Eucharist, Divine Liturgy, Breaking of the Bread, the Lord's Supper, and Holy Sacrifice. *Eucharist* in Greek means thanksgiving. This refers to the fact that Jesus gave thanks before He broke the bread at the Last Supper. As sacrifice, the Mass is the unbloody reenactment of Jesus' sacrifice made at Calvary. "Lord's Supper" refers to the night Jesus instituted this sacrament, which was the night before He died. In fact, Holy Thursday (the day of the Last Supper), Good Friday (the day our Lord died on the Cross), and Easter Sunday (the day of our Lord's resurrection) are all intertwined in the Mass. "Divine Liturgy" is derived from a Greek term meaning work. The work being done in the Mass is redemption brought about by our savior, and we share in the fruits of this work by our reception of Communion. "Breaking of the bread" is a term the early Church used for the Eucharistic Liturgy originating in the Gospel when our Lord met two of His disciples on the Road to Emmaus on the first Easter evening. They did not recognize Him until he was known to them in the breaking of the bread (see Luke 24:35). Luke 24:30–31 says, "When he was at table with them, he took the bread and blessed, and broke it, and gave it to them. And their eyes were opened and they recognized him; and he vanished out of their sight."

What we learn from these various names is that the Mass is a sacrifice and a banquet. A holy sacrifice because it is the same sacrifice of Jesus on the Cross, a sacred banquet because we receive the Body, Blood, Soul, and Divinity of the living, and glorified Jesus. Jesus is priest and victim at every Mass (he is the one offering and the one being offered), and He uses the priesthood to perpetuate His holy sacrifice. Through the words the priest uses at the consecration, "This is My Body…This is My Blood," Christ is made present. Bread and wine cease to exist, and they become the Body and Blood of Christ; this doctrine is called Transubstantiation. Holy

Communion is truly the substance of the Body and Blood of the Risen and Glorified Savior under the appearances of bread and wine so that we can receive Him.

Question 105. Can deacons or nuns say Mass when there is no priest?

Only a validly ordained priest can offer up the Holy Sacrifice of the Mass. At every Mass, it is Jesus Who is both priest and victim. Since there is no time in God and He is an eternal "now," Calvary is brought to us through the centuries. Jesus perpetuates His sacrifice through the sacramental priesthood. At the Last Supper, after instituting the Holy Eucharist, He also ordained the apostles to the priesthood with the words, "Do this in memory of me."

Christ ordained a male priesthood because the priests are to act *In Persona Christi*, or in the Person of Christ. The priests are the vehicles through which Christ continues His saving work. At Mass it is Christ who takes the bread, blesses it, breaks it, and gives it to the world. The priest is the mere instrument of Christ.

Deacons may proclaim and preach the word of God and distribute Holy Communion that was consecrated at a Mass previously. A religious sister, brother, or nun may also lead a celebration outside of Mass and also distribute Holy Communion consecrated at another Mass. This permission was given by the Holy See to areas where a priest may only celebrate the Mass infrequently so as not to deny the people the graces of the sacrament of Holy Communion.

Question 106. Can grape juice and rice cakes be used at Mass for those who are alcoholic or who have a wheat or gluten allergy?

The matter of the material served as Holy Communion is determined by Christ Himself and reaffirmed by the Church. At the Last Supper, Christ used wine and unleavened bread. This is important for many reasons. First, the Last Supper was believed to be celebrated in the context of the Passover Meal. At Passover Meals, matzo (unleavened bread made from wheat) is used and wine is blessed and taken. Passover marked the liberation of the Jews from the slavery of the Egyptians. It is in this context that Jesus, Who is the Author of the New Covenant, is the new Passover. By His death and resurrection He liberates us from the slavery of sin. Jesus took bread and wine and consecrated them into His Body and Blood and prefigured His death and resurrection, so that the apostles consumed the Glorified and Risen Savior under the appearances of bread and wine.

In the time of Christ, bread and wine were considered common elements by those who lived in the Mediterranean section of the world. Indeed, wine was drunk more than water, because often water was not clean or pure. When our Lord used these common elements, He was indicating that the Eucharist was for all people, for all times even until the end of time. Bread and wine refer to the universality of God's redemption and plenteousness of grace that He offers to humanity.

The Church continues the commission of Jesus to "do this in memory of me." The magisterium of the Church taught in creeds, doctrines, Canon Law, and Ecumenical Council that for the validity of the mass, the matter that is used must be unleavened wheat bread and wine. The Holy Eucharist is referred to as a Holy Banquet. Even in today's society, the two things commonly on every table at a celebration are bread and wine. Bread conveys nourishment, and wine, health and prosperity. The Eucharist gives us all three; it nourishes our souls and gives us spiritual health, and the grace of the sacrament is our prosperity.

That said, there are certain times the Church allows a slight variation of the matter of bread and wine. For example, if a priest is a recovering alcoholic, he may apply for permission to use mustum, which is grape juice that has no sugar added and is beginning to go under the fermentation process. It is fermentation that makes grape juice into wine, turning the sugar in the juice into alcohol, so mustum contains a very low percentage of alcohol—less than a half percent. Many recovering alcoholics may take a minute sip of this and not fall off their recovery, yet it is still considered wine or wine in the making.

Second, a person who is allergic to wheat (provided he is not a priest) is encouraged to receive from the chalice which contains the Precious Blood. If this is not possible, a special host that is made from very low gluten, again less than one percent, can be used as valid matter which results in incredibly little side effect.

Any other types of matter such as rice, oats, or different kinds of juices or spirits would invalidate the presence of Jesus in the Eucharist.

Question 107. Why was Mass once said only in Latin?

The celebration of the Mass can be still said in Latin, as it is the official language of the Church. In many oratories, shrines, chapels, and even parishes, Masses continue to be celebrated in this language. In fact, the Second Vatican Council encouraged the use of Latin. Latin hymns and prayers were to be retained even in Masses during which the vernacular languages are used.

Mass was first celebrated in the language of our Lord, the ancient Aramaic. When Peter, the first pope, went to Rome—the center of the Empire—Greek was the language used by scholars, and it then became the language of choice for many centuries in the Liturgy. Theology and philosophy were all taught in this language. Latin was considered the common language of the people. The theological opinion of the time said that Divine Liturgy, the Mass, should use the language of scholars, which was a sign of dignity.

After the Peace of Constantine, the Church became legitimate and expanded tremendously. Roughly, this coincided with the fall of the Roman Empire in the West and the development of the vernacular languages. Latin then became the language of scholars, theologians, and philosophers, and so the Mass was then translated into it. In the Eastern Empire, which was centered in Constantinople, Greek was retained.

For centuries, Latin was commonly used in Church documents, Canon Law, reading of scripture, and the celebration of the seven sacraments and prayers. Latin was and is the official language of the Church. It was only in recent times that the Holy See allowed the vernacular languages to be used in its celebration of the Sacraments. However, this usage in no way diminishes the importance of Latin in the Liturgy.

Question 108. Is the Mass a memorial or a sacrifice?

The Mass is both a memorial and a sacrifice. Our Lord instituted the Holy Eucharist at the Last Supper on Holy Thursday, and the Mass gets its liturgical makeup from this event. Holy Thursday was the night before Jesus died. He gave this sacrament to his apostles at the Last Supper: "Do this in memory of me." By these words, Jesus ordained the twelve apostles priests. He did so to perpetuate the sacrament of the Holy Eucharist until the end of time. In this way the Mass is a memorial. It makes new Christ's sacrifice. The Holy Sacrifice of the Mass is not a new sacrifice or a sacrifice like the ones Jewish or pagan priests would perform. Rather, it is the sacrifice of Jesus on the cross. One big difference is in the unbloody manner that the sacrifice is made present.

The separate consecrations at the Mass denote the crucifixion of Christ. In the Jewish understanding, death is brought about by the separation of the blood from the body. At the Mass when the priest consecrates the bread, genuflects in adoration, and then consecrates the wine, and genuflects in adoration, this is signifying the separation of blood from the body, that is, death. The Holy Sacrifice of the Mass is also the resurrection. After the consecration, but before Holy Communion, the priests place a small piece of the host into the Precious Blood in the chalice. This indicates resurrection. At the Mass, Catholics do not receive the dead Christ, but rather the risen and glorified savior. Every minute piece of the Host, every drop of the Precious Blood is the whole risen Savior. How this all happens is a mystery of faith.

Not only are parishioners receiving the Body and Blood of Christ, but also His soul and Divinity. Wherever the Son is, the Father and the Holy Spirit are as well. Therefore, Catholics receive the Triune God in Holy Communion but Christ remains present after the Sacrifice of the Mass. His presence remains as long as the appearance of bread is recognizable. Once the appearances of bread deteriorate beyond recognition, it is believed that the real presence of Jesus is gone. This is especially true when a host drops to the floor and cannot be consumed. It is then placed in a glass of water. Once it is dissolved, it may be placed in the sacrarium, which is like a sink except that it drains into the ground.

Question 109. Are Masses for the living or the deceased?

Mass can be celebrated for the living members or those of who have passed away. Why? Because it is the eternal merits won for us by Christ on the cross that are applied to the soul who is either alive or dead. We are one big church with three divisions. The first is Church Triumphant. This church consists of all the angels and saints who sit at the eternal banquet which Christ prepared for them in paradise. It is very much an interactive community of joy. The second is Church Suffering. This church consists of the Holy Souls of purgatory. These souls died as friends of God, but needed further purgation or cleansing because they either didn't finish their penance from their forgiven sins or still had earthly attachments that they needed to work out. Last is Church Militant, the baptized faithful who keep up the fight of good against evil.

All three churches are united in praise around the altar at Mass. Since there is a suspension of time and space at Mass, Calvary is brought through the ages and every soul, either in heaven, in purgatory, or on earth at Mass, offers praise and worship of the Triune God. Mass is the most perfect prayer. It is the offering of the eternal Son to the Father in union with the Holy Spirit on behalf of the faithful. The fruits of the Sacrifice are the grace of the sacrament.

The saints in heaven and the faithful on earth can help the holy souls of purgatory by their prayers. The saints can intercede to God on their behalf, and the faithful, through the mediation of the priest, can offer the Mass on their behalf. The infinite merits that Christ won on the cross are applied to their souls during the Mass. The spiritual graces then aid the holy souls in purgatory and reduce their time there. This is why Catholics will seek an intention for the Mass for the faithful departed. Usually this is done on their birthdays and the anniversaries of their passing. If a certain Mass is being celebrated for a deceased person and this person is indeed in heaven, the fruits are not wasted. Rather, the next soul in purgatory will then benefit from this Mass.

Masses can also be said for the living. One Mass celebrated in someone's honor is worth many after they die. It is customary to have a Mass celebrated in honor of a birthday, wedding anniversary, or some other joyous occasion.

What a beautiful gift to give someone the Holy Sacrifice of Jesus for their intentions.

Question 110. Can non-Catholics receive Communion?

Communion means being in union with God and with one another in our beliefs. If there isn't unity in faith, morals, and sacramental life, then common reception of the Blessed Sacrament is prohibited. The United States Catholic Conference issued a set of guidelines for the reception of Holy Communion which has to be printed in every missalette and Mass program. The guidelines basically point out what the Code of Canon Law directs Catholics, Protestants, and non-Christians to do at Mass.

Canon 916 reminds us that Catholics are encouraged to receive Holy Communion provided that they are properly disposed to reception. What is proper disposition? A Catholic should not be conscious of any mortal sins and should have fasted for one hour before Communion. If they are conscious of grave sin, then the Catholic must go to Confession before reception. There is one exception which the canon points out: "unless there is grave reason and there is no opportunity to confess; in this case the person is to remember the obligation to make an act of perfect contrition, which includes the resolve to go to confession as soon as possible."

Baptized non-Catholics are certainly welcome to attend Holy Mass. Baptism makes us members of the Church, and so there is the hope of baptized non-Catholics one day being in full communion with the Church. Since unity of belief does not yet exist, though, reception of Holy Communion is not possible. Canon Law provides a few exceptions. Canon 844, Paragraph 4 states, "If there is a danger of death or if, in the judgment of the diocesan bishop or the Bishop's Conference, there is some other grave and pressing need, Catholic ministers may lawfully administer those same sacraments to other Christians not in full communion with the Catholic Church, who cannot approach a minister of their own community and who spontaneously ask for them, provided that they demonstrate the Catholic faith in respect of these sacraments and are properly disposed."

Members of the Orthodox Churches, the Assyrian Church of the East, and the Polish National Catholic Church are directed by Canon 844, paragraph 3, "Catholic ministers may lawfully administer the Sacraments of Penance, the Eucharist, and Anointing of the Sick to members of the Eastern Churches not in full communion with the Catholic Church if they spontaneously ask for them and are properly disposed."

Finally, non-Christians are certainly welcomed to Mass but are not allowed to receive Holy Communion under any circumstances, since they do not share the same belief in Jesus Christ.

Catholics who cannot receive Holy Communion because of mortal sin should make a Spiritual Communion and go to the sacrament of Penance as soon as possible.

Question 111. What are Forty Hours and Corpus Christi?

The Holy Sacrifice of the Mass is the source and summit of Christian living. Everything that flows from the Mass, such as public prayer of the Liturgy of the Hours, Forty Hour devotions, and Corpus Christi Procession, augment our beliefs in the real presence of Jesus in the Most Blessed Sacrament. Private prayer, such as the rosary, novenas to saints, Stations of the Cross, and litanies all aid in our worship of the one true God. They prepare our souls to be receptive to God.

Forty Hours is a devotion in which the Blessed Sacrament remains on the altar for roughly forty hours. Eucharistic adoration is the extension of the consecration of the Mass, when the priest holds the sacred host and chalice of the precious blood after the consecration for people to adore. This adoration is extended in the exposition of the Blessed Sacrament. Forty Hours was made popular in this country by Saint John Neuman, Archbishop of Philadelphia in the late nineteenth century. In fact, in the Province of Philadelphia, which includes all the dioceses of Pennsylvania, this custom is still practiced to this day. During Forty Hours, people of the parish that is hosting this devotion sign up for adoration, which lasts during the night. Over the course of three evenings there might be special communal services of prayers, processions, Penance celebration, and benediction. Benediction is Latin for blessing. Jesus blesses the faithful by His Sacred Presence in the host, and the priest or deacon takes the host in the monstrance and makes the sign of the cross.

Corpus Christi is a solemnity that is celebrated at the end of the Easter season after the Feast of the Blessed Trinity, and has its roots in a Eucharistic miracle which took place in the town of Orvieto, Italy, in the thirteenth century. Eucharistic miracles can take many forms. Usually, the "accidents" or the externals of bread and wine remain the same even though the substance of bread and wine cease and become the Body, Blood, Soul, and Divinity of Jesus. In cases of Eucharistic miracles, the accidents even change into the physical looking flesh and blood. Miracles of this nature boost the belief in the real presence of Jesus and in the doctrines of transubstantiation and concomitance.

In the case of the miracle of Orvieto-Bolsena, a German priest stopped in Bolsena on his way to Rome in 1263. He had doubts about the real presence of Jesus in the blessed sacrament. While celebrating Mass and at the consecration, blood started to drip from the consecrated host onto a cloth known as a corporal. Pope Urban IV, who was visiting Orvieto, asked to see this relic. Upon investigation it was regarded as an authentic miracle. It became enshrined in the cathedral in Orvieto. Pope Urban wanted to mark this miracle with a feast and commissioned the great Saint Thomas Aquinas to compose prayers and music that would form the Liturgy of the Mass of Corpus Christi. Corpus Christi became an official feast of the universal Church in 1264. On the seven hundredth anniversary of the institution of the feast, Pope Paul VI celebrated Mass at the altar where the blood-stained corporal is kept.

On the feast of Corpus Christi, it is traditional to form a procession from the parish church through the streets of the town. Along the way, the priest stops and offers benediction of the Blessed Sacrament. Finally, the procession ends in the Church with solemn benediction of the Blessed Sacrament. These external signs of devotion instill fervor, belief, and worship among the faithful.

Pope John Paul II dedicated the whole year in which he died to the Eucharist. It was his hope that processions, Forty Hours, Nocturnal Adoration on First Fridays, and Perpetual Adoration would once again flourish in the church, because the fruits of the Eucharist—which are an increased union of Jesus and His Church, a renewal in the life of grace, and a growth in the love of our neighbor—are tremendous.

Question 112. How many times can I receive Holy Communion in one day?

Canon 917 says that Catholics may receive Holy Communion twice on the same day only within a Eucharistic celebration (Mass) in which that person participates. The Latin uses the word *iterum* which not only means "again" but more specifically, "one more time."

If a Catholic goes to a morning Mass and receives Holy Communion, he or she can attend another Mass and receive a second time. Were they to attend a third or fourth Mass, they could not receive any more Communion that day. This prevents people from cultivating a numerical or quantitative theology, which the Church vehemently opposes.

One of the six precepts of the Church is that Catholics are expected to receive Holy Communion at least once during Easter season, if not more often (like once a week on Sundays, or even on weekdays).

Question 113. When is a person *not* allowed to go to Communion?

A Catholic is never permitted to receive Holy Communion in the state of mortal sin. A person in this state must receive the sacrament of Penance. A Catholic is never permitted to receive Holy Communion while under the penalty of excommunication until it is lifted by competent authority, which includes priest, bishop, or pope, depending upon the severity or nature of the excommunication.

Catholics living in a perpetual sinful state should also not receive Holy Communion until it is rectified. For example, a person who is married, divorced, and remarried outside the Catholic Church without an annulment is living in a perpetual state of mortal sin. The only exception to the rule is if the remarried couples live as brother and sister and not in a conjugal union, until the annulment is procured and the marriage is convalidated in the Catholic Church. Another example is if a baptized Catholic marries outside the Church without dispensation or permission obtained from the bishop, then the marriage is not recognized by the Church and the couple must refrain from reception of Holy Communion until this is ratified. A person who is dealing with a habitual sin in the sacrament of Penance might not be in the state of mortal sin because the freedom of the will has been reduced.

Question 114. What are a tabernacle and a monstrance?

Tabernacle, monstrance, chalice, ciboria, paten, corporal, and purificator are items integral to the Blessed Sacrament. The chalice is the vessel that holds the wine which will become the blood of Christ; the paten and ciboria hold the hosts which will become the body of Christ at the Consecration of the Mass.

The tabernacle is the suitable receptacle in which the Blessed Sacrament is reserved in the Church. Christ remains present in the Blessed Sacrament long after Mass is over. Only the Sacred Host is allowed to be reserved. Tabernacle is derived from the Latin word for tent. It has its origins in the Old Testament Ark of the Covenant.

The monstrance, or ostensorium, is a sacred vessel designed to expose the consecrated host for adoration and benediction. The word's origin is from the Latin word for "to show." A monstrance usually is a tall vessel made of precious metal that is placed on the altar. The luna, which is a piece of glass in the shape of a moon, contains the Blessed Sacrament, previously consecrated. The luna is then placed in the middle of the sunburst of the monstrance.

Chapter 11

SACRAMENTALS

This chapter answers questions about sacramentals and other man-made elements of the church in distinction from divinely instituted sacraments mentioned previously.

- Question 115. What is holy water?
- Question 116. What is holy oil?
- Question 117. Why pray a rosary? Isn't it just repetition?
- Question 118. What is the difference between a statue and an idol?
- Question 119. Is it good luck to wear a religious medal?
- Question 120. Are there really exorcisms?
- Question 121. How many scapulars are there?
- Question 122. What are Catholic blessings about?
- Question 123. Who can bless a home?
- Question 124. What happens at a Catholic funeral?
- Question 125. Can Catholics be cremated?
- Question 126. What is the meaning of burning incense?

Question 115. What is holy water?

Usually, regular water is taken from the tap and then blessed either at Mass or afterward. Holy water is blessed by an ordained minister. There are no specific regulations concerning the drinking of blest water; however, sometimes the water sits in a holding tank for days, and therefore it wouldn't be advisable to drink. Holy water is a sacramental, meaning it is related to a sacrament. Baptism employs the usage of holy water to confer the sacrament.

In the blessing of water at baptisms, the prayer traces the long history of water as a purifying and cleansing substance. It mentions, for instance, the parting of the Red Sea in which the Israelites were lead out of slavery. Through the water of baptism, Jesus leads us out of the slavery of sin. The usage of holy water outside of Mass has many different forms. Priests use holy water to bless people, objects, and places. At the beginning of Mass, holy water is sprinkled on the people. Holy water, when consciously used, removes venial sins. When objects are blessed with holy water by a priest or deacon they become reserved for sacred use and should be disposed of in a dignified way. When palms are blessed on Palm Sunday, they cannot be thrown into the waste paper basket after they become old and withered; rather, they may be buried or burned.

The verse from the Old Testament Exodus 12:22 refers to hyssop. Hyssop was a plant used by the Israelites for sprinkling the blood of the Passover lamb on the lintels of Jewish homes. Hyssop had medicinal properties and was used for healing. In the New Testament, holy water is referred to as hyssop. The blood of the Lamb, Jesus Christ, which was poured out on Good Friday, is passed to our souls through the waters of baptism. When holy water is used at Mass, it reminds the faithful of the saving blood of Jesus.

Many people store and use holy water in their homes. Homes can be seen as little churches. When we take holy water before leaving home, this reminds us of the rich blessings God bestows on His people. Often, people bless their homes during storms to invoke God's blessings in time of calamity. When Catholics enter or leave church, they take holy water by their fingers and make the sign of the cross over themselves. When sprinkled at Mass or at a blessing, they make the same sign of the cross. Again, they are reminded of the rich blessings of God.

Question 116. What is holy oil?

Holy oil is the tangible matter used in the sacraments of Confirmation, Anointing of the Sick, and Holy Orders. While holy oil is used in baptism, it is not essential to the sacrament. Like water, oil is an ancient symbol from the Mediterranean world. Olive oil was healthy to ingest and was used as a component in topical medications. Athletes and soldiers would anoint themselves with oil before they entered competition or combat. Borrowing these themes, holy oil is a means by which Christ strengthens Christians. Often the term "Soldier of Christ" would be applied to a person who received Confirmation. As a healing theme in the sacrament of the Anointing of the Sick, blessed oil is used as the matter of the sacrament. Jesus is the divine physician who comes to heal us both physically and spiritually in the anointing.

There are three kinds of blessed oil—catechumen, the sick, and Chrism. The oils are blessed at a special Mass during Holy Week, usually held on the morning of Holy Thursday, known as the Mass of Chrism. At this Mass, the priests of the diocese gather around their bishop and renew their priestly commitment. The bishop blesses these oils, which will later be divided among the parish for the sacramental life. Great symbolism of unity is expressed since the oil is blessed at the mother church of the diocese, the cathedral, with all the bishops' representatives to the parishes (the priests), and then dispersed from this central place.

Oil of catechumens (*oleum sanctorum* in Latin) is used as a prebaptism anointing. In the case of baby baptisms, it is done right at the celebration of the sacrament. For adult converts, this anointing can take place months beforehand. This idea comes from the fourth century, when the church was receiving many converts and baptism could require several months or even many years of preparation. Oil, which has the spiritual meaning of strengthening, was used to strengthen the convert with Christ as he or she journeyed to the sacraments.

Oil of the Sick (*oleum infirmorum*) is used in the Sacrament of the Anointing. It is the outward sign that confers grace. After the priest imposes hands on the sick person, he then anoints the candidate's forehead and hands with the oil. Inwardly, if the person is receptive, healing takes place. It may be only spiritual healing and strengthening of the infirm to deal with his maladies. At times, physical healing can also occur.

Chrism Oil (*sacrum chrisma*) is quite special and set apart from the other two. Chrism derives its name from the Greek word *Christos* from which we get Christ. "Christ" means "the Anointed One." This oil is used in the sacraments of Confirmation and Holy Orders to confer the sacrament. It is also used in the sacrament of Baptism when confirmation will not immediately follow. Chrism is a mixture of balsam and olive oil. Balsam is an aromatic scent derived from special trees in the Mediterranean world, formerly reserved for royalty and priests. This is fitting in the sacramental sense, since Baptism makes us adopted children of God and we share in the priesthood of the laity.

All three oils are stored in a wall cupboard, known as an ambry. In light of the Second Vatican Council the ambry has taken on a significant role in church architecture. The ambry was once hidden in the sacristy or side chapel, but now it is placed in the sanctuary and made of glass with lights inside to show off the containers, which are also made glass.

Question 117. Why pray a rosary? Isn't it just repetition?

Beads for counting prayers are common in many religions. In Christianity, the Orthodox Church has Jesus beads. In Catholicism, there are different kinds of chaplets, such as Divine Mercy, Infant of Prague, Saint Michael the Archangel, and of course the rosary. The rosary is a sacramental and should be blessed by a priest or deacon. Once blessed, it is set apart for spiritual use.

Saint Dominic is attributed as the one who received the first rosary. He did so by way of an apparition of our Blessed Mother. Mary gave him the rosary as a spiritual tool to fight the heresy of Albigensianism, which denied the humanity of Christ. His preaching was not able to fight the errors prevalent in the thirteenth century, but the simple rosary, whereby the believer meditated on the Joyful, Sorrowful, and Glorious Mysteries of Jesus Christ, helped convince the people of Spain and France that Jesus was truly God and Man, human and divine. The Sorrowful Mysteries especially underscore the human nature, since Jesus felt real pain and died a real death which only a human could experience. The Glorious accentuate the divine nature since only divinity can rise from the dead and ascend into heaven. The Joyful bridge the gap of heaven and earth, divine and human in that Jesus had a real human mother in Mary but she conceived miraculously by divine power of the Holy Spirit.

The rosary consists of twenty mysteries which center on the life of Christ. These mysteries were taught to people who could not read and write, and soon they began to learn their faith. A famous painting that is enshrined in a church in Pompeii is said to be the miraculous depiction of Our Lady of the Rosary. In the painting our Lady is giving the rosary to Saint Dominic and Saint Catherine of Sienna. Saint Catherine is cofounder, along with Saint Dominic, of the Dominican Sisters.

The twenty mysteries of the rosary are divided into four categories. First are the joyful mysteries, which include the Annunciation, Visitation, Nativity, Presentation, and Finding in the Temple. The second category centers on the passion of Christ, known as the sorrowful mysteries, which include the Agony in the Garden, the Scourging at the Pillar, the Crowning of Thorns, the Carrying of the Cross, and the Crucifixion. Third, the glorious mysteries comprise of the Resurrection, Ascension, and Descent of the Holy Spirit, Assumption of Mary, and Coronation of Mary. Pope John Paul II dedicated the year 2003 to the rosary and composed the last five mysteries of light, known as the Luminous Mysteries, which consist of the Baptism of the Lord, Wedding Feast of Cana, the Preaching of the Kingdom, the Transfiguration, and Institution of the Holy Eucharist.

The contemporary rosary is comprised of fifty beads, and for each bead a prayer is said. It begins on the crucifix with the Apostles Creed followed by one Our Father, three Hail Marys, and one Glory Be to the Father. Then the first mystery is announced followed by one Our Father, ten Hail Marys, and one Glory Be to the Father. This is repeated five times and concludes with the Hail Holy Queen. (See also Question 194.) The rosary can be repetitious if it is not prayed in the proper spirit. When one meditates on each of the mysteries, the Hail Marys become the background for one to meditate on a certain scene. Every pope in the last 400 years has written some point on the power of this spiritual tool. It is a great preparatory or thanksgiving tool for Mass. When said in public in front of the Exposed Blessed Sacrament, the Church grants a plenary indulgence, provided the person follows the norms for this spiritual instrument.

Question 118. What is the difference between a statue and an idol?

There is quite a bit of difference between a statue and an idol, and it has to do with mentality. The Catholic Church allows statuary of Jesus, His Mother Mary, and the saints to be placed in Churches and in homes. The understanding is that Catholics venerate the saint in heaven by honoring their picture. Catholics do not worship statues. They know they are only made out of wood, plaster, or marble. Just like someone has a picture of deceased relative in their wallet, so many Catholics have a picture of a certain saint. We praise God through the five senses, and sight (through which we look upon and then contemplate religious images) is one of these senses.

Idols, such as the golden calf constructed by the Israelites, were worshipped as gods and divine powers were attributed to them. In no way are statues or icons given this status. However, as a spiritual tool and sacramental, the faithful can think of the person in heaven as a visual reminder when they are praying. In the ninth century in the Eastern Church, there was a great battle about whether to keep icons in churches, but it was eventually decided that devotional items would remain in churches. That decision is commemorated to this day in a feat known as the Triumph over Iconoclasm. In the sixteenth century, Protestants who hearkened to the Book of Exodus and admonishments over the Israelites' golden calf rid all of their churches of any statuary. Even the corpus was taken off the cross. During the Council of Trent and the Counterreformation period, the Church continued to teach that statues were perfectly acceptable in homes and churches, reminding us that Catholics do not worship the art but revere the saint in heaven through the art.

Question 119. Is it good luck to wear a religious medal?

A Catholic does not wear a medal for luck. Rather, they wear a medal to remind themselves either of the saint that the medal represents or of Jesus and His Mother, Mary. Many religions have external signs of devotion that believers wear. For example, Jewish and Muslim men wear skull caps. Muslim women veil themselves in public. Catholics wear medals, crucifixes, and scapulars. Often, this sacramental is placed under one's clothing, but can be worn externally as well.

A Catholic who wears a medal is not looking for luck, but for God's blessing through the intercession of the saint. One famous medal Catholics wear is that of Our Lady of the Miraculous Medal. It is believed that Our Lady appeared to a French Visitation Cloister Nun in Paris in the nineteenth century. She asked this nun, Sister Catherine Labore, to construct a medal with Mary's image on it with the words on the back, "O Mary conceived without sin, pray for us who have recourse to thee." The medal also comes with a novena book to Our Lady of the Miraculous Medal. This perpetual novena is often prayed weekly in Catholic parishes.

A scapular consists of two pieces of cloth attached by a string; it is placed over the scapular bone. The most famous of all the scapulars is that of Our Lady of Mount Carmel. It is believed that the Blessed Mother gave this devotion to Saint Simon Stock, a member of the Carmelite order, in the twelfth century. The scapular is like a habit of the order. Once a Catholic is enrolled into the scapular, he receives the spiritual benefits of the order. Also, the scapular is a visual reminder of the duty of the Catholic to live out the baptismal call to be a saint.

Finally, Catholics wear crucifixes either around their neck or as a ring on their fingers. The crucifix reminds the faithful daily of the price of salvation and how much God loves them.

Question 120. Are there really exorcisms?

Yes. Exorcism refers to a religious ritual in which an officially delegated priest casts out the devil from a person, object, or place in the name of the Triune God. The delegated priest acts in the name of Jesus Christ. This designation from Christ can be found in Luke's Gospel 9:1, "And He (Jesus) called the twelve (apostles) together and gave them power and authority over all demons and to cure diseases, and He sent them out to preach the Kingdom of God and to heal."

The ability to perform public exorcisms is related to the sacrament of Holy Orders. By this sacrament, any priest or bishop has the sacramental power to perform exorcisms; however, the jurisdiction to do so is limited to an appointment by the bishop of the diocese. When the bishop goes about appointing an exorcist, he looks for qualities of holiness and strength. Before 1972 there was a formal Minor Order of Exorcists. As part of the reforms of the Second Vatican Council and suppressions of the Minor Orders, the 1983 Code of Canon Law, Canon 1172, states the current understanding of an exorcist: "No one can legitimately perform exorcisms over the possessed unless he has obtained special and express permission from the local ordinary."

Formal public exorcisms are rare. Diabolical possession (where the devil inhabits a person's body) or diabolical obsession (where the devil attacks a person's body from the outside by flying objects around the room or trying to injure the body) requires this special and ancient ritual of the Catholic Church. The movie *The Exorcist* accurately depicts the exorcism ritual. The Hollywood effects, however, of throwing up pea soup, floating in the air, etc., while real and possible, are rarer. Speaking in foreign languages the person never knew, or mysterious and bizarre voices coming from the person, occasionally occur. The process of exorcism only takes place *after* the local bishop has concluded an official inquiry. All medical and psychological explanations and treatments must be attempted first. Only after the doctors and scientists cannot remedy the situation through modern medicine and psychiatry is the exorcist allowed to get involved. This prevents hysteria and superstition. The failure of medicine and science to solve the mystery can be a sign of the supernatural.

The Psalms and passages from the Bible, especially the Gospels where Jesus expelled demons from the possessed, are recited by the priest performing the exorcism and the other priest or deacon who accompanies him. Holy water is sprinkled frequently on the person, rosaries are prayed, the Bible is read aloud again, and the formal prayers of exorcism are said. Usually, this is done completely in Latin. This whole process can take several hours, if not days, and, in some cases, weeks. Doctors and nurses are kept nearby should the possessed person need immediate medical treatment. The possessed rarely become possessed because of something they have said or done. Just like physical injury can indiscriminately hit the good and bad alike, one should never think or conclude that only sinful, evil, or immoral people get possessed. The only reason why these things happen is so that the power and majesty of God can be manifested when the possessed are delivered from their bondage, and we see clearly that good triumphs and is victorious over evil.

In addition to the formal exorcism that is reserved only to a priest or bishop, there are minor ones in which all the faithful can participate. Usually, these types of exorcisms involve holy water. When objects are blessed they are often reserved for good and all evil is asked to be removed. Taking of holy water, making the sign of the cross, and sprinkling of Holy Water on objects or in the home can all be done by lay people. The water is blessed by a priest, but then can be used by laity.

The prayer to Saint Michael the Archangel is considered to be a prayer of exorcism. This prayer used to be said by Catholics at the end of Mass:

Saint Michael the Archangel, defend us in battle, be our protection
against the wickedness and snares of the devil; may God rebuke
him, we humbly pray and do thou, O Prince of the heavenly host,
by the power of God, thrust into hell Satan and all evil spirits
who wander through the world for the ruin of souls Amen.

Finally, the wearing of the medal in honor of Saint Benedict is also seen as a devotion and prayer of exorcism.

Question 121. How many scapulars are there?

The scapular was originally a garment that went over the shoulders and covered the wearer on both sides. The word is from the Latin, *scapula*, which means shoulder blades. Many different religious communities, both male and female, wear these outer garments, which are considered part of their religious habit. In the thirteenth century, lay people began to wear scapulars as a sign of being attached to a religious community through prayer and devotion. The scapular became reduced in size and could be worn underneath street clothes.

There are many different kinds of scapulars. For example, the red scapular is for the passion of Christ, the black is in honor of the seven sorrows of Mary, the blue is devoted to the Immaculate Conception of Mary, the white is for the Holy Trinity, and the green is for healing. The most famous of all scapulars is the brown attributed to Our Lady of Mount Carmel.

This scapular is brown because the Carmelite priests and nuns wear a brown habit. The devotion to the scapular of Our Lady of Mount Carmel goes back to Saint Simon Stock of England, who received the scapular in a vision from Our Lady. By wearing the brown scapular, one becomes a member of the Confraternity of Our Lady of Mount Carmel. Those who have been enrolled in the confraternity have a spiritual relationship with the Carmelite order. With this affiliation one observes certain practices: frequent participation in the Mass and reception of Holy Communion; frequent reading of and mediation on the Sacred Scriptures; the regular praying of at least part of the Liturgy of the Hours; imitation of and devotion to Mary; and the practice of the virtues of charity, chastity, and obedience to the will of God.

The brown scapular is not a magical charm to protect you, an automatic guarantee of salvation, or an excuse for not living up to the demands of the Christian life. It is, however, a sign which has been approved by the Church that stands for the decision to follow Jesus like Mary: open to God and to His will; guided by faith, hope, and love; close to the needs of people; praying at all times; and discovering God present in all that happens around us. Those who wear the scapular are reminded daily of their vocation to be saints.

Question 122. What are Catholic blessings about?

The celebration of blessings holds a privileged place among all the sacramentals created by the Church for the pastoral benefit of the Church. As a liturgical action, the celebration leads the faithful to praise God. By celebrating a blessing, the faithful can also sanctify various situations, events, persons, and things in their lives. Blessings are signs that have God's word as their basis and that are celebrated from motives of faith. They are meant to declare and to make manifest the newness of life in Christ that has its origin and growth in the sacraments of the

Church. Above all, blessings are signs of spiritual effects that are achieved through the Church's intercessions.

In the present Rite of Blessings, the celebration consists of three parts: first, the proclamation of the Word of God, and second, the praise of God's goodness and the petition for His help. Finally, there are prayers and rites proper to each celebration. Outward signs that are often employed are the outstretching and laying on of hands, the sign of the cross, the sprinkling of holy water and, at times, incensation, which is a sign of veneration and honor.

The quality of life is enhanced by the various means of overcoming distance and of making it possible for people to come together for meetings, visits, and other forms of social contact. A blessing provides an opportunity to praise God for giving us such benefits and to pray for the safety of those who will use them.

In the Book of Blessings, elements are provided for special celebration to present a car or other means of transportation at a church, in order to ask for a blessing as a pledge of God's protection during travel. The rite is ordinarily used by a priest or deacon, but can be used by a lay minister or a lay person, though a benediction cannot be employed. Lay people should always use holy water that has been blessed by a priest or deacon.

Blessings of common objects, such as cars, are a rich symbol of faith. Everything has been given to us by God, and we are merely the custodians of material things. When an object is blessed, we are reminded of the many graces and privileges God bestows upon us. Without the grace of God, we could not exist, nor would we be in possession of these material things. Therefore, everything gives glory and honor to the Almighty. Blessings of objects must flow from a person's deep faith. It is an external sign of a practicing Catholic's belief in the Fatherly protection.

Question 123. Who can bless a home?

Normally, anyone can walk through a home with holy water and say prayers. In the past, it was customary in Catholic homes for fathers to bless their children before they retired to bed. In case of storms, many people say prayers and sprinkle their homes with holy water. Holy water is encouraged to be stored in fonts at the entrances to homes, so that the faithful may bless themselves as they enter or leave the house.

Formal blessing of a home, however, is usually reserved to the ordained ministry. Although there are provisions for lay ministers and people to say the prayers, it is traditional for a deacon or a priest to bless a home, especially when a family moves in. Other times during which deacons or priests bless homes are the Christmas and Easter seasons. In Nordic countries, such as Poland, Ukraine, and Czech Republic, priests visit the homes of the faithful—especially on the Feast of Epiphany. Catholics in Nordic and Mediterranean countries often have their homes blessed with the new water blessed at Easter. It is also a way for the parish priest or deacon to visit and get to know his parishioners. In America, these customs have fallen away, with the exception of a blessing for a family who moves into a new home.

The ministry of blessing involves a particular exercise of the priesthood of Christ. The general instructions of the Book of Blessings spell out the different ministers who may preside, in which the first is the bishop. When the celebration involves the entire diocese, the bishop may reserve certain celebrations to himself. Second, it belongs to the ministry of the priesthood when the celebration involves the local parish community, unless the bishop is present. Third, it belongs to the ministry of the deacon, because as the minister of the altar, of the word, and of charity, the deacon is the assistant of the bishop and priests. Yet whenever a priest is present, it is more fitting that he presides at the blessings. Finally, there are provisions for lay people, the priesthood of the faithful. This is especially appropriate when parents bless their children or food at meal time; however, whenever a priest or deacon is present he should preside.

When any of the faithful wish to mark their moving into a new home with a religious celebration, the parish priest should provide the occasion to gather the members of the household to thank God for the gift of their new home. The blessing usually recalls the Holy Family of Nazareth, Jesus, Mary, and Joseph, who inspire Christian families to live according to the virtues.

Question 124. What happens at a Catholic funeral?

Catholic funerals usually begin the night before the burial at a wake service in a funeral home. Wake service consists of readings from Sacred Scripture, prayers, intercessions, litanies, responses, hymns, and often homilies. Normally, a deacon or priest performs the service, but a lay person may also pray the service.

Mass of Christian burial is celebrated in the Church of the deceased. It is a special Mass that calls to mind our special destiny to be with God for all eternity. It is also a formal way to recognize family grief through prayer. The body is greeted at the door of the church with holy water, which calls to mind our Baptism. It is in baptism that we have been given a calling to be with God for all eternity. During the Liturgy, it is the hope of all present that the faithful departed is sharing in this eternal destiny. It is also a time of prayer for the faithful departed who might be in purgatory.

The casket is then covered with a pall, which is a long flowing piece of material. Again, it is a reminder of Baptism, when the grace of Jesus Christ envelopes the soul. On top of the casket a crucifix and Bible may be placed. Then all enter the church. Mass does not begin with the sign of the cross, because Mass began with the sign the night before at the wake service. Readings from Sacred Scripture (one passage from each: Old Testament, Psalms, New Testament and the Gospel) are followed by a homily. The homily is not meant to be a eulogy; rather, a recounting of our beliefs in the afterlife. The General Intercessions round off the Liturgy of the Word.

The Liturgy of the Eucharist follows with the offertory, preface, sanctus, and canon of the Mass. At the canon, all pray through the priest for the departed loved one. Our Father, Agnus Dei, and reception of Holy Communion follow. After the post Communion prayer, the final condemnations are prayed. The casket is then processed out of the church and taken to its place of burial. Burial concludes the funeral liturgy, with a special blessing of the grave or tomb, intercessory prayers, and a reading from Sacred Scripture. Upon the completion of the final blessing, the Catholic funeral finishes. White, purple, or black vestments may be worn by the priest or deacon. White symbolizes the resurrection, purple symbolizes penance, and black denotes sorrow.

Question 125. Can Catholics be cremated?

At one time, cremation was not permitted for many reasons. First, pagans often cremated their dead, so for Christians to bury the dead in sacred ground was a firm statement of belief in resurrection of the dead and the afterlife. Second, the remains of the dead were often not buried. Sometimes they would be used as amulets or kept in homes. The old Code of Canon Law of 1917 forbade the practice of cremation as recently as 1963. In 1963, a concession was provided in limited circumstance as long as the Christian did not deny the resurrection of the dead and the immortality of the soul.

With the scarcity of cemetery space in certain parts of the world, the Church over the years has allowed cremation. However, once the body is cremated, it must be interred in sacred ground, either in a Catholic cemetery or in a non-sectarian one, in which the grave is blessed by a deacon or priest. Cremated remains cannot be kept in urns or other containers around the home.

In 1997, the Catholic Church allowed cremated remains to be brought into the Church for the Mass of Christian burial. Before this date, the body had to come to the church first for the funeral Mass, and then sent to the crematorium. Later, the remains would have to be interred. Although cremation is now permitted by the Church, it does not enjoy the same value as burial of the body. The Church clearly prefers that the body of the deceased be present for the funeral rites, since the presence of the human body better expresses the Christian values regarding the resurrection of the body and the dignity of the human body which, through baptism, was a Temple of the Holy Trinity when it was alive.

Cremated remains of a body should be treated with the same respect given to the human body. Selecting a worthy vessel to contain the ashes, carrying them in a respectful manner, and paying great care and attention to the appropriate placement, transport, and final disposition are all required from the living. The practice of scattering remains in the ocean or some other location from the air or ground is never permitted. Whenever possible, appropriate means for memorializing the deceased should be employed, such as with a plaque or a stone that records the name of the deceased.

Cremated remains of a body of a deceased person is permitted in the United States in the following instances according to Canon 1176, paragraph 3: "The Church earnestly recommends that the pious custom of burying the bodies of the dead be observed; it does not, however, forbid cremation unless it has been chosen for reasons which are contrary to Christian teaching." Second, each diocesan bishop will judge whether it is pastorally appropriate to celebrate the liturgy for the dead, with or without Mass, with the ashes present, taking into account the concrete circumstances in each individual case.

Question 126. What is the meaning of burning incense?

First, there is not scientific research that concludes that the usage of incense is carcinogenic. Second, most churches are large and airy, and the fragrant smoke dissipates as quickly as it is used.

Incense has a long tradition in the area of worship. Not only did pagans use this, but Jews in the Temple service employed incense at the sacrifice of the animals.

Psalm 141 makes an analogy of incense and prayer when it says, "like burning incense let my prayer rise to you O Lord." Moses commanded that in addition to sacrifices of animals, incense should burn before the Ark of the Covenant, which contained the Ten Commandments. The sweetness of incense reminds the worshipper of the sweet mercy of God.

In the Middle Ages, incense had a more practical use. Churches, cathedrals, and monastery chapels were often used as hospitals, and poor hygiene resulted in smells which were less than heavenly. Incense was employed as an ancient form of potpourri. In the Shrine of Saint James of Compostelo in Spain, one of the oldest and most traveled to pilgrimage sites, a huge thurible (incensor, a metal container on a chain that burns hot charcoals onto which incense is placed and burned) that swings from the rafters of the church is in constant use.

The Church has always used incense in the Liturgy during the Holy Sacrifice of the Mass, the benediction of the Most Blessed Sacrament, and the solemn celebration of Vespers. Biblically, it was one of the three gifts given to the Christ child by the Magi. It symbolized the royal priesthood of Jesus. At Mass, incense is burned at the four presences of Christ—the proclamation of the Gospel, the gifts that become the Body and Blood of Christ, the priest, and the faithful. At funerals the body is incensed, because it was the Temple of the Holy Trinity through baptism when the person was alive.

WHICH TEN?— THE TEN COMMANDMENTS

THIS SECTION HANDLES CATHOLIC MORALITY, FROM THE COMMANDMENTS TO THE ETHICAL TEACHINGS OF THE CHURCH.

Chapter 12

MORAL QUESTIONS FROM A CATHOLIC PERSPECTIVE

This chapter answers questions about ethical behavior and Christian morality.

Question 127. How do I get to heaven?

On the one hand, no one "gets" to heaven in that you can't "earn your wings," so to speak. The heresy of Pelagianism was condemned by Saint Augustine and the Church in the fifth century. Basically, it was the teaching that there was no original sin, and therefore mankind did not need to be saved or redeemed and anyone could merit heaven on their own efforts and accomplishments.

Augustine opposed this error vehemently, and his teaching became the official teaching of the Catholic Church. He maintained that the sin of Adam and Eve (original sin) is in fact transmitted by human nature to every man and woman. Only the divine grace of God (which he called sanctifying or habitual grace) can justify a person by removing original sin and making them capable of receiving more divine grace. Sanctifying grace only comes through baptism (whether by water, blood, or desire) and it alone makes us children of God.

Heaven is not a reward but a gift from God. He does not owe us heaven and we do not deserve it, nor can we earn it. Out of pure love, God offers us heaven, and by his divine grace we can accept the gift or, because of free will, we can reject it. Augustine denied Pelagius' claim that one could merit or earn their way to heaven. On the contrary, without divine grace, Augustine said, it is impossible for man to perform good works. Actual grace is the divine grace given after the sanctifying grace of baptism. Actual grace empowers and enables us to do good works and have those works become efficacious. Augustine did not refute the necessity of good works (as would Luther), but he denied that works alone (as espoused by Pelagius) could save you.

Those who believe and regularly practice their faith trust in the gift of salvation, but they never presume it or take it for granted. Catholicism teaches that the Christian is never a spectator but is always a participant. Jesus commanded that we deny ourselves, take up our crosses and follow Him (Matthew 16:24). If we each follow Him to Calvary by carrying our own cross, and are buried with Him, we shall also rise with Him and join Him in heaven. Not because we earned it, but because God's grace is at work in us.

Question 128. What is a good life?

Living a good life in this world should be the goal of every Christian since it ensures eternal happiness in the next. Being nice or friendly is not the same as being good. Being good means doing good. Practicing the moral virtues of prudence, justice, fortitude, and temperance helps a person become good and virtuous. A good Christian life, as Catholicism understands it, is a lifetime commitment to doing good and avoiding evil. That makes you a good person. To get to heaven, however, there is another step involved.

It is not enough to be good—one must also be holy. Today's world, however, loves and lives extremes. Many people only equate holiness with the heroic virtue of someone like Mother Teresa of Calcutta. They say, "I could never be as good as she was." So, they never try. Yet we are not supposed to be moral or spiritual clones of Mother Teresa. We are called to be saints, or people who live holy lives. That does not mean perfect or sinless lives. Saints were never perfect and they were not sinless. They made mistakes, and they committed sins. They just did not rationalize or make excuses for them. Saints are sinners who never stopped trying to do and to be better Christians, no matter how often or how many times they failed.

Living a good and holy life means never giving up the struggle to do good and to avoid evil by keeping the Commandments. It means aggressively seeking sanctity by regularly practicing the corporal and spiritual works of mercy, praying daily, and constantly seeking to know and to do the Will of God.

The Catechism lists the Works of Mercy in paragraph 2447. Traditionally, based on the Last Judgment scene in Matthew 25:31–46, there have been seven corporal and seven spiritual works of mercy. These are deeds of compassion Christians are obligated to perform throughout their life. The corporal deal with providing physical or bodily assistance to those in need, whereas the spiritual deal with giving moral and religious aid to others.

Corporal Works of Mercy
1. *Feed the hungry.*
2. *Give drink to the thirsty.*
3. *Clothe the naked.*
4. *Shelter the homeless.*
5. *Comfort the imprisoned.*
6. *Visit the sick.*
7. *Bury the dead.*

Spiritual Works of Mercy
1. *Admonish (warn) sinners.*

2. *Instruct the ignorant.*
3. *Counsel the doubtful.*
4. *Comfort the sorrowful.*
5. *Bare wrongs patiently.*
6. *Forgive others.*
7. *Pray for the living and the dead.*

Question 129. What is the Natural Law?

The Natural Moral Law was defined by the Ancient Roman and Stoic philosopher Cicero, who wrote in 52 BC, "For there is a true law: *right reason*. It is in conformity with nature, is diffused among all men, and is immutable and eternal; … [it is the] supreme law which existed through the ages, before the mention of any written law or established state … Nor may any other law override it, nor may it be repealed as a whole or in part, nor have we power through Senate or people to free ourselves from it … Nor is it one thing at Rome and another at Athens, one thing today and another tomorrow, but one eternal and unalterable law, that binds all nations forever."

Saint Paul said in his epistle to the Romans (2:14), "For when the Gentiles who do not have the law by nature observe the prescriptions of the law, they are a law for themselves even though they do not have the law. They show that the demands of the law are *written in their hearts*."

The Natural Moral Law is the universal set of basic ethical norms every man and woman knows by virtue of reason. No rational person can be ignorant of it, nor can they claim ignorance. It applies to everyone, always and everywhere. There are no exceptions.

This was the basis for the Nuremburg Trials after World War II and for all trials of those charged with crimes against humanity. The Nazis, who participated in the slaughter of six million Jews, could not excuse their guilt; whether they were generals, privates, judges, or laborers did not matter. Any human being is expected to know it is gravely immoral to intentionally kill one innocent person. Helping murder six million innocent people is a crime against humanity. Regardless of religious, political, ethnic, academic, or economic background, every human person knows the basic fundamentals of the Natural Law: murder, theft, lying, adultery, and the like are intrinsically immoral and evil. People still commit these sins, but no one can claim ignorance of knowing they are wrong.

Catholic morality is governed by both the Natural Moral Law (known by reason) and the Divine Positive Law (revealed by God in the Ten Commandments). The principles of the Natural Law shaped and formed the Catholic teachings on the immorality and sinfulness of acts such as abortion and euthanasia, as well as the evils of social ills such as racism, anti-Semitism, and the exploitation and abuse of women and children.

Question 130. What is a moral act?

Moral theology distinguishes between human acts (*acti humani*) and acts of man (*acti hominis*). Any voluntary, deliberate, and conscious act freely committed by the person is a human act. Any activity which involves the human free will is considered a human act, and all human acts are de facto moral acts. Anything which is done by virtue of our nature or specific to our species is an act of man, like walking on two legs or speaking.

The physical act of walking is an act of man, unless one deliberately chooses to walk to a place one should not go; for example, if a married man walks to a house of ill repute. His freewill choice was to commit sin, and he employed means to achieve it. Whether he drove a car, took a bus, or walked to the bordello is irrelevant. The act of the will to use walking to enable him to go and sin made this particular act of man a sinful human act. Likewise, learning to swim is an act of man. Jumping into a lake to save a drowning person is a human act because the person had to freely choose to swim out and rescue the person.

Things done while asleep are not human acts because you must be conscious in order to use your free will. All free-willed acts are human acts and therefore are moral acts. Animals act on instinct, so when they attack out of fear or when they mate while in heat, it is nothing more than animal nature at work. When human beings have sex, it is not because they are compelled to from instinct. It is a voluntary and deliberate choice to engage in that activity. Therefore, it is a human act and a moral act. When done outside of marriage, it is sinful.

The act itself, that is, the *object* of the will, the *intention*, and the *circumstances* make up the "sources" of the morality of human acts. All three determine the morality of any human act. Hence, if the object were the deliberate and intentional killing of an innocent person, it is never justified, no matter how good the intention—even saving hundreds of lives—since the ends never justify the means. Likewise, evil intentions can corrupt good objects; for example, criminals donating money to charity to appear respectable merely to get a light sentence if convicted. One should never deliberately do evil no matter how much good it is thought may come from it. Some objects or acts are intrinsically evil and are always immoral to perform. Circumstances can diminish or increase culpability or the moral goodness or moral evil of an act but they can never make what is intrinsically evil change into good. Even if I am in a very desperate situation or set of circumstances, this cannot change the evilness of an evil act, such as murder (deliberately killing an innocent person).

Question 131. Is conscience sacrosanct?

Conscience is a "judgment of reason whereby the human person recognizes the moral quality of a concrete act that he is going to perform, is in the process of performing, or has already completed. In all he says and does, man is obliged to follow faithfully what he knows to be just and right" (Catechism #1778).

Conscience is not a little man or woman on your shoulder, or some little voice in your head telling you what to do or not to do. It is a judgment made by your intellect that some action is good and should be done or is evil and should be avoided. Since our judgment is human, it is not perfect. We can make bad judgments even in good faith and with the best of intentions. Knowing that, we are obligated to form a good conscience.

Forming a good conscience involves prayer, study, and dialogue. Prayer is communicating with God. Listening to Him helps form a good conscience. Studying the Bible and the Catechism are also indispensable tools to forming a good and correct conscience. Not only is our judgment imperfect, but so is our knowledge. No one knows everything (except for God). Therefore, it is crucial to read and study Sacred Scripture (Bible) and Sacred Tradition (Catechism) to have a correct and informed conscience. Talking to good, moral people when we are uncertain or doubtful is also vital to forming a good conscience. Sometimes others can see more clearly and more objectively than we can due to our emotions, personal history, and other factors.

Someone might erroneously think it is morally permissible to steal from the rich to give to the poor. They must follow that conscience *only* if it is certain and there are no doubts. Furthermore, that person has a moral obligation to form a correct conscience, which means he or she must verify their position and not just claim "I was following my conscience." They must test their conscience by comparing it to what the Church teaches. In any conflict, the Church's teachings must prevail since she has 2,000 years of wisdom and grace; we don't.

The Church also teaches that we should always follow a certain conscience (as long as we do not know or do not suspect it is erroneous), but we should never act on a doubtful conscience. It is also our duty to form a correct conscience that can be tested by comparing our judgment to what is taught in the Bible and in the Catechism.

There is no carte blanche on lax or improperly formed consciences. God will judge us according to our conscience and how well we formed it.

Question 132. How does one cooperate in evil?

There are different levels of cooperation in evil, and each one has a different degree of culpability. First, there is formal cooperation in evil. That is when you deliberately, consciously, and willingly intend the evil to happen. Civil law calls it being an accessory to a crime. If you know a murder is going to happen, you say or do nothing to prevent it, and you really want it to take place, that is formal cooperation. There is knowledge of the evil beforehand or while it is happening, and consent to it being done. This is always sinful and immoral.

Material cooperation in evil is when you provide the means for the evil to be done. Supplying weapons to terrorists, giving alcohol to minors, lying to the police to provide an alibi for a suspected criminal—these are all examples of material cooperation. You did not commit the act itself, but you helped make it possible by providing material cooperation.

Moral theologians also further subdivide material cooperation into two more categories: proximate and remote. Proximate material cooperation would be giving or selling nuclear weapons or biological toxins to terrorists groups. You are directly giving material cooperation without which the evil could not be done. Proximate material cooperation requires the level of necessity; your assistance was necessary for the crime to take place. Providing proximate material cooperation while withholding formal cooperation is still immoral and sinful. You can't say "I am personally opposed to abortion" but then provide someone the money or transportation to get one.

Remote material cooperation is further down the line and often can indicate no culpability, or at least a reduced level. Buying stolen goods is remote material cooperation, and it is immoral if you are aware that the items are stolen. If you are scammed by a con artist and unknowingly buy stolen goods, your guilt is minimal to nonexistent, depending on whether or not it would have been possible to ascertain if the items for sale were stolen.

The more remote the material cooperation, the less the culpability. Buying confiscated cars and homes from the police that were seized from drug dealers is permissible. Even though you know the property was obtained through illegal and immoral means, your purchase is not going to encourage further criminal acts.

Obviously, if force is used to coerce you to provide material cooperation, then by withholding formal cooperation (not giving internal consent to what is being done), your culpability is also greatly reduced.

Question 133. Why Ten Commandments?

Every day we get emails about why there are Ten Commandments, no more and no less. God was not limited to only giving ten. Moses did not drop a tablet of stone and thus lose five, as portrayed in the comedic film by Mel Brooks *History of the World*. There are ten because God gave Moses ten. The number ten is referred to in Hebrew scriptures as the ten words, *Debarim* or *Devarim* (from *dabar* in Hebrew meaning "word"). The ten words are what we now call the Ten Commandments.

Ancient Jewish mysticism taught that God created the world not just in six days, as is told in Genesis, but in six words as well. No one knows these words—just that the very act of God speaking them created the world and all that is in it. This concept is also seen in the Christian idea of the creative power of the Word of God, the spoken and written word, and most of all, the Word made flesh (Jesus).

Why did God give these ten words or Commandments to Moses? Didn't people already know it was immoral to murder, to steal, to lie, and to commit adultery? What was the purpose? Every human being has a rational intellect, and therefore it is presumed that he or she is capable, regardless of their IQ or education, of knowing the fundamental basics of the Natural Moral Law, which is the system of ethical rules every sane person knows intuitively.

When Cain murdered his brother Abel in Genesis 4:1–17, he knew it was wrong before and after he committed the crime. He needed no Commandment to tell him so, otherwise, he would have been excused of all guilt and culpability since the Commandment "Thou shalt not kill" was not handed down to Moses until many centuries later.

If basic morality and ethics, like "do good and avoid evil," are knowable to anyone with the use of reason, why reveal Ten Commandments? The first three deal with our relationship with God; the last seven deal with our relationship with our neighbor. Anyone and everyone *can* know what is morally good and what is morally evil and sinful, but because of original sin, not everyone has the same intellectual abilities. Some people will know before others. Some need more time or assistance understanding.

The Commandments even the playing field. Since we all have different intellectual abilities, God provided help to ensure that everyone could and would know what is morally good and what is morally evil and sinful. The Commandments are like prescription directions on a pill bottle. They tell you what to do or not to do to stay alive and healthy.

Question 134. Whose Ten Commandments?

Did you know that if asked what the Fourth Commandment is, a Catholic will answer differently than a Protestant (except for Lutheran)? Yes, there is a different numbering system for the Ten Commandments depending on who did the counting. The Bible itself never numbers the Commandments. There were not even any chapter or verse numbers until a thousand years after the last book was written. So, how were the Ten Commandments delineated?

Saint Augustine (fifth century AD) was the first one to give a definite number to each Commandment. Until then, everyone knew the Commandments; they just did not refer to them as the fourth, fifth, or sixth as people do today.

Exodus 20:1–17 and Deuteronomy 5:6–21 list the Commandments with slight variations each. Without the sacred author telling you where number one begins or ends (remember that ancient Hebrew, Latin, and Greek had no punctuation marks), it is anyone's guess. Augustine numbered them this way:

I am the Lord, thy God, thou shalt not have any strange gods before me.
Thou shalt not take the name of the Lord thy God in vain.
Remember to keep holy the Sabbath Day.
Honor thy father and mother.
Thou shalt not kill.
Thou shalt not commit adultery.
Thou shalt not steal.
Thou shalt not bear false witness.
Thou shalt not covet thy neighbor's wife.

Thou shalt not covet they neighbor's goods.

Martin Luther, even though he initiated the Protestant Reformation (1517), had been a Catholic priest (Augustinian monk) and retained this numbering system. It was John Calvin (1536) and the Swiss Protestants who changed the numbering to be as follows:

I am the Lord, thy God, thou shalt not have any strange gods before me.
Thou shalt not make unto thee any graven images.
Thou shalt not take the name of the Lord thy God in vain.
Remember to keep holy the Sabbath Day.
Honor thy father and mother.
Thou shalt not kill.
Thou shalt not commit adultery.
Thou shalt not steal.
Thou shalt not bear false witness.
Thou shalt not covet thy neighbor's house, nor his wife nor anything that belongs to him.

Both lists have Ten Commandments. The main difference is in how the first two and last two commandments are broken up. The Catholic and Lutheran list (based on Saint Augustine) considers the injunction against graven images just a continuation of the first Commandment, which prohibits all kinds of idolatry or false worship. The Swiss Reformed list considers the proscription of idols to be a completely distinct Commandment. Coveting thy neighbor's wife is number nine in the Catholic/Lutheran system but it is part of number ten (along with coveting thy neighbor's goods) in the Calvinist system.

The older system (Augustine's) makes a connection between the sixth and the ninth and between the seventh and the tenth Commandments. Number six forbids the act of adultery, while number nine forbids the desire for it. Number seven forbids the very act of theft, while number ten forbids the desire to take what someone else has.

The discrepancy between the two lists is one reason why it can be problematic to post the Ten Commandments in public—if you use one system over another, one group is going to feel discriminated against. Better to just put the text with no numbers as originally found in the Bible.

ICE AND
IRTUE

struggle to live a virtuous life.
?

Question 135. Isn't it enough not to sin?

Is keeping the Ten Commandments all that is required of us by God? No. Avoiding sin is a good thing and necessary for happiness in this life and in the next; however, it is only one half of the equation. If you go to the doctor and are told the good news that you have no disease, does that mean you are completely healthy? Being free of disease or injury is very important, but any good physician will also tell you to cultivate healthy behavior. Lacking the negative must be accompanied by adding the positive. Exercise, rest, and eating properly will promote and sustain good health and will help fight disease.

Both doing good *and* avoiding evil make up the entire formula. One side is not enough. We must do both, just as we must avoid what is unhealthy and do what is healthy to keep our bodies in optimum shape. Look at sin as a disease of the soul. Mortal sin is a deadly sin as it kills the life of grace. Grace is to the soul what blood is to the heart or oxygen is to the lungs. Mortal sin removes life support from the soul by killing the grace that was there. It is like a malignant tumor on the soul. Venial sin is less lethal and is like a benign tumor. Even though benign, no one wants a non-lethal growth on their face. Similarly, the Christian needs to be equally concerned about his venial sins and not just the mortal ones.

The Ten Commandments help us avoid sin, but what helps us do good? This is where the moral virtues come to our rescue. Even the pagan Greeks and Romans realized the value of living a virtuous life. For example, the Roman philosophy of Stoicism endorsed living the private and public virtues to promote harmony within the person, the family, and the state (or empire).

The ancient philosophers and early Christian theologians distilled four cardinal virtues which were invaluable to a morally good life. They are called "cardinal" from the Latin root of the word, *cardo*, meaning "hinge." The virtuous life hinges on these four moral virtues. They are *prudence* (*prudentia* in Latin; *phronésis* in Greek), *justice* (*iustitia* in Latin; *dikaiosyné* in Greek), *fortitude* or courage (*fortitude* in Latin; *andreia* in Greek), and *temperance* or moderation (*temperantia* in Latin; *sóphrosyné* in Greek).

Question 136. What is prudence?

Prudence is nothing more than the wisdom to make the right judgment regarding what to say or not to say, what to do or not to do, when, where, and how. Prudence is the prince of all virtues. Saint Thomas Aquinas (thirteenth century AD) said prudence was right reason in action.

Prudence not only tells us when it is appropriate to act or speak but to what degree, in what way, and with what limits. It also judges when it is best to wait, or to do or say nothing. A prudent person does not speak when he or she is angry lest what they say be tempered by their emotion. Prudence will say it is better to talk to someone when both of you have cooled off and are more objective. Prudence also says that urgency and emergency may warrant drastic measures, like yelling at someone who is in imminent danger. There may not be time for polite discourse.

Arguing with a criminal or terrorist who has a lethal weapon pointed at you or at others is not prudent. Calmly trying to negotiate a peaceful and nonviolent resolution could be prudent, depending on what was being negotiated. Using proportionate force is prudent, for example, wounding a criminal instead of killing him if he refuses to surrender. Prudence also helps nations avoid war by working to resolve differences diplomatically or economically before resorting to physical force.

Question 137. What is justice?

Justice is giving each person his or her own due. An employer pays an employee a fair wage out of justice. An employee gives a full day's work for a full day's pay out of justice. Convicted criminals pay fines and/or go to prison as punishment for their crimes out of justice. Good is rewarded and evil punished because of justice.

There are three subcategories of justice: *commutative*, *distributive*, and *social*. Each one depends on the relationships involved. *Commutative* justice is between two persons or two equal entities, like two nations, two businesses, or two families. *Distributive* justice is between the one and the many. A citizen pays taxes to the government, which in turn protects the individual from domestic and foreign dangers as far as possible. *Social* justice is concerned with the whole of humanity and groups of people, and the responsibility of the individual and the state to work for the common good. Protecting the environment, defeating terrorism, respecting the human rights of all persons, defending the innocent and the helpless, and helping the poor and the needy are all examples of social justice. Prudent use and management of natural, economic, military, and human resources is also a function of social justice.

Gratitude, piety, and *religion* are also considered by-products of justice. It is only fair to be grateful; showing gratitude is not only good manners but a requirement of justice. Giving thanks and accepting thanks are required by justice, so saying "thank you" and "you're welcome" are morally good and necessary to preserve harmony and peace. Piety is defined as the duty or devotion one has to one's parents or country (patriotism). It comes from the same principle, and many cultures refer to the home nation as the motherland or the fatherland because it was the place that gave birth to and sustains the lives of the people who live there. Piety means showing respect and providing support and defense when needed. It also entails *obedience*, such as that of minor children to their parents or from adults to those in authority—be it civic, military, or ecclesiastical. Elderly or sick parents require support from their adult children because of the virtue of piety, which stems from justice. Defending your country from foreign or domestic enemies (unless the nation acts immorally) is a demand of justice and piety. Religion is the duty and obligation of people to worship the divine Creator. Justice demanded that some form of religion exist even before there was a supernatural religion revealed by God. The fact that every culture and society which ever existed had some form of religion, pagan or otherwise, comes from man's realization that it is just and right and necessary to worship the Almighty Supreme Being.

Question 138. What is courage?

Fortitude or courage is the virtue whereby, rather than abandoning one's moral responsibility, duty, or obligation, one has the ability and strength to endure difficulties, obstacles, opposition, and persecution. It is the power to persevere in times of trial and tribulation. Fortitude can even give someone the heroic strength to sacrifice his life for a greater and higher good, for example, to save innocent victims. This virtue does not eliminate fear but it allows a person to overcome fear.

Pain, hardship, danger, and even threat of death deter many people from doing the morally right thing. Fortitude gives them the power to conquer those hurdles and remain faithful. Cowardice is the defective absence of courage or fortitude. Rashness or foolhardiness is the excess. There is a saying *"Only fools rush in where angels fear to tread,"* which means, it is not a lack of courage or fortitude to move slowly, carefully, and cautiously when possible.

Patience and *perseverance* are by-products of fortitude and help a person remain courageous for longer periods of time. They also build up stamina and promote the ability to bear wrongs patiently, which is a spiritual work of mercy.

Question 139. What is temperance?

Temperance, or moderation, is the moral virtue of knowing when to stop. Temperance allows legitimate pleasure without degenerating into hedonism or debauchery. Excessive drinking can lead to drunkenness, which can then lead to a number of unpleasant outcomes, for example, an accident in which someone gets hurt or killed. A social drink is temperate unless someone is an alcoholic or under-age, then temperance dictates abstinence. Working too little can produce laziness or sloth (*acedia*), whereas doing too much work can indicate that someone is a worka-holic. Temperance or moderation seeks a happy balance in morally allowed enter-tainment and pleasure.

Abstinence (moderation in eating food), *sobriety* (moderation in drinking alcohol), and *chastity* (controlling sexual appetites) are three effects of temperance. If some-one has little or no self-control, then complete abstinence or total sobriety may be the prudent course. Temperance is not the denial of pleasure (severe asceticism) nor the excess of or obsession with pleasure (hedonism or epicureanism).

Eutrapelia is a form of temperance related to sports and athletics. Excesses in sports can result in cheating, rioting, violence, and exploitation. Eutrapelia involves good sportsmanship, fair play, and not getting obsessed with the game, either on the part of the team or the fans. It allows players and spectators to have wholesome fun.

The Seven Deadly Sins as they have been known through the ages are: lust, glut-tony, greed (avarice), sloth (laziness), wrath (anger), envy, and pride. They are called deadly or capital because they will kill the life of grace. They can merit the pains of hell and eternal damnation unless one obtains the grace of forgiveness provided in the sacrament of Confession (Penance).

Question 140. What is lust?

The vice of lust is the desire for immoral or sinful sexual pleasure. Having a desire for sex is normal and human. Controlling it is also human, since men and women have a free will and rational intellect. Animals have sex because of instinct. Human beings freely choose to have sex and thus, as a conscious and deliberate act of the free will, it is a moral act. Human sexuality is not intrinsically evil, and when it occurs between a husband and wife and is oriented to love (unity) and life (procre-ation), it is a holy and sacred act of marriage. When human sex occurs outside or before marriage, with members of the same sex or by oneself, it is sinful and immoral, as it is an abuse of a gift reserved for those in marriage.

Jesus said in the Gospel, "You have heard that it was said, 'You shall not commit adultery.' But I say to you, everyone who looks at a woman with lust has already committed adultery with her in his heart" (Matthew 5:27). The Church interprets this to mean that the sixth Commandment forbids not only acts of adultery, but also willful and deliberate thoughts as well. Sin can be committed in thought, word, or deed. Lust is the intentional and conscious desire to have immoral sexual pleasure. Involuntary and spontaneous impure thoughts that plague everyone at some time or another after puberty are not subjectively sinful since there is no deliberate act of the free will.

Intentionally arousing dirty thoughts or cultivating sexual fantasies while fully awake is considered sinful. Pornography and frequenting strip clubs are also deemed immoral, as they divorce sexual intimacy from the sacredness of marriage and degrade the person being looked at by presenting him or her as a sex object—not as a person made in the image and likeness of God.

Question 141. What is pride?

Pride is often called the source and epicenter of all sin. It is inordinate self-love and self-importance. Pride makes us feel superior and better than others, and tempts us to disdain and look down upon those we deem inferior. Pride is the refusal to submit to a higher authority. Arrogance is the companion to pride.

Pride prevents us from admitting our mistakes, making apologies, or seeking forgiveness. Love of self is not a bad thing, as long as it does not diminish love of neighbor and as long as it is secondary to love of God. Pride not only makes self-love the priority but eventually eliminates love of God and love of neighbor.

Theologians speculate that it was the sin of pride which the angel Lucifer succumbed to that led to his downfall and casting into hell as the Devil. John Milton's *Paradise Lost* (1667 AD) is a classic poem, and one line of the poem in particular demonstrates the depth of Lucifer's pride when he says, "Better to reign in Hell than serve in Heaven." Vanity made Lucifer think he was the most intelligent and most beautiful of all God's angels.

There is a good type of pride, as when people take pride in their work, their family, their culture, their nation, or their religion. It stops short of feeling superior to others. Unlike the sin of pride, healthy pride is showing interest and appreciation without degenerating into being condescending or patronizing.

Question 142. What is greed?

Greed or avarice (covetousness) is the inordinate desire to have things or money and to get them at any cost. It is the inordinate desire to have what someone else has merely because they have it and we don't. Envy is similar, except that it also fosters resentment toward those who have what we do not. There is a sense of injustice that what they have should be ours, not theirs. Greed is simply the desire to have the most. Greed is the source of much pain and misery in families, marriages, and friendships. It is not limited to the acquisition and possession of things, especially money, but also includes power. Greed has an insatiable appetite; it is voracious in that it is never satisfied. The more one has, the more one wants. Greedy people will do anything to obtain what they want: lie, steal, cheat, threaten, hurt, or even kill.

Greed distorts possessions from being tools, means, or instruments for achieving one's goals into being ends in themselves. Just wanting to have stuff, regardless of how or even if it is used, is greed. Greed refuses to share and resents any kind of generosity whatsoever. The object of desire need not be monetarily valuable, either. Greed makes us want what we want merely because we want it.

Question 143. What is envy?

Envy is often confused with jealousy, which is the fear of losing what we do have (like a jealous husband who is afraid he will lose his wife and unfairly suspects her to be unfaithful). Envy, on the other hand, is the inordinate desire to have someone else's talents, honors, status, abilities, character traits, etc. It can also be the resentment and hatred of someone for having what we cannot or do not have.

Envy can also be a sorrow for other people's good fortune instead of the Christian response to rejoice with them and for them. The worst form of envy is spiritual, where a person resents the moral improvement of another or becomes angry that someone else is achieving holiness and sanctity in their lives. Bad enough to envy a millionaire for being wealthy, or a movie star for being beautiful, but it is horrible to disdain a saintly person merely because they are improving in the spiritual life. Many of the great saints were envied by their contemporaries.

Wanting to emulate or imitate someone is not envy. However, resenting what someone has or wanting their gifts and talents just for ourselves is real envy. I might be envious of my coworker's promotion, whether they deserve it or not. I could be envious of the fruits of someone's hard labor, for example, a neighbor who saved money for many years in order to have a comfortable retirement. Often, those who did not exercise prudence when they had the opportunity to do so come to envy those who did.

Question 144. What is anger?

Anger is the inordinate desire to hurt someone, to seek revenge, to vandalize property, or to ruin a reputation. Anger or wrath is different from righteous indignation, which is the moral outrage at a gross injustice, such as genocide, racism, exploitation, child abuse, abortion, or terrorism.

Often we hear of people committing a crime in the heat of anger. You and I have no control over *what* makes us angry, but we do control our *response* to it. Rage is a form of anger where irrational thoughts of violence overcome a person. Anger as a deadly sin must be deliberate and intentional. The momentary desire to punch someone who has just waved one finger at me is not the capital sin of anger. Once my reason kicks in, I need to chill out and cool off and look at the situation objectively and dispassionately. (Road rage is an example where anger left unchecked leads to violence.) Making a decision while one is still angry is ill-advised.

Jesus did not show anger but demonstrated righteous indignation when he threw the moneychangers out of the Temple (Matthew 21:12). He did not commit any violence, but He did use what some might call tough love.

Question 145. Is overeating a sin?

Gluttony (from the Latin *gluttire*, meaning to swallow or to gulp down) is not only making a pig of yourself, but it is the inordinate desire to eat or drink more than you need to or should. It is usually associated with a fear or concern that someone else might eat or consume the portion of food before we do.

Eating disorders such as anorexia or bulimia are not gluttony since they are illnesses. Deliberate and conscious overeating just to prevent someone else from having it for their meal is gluttony. The Romans perfected the sin with their vomitoriums, where the elite could regurgitate their recently consumed meal and start all over again. Fortunately, it was not as popular or prevalent as portrayed in the movies.

Animals will often eat until they throw up, but when human beings do it intentionally and not because they have an eating disorder, it is gluttony. This vice abhors any type of abstinence or fasting, whether for medicinal or spiritual purposes. The sin also leads to injustice if someone eats more than they need to survive or to satisfy their hunger while depriving someone who truly needs that food. Unnecessary waste of food is unjust even if it cannot be transported to those who truly need it.

Chapter 14

SIN

This chapter answers questions on sin—kinds and degrees.

Question 146. What is original sin?

Original sin is the name given to the first sin committed by the first human beings, Adam and Eve. Genesis 3 tells how God placed Adam and Eve in the Garden of Paradise, telling them that they could eat of any tree in the garden *except* the one in the middle, the Tree of Knowledge of Good and Evil. Later, the serpent tempts them to eat fruit from this tree.

Sacred art has traditionally portrayed Eve handing her husband Adam an apple, but the Bible does not identify the kind of fruit or tree. At some point in the past, someone depicted the Fall of Adam and Eve in art, using an apple to represent the fruit, and everyone has followed suit since.

The key here is not what kind of fruit, but that it was the sin of disobedience. Notice how God gave them all kinds of alternatives. There were many other trees in the Garden, but only one was forbidden. The one forbidden fruit was more appealing than all the rest. That is the insanity of sin: it often makes no sense.

Once our first parents sinned, human nature itself was wounded. That is because sin is not just a violation of divine law, but is also a spiritual disease, an infection, a bacterium, and an injury to the soul. Punishment was swift after God discovered that man and woman had sinned. "To the woman he said: 'I will intensify the pangs of your childbearing; in pain shall you bring forth children. Yet your urge shall be for your husband, and he shall be your master.' To the man he said: 'Because you listened to your wife and ate from the tree of which I had forbidden you to eat, Cursed be the ground because of you! In toil shall you eat its yield all the days of your life'" (Genesis 3:16–17).

Not only were they exiled from the Garden of Eden, but the aftereffects of sin now infected human nature. Original sin had the consequences of:

1. Loss of the gift of immortality: death became part of human nature.
2. Loss of the gift of impassibility: pain and suffering became part of human nature.
3. Loss of sanctifying grace: heaven would be closed to man until he was redeemed by the Messiah.

Original sin not only hurt our relationship with God, but it deeply wounded human nature the same way a horrible virus or bacteria harms our bodies. Some diseases or their effects can be inherited by subsequent generations. Every human being since Adam and Eve inherited a wounded human nature. What was that wound? Martin Luther (1483–1546) thought original sin destroyed human nature, or at least made it so putrid and repugnant that God had to cover us with grace to hide our ugliness. The Council of Trent (1545–1563) repudiated that idea and taught that human nature was not decrepit or corrupt, merely wounded. What is wounded can be healed.

Trent also taught that the effects of original sin were threefold:
1. Darkening of the intellect: sometimes we cannot reason clearly when tempted.
2. Weakening of the will: sometimes we know what we should do, but lack the courage or strength to resist temptation.
3. Disordering of the lower passions: often our emotions overpower our reason.

The only remedy for original sin and its effects is divine grace, a supernatural gift from God to help our souls. The grace of baptism is sanctifying grace. It washes away original sin and restores the broken relationship between the created (man) and the Creator (God). Baptismal grace also makes one a child of God by adoption. It enables us to receive more divine grace from the other sacraments.

Divine grace also treats the wounded human nature by enlightening the intellect, strengthening the will and reordering the lower passions. Concupiscence is the theological word used to describe our natural inclination or proclivity to sin, which is another effect of original sin.

Question 147. What is actual sin?

Actual sin is the sin human beings commit once they have reached the age of reason (seven years old). It is an intentional, deliberate, conscious, and willful act to oppose the will of God. Sin is more than just breaking the divine law; it is a spiritual disease that harms the life of grace. Some sins are so dangerous that they can kill the life of grace and permanently destroy our relationship with God for all eternity. These deadly sins are called mortal sins. Venial sin is not as deadly.

Some Catholics try to understand sin through a legal metaphor, as though mortal sins are felonies and venial sins are misdemeanors. While this analogy may help, it has its limitations. It is better to think of mortal sin as a malignant tumor which, if left untreated (no confession), will eventually kill the spiritual life of the person. Venial sin in this model is a benign tumor, although not a life-threatening condition.

(See Question #161.)

Sanctifying grace heals original sin, and actual grace heals actual sin. Sanctifying grace comes only through the sacraments, first and foremost Baptism and Penance (Confession). Actual grace comes just by asking for it, by reading the Bible, using a sacramental (see Chapter 12), or by God's divine mercy.

Actual grace helps us resist temptation and empowers a person both to want to do and to do good works. Without this grace, man cannot do any holy deed. He can do good and virtuous deeds, but not easily. He cannot do any supernatural work without divine grace.

Actual sin can keep us from heaven if serious enough, but even minor sins over time will weaken and discourage the most dedicated person.

Question 148. What is the difference between mortal and venial sin?

Mortal sin kills the life of grace, and venial sin inflicts a wound on the life of grace. In the case of a mortal sin, there are three necessary requirements for a person to have full guilt and culpability:

1. Grave matter
2. Full knowledge
3. Deliberate consent

If one, two, or all three are missing, then there is only the guilt of venial sin. Grave matter means that the *act itself* must be serious. Throwing a spitball may not be nice or polite, but it is not a grave matter. Stealing a valuable object or a large amount of money, committing murder, committing adultery or fornication, and committing perjury, for example, are all considered acts of grave matter.

Full knowledge means the person must *know* before and while he is committing the act that it is objectively wrong and sinful. Deliberate consent means that the person *freely* committed the sin. They were not drunk or stoned; they were not having a psychotic episode or hallucination, either. Being under the influence of drugs or alcohol impairs not only your judgment, but can also diminish your culpability, since you need to be fully conscious and sober to make moral decisions. However, freely and deliberately getting under the influence is immoral and sinful. A drunk may not fully know what he is doing, but when he was sober and chose to get drunk or have those drinks, he made a moral decision to risk having his judgment impaired. Everyone is responsible for their actions, but especially when we have the consciousness and sobriety to know better. Driving under the influence of drugs or alcohol is a mortal sin at the moment the person decides (while still sober) to get high or intoxicated and makes no provision for a designated driver or for a cab ride home. The full culpability occurs when the sober person chooses to take a chance to drive later when he or she should not get behind the wheel.

Ignorance, force, fear, and *habit* do not destroy freedom, but they can greatly weaken or eliminate culpability. For example, I may be under the erroneous notion that you are a terrorist and part of a cell working here to carry out some nefarious plot. Instead of reporting you to Homeland Security, I take matters into my own hands and rough you up so you will admit your true identity. My ignorance of the truth (that you are an innocent citizen of this country and are not a terrorist) and my fear of al Qaeda may be so strong as to vitiate my freedom and culpability. It is no carte blanche, but it keeps things in perspective.

Question 149. What is concupiscence?

Concupiscence is an effect of original sin which created a proclivity in our human nature to sin. It is a spontaneous movement of our sensual appetite toward what we imagine as pleasant and away from what we imagine as painful. *Concupiscence of the eyes* is an unreasonable desire to see, hear, and know what is harmful to our virtue, inconsistent with our state in life, or detrimental to our higher duties. *Concupiscence of the flesh* is when sensual pleasure is desired as an end unto itself, apart from its divinely intended purpose: to facilitate our practice of virtue and to satisfy our legitimate desires.

Concupiscence explains why it is often easier to sin than to practice virtue or seek holiness. It is not an excuse for sinful behavior but explains why we often commit the same sins over and over again, no matter how hard we try to do otherwise. Concupiscence can only be overcome by grace and mortification (penance).

Question 150. Is the Internet evil?

That depends on what you use the Internet for. If you use it to access pornography or to cultivate an adulterous relationship, it is immoral. If you use it to enlighten your mind with wholesome facts and truths, then it is beneficial. Like television, cable, VCRs, DVDs, cell phones, and all technology, the Internet can be easily abused and used for sinful purposes, or it can be used to evangelize and catechize as is done, for example, on the Eternal Word Television Network (EWTN) web page: www.ewtn.com. Books can be used for good or for evil, so one is not limited to the world wide web as a potential source of immorality.

Parents are strongly urged, however, not to trust anyone else in cyberspace no matter how good and trustworthy their teenagers are,. Your son or daughter may not have obscene desires, but pedophiles and child abusers do, and they often impersonate being a teenager themselves to prey on children and adolescents. That is why the Internet is good for young people *only* if they are supervised. One Internet connection in the house should be attached to one computer which is in full, conspicuous view of everyone in the house at all times.

Chapter 15

CONTROVERSIAL MORAL ISSUES

This chapter answers questions on the Church's view of controversial moral issues.

■ Question 151. What is a just war?

■ Question 152. Is capital punishment immoral?

■ Question 153. Why is contraception considered sinful?

■ Question 154. Is abortion always wrong? What about in cases of rape or incest?

■ Question 155. What are ordinary means?

■ Question 156. What is euthanasia?

■ Question 157. What is wrong with in vitro fertilization?

■ Question 158. Why can't scientists use embryonic stem cells for research if they might cure disease?

■ Question 159. What about cloning?

■ Question 160. Is sex before marriage wrong if a couple truly loves each other, is faithful, and eventually marries anyway?

Question 151. What is a just war?

The Just War Doctrine is an ethical criterion to ascertain if a particular war is indeed morally permissible. If it is evidently clear that a war, battle, or specific order is immoral, then it must not be complied with, lest the person become a material cooperator in evil.

Saint Augustine (fourth century AD) and Saint Thomas Aquinas (thirteenth century AD) developed a system by which any citizen or leader can ascertain the morality of a war in question.

Since moral theologians have always believed it was morally right to defend yourself and your family from unjust aggressors, then it was not too difficult to see that nations had a similar right to defend their citizens from foreign or domestic enemies. The issue of warfare, however, can sometimes get complicated.

The Catechism (#2309) lists the four requirements of a just war:

Damage inflicted by the aggressor on the nation or community of nations must be lasting, grave, and certain;

All other means of putting an end to it must have been shown to be impractical or ineffective;

There must be serious prospects of success;

Use of arms must not produce evils and disorders graver than the evil to be eliminated. The power of modern means of destruction weighs very heavily in evaluating this condition.

More elaborate refinements can be found in Catholic textbooks on moral theology and ethics. Refined distinctions have been made for the period prior to going to war *(ius ad bellum)* and for what happens once war has begun *(ius in bello)*.

Before going to war *(ius ad bellum)* there must a just cause to initiate war; the decision to go to war must be made by a competent authority; there must be comparative justice *(is this particular war worth the risk of life and property?)*; right intention *(it must not be a war of revenge or retaliation nor to gain territory, but to defend against an unjust aggressor)*; the option must be the last resort *(diplomatic and economic measures must be tried first)*; and probability of success *(fighting an unwinnable and impossible war is wrong)* and proportionality must be considered.

During war *(ius in bello)*, there must be proportionality *(only as much lethal force as is necessary to achieve success)* and discrimination against non-combatants *(formerly this referred to distinguishing civilians from military personnel but this is no longer applicable since often enemies do not wear uniforms as such and sometimes civilians have guns, making them combatants as lethal as armed soldiers).*

Question 152. Is capital punishment immoral?

The Catechism (#2267) says, *"The traditional teaching of the Church does not exclude recourse to the death penalty, if this is the only possible way of effectively defending human lives against the unjust aggressor."* While in theory the state (civil government) has the right to impose capital punishment, it is neither an absolute nor an unrestricted right. Just as there are legitimate limitations on free speech (for example, it is immoral and illegal to commit perjury), there are limitations on the moral use of the death penalty.

If non-lethal means are sufficient to defend and protect the common good and public safety, then the necessity of capital punishment begins to diminish greatly. Today, in view of more effective crime prevention, more secure prisons, and the technology to monitor movements of released prisoners, the justifications for execution (in the words of Pope John Paul II in *Evangelium Vitae*, Gospel of Life, 1995) "are very rare, if not practically nonexistent."

Therefore, without denying in principle the right of the state to impose the death penalty, the moral justifications may not always be present. Another problem besides the debate on whether or not capital punishment is truly a deterrent is the inequitable application in many instances. Each state in the US decides for itself whether or not it will execute certain criminals and which crimes warrant this extreme punishment, so it is not just the crime itself, but also where it took place that often determines if you are subject to the death penalty. Often, if you are a celebrity or someone with vast financial resources, you can hire an expensive and qualified legal team to defend you, whereas the poor person gets a public defender, who may be extremely qualified but is also usually overworked.

Since there is no universal application (same crime, same punishment), the previous pope and the Catechism seem to dissuade public opinion from capital punishment. It is not condemned as never being applicable; rather, the criteria for it do not seem to be present at this point and time in history. The prudential judgment of whether or not the moral principles have been fulfilled to make it a morally permissible act (war or death penalty) rests with those in authority who are authorized to care for the common good. There may be disagreement even among or with some church leaders in terms of practical or specific implementation or application as long as the general principles are respected and upheld.

Question 153. Why is contraception considered sinful?

The Catholic Church does not command couples to have as many babies as is reproductively possible. The husband and wife, as mother and father, have a right to make moral and reasonable plans in terms of the size and spacing of their children. As long as moral means are used, then it is up to the couple to decide when and how many children to have with the constant proviso that God may have other plans.

While many erroneously still call it the Rhythm Method, Natural Family Planning (NFP) is as effective as any artificial means of contraception when used properly. The only difference is that this method is extremely inexpensive, involves minimal inconvenience, and is completely moral to use. Artificial contraception is immoral for several reasons, and it can be very expensive and potentially dangerous to the woman over a long period of time.

Pope Paul VI issued his encyclical *Humanae Vitae* in 1968, in which he spoke of the intrinsic connection of the unitive (love) and procreative (life) faculties of marriage. He saw contraception as something which created a wall that separates the two; when that happens, the sex act is no longer a sacred sign of the covenant of marriage. Instead, it reduces the sex act between husband and wife to a purely physical—not spiritual—activity. When done within marriage as a sign of the unity of the couple and their openness to God's will should He want to bless them with new life, then human sexual intercourse is a sacred and holy act. When done purely to satisfy sexual fantasies and desires, then it reduces the couple to mere sex objects for one another.

Another concern the Church has is that many so-called contraceptives do not prevent conception; rather, they force a premature ejection of a fertilized egg. Once the sperm and egg have united, conception has taken place, and an immortal soul has been infused by God into that new human life. DNA proves that the "zygote," "embryo," or "fetus" is actually a distinct and separate human person. There are only human genes present, and this human DNA is unique from the mother and father in that it constitutes another complete human being and is not merely an extension of the mother's own tissue. Many so-called birth control pills act in reality as abortifacients, that is, they cause a very early abortion of a fertilized egg (now considered a conceived child) from the mother's womb. Conception was not prevented, but implantation was. What is ejected is very tiny, but very human nevertheless.

Finally, recent studies have shown that long-term use of birth control pills has increased the risk of breast and uterine cancer in many women. Natural Family

Planning needs no prescription, has no health risk, costs nothing, and involves both the husband and wife (so that one spouse isn't taking it easy while the other assumes all the responsibility). It can be used to space out births, and to avoid pregnancy or to facilitate it, since it is based on using the unique and personal fertility cycle of the woman.

The three- to seven-day abstinence from sexual relations involved for the couple using NFP allows them to foster nonsexual but very romantic encounters to bring them spiritually and emotionally closer together while avoiding the physical intimacy of sexual intercourse.

Question 154. Is abortion always wrong? What about in cases of rape or incest?

"Therefore, by the authority which Christ conferred upon Peter and his Successors...I confirm that the direct and voluntary killing of an innocent human being is always gravely immoral." —Pope John Paul II, *Evangelium Vitae*, Gospel of Life, #57.

Abortion is always considered evil, sinful, and immoral because it is the deliberate and intentional killing of an innocent human life.

The Catechism teaches, "Since the first century the Church has affirmed the moral evil of every procured abortion. This teaching has not changed and remains unchangeable. Direct abortion, that is to say, abortion willed either as an end or a means, is gravely contrary to the moral law" (#2271).

The ends can never justify the means, so no evil act should ever be done deliberately, willingly, and knowingly no matter how much good may come from it or how much evil may be prevented. The reason for this absolute is that if you make one exception and allow any evil to be done for whatever lofty reason, then anyone can find sufficient reason to commit almost any evil in the name of higher good or the prevention of greater evil. If murdering one man would save a hundred, then using the same moral logic, someone could murder a million to save a billion. Any exception would open the door to a Pandora's Box of moral relativism, situational ethics and consequentialism, where the outcome or circumstances determine the morality of any act.

Since it is not morally permissible to directly will or perform evil, abortion is never permitted—even to save the life of the mother or in response to rape or incest. Medically, there are few, if any, instances where a physician would even be in the situation where killing the unborn child would be the only and safest way to save the mother. If the mother is in danger, so is the child.

Rather than directly aborting and thus unjustly killing the unborn, doctors can do what is necessary to treat the mother, and if in the course of the treatment or procedure her own body causes a premature ejection of the fetus, then that is considered a natural abortion in that it was not directly willed or intended even though it may have been known to be possible, probable, or even inevitable. Once the baby comes out of the womb, everything must be done to assist him or her. If the baby happens to die anyway, it is morally acceptable because it was an act of human nature that caused the natural death, not a direct act of killing as in the case of partial birth abortions or craniotomies. Modern science and medicine do not need to directly kill any unborn child to save the life of the mother. The baby may not be viable outside the womb for too long, but a natural death is preferred to the violent, intentional killing of an innocent life.

Question 155. What are ordinary means?

Medical bioethics uses the term "ordinary means" to refer to all medical procedures which are normally and typically performed to save and sustain life. Ordinary means are always obligatory and can never be refused unless a specific procedure will have no effect whatsoever. Nutrition (food) and hydration (water) are always ordinary means and must be given as long as the patient's body is able to absorb or ingest them. Use of a feeding tube or insertion of a tracheotomy are also considered ordinary means and both were administered to Pope John Paul II a month before his death and one year after he issued a statement clarifying that ordinary means and ordinary medical care (shelter, warmth, and dignified respect) must be given to all patients, even those in a persistent vegetative condition.

Extraordinary means are those experimental, expensive, unusual, or rare treatments which may or may not have the desired effect of saving or sustaining life. These can be refused by the patient or their family. Extraordinary means are usually very new, very costly, and can be very painful. The risk is that the cure could be worse than the disease or injury.

In some cases, procedures and treatments which were considered extraordinary means in the past are now considered ordinary means. Blood transfusions, intravenous medication, and even antibiotics were initially experimental, unproven, and potentially dangerous until perfected. Now, they are standard and ordinary procedures. If a dying person's stomach has shut down and he is incapable of digesting anything, then a feeding tube is redundant. If an IV would work to give his body nutrients, however, then it is considered ordinary means. Ordinary does not mean just what is natural, but includes all modern medical procedures which are typically, routinely, and successfully performed.

Question 156. What is euthanasia?

Euthanasia (from the Greek *eu thanatos* meaning good death) is the intentional and deliberate ending of a human life by either withholding necessary, viable, and ordinary treatment (called passive euthanasia) or by introducing a substance (such as a poison) or procedure that directly causes death (called active euthanasia).

Both passive and active euthanasia are considered gravely evil and immoral and in the same moral category as abortion in terms of being the unjust killing of an innocent human life.

Patients are never obligated to endure painful procedures which are worse than their current condition and which do not have a reasonable hope of success. During the Civil War, many soldiers died not from war injuries but from the results of medical procedures, for example, infections from botched amputations. In such cases, refusal of these "extraordinary means" would not be considered euthanasia. Today, however, with the progress of medicine, technology, and rehabilitative treatment, drastic procedures like amputation can be done, and survivors usually live and adapt to their disability and are able to function in society, have a family, maintain employment, and live a relatively normal life.

Dying patients are allowed to be given as much pain medication as their bodies can tolerate as long as the dosage itself does not directly cause death. Too much morphine can stop breathing, whereas monitored amounts can keep a person relaxed and comfortable, rather than in excruciating pain and misery.

So-called mercy killing and the efforts of Doctor Kevorkian and the Hemlock Society to make euthanasia socially acceptable are condemned by the Church. God alone should decide when someone leaves this earth—not the patient, doctor, or caretaker. Keeping the dying patient pain-free, comfortable, clean, nourished, and hydrated, so as not to starve him to death, and just allowing the natural death process to take its course is how human beings die with dignity.

Question 157. What is wrong with in vitro fertilization?

Just as contraceptive sex is wrong because it divides what God intended to be integrated (love and life; unitive and procreative), so, too, conception outside the womb is equally wrong for the same reasons. There is no absolute right to have sex whenever and with whomever, and neither is there an absolute right to become a parent. While marrieds should be open to the possibility of children, no one has an inalienable right to be a father or mother. A child is a gift from God, not a commodity or bargaining chip.

Medical procedures which enhance and promote the natural biological process within the woman to have her egg fertilized by the husband's sperm must take place within the context of the married sex act and not in a test tube or Petri dish. In vitro fertilization not only takes the eggs and sperm from the bodies of the parents and conceives a human being in a test tube, but the procedure also takes more than one egg and fertilizes it so that there are several embryos conceived artificially. Each one has an immortal soul and is a human person. In vitro uses the "best" pick of the litter and discards or freezes the remaining embryos, each of which is a unique human being.

When the Virgin Mary visited her cousin Elizabeth in Luke 1:39–45, Elizabeth was six months pregnant. Her unborn son was John the Baptist. Mary was only a few days pregnant since she "went in haste to visit her cousin." Both the unborn John the Baptist and the unborn Jesus would be considered "embryos" or "fetuses" today. Yet the unborn John the Baptist leapt in his mother Elizabeth's womb for joy since he miraculously recognized the presence of the Savior in the womb of his mother Mary.

Question 158. Why can't scientists use embryonic stem cells for research if they might cure disease?

The ends never justify the means. It is a sin to directly kill innocent human life, no matter what advances science or medicine could gain from the remains left after the innocent life was unjustly taken. Some ask, "What about the already aborted embryos which are dead anyway? Why not use their bodies the way medicine uses corpses today for organ donation?" The method by which the embryonic stem cells are obtained is still sinful and immoral whenever it involves the destruction of a human embryo since that would be the unjust death of an innocent person. If an immoral government unjustly takes your property and offers to sell it to me at a very cheap price, I cannot in conscience buy the stolen property no matter what good use I could make of it.

Likewise, murdered embryos are still victims of direct and unjust killing. Furthermore, though potentially lucrative for some pharmaceutical companies, the prospect of embryonic stem cells is neither foolproof nor risk free. There is credible research which shows that adult stem cells and umbilical cord stem cells are just as viable as embryonic stem cells, if not more so.

Question 159. What about cloning?

Cloning is as immoral as in vitro fertilization since it, too, separates the unitive (love) and procreative (life) faculties from married sexuality. It is not even sexual reproduction by biological duplication. The dangers of creating a race of clones that might dominate the earth is the stuff of science fiction, but the real potential for the manufacturing and distribution of clones to harvest spare body parts is macabre at best and grossly immoral at worst.

Just because science *can* do something does not make it morally permissible to actually do it. Genes, chromosomes, and DNA are potentially alterable, but we do not know the impact and long-term effects of tinkering with the genetic code of life itself. The Sacred Congregation for the Doctrine of the Faith issued a document in 1987 entitled *Donum Vitae* (Gift of Life) which reminded Catholics not to take human life for granted and that each and every human life is a gift from God, not a product to be made or manipulated.

Question 160. Is sex before marriage wrong if a couple truly loves each other, is faithful, and eventually marries anyway?

Premarital sex is still considered fornication and is a mortal sin against the sixth Commandment. A couple that is truly in love wants what is best for each other individually and as a couple. So for example, a couple in love wants both partners to be at their optimum health, and they will mutually avoid what is harmful and dangerous to their health.

Morally speaking, sin is a disease of the soul, so a couple truly in love should want neither party to willingly and knowingly engage in sinful activity, for the sake of their spiritual health and well being.

Sex before marriage is not an act of love—it is an act of selfishness since there is no full or final commitment as there is in marriage. Sex before or outside of marriage cheapens the sacred act of covenantal love into a merely biological process to produce pleasure. It in essence becomes mutual masturbation, since the sex act becomes more important than the person with whom one is having sex. Why jeopardize the spiritual and moral health of someone you claim to love just so you can sleep with them? Making sacrifices is what people in love do for each other. Parents sacrifice for their children. If one or both persons in a relationship are not willing to sacrifice and wait until the wedding night to have legitimate sexual relations, then they are saying that the relationship and the other person are not worth the effort to sacrifice and abstain.

Chapter 16

HONORING GOD

This chapter answers questions on the first three Commandments which focus on our relationship with God.

Question 161. What is idolatry? What is iconoclasm?

Idolatry is the worship of false gods. Judaism, Christianity, and Islam are monotheistic religions, which means that they support belief in only one God; polytheistic religions support belief in many gods or goddesses. The Ten Commandments prohibit polytheism, which is considered a grave and serious sin.

One of the most common forms of idolatry has been the worship of idols themselves. Pagan religions of antiquity worshipped the sun, the moon, the sky, the earth, wind, fire, and the sea as deities. Many polytheistic religions also worship statues and idols as being divine.

Whenever the Hebrew people in the Old Testament dabbled in the idolatry promoted by their neighbors, God would severely punish them. Canaanites, Babylonians, Assyrians, and other ancient peoples practiced some form of Baal worship, which involved a statue of the god and usually some form of ritual prostitution. The Egyptians, Greeks, and Romans were famous for their myriad of idols to their false gods.

Not every statue or image is an idol, however. Idols are graven images intended for worship. Washington, D.C., is punctuated with statues of George Washington, Thomas Jefferson, Ben Franklin, and Abraham Lincoln. We do not worship those statues or the men they represent, so they are not considered idols. Similarly, statues and pictures (also called icons) of historical people in religion are not idols if no one worships them. If these sculptures and images are mere reminders of holy people in the past, then no one is violating the Commandment against idolatry.

Jewish custom, however, was that no image of God was ever to be made and His proper, sacred name could only be spoken once a year on the Day of Atonement, Yom Kippur. Early Christians, being mostly converts from Judaism, were hesitant and squeamish about making any image of Christ, even though they professed their belief that He was human and divine and that in his divine personhood, he deserved the same worship and adoration reserved for God alone.

Only after Christianity was legalized in 313 by the Roman Emperor Constantine, with his Edict of Milan, did Christians begin to portray Jesus and His mother, the Virgin Mary, in sacred art. Purists would condemn these things as being graven images, and accuse those who had them of being guilty of idolatry. Catholics, however, do not worship the statues, icons, images, or the many saints depicted in them, including the mother of Jesus. These items are akin to the photos of loved ones, living and deceased, that people today keep in their wallets, in their purses, and in their homes.

Iconoclasm (from the Greek *eikonoklasmos*) literally means "the breaking of icons." Icons are images of God or of any saint, painted onto square or rectangular pieces of wood. They depict either holy people like the saints, or holy events from the Bible (like the miracles of Jesus) or holy occasions (like the Assumption of Mary into heaven). Iconoclasts, then, are those who would promote the destruction of all images of God or the saints.

Judaism and Islam are not the only religions with a strong and absolute prohibition of any type of images, whether of holy people or of God Himself. Certain factions of Christians have historically held similar views that not only are false gods not to be memorialized into stone or metal, but neither can the One True God.

Emperor Leo III (717–741) was a Byzantine Emperor of the East and a staunch iconoclast who advocated and ordered the smashing of all icons, be they pagan idols or Christian images of devotion. The common people and the monks of the monasteries (the ones who actually painted the Christian icons for use in church or at home) did not share the Emperor's zeal and conviction that any and all icons were evil. Many of the peasants and lower clergy (below the rank of patriarch or bishop) popularized icons because they helped them remember holy people or holy themes. Just as stained glass in the Middle Ages of Western Europe was first used as the common catechisms for the illiterate lower classes of the day, icons in the Eastern Byzantine Church were used likewise.

The Catholic Encyclopedia says, "Persecution raged in the East. Monasteries were destroyed, monks put to death, tortured, or banished. The iconoclasts began to apply their principle to relics also, to break open shrines and burn the bodies of saints buried in churches." It took an ecumenical council, Nicea II, summoned by the Empress Irene in 787, to officially condemn as heresy the notion of iconoclasm.

Question 162. What about blasphemy?

Blasphemy (from the Greek *blaptein*, meaning "to injure," and *pheme*, meaning "reputation") is the sin in which one thinks, speaks, or writes "against God—inwardly or outwardly—words of hatred, reproach, or defiance; in speaking ill of God; in failing in respect toward Him in one's speech; in misusing God's name" (Catechism #2148). It is a violation of the Commandment "Thou shalt not take the name of the Lord thy God in vain."

Using God's name to curse or swear is the most common form of blasphemy. This includes using the word "God" and combining it with a curse phrase such as "damn it" or "damn you." Saying the name of Jesus Christ while in anger is blasphemous, as are depictions in so-called art where God or the saints are ridiculed, mocked, or shown great disrespect and dishonor. Blasphemy also extends to the vandalism or desecration of churches and of holy items, like relics and sacramentals.

Question 163. When is the Sabbath Day?

The last day of the week is the Sabbath Day in the Jewish religion and is observed from sunset on Friday to sunset on Saturday. It is a day of rest and no unnecessary work is allowed to be done in honor of the Commandment to keep the Sabbath Day holy.

Jewish Christians, like the Apostles and early converts, observed the Sabbath regulations and also celebrated the "breaking of the bread" (the most ancient term used for the Mass or Eucharistic Liturgy) the following day, Sunday, to honor the Resurrection of Christ on Easter Sunday. When more Gentiles came into the Church, and after the expulsion of Christian Jews from Judaism (in response to the destruction of the Temple of Jerusalem in 70 AD by the Roman Emperor Titus), Christianity as a separate religion abandoned the Jewish observance of Saturday Sabbath. Sunday worship of God replaced it, since it was considered the "day of the Lord" (day of Resurrection), and, in fact, in many languages the word for Sunday means "day of the Lord" (e.g., in Italian, *domenica*; in Spanish, *domingo*; in French, *dimanche*) whereas Saturday is translated as sabbath (Italian: sabato; Spanish: sábádo; French: samedi).

Christians maintained the tradition of going to church on Sunday as it is the "day of the Lord," but even when the Julian Calendar (devised by Julius Caesar in 45 BC) was replaced by the Gregorian Calendar (by Pope Gregory XIII in 1582 AD) the first day of the week remained Sunday, and Saturday remained the end of the week, the Sabbath day. Catholics, can, however, go to church on Saturday evening after sunset and have it count as going to church on Sunday, since liturgical time is based on the Hebrew practice of counting from sunset to sunset rather than from midnight to midnight.

Question 164. What is sacrilege?

Sacrilege (from the Latin *sacrilegium*, meaning "temple robber") is the sin of profaning any religious item or any person, place, or thing consecrated to God or to His Church (Catechism #2120). Desecrating a church or house of worship is one of the worst kinds of sacrilege, but the most grievous and heinous act of sacrilege is the desecration of the Blessed Sacrament (also called the Holy Eucharist or Holy Communion, the consecrated wafers of bread kept in the tabernacle in church) since Catholics firmly believe it is the real Body and Blood, Soul and Divinity of Christ.

Canon #1367 of the 1983 Code of Canon Law imposes an automatic excommunication on anyone who desecrates the Blessed Sacrament, and only the Pope can remove this penalty after one repents. Often, political activists will commit sacrilege by desecrating the Host (consecrated wafer) to make a political statement against the Catholic Church. That action is as obscene to Catholics as would be the spray painting of swastikas inside a Jewish synagogue or the burning of a Bible to a Fundamentalist Protestant.

Sacrilege can be personal, local, or real. Personal sacrilege is irreverence shown to a person consecrated by religious vows (monks, nuns, etc.) or by holy orders (deacons, priests, bishops). Ridiculing, mocking, or abusing members of the clergy is considered personal sacrilege, as often the animosity is directed not at the person themselves but at the Church or at God whom they represent. Whenever those in religious or clerical life violate the sixth Commandment and break their vow of chastity, it is considered a personal sacrilege on their part. Laying violent hands on a cleric used to incur an automatic excommunication from the 1917 Code of Canon Law. Since 1983, only someone who physically attacks the pope is excommunicated.

Local sacrilege is the violation and desecration of sacred places and space. Robbing or vandalizing a church, chapel, oratory, convent, or monastery would be of this category. It could also be committing immoral and sinful acts inside a sacred building, such as committing murder or engaging in sexual acts. The previous law (1917 Code) considered the burial of a publicly excommunicated person in a Catholic cemetery or blessed grave to be sacrilege. The current law (1983 Code) makes no mention of it.

Real sacrilege is the contemptuous irreverence shown for sacred things, especially the seven sacraments or anything used for divine worship (altars, vestments, chalices, tabernacles, et al). Using sacred vessels for secular use, such as a chalice to drink cocktails, or using common items like paper plates and Styrofoam cups for liturgical worship, are also examples of real sacrilege. The worst kind, again, is the desecration of the Blessed Sacrament, as it is the most important and most sacred item in Catholicism (far more than any relic or historical artifact whatsoever).

Question 165. Why can't I worship God privately?

Catholics are not forbidden from praying in private. In fact, the Church encourages her members to pray daily, both in private and in public. Private prayer, whether spontaneous or formal, is essential to the spiritual life. Public prayer is equally important. The highest form of public prayer is called liturgical prayer, for it is the Church at prayer. What one member or a few members do benefits all because of the doctrine of the Mystical Body of Christ, which basically states that each person is as integral a member of the Church as each organ is to a person's body.

The symbol of Christianity is the cross, which is the intersection of a horizontal and a vertical line. The vertical line can symbolize our individual relationship with God. All Christians, including Catholics, are asked to have a personal relationship with Jesus Christ.

The horizontal bar represents the communal or ecclesial relationship of the member to the Church, be it the universal church around the world, the diocese, or the local parish. The apostles gathered together for the "breaking of the bread," as the Mass was originally called. The disciples and other Christians gathered together in an assembly, and this was called in Greek *ekklesia* (in Latin *ecclesia*), which we translate into English as "church."

Sunday (or Saturday evening) worship of God must be ecclesial since it has been the norm for Christians from day one. Private worship of God is allowed and encouraged on any and all days of the week. It is not a question of choosing one or the other. Catholic Christians are expected to go to Catholic Mass each and every Sunday (or weekend) and holy day of obligation to join in communal worship of God. Private prayer is in addition to this requirement, but can take place at the person's own discretion and choice.

Question 166. Where did these holy days of obligation come from?

Saturday is the Sabbath, but Sunday is the day of the Lord (the day of Resurrection), and Christians worshipped Christ as the Son of God on Sunday from the very beginning, even when they were still part of the Jewish religion.

But where did the other days come from? Christianity was born from Judaism and the Jewish religion is loaded with religious feasts and holidays that commemorate a religious event in salvation history, seek God's blessings on seasons of the year for bountiful harvest, or celebrate mysteries of faith.

Likewise, the Christian Church developed its own religious feasts and holidays in addition to the regular Sunday worship of God. The first and foremost holy day is Easter because it is the day of Resurrection. Forty days after Easter, Jesus ascended into heaven, so the feast of the Ascension soon followed. Ten days later, and fifty days after Easter, the Holy Spirit came upon the apostles and the Virgin Mary in the upper room at Pentecost. That feast was also celebrated very early on.

After deciding on a liturgical celebration of the birth of Christ (December 25), eight days later would have been his circumcision, so January 1 was initially when that feast was celebrated. Later, that date changed to the feast of Mary, the Mother of God (after the Second Vatican Council). Twelve days after Christmas (January 6) is the feast of Epiphany, which is a holy day in most of the world; in the United States, it is celebrated on the first Sunday after New Year's. The Assumption (August 15) and Immaculate Conception (December 8) of the Virgin Mary go back to antiquity, but are not considered the actual historical calendar dates since those specifics are unknown. All Saints Day (November 1) is better known by the secular world as the day after Halloween; the word Halloween actually means "All Hallows' Eve." Hallows is an old English word for Saints.

Catholics in England and in the American Colonies until 1777 had thirty-four holy days of obligation. The following year, Pope Pius VI reduced them to eleven. The 1983 Code of Canon Law lists ten universal holy days, but national conferences of bishops can ask for dispensations from particular holy days for their countries.

The ten universal holy days are:

Immaculate Conception (December 8)
Christmas (Nativity of Our Lord) (December 25)
Saint Mary, the Mother of God (January 1)
Epiphany (January 6)
Saint Joseph (March 19)
Saint Peter and Saint Paul (June 29)
Assumption of the Blessed Virgin Mary (August 15)
All Saints (November 1)
Ascension of Our Lord (forty days after Easter)
Corpus Christi (Body and Blood of Christ) (sixty days after Easter)

The USA is exempt from four of those ten and therefore has six holy days of obligation:

1. *January 1, the Solemnity of Mary, Mother of God.*
2. *Forty days after Easter, Thursday of the Sixth Week of Easter, Solemnity of the Ascension.*
3. *August 15, the Solemnity of the Assumption of the Blessed Virgin Mary.*
4. *November 1, the Solemnity of All Saints.*
5. *December 8, the Solemnity of the Immaculate Conception.*

6. *December 25, the Solemnity of the Nativity of our Lord Jesus Christ.*

Whenever January 1, August 15, or November 1 fall on a Saturday or on a Monday, the requirement to attend Mass does not apply.

Here are what some other English-speaking countries have as their holy days of obligation:

Canada
Christmas
Saint Mary, the Mother of God
Epiphany (observed on the following Sunday)
Ascension of Our Lord (observed on the following Sunday)
Corpus Christi (observed on the following Sunday)
England and Wales
Christmas (December 25)
Epiphany (January 6)
Saints Peter and Paul (June 29)
Assumption of the Blessed Virgin Mary (August 15)
All Saints (November 1)
Ascension of Our Lord
Corpus Christi
Ireland
Immaculate Conception (December 8)
Christmas (December 25)
Epiphany (January 6)
Saint Patrick's Day (March 17)
Assumption of the Blessed Virgin Mary (August 15)
All Saints (November 1)
Australia
Christmas (December 25)
Epiphany (observed on the following Sunday)
Assumption of the Blessed Virgin Mary (August 15)
Ascension of Our Lord (observed on the following Sunday)
Corpus Christi (observed on the following Sunday)

Chapter 17

HONORING YOUR NEIGHBOR

This chapter answers questions on the remaining seven Commandments, which focus on our relationship with one another.

Question 167. Do you have to honor an abusive father or mother? What happens when your parents get elderly, and you have your own family?

The fourth Commandment (Honor thy father and mother) seems simple enough. Children are taught early on that God expects them to honor, respect, and obey their parents. Today, however, we unfortunately read and hear about abusive fathers or mothers, or deadbeat dads and moms who abandon their kids. When a father or mother uses physical abuse, how does this Commandment apply?

Again, the Natural Moral Law tells us that immoral or sinful commands (or orders), be they from a parent, teacher, coach, priest or minister, employer, police, or military superior, must not be obeyed whatsoever. Likewise, if someone in authority is immorally inflicting pain and punishment on us or abusing anyone, the victim, if possible, is to resist and either defend themselves or flee for safety.

Victims of abuse can and ought to testify to the truth when questioned by the police or in a court of law. They are not being disrespectful, nor are they dishonoring their mother or father or the person in authority merely by telling the truth.

It may take a long time for such victims to forgive their abusers, but it is something every Christian is asked to try to do no matter how long it takes or how difficult it may be. The first stage is to not hate the perpetrator and not wish him or her evil. Justice is not revenge, so wanting and seeking justice—that the guilty be convicted and imprisoned—is an honorable objective. Wanting to see the accused suffer, however, is not a Christian perspective. Jesus commanded us to love our enemies and pray for those who persecute us. He showed us how to forgive those who hurt and offend us. At the same time, God does not want us to neglect prudence and common sense. Serial abusers cannot be cured, so they must be stopped and avoided.

What about when mom and dad get older and the adult child or children must become caretaker(s) of the one who cared for them when they were little? Sadly, even in families where there are several sons and daughters, often only one or two will arise and offer their services. A husband or wife's first duty and obligation is to their spouse and to their own children, and then to their own parents. If someone has a spouse who is disabled or ill or has a child with special needs, then the ability to devote the time and energy necessary to care for a parent may be limited. Usually, however, the adult children do not have equivalent or surpassing responsibilities at home, so they ought to do what they can to help their (or their spouse's) mom and dad.

Inconvenience is something Christians should never see as an obstacle to doing good or practicing the corporal works of mercy. Only when it becomes painfully burdensome should someone refrain from giving assistance to an elderly or infirm parent. Sometimes the care that is needed cannot be provided adequately by the adult child, and either a visiting nurse or a nursing/convalescent home may be the only possible solution. That said, the duty and responsibility of maintaining regular and frequent contact, communication, dialogue, and whatever support can be offered, is expected as a matter of justice.

Question 168. Is murder the only sin involved in the fifth Commandment?

The fifth Commandment actually uses the word "murder," which is *rasah* in Hebrew, *phoneuo* in Greek, and *occides* in Latin as found in original Biblical manuscripts. The word "kill" would be *harag* in Hebrew, *apokteino* in Greek, or *interficias* in Latin. This means that the commandment literally says, "Thou shalt not murder" and not, "Thou shalt not kill." Murder is the deliberate killing of an innocent person. Self-defense is not considered murder, and killing in self-defense is neither sinful nor immoral.

Murder can be premeditated (first degree in civil law), spontaneous but deliberate deadly assault (second degree), or it can be an unlawful killing of a human being without malice (manslaughter). These are all forbidden by the fifth Commandment.

Equivalent acts would also include any and all unjust killing, such as abortion or euthanasia, where the death is directly intended and achieved—regardless of the motive or consequences. Intentionally ending the life of an innocent person is always considered unjust killing and is immoral and sinful. Gross acts would be genocide, terrorism, and unjust wars, or indiscriminate use of deadly force.

Extended acts would include physical violence or abuse, verbal or emotional abuse, harboring hateful thoughts, racism, bullying, intimidation, and blackmail. Jesus said in the Gospel of Matthew 5:21–22 that he who is angry with his brother is guilty of murder. What Christ is speaking of is the willingness to commit murder. The desire to murder someone is a sinful act of the will. Let's say I buy a gun and plan to kill my annoying neighbor, but someone or something prevents me from leaving the house to get to his home or, when the moment arrives and I pull the trigger, I discover there are no bullets in the gun, or that I missed the target, or that

I left the safety on by mistake so the gun does not fire. All these obstacles may prevent the physical act of murder, but I have already committed the sinful desire to murder when I took the gun in my hand. I committed murder in the heart if not in the flesh. My act of the will was that I commit murder.

Question 169. Is sex always sinful?

Human sexuality may have some mechanical similarities to animal sexual reproduction, but remember, any act which involves the human free will makes it a human act and not just an act of man (a biological function). All human acts are moral acts. A man or woman must freely choose to have sex, and that act of the will makes this a moral act. When human sex is used properly, it is a holy and sacred sign of the covenant between husband and wife. When done to promote love (unity) and life (procreation), it is a marital act and is sacred in the eyes of God.

When unmarried people have sex, before or outside of marriage, it is the sin of fornication. When one or both persons is married to someone else, then it is the sin of adultery. When done by yourself, it is the sin of masturbation. When it involves explicit media (Internet, telephone, television, photos, videos, or text), it is the sin of pornography. When done with persons of the same gender, it is considered the sin of homosexuality. (While the sexual inclination and orientation may be inculpable, all sexual activity between individuals of the same gender is considered immoral, just as all sexual activity of unmarried heterosexuals is considered immoral and sinful.)

Any and all sexual activity outside of marriage (that is, the marriage of one man and one woman in a permanent, faithful, and fruitful union) is considered immoral and sinful. Modern culture portrays sex as a human right. The Bible and the Church say otherwise. Sex is a gift from God; what distinguishes human sex from animal sex is that human beings act morally—with their free will and not out of blind instinct. People choose to have sex, whereas animals just do it when they are so inclined.

Human sexuality is reserved for marriage alone. We reserve the consumption of alcohol for persons over the age of twenty-one. It is illegal to buy or sell dangerous drugs such as heroin, cocaine, or other controlled substances. None of these is a denial of human rights or freedom. Even married couples cannot perform the conjugal act in a public place, and no one considers that unreasonable or unconstitutional.

The Church does not see human sex as intrinsically evil or sinful. The heretical sects, like the Gnostics and Manicheans, were that fanatical. The Church merely reiterates what the Natural and Divine Laws already make clear: sex is reserved for husband and wife. Even then, spouses should not be seen or used as mere sex objects or sex toys; rather, married men and women ought to see their spouses as their beloved to whom they are covenanted for life.

Question 170. When does stealing become a mortal sin?

Stealing violates the seventh Commandment. There is no specific price range at which theft goes from being a venial sin to a mortal sin. Civil law makes arbitrary parameters to delineate misdemeanor theft from felony theft. Moral theology does not assign a particular monetary value. It is based on the condition of the person who was robbed and the person who committed the theft. If an employed man robs a homeless woman of her one and only dollar, that would be a mortal sin. Were the same person to rob a millionaire, it would still be sinful, but only venial sin. The more sinful intention is to steal what is known as very valuable or needed by the owner. It does not mean I can steal small amounts from the rich rather than rob the poor, however.

If I rob my cousin and take his valuable and rare coin or stamp collection, thinking I have stolen at least $100,000 or more, but then find out from Joey the Fence that none of the collection is rare and the whole things is only worth $50, I am still guilty of a mortal sin. My intention was to steal a large amount of money or something worth a lot of money.

Cheating on income taxes, charging citizens unfair taxes, denying employees a fair wage, or not giving a full day's work for a full day's pay, are all sins against the seventh Commandment. The Romans may have said "*et caveat emptor*" (let the buyer beware), but price gouging and overcharging the customer are still immoral acts. Trying to swindle or defraud the seller is similarly immoral. Getting a good deal or taking advantage of a sale is no problem. When you know someone is being taken advantage of, that is a good indicator that the sale or purchase is probably sinful.

Pirating music or videos and not paying for cable or Internet by deceit are also sins against this Commandment, as is insurance fraud. Embezzlement of company funds and squandering worker's pensions would be a gross case of immoral theft.

Question 171. Can telling the truth ever be a sin?

The eighth Commandment forbids lying (false witness). People use the term "white lie," but there is no such thing in moral theology or ethics. There are major lies and minor lies, but all lies are sinful—some venial, others mortal. Lying under oath in court (perjury) is a mortal sin. Lying about someone in print (for instance, in the newspaper) is called libel in civil law, and if only verbal, then it is called slander or calumny. Both are sinful and immoral, since the person telling the lie knows that what he or she is saying is not true and that these lies can ruin someone's reputation.

Lying is the telling of a falsehood with the direct intention of deceiving another (Catechism #2482). Subjective lies are statements which contradict what is known or believed in the mind (intellect). It is not speaking what you know to be the truth. Objective lies are statements which are not true in fact (reality). In both cases, however, there must be an intent to deceive. Error of fact or inaccurate information is not lying if one innocently has the wrong information.

Can you lie about your age? No. Lying would be the intentional deception of your age, as in the case of filling out an official financial, government, or business form, or when asked in court. When someone at a social gathering asks how old you are, and you reply "Thirty-nine" when you are actually forty-seven, there is no presumption of accuracy and no intention of deception, since social convention is that anyone who says they're thirty-nine is merely replying that they do not wish to answer your question. There is no expectation, either, that the answer is truthful when the reply is "Thirty-nine" and the person obviously looks much older. While some might call this a white lie, it is not lying since there is no intention of deception, rather, someone is merely withholding information that someone else is not entitled to know. Since the questioner, upon hearing the answer, realizes that the person answering is being evasive, there is no deception and therefore no lie. The phrase white lie is a misnomer since it implies that some lies, albeit minor ones, are not immoral. All true lies are immoral; some are more grave than others. Withholding the truth is not lying when there is no moral obligation to divulge it.

Likewise, telling bedtime stories and fairy tales to children is not lying since there is no intent to deceive, merely to amuse, as in the case of telling a joke or when actors perform on stage or on film. The intent is not to deceive someone who is expecting the truth or who would mistake the deception for the truth. Magicians and illusionists and special effects artists deceive, but there is no expectation that they are showing reality when the purpose is to amuse or entertain.

Lying is withholding the truth when one is morally obligated to tell it. When someone refuses to violate physician-patient confidentiality or attorney-client privilege, that is not lying—it is keeping a secret that they are legally obligated to keep.

Priests are forbidden to reveal anything they hear in confession; this is called the seal of confession.

Giving false or inaccurate information is lying when the intent is to deceive and the recipient is morally entitled to the information. Government spies, secret agents, undercover cops, and the like, are not lying but using subterfuge and mental reservation to protect the safety and welfare of innocent persons who would be at risk from an enemy knowing certain facts and information. Officials in government, business, or even individuals in church authority who deceive the public to cover up crimes, avoid embarrassment, or escape punishment are lying. Maintaining serious confidentiality, avoiding unnecessary scandal, or protecting innocent victims from possible exploitation would not be lying if there is no culpability involved, that is, the person making the statement is not at fault.

Gossip is the sin of telling statements which may or may not be true about someone with the intention of tarnishing that person's reputation or of making the person look inferior or foolish.

Detraction is the sin of telling the truth with the intention not of preventing imminent harm to another, but instead with the intention of ruining his reputation. You see Fred come home drunk. You tell your neighbor so he thinks less of Fred; that is detraction. If you tell Fred's wife so she can get him help, that is not detraction.

Withholding the truth is sinful when it is morally obligatory to tell it, for example, when parents do not tell their children it is sinful for a boyfriend and girlfriend to live together outside of or before marriage, or when loved ones do not tell an immediate family member that he or she has a serious drinking, drug, or gambling problem.

Question 172. Must Christians be pacifists?

No. Christians may be conscientious objectors but not just to avoid military service or to escape the draft. One must be totally and philosophically opposed to a particular war or to military service in principle and not just when it is convenient. There is also a moral obligation to support and defend your homeland. So conscientious objectors can be exempt from combat or military service, yet still be patriotic, by rendering civil service in some other capacity (for example, volunteering for the Red Cross, hospital, Peace Corps, or engaging in some form of public or private charity work). If someone enjoys the benefits and privileges of citizenship but does not pay taxes or is unwilling to defend the nation that protects him, that would be injustice. You can defend yourself, your homestead, or your nation, and still be a good Christian.

Saint John the Baptist told Roman soldiers to be fair and did not tell them they had to leave the army. "Soldiers also asked him, 'And what is it that we should do?' He told them, 'Do not practice extortion, do not falsely accuse anyone, and be satisfied with your wages'" (Luke 3:14). Jesus said "render to Caesar what is Caesar's, but to God what is God's" (Mark 12:17). From these two passages, the Church has historically seen no contradiction in Christians providing military service to their homeland.

Question 173. Are all lies sinful even if they save a life?

Lying is never permitted, but using mental reservation is morally allowed to preserve life or prevent injury. Mental reservation is the technique used to withhold truthful information to someone who has no right to have it. A stranger calls, and a child answers the phone. Rather than training the kid to lie when the caller asks, "Is your mommy home?" and say "yes," when in fact she is out of the house, it is better to teach mental reservation. The better response to the question would be, "She's not in the room right now" or "She's busy right now. Can you call her later?" Both are accurate and not lies.

When Aunt Clara asks you about her new hairdo or her bizarre dress, you do not have to lie and say, "It is beautiful. I love it!" when in reality you think it is ugly. You can and should say "Wow, that is some hairdo!" or "What a dress!" in which case you are not lying, but Aunt Clara's feelings are not hurt either.

Despite the bad press, Pope Pius XII (1939–1958) did work to save and protect many Jews throughout Europe during the war but did so clandestinely, since rumors abounded then (only recently corroborated by discovered documentation) that Hitler was prepared to capture the pope and put his own puppet pontiff in his place. Pope Pius ordered the monasteries, convents, and churches of Italy to issue pretend baptismal certificates to give to Jews who were hiding from the Nazis. Since these documents were not intended to deceive pastors to falsely celebrate sacraments with those who were not actually Catholic (which would have been sinful lying), they were in fact a form of mental reservation on paper. These were not real baptismal certificates that were forged, but unofficial and fictitious papers meant to look like baptismal certificates in order to protect Jews from Nazi capture and eventual extermination at a death camp.

Many religious houses took in escaping Jews in Italy and other parts of Europe with the knowledge, permission, and direction of Pope Pius XII. While many attack him for not making public denunciations in the middle of the war, he used his prudential judgment to stay neutral so as to be of some help. Had he made overt objections, then he might have been captured, arrested, and executed, as were many Protestant leaders who defied Hitler in public. Pius's fear was not for his own death or even imprisonment, but that a phony pope would be installed by the Nazis and more harm would have come upon the Church. Though today he gets bad press, and even then some complained about his supposed silence, in reality, he was able to help more Jews by his apparent neutrality. This enabled the Vatican to hide and smuggle many Jews to safety whom otherwise would have died in the Holocaust. Had Pius made very overt attacks on the Third Reich, that in itself would not have saved more lives, nor would it have deterred Hitler and his goons; it would have had no effect on non-Catholic countries like the United States or Great Britain to react differently to Nazi Germany. The Catholic countries of Europe were predominantly occupied by the Germans or were under fascist control. Those who claim that Pope Pius could have stopped or even slowed down the deportation and eventual extermination of millions of Jews do not realize the political realities of the Vatican during WWII. All religious leaders of any religion were effectively impotent to do anything since even the mightiest military and economic powers, like Britain and North America, had a long fight to win and end the war. So, Pius' reluctance to be ousted from office is not to be seen as a cowardly response. Canon Law allowed him to resign at any moment in which he would cease to be pope and would cease to be in danger or jeopardy. He chose to stay in office and work secretly behind the scenes even at the risk of appearing complacent.

The Chief Rabbi in Rome, Israel Zolli (1881–1956) knew of Pius's efforts and was so grateful that he himself converted to Catholicism and took the baptismal name of Eugenio, the baptismal name of Pius XII (Eugenio Pacelli). Ronald J. Rychlak, The author of *Hitler, the War and the Pope*, states, "On the same day that Germany invaded Poland, Pius telegraphed the papal nuncio in Warsaw with instructions to organize Polish Jews for a passage to Palestine. One of the crucial terms of the concordat with Germany was that German officials were to regard baptized Jews as Christians. Accordingly, Pius ordered his nuncio in Turkey (Angelo Roncalli, the future Pope John XXIII) to prepare thousands of baptismal certificates for refugee Jews arriving in Istanbul in the hope that such papers would gain them passage into the country. (When he was later thanked for his extensive lifesaving work, Roncalli said, 'In all these painful matters I have referred to the Holy See and simply carried out the pope's orders: first and foremost to save Jewish lives.'")   According to Rychlak, Pius also instructed Catholics, especially clergy, to shelter Jews, provide falsified travel documents, distribute food and clothing, comfort the injured, and communicate vital information to the Allies. Ironically, when he died in 1958, notable Jews like Albert Einstein and Prime Minister Golda Meir praised Pope Pius XII as a "righteous Gentile" for his clandestine efforts to help the Jewish people during World War II. Reports vary that from 300,000 to possibly 800,000 Jews were saved from the heinous evil of the Holocaust precisely because of the secret operations performed by the Catholic Church at the direction, not just permission, of Pius XII. His reputation was tarnished not by historical evidence, but by a fictional play written in 1963, *The Deputy*, which portrayed a pope reigning at the time of WWII, as a Nazi collaborator. East German and Soviet intelligence agencies used the play for their own propaganda war against the Vatican and the Catholic Church.

OUR FATHER— OUR PRAYER

THIS SECTION HANDLES QUESTIONS ABOUT CATHOLIC PRAYER AND SPIRITUALITY.

Chapter 18

PRAYER

This chapter looks at the questions about types of prayer, motives, purpose, etc.

Question 174. How many kinds of prayer are there?

What is prayer? The Catechism (#2559) quotes Saint John Damascene who said, *"Prayer is the raising of one's mind and heart to God or the requesting of good things from God."* Many spiritual writers see prayer simply as having a conversation with God or communicating with the Lord.

Traditionally, Catholicism classifies four types of prayer: adoration, petition (*supplication*), contrition, and appreciation (*thanksgiving*). Bishop Thomas Welsh, retired bishop of Allentown, Pennsylvania, often talked about how he was educated by the nuns to learn the ACTS of prayer: Adoration, Contrition, Thanksgiving, and Supplication.

The first and foremost type of prayer is that of *adoration* or *worship*. This is nothing other than giving praise to God merely because He is God, the Supreme Being and Creator, Redeemer and Sanctifier of the World. The virtue of religion requires out of justice that earthly, mortal creatures owe worship to divinity. Adoration has no strings attached. There are no deals, bargains, or promises: "If you give me this, I will…" is *not* a prayer of adoration. The angels give God the prayer of adoration constantly. Saint Thomas Aquinas (thirteenth century) taught that of the nine choirs of angels, the highest are the Seraphim whose only task is to worship God in perpetual adoration.

"Ask and you shall receive," Jesus said in the Gospel (Matthew 7:7). Petition or supplication is prayer that asks for divine assistance. Not only are we encouraged to ask, but Jesus also told us to be patient and to persevere in asking. He never promised when or how our prayers will be answered, just that they will be answered.

Intercession is a form of petition where we ask God to help someone else. We are not seeking assistance for ourselves but on behalf of others. Praying for one another is a very Christian thing to do.

Contrition or *sorrow* is the prayer of repentance. When a sinner has had a conversion of heart (*metanoia* in Greek) and regrets committing sin, that is contrition. Perfect contrition is sorrow for sin merely because the person is sad for offending an all good and loving God. Imperfect contrition is sorrow motivated from the fear of punishment. While not the best reason, fear of hell is good enough to be forgiven, but it is a worthier goal to be sorry simply because you have offended God.

Thanksgiving or *appreciation* is a prayer of gratitude for the blessings God has given. It is a spiritual way of saying "thank you" to the Lord. Not just good manners, but justice demands that we do it. Giving thanks is perfectly expressed in the Mass.

The Greek word for thanksgiving is *eucharistia*, which is the word used by the Church to describe the consecrated host (the Holy Eucharist). Holy Thanksgiving is what the people and the Church express for being able to partake of the body and blood of Christ.

There are also three ways of praying: verbal (*spontaneous* or *formal*; *private* or *liturgical*), meditation (*mental*), and contemplation (*mystical*).

Any prayer which is spoken, either memorized or made up as you go along, is verbal prayer. It can be a soft whisper, a bold proclamation, or anything in between. It can be said or sung. It is formal if someone else composed it; spontaneous if you did. Private prayer is done alone, whereas liturgical prayer requires a congregation. Jesus said, "Where two or more are gathered in my name, there shall I be in their midst also" (Matthew 18:20). Liturgical prayer is the prayer of the church (the word *liturgy* comes from the Greek word (*leitourgia*) meaning public worship. The Mass is the highest and most solemn form of liturgical prayer.

Mental prayer, or meditation, is used to focus the mind on the truths of faith or to use the imagination and picture oneself present at some incident of salvation history—pretending you were at the multiplication of the loaves and fishes, or imagining you are on Calvary watching Jesus be crucified. Using memory and imagination helps a lot of people. Christian meditation is not produced by sitting still, humming, or chanting. It is not directed toward the self or to abstract concepts. It is communicating with God by placing our conscious selves in His presence and thinking about His attributes (merciful, loving, forgiving, patient, just, et al.).

Contemplation is the most sublime way of praying in that you allow God to do all the talking. He speaks to you, heart to heart, in contemplative prayer. It is a very mystical form of prayer which takes a lifetime to achieve by God's grace. You cannot force or conjure contemplation. It is given as a gift of the Holy Spirit when and how He chooses.

Question 175. Can I pray for anything I want?

Yes and no. Theoretically, you can ask for anything. Jesus said, "Ask, and you shall receive." He just didn't say what you would get or when. It is useless to pray for anything that would be immoral or evil, since God will not give divine assistance so that we can sin, and it would be blasphemous to ask for anything sinful anyway.

Jesus shows the perfect attitude in petition prayer. Matthew 26:39 describes when Christ is in the Garden of Olives before His arrest, scourging, crucifixion, and death. During this time, called the "Agony in the Garden," Jesus prays so intensely that He sweats drops of blood. The Scripture passage quotes Him as saying, *"Father, if it is possible, let this cup pass, yet not as I will, but as You will."* That last part needs to be added to all our prayers. Catholic Christians are encouraged to pray for whatever they need but should always add the same proviso Jesus did, "yet not as I will, but as You will."

Can you pray to win the lottery? God is not Monty Hall, and life is not *Let's Make a Deal.* Praying to win at gambling, even if you promise to share your winnings or give them all to charity or to your church, is disrespectful to the Lord. Games of chance or sporting events should be amusement and nothing else. Praying that your favorite team wins the Super Bowl, the World Series, or the World Cup is not proper. God does not take sides in such things. Instead you should pray that everyone plays well, that no one gets hurt, that good sportsmanship is shown, and that the officials and referees are fair and just.

Who hasn't prayed while taking a final exam or the SAT? There is nothing wrong with praying for a clear head and that you do your best, but prayer cannot and should not be used to replace study and homework. God gave us an intellect as well as a free will; He wants us to use both.

Question 176. Why pray for others?

One comforting aspect of Catholic theology is the teaching on intercessory prayer. It is nice to know that others are praying for you, whether or not you know who or when. It is important to note that intercession is not mediation; there is only one mediator: Jesus Christ. Being true God and true man with a fully divine nature and a fully human nature, Jesus is the only one to bridge heaven and earth.

His singular mediation, however, does not prevent, exclude, or discourage intercessory prayer. If you are having gall bladder surgery tomorrow, and you ask me to pray for you, and I say, "No, you don't need my prayers. You should go directly to Jesus and pray for yourself," you might be greatly offended—and with due cause. It is true, you do not *need* my prayers. You can pray for yourself, and you should. Everyone should. But we can and ought to pray for each other, too. While we do not need other people's prayers, those prayers are never wasted. They are still efficacious. God hears everyone's prayers, so what's wrong with praying for others or asking others for their prayers? They are not necessary but helpful (by God's will). It is still a mystery that despite the fact that we are to accept and embrace the will of God, He nevertheless allows us to ask what is in our will. Since we do not know with metaphysical certitude what God's will is in our lives, we hope and trust we are at least close or near to it. Rather than us never asking for help, God wants us to ask; He also wants us to ask properly, always under the condition that our request be in conformity to His will.

The Gospel has numerous examples in which people asked Jesus for healing, not for themselves, but for others. That is intercessory prayer. When Jairus approached Christ (as described in Mark 5:22–43), he asked Jesus to heal his dying daughter. He was praying *for* her. Jesus allowed him to intercede on behalf of his daughter and cured her miraculously.

The Roman Centurion in Luke 7 sent messengers to ask Jesus to heal his slave. Here both the Centurion and the messengers were asking for help on behalf of another. Did Jesus rebuke the servants and say, "Tell your master to ask me in person himself?" No. Jesus allowed the Roman to intercede for his slave and allowed the servants to intercede as well. Intercessory prayer works, not by necessity, but by the will of God.

Catholicism not only teaches that you and I can pray for others and that others can pray for us, but the doctrine of the Communion of Saints teaches that the saints in heaven and the souls in purgatory can pray for us as well. Death does not destroy the bonds of love. The dead can pray for us, and we can pray for the dead. The saints in heaven, however, do not need our prayers since they are already in heaven and have what they want and need. The damned in hell cannot be helped, nor do they want to be. The souls in purgatory, however, can be helped by our prayers. We do not know how or when they are helped any more than we know how or when our prayers here on earth help the living. Praying for the dead is a good thing in that it shows a respect for their immortal souls.

When Catholics pray to the Blessed Virgin Mary or to the saints, they are asking for their intercessory prayers. Only adoration prayer is worship, and that is reserved for God alone. Catholics do not and are forbidden to give adoration prayer to Mary or any of the saints. We can use the prayer of petition, however, especially intercessory prayer. If I can ask you, a living person, for your prayers for me, then I can ask a saint in heaven or even the mother of Jesus for her prayers, too.

Praying is communicating with the soul. Praying to the saints is not worshipping the saints, but communicating with them in the only way possible. Praying to the saints is only intercession; it is never necessary, but it is helpful.

Question 177. What language should we use to pray?

It does not matter if you pray in Hebrew, Greek, English, or Latin. Most people pray in their native language. God not only understands every language on earth, but He knows our thoughts before we speak them. You can use the "Queen's English" or your colloquial dialect. Since God is omniscient (all-knowing), it does not matter.

Some people find it spiritually helpful to pray in their normal dialect so as to feel closer to and more intimate with God. Others prefer to keep their prayer more formal and use what some might call archaic vocabulary. Whether you pray to the Holy Ghost, the Holy Spirit, or *Spiritus Sanctus*, it is all the same.

"Praying in tongues" is technically called *glossolalia* (from the Greek words *glossa* meaning "tongue" and *lalia* meaning "to speak"). The Bible recounts in Acts 2:1–12 how the Apostles at Pentecost were able to speak in languages they did not know. Peter, James, John, and the rest spoke their native Aramaic, but each person heard their native tongue being spoken, whether it was Greek, Latin, Persian, or Egyptian.

Charismatic Catholics claim another type of glossolalia. When they pray, often some in their assembly start speaking an unknown language. Someone else who has been given the charism (gift) of interpreting tongues, translates for the rest.

Not every Catholic believes or participates in this type of prayer, just as not all Protestant Christians are Charismatic or Pentecostal. Those who do find this helpful to their spirituality. Catholics are neither prohibited from nor compelled to embrace this kind of spirituality. It is optional.

Liturgical language is more official since it is the public prayer of the Church. Recent popes have urged that Roman Catholics maintain their appreciation and familiarity with the Latin language, just as the Greek Orthodox do with Greek, even for those who live in the USA, Canada, or Great Britain. English may be our native tongue and the vernacular is allowed in sacred liturgy, but the Church also wants to maintain tradition and continuity with the past by keeping and retaining some common parts of the Mass in Latin from time to time, if not all the time. Jewish people do the same for Hebrew, and Muslims do the same for Arabic.

Question 178. What are some helps for prayer?

The best place to start is at the top. The divinely inspired, inerrant, and revealed Word of God has helped millions of people to pray through the ages. Just reading the Bible is itself a prayer when done meditatively; each word, sentence, paragraph, and chapter are studied and given proper reflection.

Since antiquity, Jews and Christians have prayed the Psalms from the Bible. Whether it is from the Breviary (Divine Office or Liturgy of the Hours) or straight from the Bible, reading the Psalms is very good prayer. The Gospels contain the words and deeds of Christ, so reading any of them (Matthew, Mark, Luke, or John) meditatively is also excellent prayer and will enhance your prayer life. The more Sacred Scripture we read and use in prayer, the better we know the Lord since we are reading His words to us.

Many non-Catholics have problems with praying the rosary, since initially they only see it as repetitive prayer. Jesus rebuked the rattling on of prayers just for the sake of quantity. Likewise, Catholics are encouraged to pray the rosary often, but *quality* is what counts, not quantity. The rosary begins with the Apostles' Creed and uses the Hail Mary (which comes from the mouths of the Archangel Gabriel and Saint Elizabeth as recounted in Luke 1:28, 42) and the Lord's Prayer or Our Father (taught by Christ Himself). It meditates on the mysteries of Christ, from His annunciation and birth to his death, resurrection, and ascension. Praying fifty Hail Marys in one rosary can be very relaxing. The repetition does not give you more grace than if you prayed ten rosaries, but the more the rosary is prayed, the better the mind can transcend the clutter and noise of this world and connect with heaven.

Joining a prayer group which meets daily, weekly, or monthly is another help, as well as reading Bible commentaries, the Catechism of the Catholic Church, the writings of the Church Fathers, and tried and true spiritual classics. Here is a list we suggest:

1. John A. Hardon, SJ, *Catholic Lifetime Reading Plan (An Anthology)*
2. Saint Francis De Sales, *Introduction to a Devout Life*
3. Saint Therese Of Lisieux, *Story of a Soul*
4. C. S. Lewis, *Screwtape Letters*
5. G. K. Chesterton, *Orthodoxy*
6. Saint Louis De Montfort, *True Devotion to Mary*
7. Saint Augustine, *The Confessions*
8. Archbishop Fulton Sheen, *Life is Worth Living*
9. Francis Fernandez, *In Conversation With God*
10. Saint Josemaria Escriva, *The Way*
11. Fr Benedict Groeschel, CFR, *Arise From Darkness*

Question 179. What is Catholic mysticism?

Mysticism is a level of Catholic spirituality not easily achieved. Traditionally, in the spiritual life, one begins with the *purgative*, fighting one's bad habits and temptations and avoiding sin. Mortification and penance are encouraged at this basic level. Next is the *illuminative* level, seeing the light of truth by cultivating the moral virtues and seeking to do good rather than simply avoiding sin. The third level is the *unitive*, in which one has an intimate communion with God. Here is where mysticism takes place.

Meditation is practiced in the second level of the illuminative, but it is contemplation where the mystic finds a home. Meditation is the intentional concentration of the mind (intellect) on the mysteries of faith in the Christian religion, for example, the Incarnation, the Trinity, and the Real Presence. It can use the senses, imagination, memory, and emotions.

Contemplation, on the other hand, is not conjured up by the person, but is a gift from God where He communicates *cor ad cor loquitur* (heart speaks to heart) in the quiet recesses of the human soul. Only intimate union with God can allow for true contemplation. Those who achieve it are considered mystics or contemplatives. Saint John of the Cross, Saint Teresa of Avila, and Saint Ignatius of Loyola are famous Catholic mystics.

The object in contemplation is not contemplation itself, as is the case in pagan and non-Christian mysticism. The goal of contemplation is holiness, to seek sanctity by getting closer to and getting to know better the source of holiness, the Holy of Holies, God Himself.

When attachments to this world, to things (possessions, money, power, pleasure) are abandoned, then attachment to other things needs to take place (recognition, thanks, affirmation, consolation, appreciation). Finally, the self (ego) must be destroyed, in what the mystics call "dying to self." One's will must be sacrificed so that it can be replaced by God's will.

Saint Catherine of Siena experienced mystical ecstasy where she levitated from the floor and would simultaneously feel pain and joy in her body and soul. Saint Francis of Assisi and Saint Padre Pio of Pietrelcina were mystics who were also blessed with the Stigmata (having the five wounds of Christ on their own bodies).

Chapter 19

OUR FATHER OR THE LORD'S PRAYER

This chapter examines the most well known and beloved of all Christian prayers, the Our Father.

Question 180. Why is the Catholic version shorter?

Anytime there is a Catholic wedding or funeral, when it gets to the point in the Mass when the Lord's Prayer is said, you can always tell who the Protestants are and who the Catholics are just by noting who keeps going while the others stop. The Catholic form of the prayer ends sooner than the Protestant version. Both religions share 95 percent of the words:

"Our Father, who art in heaven, hallowed be Thy name; Thy kingdom come, Thy will be done, on earth as it is in heaven. Give us this day, our daily bread, and forgive us our trespasses as we forgive those who trespass against us; and lead us not into temptation, but deliver us from evil."

Here is where the Catholic version ends. The Protestant version continues with the phrase:

"For Thine is the kingdom, the glory and power, forever and ever. Amen."

What's up? Well, the King James Version of the Bible has the doxology (the phrase quoted above) at the end of the Lord's Prayer in Matthew 6:9–13, but other English versions and the original Greek and the Latin of Saint Jerome (400 AD) do not have it. In the Revised Standard Version (RSV) and the New International Version (NIV), like the Catholic Bibles (New American [NAB], the Jerusalem Bible and the Douay-Rheims), the doxology is not present.

Scholars speculate that a monk was copying the text late at night while tired, and as often happens with human duplication, if tired, his mind went back to familiar territory. Since the doxology is part of the Mass ("for the kingdom, the power and the glory are yours, now and forever") that comes right after the Lord's Prayer, perhaps the copier just kept going without thinking about it.

Luke 11:2–4 has a different version than the one found in Matthew.

"Father, hallowed be thy name. Thy kingdom come. Give us each day our daily bread; and forgive us our sins, for we ourselves forgive every one who is indebted to us; and lead us not into temptation."

Question 181. Which version of the Lord's Prayer is found in the Gospels?

Some people do not realize there are two different versions of the same prayer in the Bible. The Gospel of Matthew (6:9–13) and the Gospel of Luke (11:2–4) both have the Lord's Prayer (Our Father), but use slightly different wording. Could one of them have heard it differently? Is one right and one wrong? Aren't both inspired and inerrant?

Well, there are also two different versions of the Beatitudes in Matthew and Luke. Luke (6:17–26) includes a bunch of "woes" after the "blessed are they" which are not found in Matthew. Matthew (5:1–12) describes the sermon as being given on a mount, hence the phrase, Sermon on the Mount. Luke, however, says it was a plain.

Who's right? Matthew was an original apostle, and he was there when the sermon was given. Luke was not an apostle, but he was a disciple. There were twelve apostles and seventy-two disciples. Could their memories be that different?

Scholars believe Jesus probably gave this sermon more than once. As a preacher myself and pastor of two parishes, on any given Sunday, I give a similar sermon to each congregation but modify it a little for each place. Sometimes, the modification is for the audience to make it more specific or relevant, or it may be that I thought of a variation while driving from one church to the other.

Jesus could have and probably did give similar sermons to different people in different places. John's Gospel closes with the line that if everything Jesus said and did were written down, there would not be enough room in the world to hold all the books. This fact would certainly apply to the sermons he gave.

Question 182. Trespasses or debts?

Some Christians pray the Lord's Prayer using the word "trespasses," while others use the words "debts" or "sins." The Greek word *paraoptomata* means "trespasses," while *opheilemata* means "debts" and *hamartias* means "sins." Matthew and Luke both use any one of those words in various manuscripts. The more important word in the prayer is *aphiemi* which means "forgive." The concept that Christ is communicating is that we are to "forgive," whether debts, trespasses, or sins.

One of the reasons "trespasses" has been used by so many for so long is that forgiving a debt, while a charitable deed, is different from forgiving an offense (trespass). Theologically, it is better to restrict the word "sin" to an offense against God since it involves putting one's own will against the Divine Will. If I put my will against your will, it is not necessarily sinful. If you owe me money and I dissolve the debt, there is no real forgiveness as is demanded by the Gospel.

Forgiveness is to pardon someone who offended, hurt, or attacked us. It implies there is guilt in the offender, regardless of whether or not there is repentance, sorrow, or contrition. We can forgive those who have not even asked for our forgiveness. We are asked to forgive our enemies, to love them, and to pray for them.

Using "trespasses" in the Lord's Prayer in this context, then, seems to make more sense than using "debts" or "debtors," but all three (sins, debts, and trespasses) are found in the Gospel nonetheless.

Question 183. Why "our" and not "my" Father in heaven?

First of all, Jesus instructed that we pray this way, saying "our" (*hemon* in Greek) Father. So, to be faithful to His command, we pray using the word "our" rather than "my." Secondly, Jesus wanted us to know that we never pray alone; we always belong to the family of God because we are all children of God.

My brother is not your brother, but my brother and I can say, "She is *our* mother." Using that word affirms the relationship of those who use it. The words "we," "us," and "ours" designate a communal relationship. Christ is our brother, and God is our Father. Praying the Our Father is meant to reaffirm those basic connections.

Christianity uses the cross as its most ancient symbol. The two bars, horizontal and vertical, also represent the two dimensions of our human existence. There is the transcendent personal relationship between us and God, and there is the immanent relationship between us and our neighbors.

Question 184. How do you hallow?

To hallow is to bless or sanctify, to make holy. Hallow can also be to respect and treat as holy, as sacred. To "hallow this ground," for example, means to respect the place where we bury our dead. When we pray the Our Father, the line that says "hallowed be Thy name" does not mean we are asking God to bless His own name, rather, we are making an emphatic statement that God's name *is* holy and should be treated as holy.

The Commandment that forbids us to use the name of the Lord in vain (blasphemy) is implied here, but this goes much further by insisting not only that we don't take His name in vain, but also that we respect it and treat it as holy. Someone's name is more than just a word. It is how they are known to others, friend and foe alike. The sacred name of God as revealed to Moses in Exodus was the tetragrammaton; transliterated from the Hebrew, it is YHVH and it is the personal and sacred name of God the Almighty. No one could speak it but the high priest in the Temple of Jerusalem once a year, on the day of Atonement (Yom Kippur), while he stood behind the veil in the sanctuary that preceded the Tabernacle, wherein lay the tablets of stone containing the Ten Commandments.

So sacred was the name that devout Jews to this day do not speak it, instead using the terms *Adonai* (Lord) or *Elohim* (God). Nowadays, Christians use the name of God and Jesus to swear and curse with no shame or embarrassment. "Hallowed be Thy name" is something Christians should rediscover. Keeping God's name, God's day (Sunday), and God's will holy is how we "hallow" or sanctify our lives.

Question 185. Where is the kingdom of God?

Basileia tou theou (Greek) or *Regnum Dei* (Latin) means "Kingdom of God," and it is a consistent theme. The phrase "the Kingdom of God" is used at least fifty times by Jesus in the Gospels, and it appears almost a hundred times in the entire New Testament. It must be an important idea to be mentioned so often.

When Jesus says that "the Kingdom of God is at hand" in Mark 1:15, He is not speaking of an earthly kingdom or of a territory or place as we know it. Rather than being limited to a geographical location, the Kingdom of God is wherever the Reign of God exists. Wherever men and women accept the dominion of God, that is, allow Christ to reign in their hearts and allow themselves to be governed by God's will rather than by their own, then the Kingdom of God is present.

An analogy to this would be the Roman Empire if we describe it not in territorial terms but in terms of Roman Law, Roman culture, Roman roads, Roman language (Latin), Roman currency, etc., throughout the Empire. Territorial boundaries are artificial delineations. Likewise, the Kingdom of God is not limited to heaven but is anywhere and everywhere the Reign of God is embraced. Hell is one place where no one accepts the dominion of God.

The Kingdom of God is in our hearts, our minds, and our souls. At the time Jesus walked this earth two millennia ago, people were expecting an earthly or political Messiah who would restore the regal might of Jerusalem and the Kingdom of Israel to something resembling the days of King David and King Solomon. Christ did not come to establish an earthly kingdom but a spiritual kingdom.

The phrase "thy kingdom come" in the Lord's Prayer refers to the two comings of Christ. Historically, Jesus came two thousand years ago and established His kingdom in the hearts of all the baptized. Eschatologically, (a fancy theological word meaning "at the end of time"), there will be the Second Coming of Christ. At that time, the Devil and those who choose his reign will be cast from this earth into hell, never to escape. The righteous, who have chosen the reign of God, will be with Him forever. The prayer reminds us that there is an end of the world; there is Judgment Day and a Day of Reckoning. The rulers of this world will find out who is really in charge.

Question 186. If "God's will be done," then why pray at all?

"Thy will be done, on earth as it is in heaven" is the next part of the Lord's Prayer. Christians know it is important to seek to know and to accept the Will of God. The question is, though, why do we pray to Him about our desires when it is His will, not ours, that counts?

There are four types of prayer: adoration, thanksgiving, contrition, and petition. We pray to worship God, to thank Him, to tell Him we are sorry for our sins, and to ask Him favors and assistance. Why ask if He already knows what we want and what we need? Why pray to tell God what we want when we should really be asking Him what His will is for us?

Yet, Jesus said, "ask and you shall receive" (Luke 11:9). He never said *what* we would receive, and He never promised we would receive exactly what we asked for. He does say in verses 11–12, "What father among you would hand his son a snake when he asks for a fish? Or hand him a scorpion when he asks for an egg?" Often, we may be asking for a snake or for a scorpion, and God who loves us and knows better what we need, gives us a fish or an egg instead. We may not get what we asked for, but we can ask and trust that we will get something much more important and valuable.

Philosophers and theologians tell us that God exists outside of time, so He knows what you will ask Him even before you ask it. His Will is already decided, so we cannot change the mind of God. Prayer should really be our request that God change us, change our minds and our hearts, instead of some negotiating and bargaining we do with the Lord to try to persuade Him to see things our way.

Spiritual writers tell us that we not only need to *know* the will of God and to *accept* it but to strive to *embrace* it and make it our own.

Question 187. Is "daily bread" from a bakery?

Epiousion (Greek) and *quotidianum* (Latin) in the Gospels means "daily." "Give us this day our daily bread," as is said in the Lord's Prayer has two meanings according to Saint Augustine of Hippo (354–430 A.D.). It is not the bread you get at the bakery; rather the "daily" bread, Augustine says, is the Word of God and the Word made flesh.

Jesus said "one does not live by bread alone, but by every word that comes forth from the mouth of God" (Matthew 4:4). Augustine said the revealed Word of God is our "bread," and we should therefore partake of it daily.

Catholics, contrary to what some believe, are encouraged to read the Bible daily. At daily Mass and daily praying of the Breviary (Liturgy of the Hours), Sacred Scripture is read. Listening to and reading the Word is food for the soul.

Augustine also understood "daily bread" to mean the Word made flesh, the consecrated bread which Catholics believe is the real, true, and substantial body of Christ. Jesus said in the sixth chapter of Saint John's Gospel that He *is* the "bread of life," and he who eats this bread will never die. The daily bread for Catholic Christians is the Holy Eucharist (Blessed Sacrament or Holy Communion), which can be received each day if the person is properly disposed (by being in the state of grace).

It is because of this connection that the Church inserted the Lord's Prayer into the Mass (Eucharistic Liturgy), and it is prayed just before Holy Communion is given to the congregation. Jesus also mentioned in the sixth chapter of John that just as God gave the Hebrews manna in the desert to keep them physically alive, Jesus Himself was the "bread from heaven," and He commanded that we "eat His body" and "drink His blood."

Daily Communion is a privilege, honor, and blessing many Catholics wish they could have. Mother Teresa of Calcutta spent a holy hour before the tabernacle containing the Consecrated Host each day before she began her work in the streets of Calcutta among the poorest of the poor.

Question 188. Can we really forgive and forget?

"Forgive and forget" is not in the Bible. If you could forget what someone did to you, there would be no need to forgive them. It is precisely because we do remember vividly and with detail the words and action of others that have offended us that forgiveness has value and merit.

Jesus asked His followers to forgive their enemies, to love those who hate them, and to pray for those who persecute them. Not easy to do when you can remember what your enemies said and did. Some Christians think forgetting is the same as forgiveness. It is not. Forgiveness *does* mean that I stop reminding those I have forgiven that I have forgiven them.

Christian forgiveness not only means not seeking revenge or a vendetta, but also that we try not to keep thinking about and dwelling on what happened in the past.

It means giving someone another chance, just as we ask God to forgive us and give us another chance. Forgiveness does not mean we deny the past or pretend there are no consequences to our choices and actions. Besides the great act of forgiveness shown by Christ on the cross as He is being crucified: "Father, forgive them, for they know not what they do" (Luke 23:34), the following are two other examples that have relevancy.

In July of 1902, when Maria Goretti was almost twelve years old, a nineteen-year-old boy named Alessandro fatally stabbed her when she refused to be sexually seduced by him. As she was dying, she told her mother and the doctors and nurses that she forgave her assailant what he had done to her. At not even twelve years of age, she showed an abundance of heroic virtue.

Alessandro was convicted and sentenced to thirty years hard labor. (He was considered a minor since he was only nineteen when he committed the gruesome killing, and at that time, twenty-one was the age of majority.) While in prison, after serving six years of his sentence, he had a vision of Maria Goretti telling him that she forgave him. He called for a priest and confessed his heinous sin and received sacramental forgiveness. When released in 1932, Alessandro went to the home of Mrs. Goretti to ask her forgiveness. She opened the door and saw face to face, eyeball to eyeball, the man who had murdered her little eleven-year-old daughter Maria thirty years before. She said if Jesus could forgive him and if her daughter Maria could forgive him, she had to forgive him, too. They both attended Christmas Mass the next day, and he asked the people of the parish and of the town if they would forgive him, too. He spent the rest of his life in silence as a lay brother in a Franciscan monastery.

Pope John Paul II forgave his would-be assassin, Mehmet Ali Agca, in 1981 and visited him in his prison cell after the pontiff had recovered from his wounds. Documents recently released from the Stasi, the former East German spy agency, show that the KGB and the Kremlin were in fact the ones behind the plot to kill the pope. They had feared that his influence on Solidarity and the Polish people was so great that he could and would eventually become a catalyst to undermine the fifty years of imposed Soviet domination. If Communist Poland fell to democracy, then the entire Warsaw Pact was in danger. Little did they know that the entire Soviet Union would itself soon disintegrate.

Agca, a twenty-three-year-old Turk, was used by the Bulgarian branch of the KGB (according to a 2006 Italian parliamentary commission) to assassinate Pope John

Paul II. On May 13, 1981 (the anniversary day of an apparition of the Virgin Mary which appeared to three children in Fatima, Portugal in 1917), he came to Saint Peter's Square in Rome and blended into the audience of 20,000 during a regular outdoor papal address. After the talk, as the pope was being slowly driven through the crowd in a white car (affectionately called the Popemobile), Agca fired four shots from his 9-mm pistol from a distance of fifteen feet and into the pope.

Despite nearly fatal wounds, the pontiff (pope) survived the shooting. From his hospital bed he told the press that he forgave Agca. After recovering from his surgery and fully recuperating, the victim visited his would-be assassin in prison. He went into the cell where Agca was incarcerated and personally expressed words of forgiveness. Agca never converted to Catholicism, but the pope kept contact with his family, especially after he was deported to Turkey to fulfill a prison sentence he had escaped from prior to the papal shooting.

Pope John Paul II, like Maria Goretti, showed the world that forgiveness is possible.

Question 189. Why would God lead us into temptation?

"Lead us not into temptation" sounds odd to many Christians. Why would God lead us into possible sin anyway? What does this mean? The structure of the phrase is a Greek language construct that really means "lead us so that we do not fall into temptation" or "lead us away from temptation." Often the original languages of Scripture (Hebrew or Greek) have odd ways of saying things, which made sense to them at the time but which we may be a little puzzled by two thousand years later.

God would not and could not lead us into temptation, since temptation is the suggestion that someone disobey God and commit sin. God does not carry out sting operations, and He is never guilty of entrapment, either. The Devil is the tempter, not God. This phrase, put clumsily in English, merely asks God to protect us when we are tempted and asks that once we discover we are being tempted, God help us to resist and fight the temptation or get us away from it.

The Catechism says in # 2848: "'*Lead us not into temptation' implies a decision of the heart: 'For where your treasure is, there will your heart be also… No one can serve two masters.' … God is faithful, and he will not let you be tempted beyond your strength, but with the temptation will also provide the way of escape, so that you may be able to endure it.*"

Question 190. From what evils can we be delivered?

The original Greek text says *ponerou* which translates to "the Evil one" rather than just "evil." The Evil One is the Devil, the Prince of this World, the Prince of

Darkness, the Author of All Lies, the Son of Perdition, the Accuser, etc. This last part of the Lord's Prayer is a request for deliverance from the power of the enemy. Satan hates mankind, since God took on a human nature and not an angelic one. Humanity, although inferior to angelic nature, has been raised above the angels since we can call Jesus brother, but they can only call Him King.

This is not a request for exorcism but a prayer for protection from the influence of the Devil. When he tempted Adam and Eve, he distorted the truth; and when he lies to us, it is the same principle.

Evil is not the opposite of good, and it is not equal to good. Evil is the privation or absence of a good where it belongs. If a rock is blind and cannot see, that is not a physical evil, since rocks have no eyes are not supposed to see. If a man or woman commits sin, that is evil since we are supposed to and are intended to do good.

This part of the prayer asks that physical, moral, and spiritual evils be placed out of our path. The Devil will use whatever he can to tempt us, but his power is not unlimited. By contrast, God's power always prevails.

Chapter 20   HAIL MARY

This chapter answers questions on the prayer known as the Hail Mary.

- Question 191. Where does this prayer come from?
- Question 192. Was Mary really "full of grace"?
- Question 193. What is the Angelus?
- Question 194. What are some other Marian prayers Catholics know?

Question 191. Where does this prayer come from?

Certainly the most Catholic of all prayers is the Hail Mary (or *Ave Maria* in Latin). Many non-Catholic Christians do not realize just how biblical this prayer truly is.

"Hail Mary, full of Grace, the Lord is with thee. Blessed art thou amongst women, and blessed is the Fruit of thy womb, Jesus. Holy Mary, mother of God, pray for us sinners, now and in the hour of our death. Amen."

Latin Version, Ave Maria:

"Ave Maria, gratia plena, Dominus tecum. Benedicta tu in mulieribus, et benedictus fructus ventris tui, Iesus. Sancta Maria, Mater Dei, ora pro nobis peccatoribus, nunc, et in hora mortis nostrae. Amen."

The first line comes directly from the Gospel of Luke and from the mouth of the Archangel Gabriel himself in Luke 1:28. The second line comes from the mouth of Saint Elizabeth, the cousin of Mary in Luke 1:42. The rest of the prayer was added over time, but the substance and essence is from and is based on the Scriptures. Praying to the Virgin Mary is not considered idolatry, since it is not a prayer of adoration or worship. Only God can be worshipped or adored. Supplication or petition is another form of prayer which is nothing more than asking for assistance. All prayers to Mary and to the saints are considered prayers of petition asking those in heaven to ask God on the praying person's behalf for His divine help.

A Syriac ritual attributed to Severus, Patriarch of Antioch (513 AD), is one of the oldest references to this prayer.

The Catechism quotes this ancient Marian prayer in #2676– 2677.

"Ave Maria, piena di grazia, il Signore è con te. Tu sei benedetta fra le donne, e benedetto è il frutto del tuo seno, Gesú. Santa Maria, Madre di Dio, prega per noi peccatori, adesso e nell'ora della nostra morte. Amen." (Italian)

"Dios te salve, María, llena eres de gracia, el Señor es contigo. Bendita tú eres entre todas las mujeres, y bendito es el fruto de tu vientre, Jesús. Santa María, Madre de Dios, ruega por nosotros pecadores, ahora y en la hora de nuestra muerte. Amen." (Spanish)

"Je vous salue, Marie, pleine de grâce, Le Seigneur est avec vous. Vous êtes bénie entre toutes les femmes, et Jésus, le fruit de vos entrailles, est béni. Sainte Marie, Mère de Dieu, priez pour nous, pauvres pécheurs, maintenant et à l'heure de notre mort. Amen." (French)

Question 192. Was Mary really "full of grace"?

Chaire kecharitomene (Greek) is the salutation the Angel Gabriel gives to Mary in Luke 1:28. *Ave gratia plena* is how Saint Jerome translated that phrase into Latin.

Greek and Latin give the same meaning: Hail, full of grace.

Kecharitomene comes from the root word *charis*, meaning "grace." Grace is a supernatural gift from God given to man. If Mary is full of grace, it is by the power and the will of God. The Angel does not give her the grace, he merely states a fact that she is full of grace; this is *before* she conceives in her womb the child Jesus, the Son of God.

"Full" means one is at one's capacity. It does not mean that Mary is the source of grace or that she has all the grace in the universe, merely that she herself is filled with God's grace.

Since the sin of Adam and Eve, no children or descendants of theirs had sanctifying grace, which makes one a child of God and able to enter heaven. Grace was lost by sin. So, how did Mary get it? She got it from God.

Jesus Christ redeemed the entire human race, including His human mother, Mary. He, being God, could also apply to her the benefits and fruits of His work of redemption backward in time so that Mary could receive grace at the moment of her conception in the womb of her mother, Saint Ann (grandmother of Jesus).

The doctrine of the Immaculate Conception is merely that God applied or gave to Mary the fruits of what her Son Jesus would do in her future by having Jesus give backwards in time from His Passion and Death on Good Friday. In other words, what Jesus did in Mary's future, He gave her the application of in her past.

She was conceived without original sin so she could give her Son an untainted human nature. This gift came from her Son, who would become the Savior and Redeemer of mankind.

Mary did not know this had happened to her. She did not glow in the dark, and there was no sticker or label on her telling anyone about it. Only when the angel told her she was full of grace did she find out. Once she said yes to Gabriel, the Holy Spirit overshadowed her, and she conceived Christ in her womb without the assistance of any human father. To be "full of grace" meant she was filled with the source and author of grace, God Himself.

Question 193. What is the Angelus?

There is an old joke that goes like this: A simple farmer went into town to make his annual confession to the parish priest. After hearing the man's confession and giving absolution, the clergyman gave the man his penance. A couple hours later, the priest was outside taking a walk before lunch when he saw the very same man standing in the town square yelling, "Bong! Bong! Bong!" The clergyman asked a parishioner what was going on, and was told "Fred went to confession this morning and is doing his penance. He was told to do the Angelus."

The Angelus is not the ringing of bells but the prayer people are reminded to pray by the bells rung three times a day—at dawn (6 a.m.), midday (noon), and dusk (6 p.m.). It is an ancient prayer based on the biblical account of the Annunciation and the Incarnation of Christ. Taking lines from the Gospels of Luke 1 and John 1, the prayer goes as follows:

"The angel of the Lord declared unto Mary" (said by the leader or by self if in private).

"And she conceived by the Holy Spirit" (response by congregation or by self if in private).

*** At this point the *Hail Mary* is said in its entirety by everyone. ***

"Behold the handmaiden of the Lord" (taken from Luke 1:38).

"Be it done unto me according to thy word" (taken from Luke 1:38).

*** At this point the *Hail Mary* is said again in its entirety by everyone. ***

"And the Word became Flesh" (taken from John 1:14).

"And dwelt among us" (taken from John 1:14).

*** At this point the *Hail Mary* is said again in its entirety by everyone. ***

"Pray for us O most holy Mother of God"

"That we may be made worthy of the promises of Christ."

"Pour forth, we beseech thee, O Lord, thy grace unto our hearts, that we, to whom the Incarnation of Christ, thy Son, was made known by the message of an Angel, may by His Passion and Cross be brought to the glory of His Resurrection, through the same Christ, our Lord, Amen."

Question 194. What are some other Marian prayers Catholics know?

Catholics call any prayer addressed to the Virgin Mary (often she is just called the Blessed Mother) "Marian" prayers. The Hail Mary (*Ave Maria*) is the most famous.

The *Salve Regina* (Latin for Hail Holy Queen) is prayed at the end of the Rosary and is chanted in Latin at the funeral of a deacon or priest and at the funeral of the mother or father of a priest.

"Hail Holy Queen, our life, our sweetness, and our hope. To thee do we cry, poor banished children of Eve. To thee do we send up our sighs, mourning and weeping in this

valley of tears. Turn then most gracious Advocate thine eyes of mercy towards us and after this our exile, show onto us the blessed fruit of thy womb, Jesus. O clement, O loving, O sweet Virgin Mary. Amen."

Here it is in Latin:

"Salve Regina, Mater misericordiae, Vita dulcedo et spes nostra salve. Ad te clamamus exsules filii Hevae. Ad te suspiramus gementes et flentes, in hac lacrimarum valle.

Eia ergo advocata nostra, illos tuos misericordes oculos ad nos converte. Et Jesum benedictum fructum ventris tui nobis post hoc exsilium ostende. O clemens, o pia, o dulcis Virgo Maria. Amen."

The *Magnificat* is prayed at Vespers (Evening Prayer) and comes from Luke 1:46–55. This is the prayer the Virgin Mary herself prayed as recounted in the Gospel.

"My soul proclaims the greatness of the Lord, my spirit rejoices in God my Savior; for He has looked with favor on His lowly servant; From this day all generations shall call me blessed. The Almighty has done great things for me, and holy is His name. He has mercy on those who fear Him in every generation. He has shown the strength of His arm, He has scattered the proud in their conceit. He has cast down the mighty from their thrones, and has lifted up the lowly. He has filled the hungry with good things, and the rich He has sent away empty. He has come to the help of His servant Israel, for He has remembered His promise of mercy, the promise He made to our fathers, to Abraham, and his children forever. Amen."

The *Memorare* was composed by Saint Bernard of Clairvaux (1090–1154 AD).

"Remember, O most gracious Virgin Mary, that never was it known that anyone who fled to thy protection, implored thy help, or sought thy intercession, was left unaided. Inspired with this confidence, I fly unto thee, O Virgin of virgins, my Mother! To thee I come; before thee I stand, sinful and sorrowful. O Mother of the Word Incarnate, despise not my petitions, but in thy mercy hear and answer me. Amen. "

Chapter 21

PIETY AND DEVOTIONS

This chapter answers questions about personal acts of piety and devotion as distinct from public worship in church.

- Question 195. What are some other popular Catholic prayers?
- Question 196. What is the creed?
- Question 197. What is the Catholic fascination with bells about?
- Question 198. What is the liturgical year?
- Question 199. Why all the Catholic calisthenics?
- Question 200. Why do Catholics keep relics?
- Question 201. What are Candlemas and the blessing of throats?
- Question 202. What are some Catholic Christmas traditions?
- Question 203. Isn't public worship enough for a Christian?
- Question 204. What is piety?
- Question 205. Don't private devotions detract from healthy spirituality?
- Question 206. What is a holy hour?
- Question 207. What is special about first Fridays and first Saturdays?

Question 195. What are some other popular Catholic prayers?

Grace before meals: *"Bless us, O Lord, and these Thy gifts, which we are about to receive from thy bounty through Christ our Lord. Amen."*

Grace after meals: *"We give Thee thanks for all Thy benefits O Almighty God Who livest and reignest forever; World without end. And may the souls of the faithful departed, through the mercy of God, rest in peace. Amen."*

Act of Contrition (said in the Sacrament of Penance): *"O my God, I am heartily sorry for having offended Thee. I detest all my sins because I dread the loss of Heaven and the pains of Hell, but most of all because they offend Thee, my God, Who are all good and deserving of all my love. I firmly resolve, with the help of Thy grace, to confess my sins, to do penance, and to amend my life. Amen."*

or

"O my God, I am heartily sorry for having offended Thee and I detest all my sins because of Thy just punishments, but most of all because they offend Thee, my God, who art all good and deserving of all my love. I firmly resolve, with the help of Thy grace, to sin no more and avoid the near occasions of sin. Amen."

Guardian Angel Prayer: *"Angel of God, my guardian dear, to whom God's love commits me here. Ever this day* [or night] *be at my side, to light and guard, to rule and guide. Amen."*

Prayer to Saint Michael the Archangel (formerly said after low Mass): *"St. Michael the Archangel, defend us in battle; be our defense against the wickedness and snares of the Devil. May God rebuke him, we humbly pray, and do Thou, O Prince of the Heavenly Host, by the power of God, cast into Hell Satan and all the other evil spirits, who prowl through the world, seeking the ruin of souls. Amen."*

Fatima Prayer (said after each decade while praying the Rosary): *"O my Jesus, forgive us our sins, save us from the fires of Hell, lead all souls to Heaven, especially those in most need of Thy mercy. Amen."*

Question 196. What is the Creed?

The word creed means a system or a statement of belief, from the Latin word *credo*, meaning "I believe." There are two main creeds in Catholicism, the Apostle's Creed (from apostolic times, the first two centuries AD) and the Nicene Creed (from the Council of Nicea in 325 AD and the Council of Constantinople in 381 AD).

APOSTLE'S CREED

I believe in God,
the Father almighty,
creator of heaven and earth.
And in Jesus Christ,
his only Son, our Lord;
who was conceived by the
power of the Holy Spirit
born of the Virgin Mary,
suffered under Pontius Pilate,
was crucified, died, and was buried.
He descended into hell.
On the third day he rose again.
He ascended into heaven
and is seated at the right hand of the God
the Father Almighty, from thence
he shall come to judge living and the dead.
I believe in the Holy Spirit,
the holy catholic Church,
the communion of saints,
the forgiveness of sins,
the resurrection of the body,
and the life everlasting.
Amen.

NICENE CREED

I (We) believe in one God, the Father, the
Almighty, maker of heaven and earth,
and of all that is, seen and unseen.
We believe in one Lord, Jesus Christ,
the only Son of God, eternally begotten of
the Father, God from God, Light from Light,
true God from true God,
begotten, not made, one in Being with the
Father. Through him all things were made.
For us men and for our salvation,
he came down from heaven:
by the power of the Holy Spirit
he was born of the Virgin Mary,
and became man. For our sake he was crucified under Pontius Pilate; he suffered
died and was buried. On the third day he
rose again in fulfillment of the Scriptures;
he ascended into heaven and is seated at the
right hand of the Father. He will come again
in glory to judge the living and the dead, and
his kingdom will have no end.
We believe in the Holy Spirit, the Lord, the
giver of life, who proceeds from the Father
and the Son. With the Father and the Son he
is worshipped and glorified.
He has spoken through the Prophets.
We believe in one holy catholic and apostolic Church. We acknowledge one baptism
for the forgiveness of sins.
We look for the resurrection of the dead,
and the life of the world to come.
Amen.

Question 197. What is the Catholic fascination with bells about?

You can hear bells ringing inside and outside Catholic churches around the world. Since the sixth century AD, outdoor bells have been used to call the monks of a monastery or the people of a parish or cathedral to times of prayer. Traditionally, every three hours beginning at 6 a.m., bells would alert clergy, religious, and laity (who did not have Timex wristwatches at that time) that it was time to pray and to begin the work day. This would occur again at 9 a.m., noon, 3 p.m., 6 p.m., 9 p.m., midnight, and 3 a.m.

The traditional division of ringing the bells every three hours coincided with the Breviary or Divine Office prayed by the monks and nuns in their monasteries. *Lauds* or Morning Prayer was supposed to be prayed at dawn, so 3 a.m. was close enough and thus the bells would ring calling the religious community to common prayer. No time to take a shower, you simply went to chapel and prayed. Afterward, you could go back to your cell and catch a few winks, unless of course you had to milk the cows. *Prime* was prayed at 6 a.m., followed by *Terce* (9 a.m.), *Sext* (noon), *None* (3 p.m.), *Vespers* or Evening Prayer (6 p.m.), and *Compline* (9 p.m.) with *Matins* at midnight.

At each of these three-hour intervals, the monastics would pray some of the Psalms from the Bible and usually there was a reading from the Old or New Testament as well. The Our Father (Lord's Prayer) and canticles punctuated the major hours (Lauds and Vespers). The bells helped everyone in town and at the monastery know what time it was in addition to the call to prayer. Gradually, the hours were adjusted to suit the season, but often the bells were kept at their chronological hour since so many people in town depended on the ringing to know what time it was.

Church bells also rang to announce the sad news of death, from the pope or the emperor or king; the happy news of a new birth or marriage; an end to war; or they could ring just to alert the townsfolk of impending danger or calamity.

Since it was believed that the Devil and his demons hated the sound of church bells since they called the faithful to prayer, bells were also baptized—blessed by a bishop with holy oil and holy water, and each one given a name. They were not truly baptized since only human beings can receive any of the sacraments, but the analogy was similar since it was at baptism that parents named their children. Naming and blessing church bells was a ceremony performed throughout Europe until the time of the Reformation. Those who misunderstand the practice accused the

Medieval church of superstition, yet even today we hear of the "christening" of a ship and no one mistakes it for the christening of a baby.

Smaller bells, called the Sanctus bells, are used inside the Church to remind people to kneel. When Mass was universally celebrated *ad orientem* (facing east) instead of *versus populum* (facing the people), and before there was a microphone and speaker, people who sat in the rear of the cathedral could not see or hear what the priest was doing. The sanctus bells were rung at the part of the Mass called the *epiclesis*, where the priest invokes the Holy Spirit; at the elevation of the Host immediately after the consecration of the bread; at the elevation of the Chalice immediately after the consecration of the wine; and when the priest consumes the Precious Blood from the Chalice. Bells are also rung when the priest or deacon blesses the congregation with the Blessed Sacrament when contained in the monstrance.

Question 198. What is the Liturgical Year?

While the secular calendar year begins on January 1 and ends on December 31, and the fiscal year in most places starts on July 1, the Church calendar or Liturgical Year is completely different. Beginning on the first Sunday of Advent and ending on the Solemnity of Christ the King, the Church calendar does not have a fixed numerical date like the other two calendars. The first Sunday of Advent can fall on a day in November or in December. The only requisite is that it is four Sundays before Christmas since there are the second, third, and fourth Sundays of Advent before Christmas (which is always December 25).

The Liturgical Year refers to the designation of each Sunday as being part of a liturgical season, which reflects the cycles of life on earth and salvation history as well. Christmas and Easter are the two focal points of the Church year. The first centers on the theme of Christ our light, and the second focuses on the theme of Christ our life. Advent precedes Christmas and Lent precedes Easter. Ordinary Time occurs between these two major celebrations of the birth and death and resurrection of the Savior; all the Sundays and weekdays which have no proper celebration fall into the category called Ordinary Time.

Advent and Christmas occur in winter when there is less daylight than in the summer. During these two liturgical seasons—one preparing for Advent and one celebrating the birth of Christ—the readings and prayers recall the theme of Christ as "Light of the World," in contrast to the lack of daylight which is quite evident during this time.

Lent and Easter occur in the spring when the snow has melted; nature wakes up from its nap, and we see flowers and animals exhibiting life after the long death of winter. These two liturgical seasons center on the theme of Christ as "Life of the World," especially after His own Resurrection from the dead on Easter Sunday.

The preparation times of Advent and Lent are penitential; people pray more and engage in personal mortification, fasting, abstinence, and the like. The liturgical color for vestments for both Advent and Lent is purple or violet. Christmas and Easter, the pinnacles of the year, are the major celebrations, hence there is no fasting or abstinence and white is the proper liturgical color for vestments. Formerly the last Sunday in October and now the Sunday before Advent, Christ the King is the closing day of the Liturgical Year, since the following weekend is the first Sunday of Advent.

There are also Divine Solemnities like Ascension Thursday (forty days after Easter when Jesus ascended to heaven), Pentecost Sunday (fifty days after Easter when the Holy Spirit came upon the apostles), Trinity Sunday, Corpus Christi, Sacred Heart of Jesus, and other solemnities of the Virgin Mary like the Immaculate Conception (when Mary was conceived without original sin in the womb of her mother, Saint Ann) and the Assumption (when Mary was taken up to heaven body and soul by her son, Jesus).

Question 199. Why all the Catholic calisthenics?

Non-Catholics are amazed at the workout they get whenever they come to a Catholic Mass. Sitting, standing, kneeling, genuflecting, bowing, beating your breast, making the sign of the cross, shaking hands, going to Communion—it is a lot of movement and gesture for one hour. So why all the hustle and bustle?

Human beings are both body and soul. We are not trapped souls imprisoned in bodies until released at death, as Plato speculated. We are a union of matter and form, of body and soul, more like what Aristotle proposed. Our bodies connect to the material world and our souls to the spiritual, and since both body and soul are united into one human person, we are citizens of both worlds, living in both realms simultaneously.

Catholic worship engages the whole person, body and soul. We hear the Word of God preached, we verbally respond and sing, we sit, stand, kneel, bow, and genuflect depending on what is happening or where we are located. We smell incense burning or the aroma of chrism oil perfumed with balsam. We taste the consecrated bread (called the Body of Christ or the Blessed Sacrament or Holy Eucharist) and we taste the consecrated wine (called the Precious Blood of Christ).

Kneeling in the Western Church is the most profound sign of reverence, whereas in the Eastern Church it is standing and bowing. A genuflection is a quick kneel on the right knee, while bending the left. It is a gesture of adoration and worship and is given to God alone. Since Jesus is God, His real presence in the Blessed Sacrament (the consecrated hosts in the tabernacle) demands a gesture reserved for God alone. Bowing is done before symbols like the cross or crucifix, the altar, the person of the bishop or priest (during Mass they act in the Person of Christ, *in persona Christi*, and as another Christ, *alter Christus*). A bow of the head is done whenever the Holy Name of Jesus Christ or the Holy Spirit are mentioned.

Parishioners sit during the Old Testament and Epistle reading from Scripture, but everyone stands at the Gospel to show its preeminence as the words and deeds of Christ. Catholics strike their breast during the Confiteor (I confess) as a sign of humility and admission of fault. The sign of the cross is the most prevalent and identifiable gesture of Catholicism (and maybe genuflection, too). The right hand is used with fingers together. First the forehead is touched and the person says simultaneously, "in the name of the Father." Then he or she touches the chest in the middle with the same hand, moving downward from the forehead, saying "and of the Son." Next, the right hand reaches over and touches the left shoulder and says "and of the Holy" and moves across to touch the right shoulder and says "Spirit, Amen."

That one gesture reaffirms two doctrines, the Holy Trinity (One God in Three Persons: God the Father, God the Son and God the Holy Spirit) and our redemption by the cross of Christ.

Question 200. Why do Catholics keep relics?

The word *relic* comes from the Latin *reliquia* (in Greek, *leipsana agia*). Relics of the saints have nothing to do with Vincent Price, Halloween, or the macabre. They are merely physical reminders of holy people that the Church has officially declared to be saints in heaven. These items have no supernatural powers of their own, and even the miracles performed by the saints to whom these relics originally belonged occurred only by the power of God working through them.

There are three classes of relics: first class, second class, and third class. Unlike the airlines, you cannot get bumped up to first class. First-class relics are any part of the body of saint, usually a small piece of bone. Second-class relics are small pieces of clothing or artifacts the saint personally wore, touched, or used. Third-class relics are anything which was touched by a first-class relic.

Relics were never worshipped, since that would be idolatry and a sin against the first Commandment. They were honored insofar as they were once part of a saintly person, now considered a spiritual hero and friend of God in heaven. The practice began when Christians buried their dead, unlike the pagan Romans who burned theirs. The dead bodies were given Christian burial with the firm and certain hope that at the end of time, when the Second Coming of Christ took place and before the General Judgment of the World, the resurrection of the dead would take place.

So Christians treated the mortal remains of their dead with respect. Roman persecutions lasted three hundred years, during which time Christians hid and worshipped in the very place where they buried their dead: the catacombs. Superstitious Romans were afraid of these graveyards, as they believed them haunted by the dead—good place to hide, then!

When Christianity became legal in 313, thanks to the Emperor Constantine and the Edict of Milan, his mother, Saint Helena, began a campaign to recover as many relics of Christianity as she could get her hands on. She even led an expedition to the Holy Land, and in Jerusalem she found the True Cross of Christ on the hill of Calvary on which the Savior had been crucified and died. This was the largest and most valuable relic known to mankind. She also found the nails that were used to crucify Jesus. Pieces were sent to the patriarch of Jerusalem, the pope in Rome, and the Emperor himself. The rest was left at the Basilica Saint Helena built on the spot.

Tiny slivers of the True Cross have been handed down to various popes, cardinals, bishops, emperors, kings, queens, and other nobility throughout Europe and the Middle East. Sadly, there were some unscrupulous charlatans who sold counterfeit relics to the innocent faithful and, on occasion, there was almost a fever pitch to accumulate as many relics as possible. The church condemned all sales of relics as being the sin of simony and frequently warned people not to base their faith on "things," but rather on the truth of revelation and on the grace of God. Nevertheless, some criminal elements made money on the gullibility of a few zealous pilgrims. Many authentic relics today are embedded in altar stones placed inside altars where Mass is frequently celebrated, just as the early Christians used to celebrate in the catacombs.

Question 201. What are Candlemas and the blessing of throats?

Candlemas is another name for the Feast of the Purification (*hypapante* in Greek), now called the Feast of the Presentation, when the Blessed Virgin Mary and Saint Joseph took the infant Jesus to the temple in Jerusalem according to the Law of Moses. The Hebrew religion considered the shedding of blood a cause of making someone ritually unclean. It was not a moral or spiritual impurity but a ritual one, even if it involved the natural menstruation of a woman or the blood involved in childbirth. Consequently, Mosaic Law requires mothers of newborn sons to wait forty days before they may be ritually purified by the Jewish priest in the temple.

Before the Second Vatican Council, Candlemas, which takes place on February 2, was considered the last day of the Christmas season; decorations were taken down at that time. This feast is distinctly different from the Circumcision of the Lord, formerly celebrated on January 1, eight days after the birth of Christ. Forty days after His birth, His mother fulfilled the requirements of the Law and she and Saint Joseph went to the temple to make the customary offering of a lamb, or, if a lamb could not be obtained, an offering of two turtle doves or two pigeons. The animals would be sacrificed on the altar and the woman would be ritually purified.

Candles made of beeswax are traditionally blessed on this feast to commemorate the candles used by Saint Joseph and the Virgin Mary at the temple. Mary's ritual purification and baby Jesus' presentation are recorded in the Gospel of Luke 2:22–40. A procession can begin the day's Mass with candles carried by the faithful, symbolizing their joining the Holy Family (Jesus, Mary, and Joseph) in walking to the temple. The candles also symbolize Christ as the Light of the World.

The readings from Scripture proclaimed at Mass that day (Luke 2:22–40) also tell of the prophecy made by Saint Simeon, an elderly Jew who lived long enough to see the Messiah. He was always in the temple, and when he saw the Virgin Mary and the baby Jesus, he knew the time had come. Simeon told the mother, *"Behold, this child is destined for the fall and rise of many in Israel, and to be a sign that will be contradicted and you yourself a sword will pierce so that the thoughts of many hearts may be revealed."* That part about a sword piercing the heart of Mary is considered a prophecy which was fulfilled thirty-three years later when Jesus died on the cross and Mary stood nearby, helpless, witnessing her Son's horrible crucifixion and death, and watching as the Roman soldier Longinus thrust a spear into the heart of Jesus to ensure He was dead. At that moment, it is believed Mary felt a pain in her own heart, which only a mother who has just lost a child can understand.

The very next day, February 3, the same candles blessed by the priest for Candlemas are used to bless throats as part of the feast of Saint Blaise. Saint Blaise was a fourth century AD bishop and martyr who, while in prison awaiting his execution during one of the Roman persecutions, miraculously healed a boy who was choking on a fishbone. The mother had brought her son to Saint Blaise for a blessing and when he gave it, the fish bone popped out of the lad's mouth and he was saved. (This was before anyone knew about the Heimlich maneuver.)

Consequently, it is traditional for Catholics to have their throats blessed by a priest or deacon on the Feast of Saint Blaise. Two blessed candles are crossed and placed against the throat while the prayer is said: *"Through the intercession of Saint Blaise, bishop and martyr, may you be protected from every ailment of the throat and from every other evil, in the name of the Father and of the Son and of the Holy Spirit, Amen."*

Question 202. What are some Catholic Christmas traditions?

Saint Francis of Assisi (1182–1226 AD) created the Christmas crèche or nativity set to help people who might never have a chance to visit the Holy Land and see Bethlehem in person. Typically, the manger is set up a day or two before Christmas and on Christmas Eve; all the figures are placed inside except the baby Jesus, which is carried in and placed in the manger during the procession at midnight Mass when the crèche is blessed.

The pope has a custom in Rome of blessing the images of the baby Jesus which the youngest child in each home brings to Mass at the Vatican on *Gaudete* Sunday (third Sunday of Advent). They then go home and wait for Christmas when the infant can be placed in the family nativity set at home.

The song "The Twelve Days of Christmas" originated in England during the reign of Elizabeth I when Catholics were persecuted for their religion. There are twelve days from Christmas to Epiphany. The song uses symbols which at first glance seem nonsensical but were actually a secret code used to teach the Catechism to Catholic children in England when it was illegal to do so. The "True Love" referred to in the song ("On the first day of Christmas, my True Love gave to me…") is God the Father.

The "partridge in a pear tree" is *Jesus Christ*.

The "two turtle doves" are the *Old and New Testaments* of the Bible.

The "three French hens" are the three theological virtues of *faith, hope,* and *love*.

The "four calling birds" are the four Evangelists: *Matthew, Mark, Luke,* and *John*.

The "five gold rings" are the first five books of the Bible, the *Pentateuch*.

The "six geese a-laying" refer to the *six days of Creation*.

The "seven swans a-swimming" are the *seven sacraments*.

The "eight maids a-milking" are the *eight Beatitudes*.

The "nine ladies dancing" are the *nine choirs of angels*.

The "ten lords a-leaping" are the *Ten Commandments*.

The "eleven pipers piping" are the *eleven faithful apostles*.

The "twelve drummers drumming" are the *twelve doctrines in the Apostles' Creed*.

Christmas trees originated in Germany in 1521. A priest put an evergreen tree into the church to represent the gift of Christ, which is always present (evergreen) not just at Christmas, but all year round. There is a legend that a monk in seventh-century Germany used the triangular shape of the fir tree to explain the Holy Trinity (God the Father, God the Son, and God the Holy Spirit).

On Christmas Eve, Polish Catholics use the *Oplatek*, which is a rectangular wafer of bread that is broken into pieces and given to each member of the family with a blessing.

Hispanic Catholics have a Christmas custom of *Las Posadas*, a reenactment of the journey of Saint Joseph and the Virgin Mary looking for a place to stay as Mary was about to give birth to Jesus.

Question 203. Isn't public worship enough for a Christian?

Worship is our duty toward God. We read in the Ten Commandments, "Thou Shall Keep Holy the Sabbath." Catholics honor Sabbath by attending Holy Mass on Sundays and holy days of obligation.

But worship is only part of the picture. In his letters, St. James mentions that faith and good works are important; they are not optional. In fact, he goes on to say that faith without works is a dead faith. Therefore, the Christian proves his or her love for God by works of charity. Look at any canonized saint from the Blessed Virgin Mary to a holy person of our present age; they are all living examples of how to live the Gospel of Christ. Christ warns the disciple that faith is a light that should not be hidden.

Missionaries have often performed works of kindness before preaching to people. Once people encounter the charity of God through Christian men and women they are more inclined to convert. Pope John Paul II, in his Encyclical on the Gospel of Life, calls for a new evangelism. By our Baptism and Confirmation, we are to be the ambassadors of Christ in our families, communities, towns, countries, and world. But it first starts at the local level with the individual.

Saint Frances of Rome, a seventeenth-century laywoman, wife, and mother, often engaged in good works just by caring for her family in a dignified and thoughtful way. Saint Therese of Liseux wrote in her "Little Way" that sanctity can be achieved in the little things we do every day. Christ went about caring for the sick, for the dying, and for the outcasts, and, as His followers, we must do the same.

Question 204. What is piety?

Piety is one of the seven gifts of the Holy Spirit that is received in baptism and fortified in confirmation. These gifts dispose the person to obey God's influence and inspiration. Along with understanding, counsel, wisdom, fortitude, and fear of the Lord, these gifts make us agreeable to the motivation of grace. Piety refers to reverence, and it moves us to worship God.

Piety should not be confused with "pietism," which was a Lutheran movement from Germany begun in the late seventeenth century. Reverend Jacob Spener sought to restore and enliven Christian devotion by promoting individual spiritual life through Bible reading and prayer. This movement also influenced other denominations, such as Methodists.

Piety can also refer to devotion. Besides the holy sacrifice of the Mass, Christian people express their belief in God in many forms of religious practices, such as novenas to Jesus, Mary, the saints, and angels; the veneration of relics of saints, prayers, and litanies; visits to shrines; processions; recitation of the rosary; and praying the stations of the cross. Piety extends the liturgical life of the church, but never replaces it.

Piety can also take on a formal look in the church. There have been many pious movements in the church. The monastic movement began in Egypt after the Fall of Rome and centered on the individual hermit. Many followers went into places far away from civilization to be alone with the Lord. The purpose was to gain a deeper relationship with God through their solitude.

In the West, monasticism took on a different form—communal. The great Saint Benedict is considered the founder of Western monasticism with his division of time. He divided the monk's time into work, prayer, and rest.   In the late Middle Ages came a radical movement of thought and prayer known as "Devotio Moderna." Christians were bored with highly intellectualized and intricate expressions of faith that seemed too far removed from their ordinary life. This new trend offered a sentimental type of spirituality which answered the practical needs of the Christian. One of the greatest classics of this movement is the *Imitation of Christ* by Thomas A. Kempis. It stressed that true spirituality is the imitation of Christ achieved by meditating on His sacred humanity.

Question 205. Don't private devotions detract from healthy spirituality?

There should never be a competition between private and public worship. Each nourishes the other. Since the Second Vatican Council there has been a strong emphasis on Christ in all devotions. For example, a prayer or novena to a certain saint should lead you into a deeper relationship with Jesus Christ. A saint is a concrete example of how to follow Christ. Seen in this light, devotions should lead to healthy spirituality.

Holy Eucharist is the source and summit of Christian living. At Mass not only do we worship God, but we also grow as a community in a bond of fraternal charity. To prepare for Holy Mass, Catholics are encouraged to pray, meditate, and read verses from Sacred Scripture. This helps the person to mentally prepare for the supernatural. In the same vein, after receiving our Lord, it is helpful to perform acts of thanks in order to be conscious of the tremendous gift of the Lord you received. In essence, private devotions should lead to the Eucharist, and in turn, the Eucharist should fortify our private spirituality.

This is especially true when a person goes on retreat, makes a pilgrimage, or visits a special place of worship, like a shrine. Through these special environments or actions the person becomes more conscientiously aware of his surroundings and becomes more open to the promptings of the Lord. One's spiritual life can be reawakened.

During Lent, many parishes foster different kinds of private devotions to rekindle spiritual life in the faithful that has gone flat during the year. Public praying of the stations of the cross, parish missions, and solemnly preached novenas can awaken the person to participate more fully in the Mass, to go to the sacrament of Penance, and thereby to become a better Catholic.

Private devotions are bad when they don't lead to Christ. A special warning should be given about chain prayers. Like chain letters, there is bargaining that is attempted with God through the saint being honored. No one ever has to sign up a certain number of people to pray a certain prayer, to do a certain action, or to publish a thank you. This belongs to superstition, which is not promoted by the Church.

Question 206. What is a holy hour?

Holy hour can trace its roots back to Jesus Christ in the Garden of Gethsemane, when our Lord asked His disciples to stay awake with Him in prayer. They fell asleep, and in Matthew's Gospel 26: 40 our Lord admonished them by saying, "So, could you not watch with me one hour? Watch and pray that you may not enter into temptation; the spirit is indeed willing, but the flesh is weak."

There has been a long biblical history of going into the wilderness to get closer to God. In the wilderness, distractions are at a minimum. Things that wrestle for a place in one's mind fall into the background. In the early church, there were many who chose to live in the wilderness as a way of life. There were called hermits. However, in the spiritual life of the Christian, this oasis from noise, civilization, and other types of disturbance can be achieved right where one lives through prayer. Whether prayer is done at church, in a shrine or chapel, in nature, or at home, the idea of calming oneself down to allow the Lord to talk to you is an important part of a serious Christian's spiritual life. Though necessary for clergy and religious, it is recommended for all who want to get to know the Lord.

The Lord speaks to us only when we are quiet. Holy hours are a great way to quiet ourselves down. This is achieved in many different ways. Holy hours prayed in Church are of course the optimal choice. First, one is in the presence of the Lord in the Most Blessed Sacrament. Churches are conducive to prayer. However, if a church or chapel is not available then one's own room is fine. Our Lord Himself said that when one wants to pray, he should go to his room and basically shut out the world of distractions.

The content of holy hour varies. What an individual worshipper does is up to him. There is no formal structure. Scripture, devotional prayers, litanies, rosary, stations of the cross, and other formal prayers can be used to quiet the mind down. Saint Ignatius of Loyola used to take a section of Scripture and place himself as one of the characters in the biblical scene as way of meditating. One who is praying the mysteries of the rosary can do the same. For example, the third joyful mystery is a reflection on the nativity. As you meditate on this mystery, you can place yourself as one of the characters you see in the nativity: a shepherd, a wise man, or an angel. Archbishop Fulton J. Sheen, a great orator and T.V. host from the last century, preached of holy hours. He said the way to get to know a friend is to spend time with him. If we want to know the Lord we have to spend time with Him as well. We should do so in prayer and silence for at least one hour a day.

Question 207. What is special about first Fridays and first Saturdays?

Something uniquely Catholic are the First Friday and First Saturday devotions. Going to Church on Sunday is definitely a Christian tradition shared by Catholics, Protestants, and Eastern Orthodox believers. Going to Mass on the first Friday and on the first Saturday of the month, however, is distinct to Roman Catholicism. It is not a custom in the Byzantine Catholic Church but is found in the Western (Latin) tradition.

First Fridays originate with Saint Margaret Mary Alacoque (1647–1690), a French Visitandine nun at the convent of Paray-le-Monial, who had experienced apparitions of the Sacred Heart of Jesus. Our Divine Lord asked her to promote devotion among the faithful to His Sacred Heart, to display a picture or statue of the Sacred Heart in the home, and told her that if someone went to Holy Communion on the first Friday of the month for nine consecutive months, these promises would be fulfilled:

"I will give them all the graces necessary in their state of life."
"I will establish peace in their homes."
"I will comfort them in their afflictions."
"I will be their secure refuge during life, and above all in death."
"I will bestow a large blessing upon all their undertakings."
"Sinners shall find in My Heart the source and the infinite ocean of mercy."
"Tepid souls shall grow fervent."
"Fervent souls shall quickly mount to high perfection."
"I will bless every place where a picture of My Heart shall be set up and honored."
"I will give to priests the gift of touching the most hardened hearts."
"Those who shall promote this devotion shall have their names written in My Heart, never to be blotted out."
"I promise thee in the excessive mercy of My Heart that My all-powerful love will grant to all those who communicate on the First Friday in nine consecutive months, the grace of final penitence; they shall not die in My disgrace nor without receiving the Sacraments; My Divine heart shall be their safe refuge in this last moment."

The first Saturday devotions originate with an apparition of the Virgin Mary at Fatima, Portugal (1917) to three children, Jacinta, Francisco, and Lucia, where Our Lady said:

"I promise to help at the hour of death, with the graces needed for salvation, whoever on the first Saturday of five consecutive months shall:

'Confess and receive Holy Communion.'

'Recite five decades of the Holy Rosary.'

'Keep me company for fifteen minutes while meditating on the fifteen mysteries of the Rosary, with the intention of making reparation to me.'"

Yesterday and Today: Church History and Common Questions

Chapter 22

CHURCH HISTORY

This chapter answers questions on the history of the Catholic Church.

- Question 208. What were the Crusades?
- Question 209. Who were the first martyrs?
- Question 210. What was the Council of Jerusalem?
- Question 211. Why did the Great Eastern Schism occur?
- Question 212. What were the important journeys of Saint Paul?
- Question 213. What is heresy? How can heresy be stopped?
- Question 214. What are ecumenical councils and what do they do?
- Question 215. What is a martyr and who are some martyrs that affected the Church?
- Question 216. Who were the Fathers of the Church and what did they do?
- Question 217. Why was Charlemagne so important to the early Church?
- Question 218. What were some fourteenth-century problems that the Church faced?
- Question 219. Did tongues of fire really appear above the apostles' heads at Pentecost?
- Question 220. How did the Black Death affect the Church?
- Question 221. In what ways did the monks of the sixth century spread the light of faith?
- Question 222. What was the Inquisition and why did it happen?
- Question 223. Why did Thomas Aquinas write Summa Theologica?
- Question 224. How was the Church alight during medieval times?
- Question 225. How did the separation of church and state come about?
- Question 226. How did the persecution of the Christians actually help spread the Good News?
- Question 227. What are some of the places that were important to early Christians?
- Question 228. Who were some great Catholic women of the Middle Ages and what are they known for?
- Question 229. What are mendicant orders?
- Question 230. What does the title Doctor of the Church mean?
- Question 231. Who are the Jesuits?
- Question 232. What was the Reformation?
- Question 233. What was the Second Vatican Council (Vatican II), and how did it change the Church?
- Question 234. What is World Youth Day?

Question 208. What were the Crusades?

At first, the Crusades were called for by the Christians to rescue the Christian shrines in the Holy Land from the Muslims. Muslim religion began in the seventh century in the area of present day Saudi Arabia. It spread throughout the Near East into the Mediterranean. Countries that once were Christian fell by the sword and became Muslim. The Eastern section of the Roman Empire (the Byzantine Empire based in Constantinople) was threatened by the invading Muslim or Ottoman Empire. Eventually, Constantinople did fall and became Istanbul.

At first, the Muslims of Palestine were peaceful toward Christians, who made pilgrimages to the various shrines dedicated to different aspects of our Lord's life. The Muslims in power saw it as economic gain for everyone, and therefore Christians were tolerated. This was not to last. A fierce fighting tribe, the Seljuk Turks, invaded Palestine. As devout Muslims, they could not tolerate Christians in their territory. Reports of churches and shrines being burnt, Christians being murdered, and all sorts of persecution were brought back to the Christian West. Appeals from the Christian Byzantine Emperor in Constantinople, Pope Urban II, and the king of France, along with the Council of Clermont, called all Christians to take up arms and capture Jerusalem from the infidels. The rewards for their sacrifice would be spiritual blessings from God.

There would be eight major Crusades in all. The first was considered the most successful. It united royalty, nobility, clergy, and common folk. It accomplished what it set out to do: liberate Jerusalem and rescue Christian shrines in Palestine. Later, Christian city-states came into existence, and pilgrims once again could travel to the area. Constantinople, which stands at the door of the Muslim empire, was spared. However, this was short-lived. By 1270, many of the Crusades' gains were lost, and Jerusalem once again came under Muslim control.

As a military campaign the Crusades were considered a failure, but they were a success in other areas. First, they united the people for a spiritual cause—to save the Holy Land Shrines. Second, they introduced the West to the finer things of the East, such as silks and spices. Third, the ancient writings of Aristotle were rediscovered, translated, and sparked a development in philosophy in the West. Finally, Christian communities, such as Maronites in Lebanon, became reconnected to the papacy.

Question 209. Who were the first martyrs?

A martyr is a person who chooses to suffer, even to die, rather than renounce his faith or Christian principles. Technically, Saint Stephen fits this definition. However, it has long been the custom to consider the "Holy Innocents" as the first martyrs. We hear about them in the Gospel of Saint Matthew, when Jesus was born in Bethlehem and the Wise Men came from the East to worship Him. They first went to Herod to seek the newborn King of the Jews. Herod was furious, as he did not want to share the limelight with anyone. He feared losing his throne so he asked the Wise Men to seek out the Savior and report back to him. Herod planned to kill the newborn King, but the Wise Men soon realized Herod's evil plot and went home another way. This infuriated Herod, and he ordered that the male children aged two years and under be killed in Bethlehem and its surroundings.   The soldiers carried out the evil mission, but Christ was spared. Saint Joseph, His foster father, took Him and Mary to Egypt.

It was Saint Irenaeus, Saint Augustine, and other early Church Fathers who gave the murdered children the title of martyrs. They have been commemorated as martyrs since the first century. These innocent victims gave testimony to the Messiah and Redeemer, not by words but by their blood. They triumphed over the world and won their crown without having experienced the evils of the world.

Saint Stephen, a disciple of Christ, was chosen after the Ascension as one of the seven deacons. His name means "crown." He was also the first disciple to receive a martyr's crown. God worked many miracles through him. He spoke with wisdom and eloquence that converted many to Christianity. The enemies of Jesus became incensed over the success of his preaching and plotted to kill him.

Many rose up against Stephen, and he was accused of blasphemy against Moses and against Yahweh. In 35 AD he was brought before the Sanhedrin, a court in Jerusalem, to be cast out of the city and stoned to death. He faced his accusers fearlessly and reprimanded his enemies for not believing in Jesus. Yet they refused to hear him and blocked their ears to the truth. Kneeling down before his murderers, he cried out with a loud voice saying, "Lord, do not lay this sin against them." The martyr died, like our Blessed Savior, with no malice in his heart for his enemies. He went to his heavenly reward with an angelic face. Due to the means of his death, stoning, he is the patron saint of stonemasons.

Question 210. What was the Council of Jerusalem?

Councils are formal assemblies of cardinals, bishops, theologians, and heads of religious orders, as well as other Church representatives that discuss matters of doctrine, discipline, or other religious matters. The Council of Jerusalem was convened because there was much dissension and disagreement among the early Christians concerning the conditions on which Gentiles should be received as members of the Church. Jewish Christians insisted that the Gentiles obey all of Jewish Law. This faction was led by Saint James. Saint Paul and Barnabas took a stand against Saint James and the opposing side. Saint Peter, the first pope and arbiter, moderated the dispute in Jerusalem. After much discussion a declaration was drawn up, which was binding in the Church everywhere. Paul's position was accepted: Jewish regulations were no longer to be enforced.

The Council of Jerusalem is important for many reasons. First, it shows the development and organization of the Church. Christ's crucifixion, when blood and water flowed from his side, is considered the birthday of the Church. The Church later received its mission when the Holy Spirit descended upon it in tongues of fire. The pope and bishops are successors of Peter and the apostles. This first Council expressed how the Church would govern itself. In a definitive way, Peter made the binding decision after reflections from both sides and from the different apostles and disciples.

The Council's decision was the definitive mark in which the Church broke from its Jewish origins and began its mission to the Gentiles. Without the many man-made legal restrictions of the Jewish faith, the Church could expand and begin appealing to a broad band of people. In this way it becomes universal instead of provincial, with the Church as a vehicle of salvation for all people, at all times, until the end of the world. The Church becomes the primordial sacrament of Christ on earth.

With the foundations laid at the First Councils, other councils in different generations have dealt with problems, made clarifications, and modified practices in a similar way. There have been twenty-one councils since Jerusalem. The last great council of the Church was in 1962, the Second Vatican Council.

Question 211. Why did the Great Eastern Schism occur?

The Great Eastern Schism is one of the darkest moments in Church history. Just like subsequent schisms, it was based on politics under the guise of Church doctrine. The Church in the East, based in Constantinople, started to become a state church of the emperor, whereas the Church in the West, based in Rome, aligned its strengths with the kings of France and emperor of the Holy Roman Empire.

The division came about in a matter of Church policy and governance. Ignatios was the Patriarch of Constantinople from 847–858, and was the son of the Byzantine Emperor Michael. He had arrived just after the second wave of iconoclasm (heresy denying the use of icons, statues, or any images of Jesus and the saints) which lasted from 814–842. In his zeal to restore icons and orthodoxy to the Eastern Church within the Eastern Byzantine Empire, he stepped on some toes, including those of the Archbishop of Syracusa who appealed to the bishop of Rome, Pope Leo IV, for help. This caused tension between the East and West of the Church. Ignatios was later deposed in 858 and replaced by Photios, who was installed by Emperor Michael III (not the same Emperor Michael who was Ignatios' father). Ignatios then appealed to Pope Nicholas I just as the Archbishop of Syracusa had done to Pope Leo IV. Photios was deposed in 867 when the emperor was murdered, and Ignatios reclaimed the office of patriarch of Constantinople from 867–877. When he died, Photios returned as patriarch from 877–886. The political intrigue back and forth between the Byzantine Emperor and the pope in Rome only continued to escalate as the patriarchs of Constantinople fell under the tight grip and control of the Eastern Emperor. The pope, on the other hand, had no secular rival, as the barbarians had defeated the Roman emperors back in 476.

Relations between the pope in Rome and the patriarch of Constantinople were at an all-time low in the eleventh century. Patriarch Michael Cerularius considered the Latin Catholics to be heretics since they used unleavened bread in their Mass whereas Eastern Christian custom is to use only leavened bread. Sicily had been under Byzantine control for centuries until the Normans conquered and established Latin (Western) Church customs and clergy. Pope Leo IX in 1048 sought to reestablish Latin control over the Italian peninsula and to encourage—or, if necessary, coerce—the Byzantines to return back to the East, at least to Constantinople, and leave the Western church to the control of the bishop of Rome.

Patriarch Cerularius retaliated in 1052 by closing all Latin churches in Constantinople in response to the Greek Byzantine churches in Sicily being "Romanized" as he called it. Pope Leo sent Cardinal Humbert as his legate to sort things out. Meanwhile, Cerularius began to stir up antagonism against the Latin Church by complaining that the Roman Pope inserted the "filioque" into the Nicene Creed (325 AD) without proper authority. While the pope has such authority as Supreme Head of the Church and Successor of Saint Peter, in reality it was the Catholic Church in sixth century Spain that inserted the filioque into the Nicene

Creed, and it became more prevalent and popular in the West over time.

To this day, the Eastern Orthodox Church and the Byzantine Catholic Church omit the words "and the Son" (*filioque* in Latin) from the part of the Creed which reads that the Holy Spirit "proceeds from the Father." The West (Latin) Church retains this phrase, however, and professes every Sunday and holy day that the Holy Spirit "proceeds from the Father and the Son." A theological controversy of minor proportions, the filioque became the smokescreen by which both Cerularius and Humbert put a final wedge between East and West.

Cardinal Humbert, legate of Pope Leo IX, entered Hagia Sophia (1054 AD) in Constantinople and left the papal bull of excommunication of Patriarch Cerularius on the altar. And thus the Schism between East and West formally began.

Question 212. What were the important journeys of St. Paul?

Saul, who became Paul after his conversion, became the apostle to the Gentiles. The New Testament is filled with testimonies, letters, and instructions to the different churches that were established by Saint Paul. The Gospel was spread through waves by Paul as he preached throughout Europe. Communities came into being at Philippi, Thessalonica, and Corinth. Paul even went to Athens, which was known as the cultural center in ancient times. Here, he debated the Gospel with the Greeks at their own philosophical level.

He traveled to Asia as well as to Europe and encountered many difficulties. The Jews were hostile to him and would not listen to his message of Jesus, the Messiah. Yet he also achieved great strides in transmitting the faith, especially in Corinth. In all, he embarked on four journeys. The last journey took him to Rome, where he was taken prisoner. On his way to Jerusalem, he became involved in a political riot, was arrested, and was sent to a prison in Caesarea. There he claimed his rights as a Roman citizen, appealed to the emperor, and was transferred to Rome. He reached the city two years after his arrest, all the while preaching the Gospel.

It is believed that he was eventually freed, traveled to Spain, and later returned to Asia Minor and Greece. The New Testament Letters to Timothy and Titus confirm this time period. Once again, Paul was taken as prisoner to Rome. He was executed in 67 AD. In his letter (95 AD) to the Church of Corinth, Pope Clement alludes to the fact that both Peter and Paul were executed in Rome. Peter, since he was not a Roman citizen, was crucified; Paul, a Roman citizen, was beheaded. Beheading was a quicker form of death and therefore considered more humane.

Paul is considered one of the pillars of the Roman Catholic Church because of his missionary activity in Rome and his eventual martyrdom.

In his letter to the Corinthians, Pope Clement gives testimony to the legacy of Paul. He said that Paul showed great endurance all through his imprisonments, exiles, and attempted stoning, and should be considered a man of noble faith. He gave his testimony before rulers, philosophers, and ordinary people. Paul was one of the greatest men who witnessed to Jesus Christ and expanded Christianity by his testimony.

Question 213. What is heresy? How can heresy be stopped?

Heresy refers to an opinion that is in opposition to the authorized teachings of any church and promotes separation from the main body of the faithful believers. In the Catholic Church, heresy refers to any baptized Catholic who denies or doubts any truth which is part of the Divine Deposit of Faith or revelation and therefore must be believed. Formal denial can lead to excommunication. Canon 1364 states, "An apostate from the faith, a heretic or a schismatic incurs a *latae sententiae* excommunication."

"Heresy" is from the Greek word for "faction." Heresy has existed since the foundation of the Church. In 2 Corinthians 11:13 we hear Paul stating, "For such men are false apostles, deceitful workmen, disguising themselves as apostles of Christ." Again in John's letters, 1 John 2:19 we hear, "They went out from us, but they were not of us; for if they had been of us, they would have continued with us; but they went out, that it might be plain that they all are not of us." Finally, Peter admonishes in 2 Peter 2:1, "False prophets also arose among the people, just as there will be false teachers among you, who will secretly bring in destructive heresies, even in denying the Master who bought them, bringing upon themselves swift destruction."

Heresy can be stopped by listening to the authentic teaching authority of the Church, the magisterium. The magisterium is made up of the pope and the bishops when they are united with the pope or when they teach the constant teachings from the Sacred Deposit of Faith. The Holy Spirit has given the awesome gift of infallibility to the pope when he teaches in matters of faith and morals. Infallibility is that gift that preserves the pope from error. This is important so that every generation to the end of time will be guided by the uncorrupted truth on the pathway to heaven.

There were many heresies that existed in the early church which lasted until the

Middle Ages. Some heresies resurface and are given new light using different words to appeal to a new generation. Some of the most dangerous heresies centered on Jesus Christ: Arianism (which asserted that the Son of God was not truly divine but created), Docetism (which held that the humanity of Christ and His sufferings were not real), and Nestorianism (a variation of Arianism).

Question 214. What are ecumenical councils and what do they do?

Technically, the council of Jerusalem was not an ecumenical council, though it was the very first church council. Ecumenical Councils are solemn assemblies of bishops and the pope. They are convened by the pope to discuss Church doctrine, discipline, and pastoral matters. The pope is the essential unifying factor at the council. The gift of infallibility in matters of faith and morals is a characteristic of an ecumenical council. Each council produces a further clarification of Christ's teachings. There have been twenty-one ecumenical councils.

Nicea in 325 AD. Condemned Arianism and formulated the Nicene Creed.

First Constantinople in 381 AD. Condemned the Macedonians and confirmed the Nicene Creed.

Ephesus in 431 AD. Condemned Nestorianism and declared Mary as the Mother of God.

Chalcedon in 451 AD. Condemned Monophysitism and declared that Christ had two distinct natures—divine and human—in one divine Person.

Second Constantinople in 553 AD. Condemned certain persons who followed Nestorianism: Theodore of Mopsuestia, Theodoret of Cyrrhus, and Ibas of Edessa.

Third Constantinople in 680–681 AD. Condemned Monothelites and declared that Christ had two wills—human and divine.

Second Nicea in 787 AD. Condemned the Iconoclasts and defended the veneration of sacred images without it being idolatry.

Fourth Constantinople in 869–70 AD. Condemned Photius as the false Patriarch of Constantinople and reaffirmed Ignatius as the authentic one.

First Lateran in 1123 AD. Issued decrees on simony, celibacy, lay investiture and confirmed the Concordat of Worms.

Second Lateran in 1139 AD. Ended the papal schism and enacted reforms.

Third Lateran in 1179 AD. Condemned Albigenses and Waldenses heresies and decreed papal elections by two-thirds majority.

Fourth Lateran in 1215 AD. Issued a decree on annual Communion and for the first time used the term "transubstantiation."

First Lyons in 1245 AD. Condemned Frederick II and planned a second crusade.

Second Council of Lyons in 1274 AD. Temporarily reunited with the Greek churches and regulated the time papal elections can begin—ten days after the death of the pope.

Vienne in 1311–12 AD. Suppressed the Knights Templar and enacted reforms.

Constance in 1414–18 AD. Condemned Wyclif and Hus and put an end to the Western Schism.

Florence in 1431–45 AD. Affirmed papal primacy and attempted to further effect unity with the Greek Church.

Fifth Lateran in 1512–17 AD. Condemned Neo-Aristotelians, who taught that the soul was mortal and there was only one for all of humanity (that is, humans all shared one soul).

Trent in 1545–63 AD. Condemned Protestantism and enacted major reforms.

First Vatican in 1869–70 AD. Defined papal infallibility and condemned pantheism, materialism, deism, naturalism, and fideism.

Second Vatican in 1962–65 AD. Promulgated sixteen documents, which reaffirmed principles of the Catholic faith and morals. Called for reforms in the Church liturgy and sacramental life.

Question 215. What is a martyr and who are some martyrs that affected the church?

"Martyr" is from the Greek word *martus*, which means witness, and refers to one who stands firm, giving a testimony or witness to the faith. For some Christians, this witnessing has lead to persecution and, ultimately, death. Unlike the non-Christian form of martyrdom, which encourages active violence against the enemy, Christian martyrdom is based solely on witness to the truth. It is the persecutor that will falsely accuse, torture, and may even kill the witness to the Catholic faith.

Every century, beginning with the infant Church in Jerusalem, the Church suffered waves of persecution. Saint Stephen is considered the first martyr in the Church. He suffered death at the hands of the Jews who wanted to stamp out this new religion. Soon the Roman Empire became involved because they saw Christianity as a threat to their pagan way of living. All of the apostles, except John the beloved disciple, were martyrs. It was during the pagan reign of the Roman Empire that Christians suffered most cruelly—death by all sorts of means, such as being eaten by animals in an arena or being flayed and burned. The English Reformation in the sixteenth century saw Catholic Mary, Queen of the Scots, killed by her Protestant cousin, Queen Elizabeth, and many Catholics subsequently lost their lives. In France, during the French Revolution of the seventeenth century, thousands of Catholics loyal to Rome, including priests and religious sisters and brothers, lost their lives at the guillotine. During revolutions in twentieth century Spain and Mexico, Catholic faithful, along with clergy, lost their lives. Pick any century and you will see the Church is persecuted. Their shed blood was the seed of the Church in the future.

Question 216. Who were the Fathers of the Church and what did they do?

The Fathers of the Church were all theologians, and some were even bishops. They wrote extensive treatises or treatments in theology especially centering on the divinity and humanity of Jesus Christ. In the first few centuries of the Church there was much confusion, and the Church Fathers wrote to curtail heresy and spread *orthodoxy*, which is Greek for correct thinking.

The deposit of faith had been taught to the apostles by Jesus Christ, and then by the Holy Spirit, after the Ascension ended with the last apostle, Saint John. After his death, no new public revelation was given. The work of Church Fathers and ecumenical councils in the promulgation of doctrine from the Chair of Saint Peter provide further explanations to the already believed and revealed truths.

Church Fathers lived exemplary lives and were often canonized saints. They lived during the time of the early church up until the ninth century. Church Fathers include, from the West, Saint Ambrose, Saint Augustine, Saint Jerome, Pope Saint Gregory the Great, Origen, and Tertullian; from the East, Saint Basil, Saint John Chrysostom, Saint Gregory Nanzianzen, and Saint Athanasius.

Saint Athanasius lived during the time of the Arian heresy, which divided the Church. His major work was in defending the fact that Jesus, the Second Person of the Blessed Trinity, was equal to the Father. Saint Gregory of Nazianzus wrote "Theological Discourses," while Saint Gregory of Nyssa was an important figure at the Ecumenical Council of Constantinople. He wrote on the origin and creation of man. Saint John Chrysostom, who was born in Antioch, was a great preacher.

Eventually he became the bishop of Constantinople. He wrote many commentaries on Scripture and different theological works on the priesthood, matrimony, and the vows of virginity. Saint Jerome is credited for translating the first complete one volume Bible (400 AD) into Latin from the original Hebrew and Greek texts.

Question 217. Why was Charlemagne so important to the early church?

Charlemagne (*Carolus Magnus* in Latin) and Carloman were sons of Pippin, the King of the Franks. When the father died, his two sons came to rule territories of equal worth. Upon Carloman's death, Charlemagne inherited the rest of the lands. At this time, the Lombards (a Germanic people originally from Northern Europe) constantly invaded the Papal States. (A note about the Papal States: for a period of time the pope was not only spiritual ruler of the Church but also a temporal ruler. After the disintegration of the Roman Empire by attacks from the Goths and Vandals, territory around Rome came under the rule of the popes, hence the term Papal States. The emperor had moved years before to Constantinople, which was the seat of the Eastern Empire. In the West, smaller kingdoms developed. The Papal States remained in existence until the unification of Italy beginning in the 1870s. They officially came to an end with the Lateran Treaty, in which Mussolini recognized the area around the Vatican as a separate country.)

Pope Hadrian appealed to Charlemagne for help with the Lombard problem. Charlemagne crossed the Alps and defeated them. After his victory, he went to Rome and received many honors from the pope. This interference of Charlemagne had its good and bad consequences in the Church. The first good consequence was that the Pope's enemies were defeated and any future enemies of the Papal States would have to fight the Frankish Empire. Second, a newly founded religion from Arabia (Islam) was beginning to sweep through northern Africa and into Spain. With centralization of power under Charlemagne and the expansion of his kingdom, Christianity could be protected.

There were bad consequences as well. Charlemagne did not know how to separate government from Church business. He constantly meddled with Church affairs and saw it as his right to do so. He micromanaged everything, from the appointing of a bishop to a diocese to accepting candidates to the monastery. From a military and even political point of view, the pope was at the mercy of the king. Later, when there would be numerous Catholic monarchs from different countries, this would also prove to be a disadvantage. What side would the papacy take?

In any event, the successor to Hadrian, Pope Leo III, was viciously attacked in 799 by enemies to the papacy and almost left for dead. Once again, Charlemagne came to the rescue by giving the pope a body guard. Later, he traveled to Rome and attended Christmas Mass at Saint Peter's Basilica, where Pope Leo III crowned him Emperor. Charlemagne was hailed the new Emperor of the Holy Roman Empire, which was a vestige of the old Roman Empire, and was given the right to be present at Papal elections and the right to hold authority over the city of Rome and the Papal States.

Question 218. What were some fourteenth-century problems that the Church faced?

In the late twelfth and early thirteenth centuries, under the rule of Pope Innocent III, the papacy attained its height in power and influence. He held the fullness of power in Christendom. All the churches were under his control and he exerted his powers in government as well, appointing a candidate as emperor and making the king of England bow to his will. But this was to change with the next pope, Innocent IV. He deposed the emperor at the Council of Lyons and weakened the empire. Vocations to the monastic life declined, institutions in the church began to decay, and disagreements arose among cardinals in papal election.

In addition, nationalism was on the rise. With the decline of the Holy Roman Empire, Western monarchies rose by writing feudal law in their favor. Eventually these monarchies would come up against papal power and conflict would ensue between them. This is highlighted in the removal of Rome as the center of the Church and replacing it with Avignon, France. This period was called the Babylonian Captivity, named after the Biblical reference to Israel being captured by the Persians. The central power of the Church was at the mercy of the French king. The French cardinals had the upper hand in papal elections, and the Papal State fell into disrepair. Before the papacy finally returned to Rome, there was a period in which three claimed to be the authentic pope. This was known as the Great Western Schism. (See Question 211.) The Schism further reduced the power of the papacy and its influence. Its credibility had sunk to new lows. The nobility in different countries used this to their benefit in attaining power, land, and money from the church.

Eventually, the Western Schism ended, and the true pope was elected. When the papacy returned to Rome the infrastructure of Rome was in ruins. A mass building project was proposed with the rebuilding of Saint Peter's Basilica and other major monuments in the Eternal City. Of course this required money, so Catholics throughout Europe were encouraged to give to rebuild Rome. This did not meet with open hands, especially with the nobility. They did not want Rome to become powerful again, because it meant they would lose power.

Another grave problem was the ignorance of the clergy. Since there were no standardized texts or seminaries for the priests to learn from, they were often uneducated. They misinformed people concerning the doctrines of the Church. Bad theology (though never the official teachings of the Church) and ignorant clergy were the impetus for Martin Luther and his 95 Theses.

Question 219. Did tongues of fire really appear above the apostles' heads at Pentecost?

Pentecost is the feast of the Spirit. "Tongues of fire" is a figurative way of explaining that the Holy Spirit descended upon the apostles. Before Pentecost, the apostles were huddled in an upper room praying the first novena for the coming of the Holy Spirit. Jesus had promised that ten days after His Ascension He would send the Third Person of the Blessed Trinity, the Holy Spirit. The apostles were quite scared and remained in prayer for nine days with the Blessed Mother. After completion of the prayer, the Spirit came and enlivened the twelve apostles.

In depicting this event, the Holy Spirit is pictured either as a dove or as a flame of fire, fire because the result of the gifts of the Spirit is motivation for the Christian. The old axiom about "lighting a fire under someone" as motivation is analogous to the effects of the Spirit. The Seven Gifts of the Holy Spirit bear twelve fruits and ultimately motivate the person to be "on fire with the love of God." Therefore, the image evoked by the tongues of fire is one of enthusiastic faith. After the reception of the Holy Spirit, the apostles could expel demons, talk in many languages, and endure torture even to the point of martyrdom.

Question 220. How did the Black Death affect the Church?

The Black Death was damaging both to the Church and to society. The Black Death was a plague that spread like wild fire through villages, towns, and entire countries throughout Europe. The primary manner of dispersal was from infected animals to human beings by means of flies. The unsanitary conditions of towns made these areas ripe for contamination. Whole families and even towns were decimated, demoralizing the people who remained alive.

One third of the population of Europe was wiped out by the Black Death; two-thirds of the clergy were killed by the same plague. Death became the primary theme of much literature and art. Great fear that spread throughout Europe became the driving force of many people. With so much death and destruction, society could not advance. The physical structures of the Church decayed. Education had to be put on the side. This is one of the reasons why the period of the Middle Ages is sometimes referred to as the Dark Ages.

The decline of the Church, the worry about one's mortality and ultimate judgment in life led to changes in the ordinary outlook of a Christian. Individualism took precedence over the structure of the church with its hierarchy and clergy. Individualism manifested itself in many ways, but in one area in particular it proved to be a major problem: superstition. Since most of the clergy died from the plague, ill-prepared, uneducated, and unsuitable candidates for the priesthood were rashly chosen and quickly ordained. The need for priests was so desperate that bishops ordained almost any young man who did not die from plague or war. The result, however, proved to be devastating, since these poorly trained clerics knew little theology and had no supervision. Their sermons and teachings were usually very bad and often heretical, and many of them behaved terribly and committed a plethora of immoral acts. Their sacraments were still valid, however, and people were still able to get baptized, confessed, confirmed, married, and anointed when needed. The downside was the superstition, heresy, bad examples, and scandal that many of these quick-fix priests produced.

The Black Death demoralized the people. Few wanted to take care of the sick. Anything foreign or different was not to be tolerated and was looked upon with suspicion. Hunting for witches became an obsession. The prime example of this is the martyrdom of Saint Joan of Arc, who was burned at the stake and falsely accused of being a witch.

The Black Death also opened the door for Muslim influence. The Christian Byzantine Empire of the East, based in Constantinople, was a stepping stone to the Muslim Ottoman Empire. The failure of the Crusades, bickering of Christians between countries which led to disunity and wars, and controversy between Catholicism in the West and East led to schism and further disunity and aided in an eventual Muslim attack. Constantinople fell and became Istanbul. The magnificent cathedral named Hagia Sophia became a mosque. The Byzantine Empire, the last vestige of the old Roman Empire, was taken over and became part of the Ottoman Empire. There was no more buffer zone between Christianity and Muslims. The threat that Christianity would be wiped away was imminent.

In addition to the Black Death, wars, and superstition, dissent from Catholic beliefs also became a problem. Ignorant clergy promoted the incorrect interpretation of doctrine. Also, the decline of papal authority due to the Great Schism furthered disunity. Heretics, such as William of Ockham, John Wyclif, and John Hus spurred people to rebel and leave the church. Dissension later sowed the seeds to the Protestant Revolt. With Christianity weakened by disease, politics, and an uneducated clergy, a complete Muslim takeover was a real possibility.

Question 221. In what ways did the monks of the sixth century spread the light of faith?

Once the seat of the Roman Empire moved to Constantinople in the East, the West went into decline. All sorts of invaders from the north, such as the Visigoths, Vandals, and the Huns, invaded Rome and sacked it. Western society plunged into the Dark Ages. Whereas under the glories of the Roman Empire there had been a period of peace and a high standard of living, cities became places of disease, crime, and filth.

In an attempt to save western civilization, classical Greek, Latin, poetry, literature, culture, and philosophy were preserved by monks in their monasteries. Western monasticism developed quite differently from Eastern by being communal. This new way of monastic life was championed by Saint Benedict. He came up with a way of life that consisted of eight hours of prayer, eight hours of work, and eight hours of relaxation.

Monasteries became centers of learning and education. By preserving the heritage of the Greco-Roman world, everything from architecture to plays was preserved for future generations. The Renaissance owes its flourishing to these monks. Artists, sculptors, and architects of the Renaissance period saw their period as a rejuvenation of the classical world. In addition to preserving this wealth of history, monks also advanced their own era. They were master artisans. This was the time before the printing press, so a book had to be laboriously hand written by someone. Manuscripts, such as the Bible, Liturgy of the Hours, and Missals, were elaborately decorated by them. Also, many famous paintings were created by monks, such as Fra Angelico.

Later, monasteries developed into universities. Many of today's oldest universities were begun as extensions of monasteries. Monks often taught the sciences in these institutions. These early universities became centers of higher learning and intellectual debate. The medieval monks and monasteries also spawned hospitals as well as colleges and universities. Science, art, logic, philosophy, music, history, grammar, rhetoric, math, and theology (the liberal arts) were the backbone of Middle Age and even Renaissance higher education.

In Ireland, another development occurred in the area of the sacraments. Until the seventh century, confession was a public matter with public penance. Increasing populations of Catholics and a more private nature of confession led to the Irish monks' development of the private confession. This is the most common form of confession to this day. The Irish monks also promoted culture, literature, and the Christian faith in the pagan, Celtic lands. As on the Continent, monasteries became centers for learning and religion.

Question 222. What was the Inquisition and why did it happen?

The Pontifical Inquisition was a Church (ecclesiastical) court that was established by Pope Gregory IX in 1230 to root out heresy. The notorious Spanish Inquisition was created by Pope Sixtus IV at the request of King Ferdinand and Queen Isabella of Spain in 1478. Pope Paul III founded the Sacred Congregation of the Universal Inquisition (called the Roman Inquisition) in 1542, which later became the Holy Office in 1908 and then the current Sacred Congregation for the Doctrine of the Faith in 1965.

Heresy is false teaching which can threaten the very foundation of the Church. Doctrinal error is the antithesis of a religion based on teaching divinely revealed truth. The Roman Inquisition was staffed by friars from the Franciscan or Dominican Orders and moved from town to town, setting up courts to try people accused of heresy. The accused were generally given a month to recant. If they did not, then a public trial was held, and if they were found guilty and still did not renounce their false teachings, they would be handed over to civil authority, which usually meant death.

In societies where church and state were one, heresy affected not only the church but also the good of society. Therefore, heresy became a crime of the state as well as of the church. Most people conjure thoughts about the Inquisition as agents of torture, and unfortunately, this is not far from the truth. The Inquisition existed in a period of time in which people were far more violent. It was not uncommon for secular society to punish with an eye for an eye and tooth for a tooth. In other words, if a man was convicted of theft, his hand was cut off. Public hangings were seen as events to attend, much like the human sacrifices in the Roman Coliseum, in which countless Christians were fed to lions. Medieval society was only a few generations removed from barbarism. It was not unusual for the civil society to use means of torture to cleanse a criminal. Pope Innocent IV in a papal bull permitted torture as a last resort in extreme cases in order to smash the stubbornness of the heretic and force them to admit guilt. The painful extraction of confessions only occurred *after* a church tribunal had enough proof and evidence that the accused were in fact guilty. If they admitted or confessed their crime, they would be given a modest punishment. If they obstinately refused to admit their guilt despite witness testimony and corroborating evidence, then torture was used to get the truth out of them.

While today we would see this as cruel and inhumane, the Medieval concept was that the salvation of souls was in jeopardy. If heretics died unrepentant, they were considered damned for eternity. If they confessed and repented, they would be absolved and would save their souls from hell. Better to save one's soul for eternity than to lose the immortal soul merely to save one's mortal life—that was their perspective. So torture was seen as a last-resort medicinal means to get the guilty to confess and, thus, to save their souls. Of course, these measures were also at times used for political advantages. Saint Joan of Arc, who was burned at the stake for being heretical and a witch, suffered from the lies of her enemies. The Catholic Church never imposed the death penalty, nor executed heretics or witches during the Inquisition. The trial was ecclesiastical and under the direction of religious orders, but the actual capital punishment and most of the torture occurred at the hands of the civil authorities under authority of the emperor, of the king, or of the local prince, baron, etc.

After the Protestant Reformation, countries which had suffered at the hands of the Inquisitions formed their own form of Inquisition, and would do much of the same in the name of God, religion, and country. Countless Catholics lost their lives because they would not convert to Protestantism. Mary, Queen of the Scots is a notable example. Queen Elizabeth I of England martyred more Catholics than her half sister before her, Queen Mary I, did Protestants. Even in the New World, the Salem witch trials were considered a type of Protestant Inquisition. Torture and the threat of death were used to obtain confession and conversion. Often the punishment for refusing to confess was burning at the stake.

After the Council of Trent with its sweeping reforms, the Inquisition was radically changed. It was made up of cardinals and became a final court of appeal. Torture was not used, and censures and excommunications would be the punishments.

In the twentieth century, the Inquisition's name became the Holy Office, where doctrinal purity was the main intention of its existence. After the Second Vatican Council in 1965, the name finally became the Congregation of the Doctrine of the Faith with its primary purpose being to guarantee the correct teaching of faith and morals.

Question 223. Why did Thomas Aquinas write "Summa Theologica"?

Saint Thomas Aquinas was a priest and doctor of theology who belonged to the Order of Preachers, known as Dominicans. As a youth he studied in Paris under the great theologian Albertus Magnus and, because of his size and shyness, was mislabeled by his peers as the "Dumb Ox." Albertus Magnus saw much more depth in Aquinas. He told the class that Thomas would be a greater scholar than he, and indeed,. Thomas held two professorships in Paris. His greatest contribution to the Catholic Church was his writings. He wrote "Catena Aurea" to help the clergy to better understand the Word of God, the "Summa Contra Gentiles" doctrinal material for missionaries to the Muslims, and a Solemn Mass for Corpus Christi. Yet his greatest work would be the "Summa Theologica," which he unfortunately did not finish.

At that time, there was a resurgence of interest in Greek philosophy. The great pagan philosopher Aristotle's writings were once again studied. During this period Aquinas wrote a theological treatise on various works of Aristotle which would become part of his famous "Summa." He used Aristotle's philosophy of metaphysics to explain Catholic doctrine. Scholasticism is the philosophy that became associated with this period, and Saint Thomas was its champion. Thomism was so popular and universal that it is even used to this date.

The "Summa" became a collection of Catholic thought and explanation of doctrine. Based on the "Sentences of Peter Lombard," the Summa explained the core of Catholic teachings, from the seven sacraments to the doctrines on Christ, the Virgin Mary, the Saints, the Church, etc. It was the first "catechism" of sorts. Using both philosophy and theology, Aquinas used reason to help explain the faith. The many volumes would also become a staple in Catholic seminaries, in order to teach and explain theology. Three centuries later, during the Counter Reformation period, the "Summa Theologica" would become an invaluable tool for clergy to learn and therefore explain doctrine in aid of converting people back to the Catholic faith. Hence, this is one of the greatest classics in the development of Catholic thought and one that is even used today.

Question 224. How was the Church alight during Medieval times?

Due to the Barbarian invasions and the sacking of Western cities, civilization was under the threat of complete destruction. The establishment of monasteries as centers of culture, art, and learning made them appropriate places in which to preserve historical documents. The patrimony of the Greco-Roman Empire, theater, music, art, architecture, political thought, and philosophy were kept in the monastic archives. The Church, even in the most difficult times of invasions, always promoted learning. Many of the monasteries developed into universities which were centers of debate and research.

In the practical realm, after the fall of the Roman Empire and subsequent Barbarian invasions, it was the Church that became involved in the everyday running of civil municipalities. The Papal States came into existence, and so the pope was not only a spiritual leader but also a civil one. Road building, hospitals, prisons, and daily functions of towns came under the auspices of the church.

Even outside the Papal States, the Church was the center of every village, town, and city. Birth certificates were registered as baptismal certificates. Marriages were both civil and religious. Even deaths were registered and recorded in the funeral books of the Church. There was no death certificate as issued today by the coroner, but an official registry of baptisms, weddings, and funerals was kept in the local parish church. Education was fostered by the church as was entertainment. Religious festivals, processions, and celebrations became a way of life. They were looked forward to as a diversion from the hard work a person living in the Middle Ages had to endure. These festivals were often colorful, musical, and bountiful since food was a part of celebrations and was shared by everyone.

Diplomatically, the Church of the Middle Ages was also involved in disputes between Catholic countries, in the Crusades to provide safe passage of pilgrims to the shrines of the Holy Land, and in treaty negotiation. Treaties with the Vatican are called Concordats. The Vatican Diplomatic corps is the oldest continuously running service in the world. Even today, the Vatican City State, which is a vestige of the old Papal States, has diplomatic relations with over 125 countries. It has full diplomatic relations with an ambassador to the United States, called the Apostolic or Papal Nuncio, and has a Permanent Observer Mission of the Holy See to the United Nations. The United States (and other nations) has its own ambassador to Vatican City distinct and separate from the American Embassy in Italy.

Culturally, the Church in the Dark Ages was a beacon of light. Music, architecture, and art were given sponsorship by bishops, cardinals, and popes. Many of the great works of arts that hang in modern museums were commissioned by Catholic hierarchy. Indeed, the Vatican library and museum is a vast and important collection of Western culture.

Question 225. How did the separation of church and state come about?

The separation of church and state is a relatively new development. When Emperor Constantine gave freedom of religion to the Roman Empire in the Edict of Milan in 313 AD, the Church was able to come out of hiding and into the public. Constantine gave many government buildings over to the Church for its use. In fact, Christianity became the state religion of the Empire. It was hard to distinguish the role of government from that of the Church.

As time went on, the relationship between church and state intensified. For many years there was only one religion, the Catholic Church. Everyone in Europe was Catholic. The height of earthly power in the Church came under Innocent III. All rulers and nobleman were subjected to the pope and looked to him for guidance. In addition, the pope was also a leader of a country, the Papal States. He looked to strong Catholic rulers for help from time to time, for example, when the Papal States were being invaded. With their aid came conditions. One of the conditions was that the emperor of the Holy Roman Empire would be in attendance at papal elections. Rulers also had a say in who could be bishops of diocese in their realm. The division of church and state was so slight that the emperor had the right to approve who could enter a religious community or order.

This interference was at its peak when the king of France kidnapped the papacy and brought it to Avignon, France. For over seventy years, the center of church government was not Rome but the back pocket of the king in Avignon. He regulated Papal elections, which undermined the central authority and power of the Church.

After the American Independence and the establishment of a new Catholic diocese, the Holy See conferred with President George Washington on his choice for the new bishop. The American government, which is built on the principles of the separation of church and state, said it was none of their business. For the first time, the Church did not need government approval on its choice of bishop. Over the years this would become the norm. Only in Communist countries would government still interfere in Church policy.

Question 226. How did the persecution of the Christians actually help spread the Good News?

There is an old axiom from Saint Augustine: "The Blood of Martyrs is the seed of the Christian Church." In other words, it is the martyrs' fidelity to Jesus Christ that would prove to be an undying demonstration of loyalty to Him. All through the centuries, the Church thrived under persecution. During the great Roman persecution of the first three centuries, this little sect known as Christians would eventually overturn the mighty Empire. They did so not with weapons or an army but with living a moral life according to the Gospel of Jesus.

In all there were ten great persecutions in the Roman Empire over the course of three hundred years. To be a follower of Christ or even to be sympathetic toward a Christian could mean torture or death. Martyrs were held in great esteem because of their heroic witness. It was this testimony that lead to many conversions. Christianity defended the rights of the poor, the elderly, slaves, women, and children. These sections of society were considered fringes and had no rights. Clergy, wealthy laymen, women who converted to Christianity, and all sorts of support structures in the Church helped to win many to the faith. Paganism was a morally bankrupt religion and did not even offer a hope in the afterlife, and eventually, the old order of paganism was not strong enough to crush the Christians. Christianity in the remaining years of the Empire eventually became the state religion.

Pick any century, and where the Church is persecuted you see a strong and vibrant Christian community. For example, Korea and Africa (mid-nineteenth century), and North America (seventeenth century), all saw a significant growth in the Catholic Church during periods of violent persecution. It was the martyrs' testimonies of faith and their moral living that won countless souls to Christianity. Even during the persecution of the Catholic Church in Catholic or former Catholic countries—such as Spain during the 1930s revolution, France during the 1790s revolution, and England during the 1570s revolution—the Church remained strong and intact. Ireland's great witness to its Protestant rulers was that it always remained Catholic. Many of the United States dioceses were headed by Irish bishops, or spiritually taken care of by Irish religious sisters, brothers, or priests. Even in Communist repression, the Church grew strong. Poland and its political-religious movement, Solidarity, overthrew the government. The Polish pope became famous for over-turning Communist governments in satellite countries and even in Mother Russia.

Question 227. What are some of the places that were important to early Christians?

Antioch is one of the five major patriarchal dioceses of the ancient world, which also included Jerusalem, Alexandria, Constantinople, and Rome. Each of the sees would have an archbishop that would be called a patriarch. Only Rome would be the first among the patriarchs, since Saint Peter and his successors governed from this city. Saint Peter and the popes have been the heads of the universal church from the time of Christ, when Jesus entrusted Peter with the Keys of the Church.

The largest city of the Eastern section of the Roman Empire, Antioch was the home to many Jewish converts. Some were intellectual men who began to teach the Gospel among the gentiles, which led to a vast number of conversions. Saint Barnabas was sent to Antioch to shepherd the Church in Antioch. It was in this city that the followers of Christ were first called Christian.

Jerusalem was important because it is where Christianity began. The sacred shrines centering on Jesus' life and death were in this city. It is there that the Holy Spirit descended upon the apostles and the missionary spirit of the Church was born. The connection with the places in Scripture, the physical attachment to specific sites in Christ's life, ensured the uniqueness of this patriarchal see. Saint Helena, mother of Emperor Constantine, in the fourth century went to Jerusalem to find the place of crucifixion and resurrection. She retrieved many of the holy relics which are enshrined in Rome today. The Crusades of the eleventh through thirteenth centuries were established to guarantee safe passage of pilgrims to the Holy Land.

Alexandria was known for its massive library and collection of ancient texts. It was a center for higher learning and education in the classical world. Constantinople became an important metropolis only when the seat of government of the Roman Empire moved from Rome to this city (named after the Emperor Constantine). Long after the breakup of the Western part of the Roman Empire, Constantinople remained a stronghold and has become known as the Byzantine Empire. After the schism from Rome, it also became the center or the Orthodox Christian religion. In the fourteenth century, Constantinople fell under the domain of Muslims and was renamed Istanbul. Rome, where Saint Peter and Paul lost their lives, remains the foundation of Catholicism. To this day, the Eternal City is central to the popes, who are the successors of Saint Peter.

Question 228. Who were some great women of the Middle Ages and what are they known for?

One of the greatest women of this period is Saint Catherine of Siena. She was a member of the Dominican Order of Nuns founded by Saint Dominic. She traveled to Avignon, France, where the pope was in residence due to the kidnapping of the papacy by the king of France. She pleaded with the pope to return to Rome, and under her influence Gregory XI left Avignon and reinstated the papacy in Rome. During the Great Schism, when there was more than one man claiming to be pope, she wrote to the cardinals and nobility who were the cause of the trouble and asked them to stop that terrible evil. Long regarded as one of the finest theological minds in the Church, Saint Catherine was given the title "Doctor of the Church." She is also patroness of Italy (Saint Francis of Assisi is patron).

Saint Bridget of Sweden was the daughter of the prince of Sweden. Her parents instilled in her a great devotion to the Passion of Christ. She married Ulfo, prince of Nericia in Sweden, and raised eight children. Later, Bridget and Ulfo took upon themselves the vow of chastity. Ulfo entered the Cistercian monastery. Upon his death, Bridget renounced her rank as princess and became a nun, founding a new order, the Brigittines. She next undertook a pilgrimage to Rome and the Holy Land. She remained in Rome where she continued her great devotion to the Passion of Christ. It is here that Christ appeared to her from the cross to strengthen her during a severe illness. A collection of prayers that are attributed to her writing became part of everyday Catholic devotion. Her religious order, to this date, still runs pilgrimage centers in Rome for travelers.

Saint Joan of Arc was born to religious parents in France, and very early on she received allocutions from Saint Michael the Archangel, Saint Catherine of Siena, and Saint Margaret. At first, the messages were personal, but later they became more political. The allocutions told her to go to the king of France and help him re-conquer his kingdom, which was being threatened by the English. She was given a small army and was victorious with a series of military successes. She was captured, sold to the English, and after months of imprisonment, was tried for heresy. Not sophisticated in theological terms, she was trapped by her captors into admitting things she did not believe. She was burned at the stake; however, her innocence was proven when it was made clear that the opposing side had spread calumnious rumors. In 1920 she was canonized a saint. She is considered responsible for saving France by uniting it.

Question 229. What are mendicant orders?

Mendicant is a term of Latin origin that means "to beg." This title was given to a type of religious order that came into existence in the Middle Ages, which consisted of a band of professed men who would go from town to town preaching the Gospel. Because they did not own any property and took strict vows of poverty, they begged for alms from the faithful. At the time, religion was reserved to monasteries. Diocesan clergy were in a very bad state, and many parishes went without priests. Due to their success, Christianity was revitalized. Through the mendicant orders, religion came to the people.

Two of the greatest mendicant orders are Dominicans and Franciscans. Both orders were founded roughly at the same time. Saint Dominic and Saint Francis were contemporaries, though they exercised their ministry in different areas.

Saint Francis was born in Assisi, Italy, into a burgeoning merchant class. After his conversion, he gave up all his worldly possessions to heed the call he heard from Christ to rebuild His Church. At first, Francis thought He meant a physical rebuild-ing of churches, but later, when he founded his order, he came to understand that it was much more. Francis and his little band of friars rejuvenated the Church by preaching missions, going from home to home and town to town bringing the Gospel.

Saint Dominic was originally from Spain. He founded the Order of Preachers more commonly known as Dominicans. A great heresy called Albigensianism flour-ished at this time. Its followers rejected the sacraments and Church authority,. lived promiscuous lives, and rejected the state's right to punish criminals. Before Saint Dominic went to preach against this heresy, he founded the Dominican Nuns to be a first line of defense and pray for the success of his mission. He also taught doctrine to the unlearned by way of the rosary. (See Question 117.) Soon this new order attracted many members and became known for its preaching and teaching.

Many of the early universities were staffed by the Dominicans or Franciscans. These orders came to the New World to establish parishes, colleges, seminaries, and other institutions for the Church. The great Juniper Serra, who is credited for being a pioneer in America, was a member of the Franciscan Order and a champion of the civil rights of the Native Americans. Christianity grew and was strengthened because of these great Orders.

Question 230. What does the title Doctor of the Church mean?

Doctor traces its root from the Latin word *docens* which means "teaching." In the church, the term Doctor of the Church refers to those writers who contributed much to the development of Catholic thought. Many of the Early Church Fathers were considered doctors of theology. They wrote extensively to repudiate heresy. These early doctors were not all saints, and their writings were not always free from error themselves. Only those who are officially declared doctors by the church have writings that are completely free from any error.

Doctors formally proclaimed by the Church are men and women who are revered for their writings, preaching, and holiness. Each proclaimed doctor made important contributions to the faith and is acknowledged for his tremendous worth.

The following have been declared Doctors of the Church:

Saint Albertus Magnus (d. 1280)
Saint Alphonsus Liguori (d. 1787)
Saint Ambrose (d. 397)
Saint Anselm (d. 1109)
Saint Anthony of Padua (d. 1213)
Saint Athanasius (d. 375)
Saint Augustine (d. 430)
Saint Basil the Great (d.379)
Saint Bede the Venerable (d. 735)
Saint Bernard of Clairvaux (d. 1153)
Saint Bonaventure (d. 1274)
Saint Catherine of Siena (d. 1380)
Saint Cyril of Alexandria (d. 444)

Saint Cyril of Jerusalem (d. 386)
Saint Ephraem (d. 373)
Saint Francis de Sales (d. 1622)
Saint Gregory of Nazianzus (d. 390)
Saint Gregory I the Great (d. 604)
Saint Hilary of Poitiers (d. 368)
Saint Isidore of Seville (d. 636)
Saint Jerome (d. 420)
Saint John Chrysostom (d. 407)
Saint John Damascene (d. 749)
Saint John of the Cross (d. 1591)
Saint Lawrence of Brindisi (d. 1619)
Saint Leo I the Great (d. 461)
Saint Peter Canisius (d. 1597)
Saint Peter Chrysologus (d. 450)
Saint Peter Damian (d. 1072)
Saint Robert Bellarmine (d. 1621)
Saint Theresa of Avila (d. 1582)
Saint Thomas Aquinas (d. 1274)
Saint Therese of Lisieux (d. 1897)

When Pope John Paul II is canonized a saint, he will very likely be given the title of "Great" and be made a Doctor of the Church. He wrote extensively in philosophy and theology, and was the greatest teacher of our time. In addition to his holiness, Pope John Paul II was an erudite teacher, who instructed not only his Church but also the world in the areas of morality. These are some of the qualities that the Church looks at when it proclaims a saint to be a Doctor of the Church.

Question 231. Who are the Jesuits?

Jesuits are priests who belong to the Society of Jesus, a religious order founded by Saint Ignatius of Loyola in 1540 AD. He had been a Spanish soldier (born in 1491) and at the age of thirty was injured in battle by a cannonball that shattered his right leg. Having no television, radio, Internet, cell phone, or iPod at his disposal, Ignatius was left to read whatever was available during his very long recuperation and convalescence. All the nuns gave him to read was the Bible and writings on the lives of the saints. When his leg did not heal properly, doctors had to break it again (without anesthesia) and reset it. That meant even more rehab time. So, he read more, too.

While in recovery, he decided it was better to become a soldier of Christ than to remain a soldier for the earthly crowned princes. Regaining his full health, he spent the night in prayer, and after making a general confession and following the tradition of knightly chivalry, he knelt on the floor of a chapel to Our Lady to show thanksgiving for his recovery. He left his sword and knife and gave his expensive clothes to the poor. He then embarked to establish a new order in the Church, the Society of Jesus (nicknamed the Jesuits).

The motto of Ignatius and the Jesuits is *ad majorem Dei gloriam* (to the greater glory of God). The Society of Jesus was founded to respond to the current needs of the Church as they occurred. In addition to taking the three vows of the evangelical counsels (poverty, chastity, and obedience), they took a fourth vow of total obedience and service to the Roman Pontiff (the pope), which earned them the moniker of "foot soldiers of the pope" or "papal stormtroopers." They never actually fought in military battles for the Papal States but did fight spiritual battles to defeat heresy and to defend the orthodox doctrines of the Catholic religion.

When the Catholic Counter-Reformation arose in the aftermath of the Council of Trent (1545–1563) to implement the decrees of the Council (which met to address the abuses in the Church exposed by the Protestant Reformers and to refute the doctrinal errors the Reformers also created in response), the Jesuits were ready and willing to go to work. Using techniques like the Spiritual Exercises, and making sure every member of the Society of Jesus was extremely well trained and educated (getting the highest of degrees if possible), they were able to preach and teach effectively and convincingly across Europe. Even today, some of the most prestigious colleges and universities were founded and are still being run by the Jesuits.

Their missionary success in Japan, China, India, and Latin America, and their strong loyalty to Rome were so well known that eventually they came under attack and suspicion in much the same way that Opus Dei is today. The order was actually suspended by Pope Clement XIV in 1773 after the kingdoms of Portugal, France, the Two Sicilies, Parma, and Spain expelled them in 1767. This was done not because of any heresy or immoral activity, rather, because of economic envy at the "connections" the Jesuits had established around the world thanks to their missionary work. Historically, a similar fate met the Knights Templar when the King of

France (Philip IV) seized their assets to compensate for his empty treasury and trumped up charges to have them suppressed, ironically by a previous Pope Clement, Clement V, in 1314. Pius VII restored the Society of Jesus in 1814.

The Superior General of the Jesuits was sometimes called the "black pope" due to the black cassock which is the habit (religious garb) of the order and to infer the influence of the Society of Jesus in the Church.

Question 232. What was the Reformation?

The Protestant Reformation took place in 1517 AD. Until then, there had been only one Christian church and religion in Western Europe and that was Roman Catholicism. Eastern Orthodoxy had split from Rome in 1054 AD but remained in the Eastern part of the Empire, called Byzantium. England, Scotland, Germany, and Switzerland were all Catholic until the Reformation.

The division of Western Christendom into separate religions can be attributed to several factors. While most people have this romantic image of Martin Luther posting his ninety-five theses on the Cathedral door as the equivalent of him burning his draft card and thus starting the Reformation, history has a different story to tell.

Internal corruption took hold among some of the clergy, including an assortment of parish priests, local bishops, cardinals, and even a few popes. Lust, greed, anger, sloth, and the other deadly sins were no stranger to many Renaissance clergy, who saw holy orders as stepping stones to an ecclesiastical career. In some cases, if Junior did not have what it took to be a military commander, then Pops would send him to a monastery (with a big donation) in the hopes that Dad's little boy would make good someday and become abbot or bishop.

The reason for the high percentage of corrupt and ignorant (poorly trained and educated) clergy at the time Martin Luther joined the Augustinian monks in 1505 (after making a deal with Saint Ann, the mother of the Virgin Mary that if he survived a lightning storm, he would enter monastic life) was due to the Black Death. Bubonic Plague (1347–1351) ravaged Europe and killed one-third of the population but also killed two-thirds of the clergy. The clergy were hit harder because they had to go and anoint the sick without protective masks or gloves; they rapidly succumbed to the disease. Desperate for clergy to administer sacraments, especially extreme unction (anointing of the sick), and to offer Mass, candidates for holy orders were not carefully examined or trained. Preaching suffered the most, and erroneous or distorted doctrines were espoused from pulpits as a result. What the ignorant clergy did not do with their superstition and inaccuracy, the immoral and corrupt clergy did with their bad example and scandal. The standards had been lowered so much to compensate for the huge vocation shortage coming from the Black Death, that men who should never have been ordained were ordained anyway, and some even moved up the ecclesiastical ladder and became members of the hierarchy.

After seventy years of the popes living in luxurious Avignon, France (referred to as the Babylonian Captivity by some historians), the pope moved back to Rome only to have two other pretenders claim to be pope, one in Avignon and one in Pisa.

Simultaneous to this phenomenon was the emergence of a middle class. The nobility and aristocracy were used to dealing with ignorant peasants, but the Middle Ages produced a middle level between the poor and the rich. The merchant class was partially educated and had some money. The medieval manorial system did not have a place for an economic offspring called the middle class.

Finally, the political scene in Western Europe was becoming a tinderbox. Since 800 AD, when Pope Leo III crowned Charlemagne Holy Roman Emperor, there had been an emperor in Europe to whom the kings and queens, princes, barons, lords, dukes, and counts owed allegiance. When the French lost the imperial throne to the Germans, the nation of France emerged as a strong power, like England, Spain, and Portugal. There was no unified Italy yet, and Germany was still a confederation of barons and princes. One faith (Catholicism), one secular ruler (Holy Roman Emperor), and one official language (Latin) kept diversified peoples and lands together.

By the end of the fifteenth century, with the discovery of the New World in 1492, gold was being sent back to Spain and Portugal from their colonies, which diminished the power of the German emperors. The German princes, barons, and other nobility wanted a separate German nation rather than a Germany which was the puppet of the empire.

When Martin Luther visited Rome from his native Germany, he was scandalized at the ill-educated and corrupt clergy he encountered along the way. His greatest shame was in finding unscrupulous clergy selling indulgences, something forbidden by the church and considered the sin of simony. His posting of ninety-five theses (propositions) on the door of the cathedral was standard practice as the door had the dual function of being the town bulletin board. He sought a debate on the theology of indulgences. Things got out of hand, tempers flared, and name calling and ad hominem attacks emerged from both sides. The princes saw an opportunity arise.

Politically, militarily, and economically, they were unable to dissolve or weaken the hold the emperor had over them, but if the ties to the empire were severed by other means, that would be to their advantage. The pope was head of the Catholic Church, and he crowned the emperor who had authority over the nobility under him. If the ties to the Catholic Church were severed, then the authority of the Catholic emperor would cease to extend to non-Catholic nobility.

Meanwhile, thanks to the printing press, the middle class read the theological tracts of Martin Luther. Unfortunately, the Catholic response was not as quick or accessible. Luther saw corrupt clergy and saw no need for a hierarchy, least of all a pope. So the ultimate authority was not the Magisterium or the Papacy but the Bible (*sola scriptura*). Since favors were being bought and sold, he saw no need for good works, hence the axiom *sola fide*, or "faith alone." No need for confession or confessors. No need for a Magisterium or a hierarchy. The Protestant faith had been born. The princes used the situation to revolt against imperial authority which was tied to the papacy and Catholicism.

When the peasants saw the lower clergy rebel against the pope and bishops, and saw the princes and barons rebel against the emperor, they thought that democracy was in the air and they sought their independence as well. The nobility were of no mind to dissolve the institution of servants, and even Martin Luther enthusiastically sided with the German nobles to crush the Peasants' War (1524–1525). Once Germany became Protestant (Lutheran), England followed in 1533 when King Henry VIII declared himself supreme head of the church in England after the pope refused his request for an annulment to his Spanish queen, Catherine of Aragon, who was unable to give him a male heir, and the Church of England (or the Anglican Church) was born. Switzerland would be next in 1541 with John Calvin in Geneva founding the Calvinist or Reformed Church that would also give birth to the Presbyterian Church in Scotland with John Knox in 1560. John Smyth broke from Anglicanism to form the Baptist Church in 1609, and John Wesley would also split from the Anglican Church to form the Methodist Church in 1739.

Question 233. What was the Second Vatican Council (Vatican II), and how did it change the Church?

Vatican II, or the Second Vatican Council as it is sometimes called, met from 1962 to 1965. It was the twenty-first ecumenical council since the first one took place back in 325 at Nicea. This latest council did not meet to address heresies as did early councils (Nicea and *Arianism*; Ephesus and *Nestorianism*; Chalcedon and *Monophystism*); rather, it was convened by Pope John XXIII to have the Church address concerns of the modern world. It was not intended to modernize the two-thousand-year-old religion, but it was the goal of the Council Fathers (the pope and the bishops) to adapt and adopt the best of the modern world and use it to further the mission of the Church. The spirit of Vatican II was to preserve and maintain the same doctrines and dogmas of faith and morals which had been espoused for two millennia, but to use modern methods, means, and manners to convey that message.

No official teachings (doctrines) were changed, nor were they meant to be changed by the Second Vatican Council. Ancient disciplines like celibacy were not abandoned, either. Updating religious garb (called habits) was allowed, but total abandonment was never even suggested. The content of faith could not be and was not altered, but the way in which the faith was explained—from the vocabulary to the tools used to transmit the teachings—was updated to take advantage of the advances of progress. The laity was not to be clericalized and the clergy laicized, but each was called to play their respective role in the church.

The sixteen documents of Vatican II were primarily pastoral and spiritual; even the Dogmatic Constitution on the Church (*Lumen Gentium*) did not issue any new doctrines and it certainly did not change or repudiate previous ones. The Second Vatican Council merely gave a new perspective and viewpoint to teach and to understand what the Church has always taught and what she has always done, especially in her public worship of God (called Liturgy).

One obvious change stemming from Vatican II was the introduction of modifications in the Mass (the Divine, Sacred, or Eucharistic Liturgy as it sometimes called). The essence of the rituals for the Seven Sacraments were not changed, but the vernacular (common tongue or language) was introduced. Latin remained and still remains the standard, universal, and official language for worship and doctrine, hence all official documents and rituals are still printed in Latin. Countries can get authorization from the Vatican to translate the Mass and Sacraments into the vernacular, and that was done once the Council closed in 1965. While the Council Fathers never intended the complete and permanent removal of Latin from the public worship and prayer of the Western Church (the Byzantine Catholic church has always used Greek, Old Slavonic, and the vernacular), in practice, most American and European countries went 100 percent vernacular after Vatican II.

Since the reign of Pope John Paul the Great (1978–2005), the true spirit of

Vatican II was reclaimed by the actual letter of Vatican II. Many innovators had tried to justify their liturgical abuses by claiming they were being faithful to the "spirit" of the law without being slaves to the "letter" of the law. On the contrary, John Paul showed that the intent of the Council Fathers can be found in the documents they issued. He also reminded people of the rich patrimony and heritage of the Church, from the Latin language to the perennial truth of Thomistic philosophy to the elegant and edifying beauty of Catholic art and music over the centuries for two millennia.

Abuses came not from Vatican II or because of Vatican II, but from those who distorted the intentions of the Council Fathers and the implementation of the documents. Optional celibacy for priests of the Latin rite, ordination of women, allowing artificial contraception by married couples, removing the obligation to attend Sunday Mass every week, forbidding Latin in any public worship, getting rid of devotions to the Virgin Mary and the saints, removing statues from churches, removing altar (communion) rails, moving tabernacles from the sanctuary, and forcing the priest to celebrate Mass facing the people were never required or mandated by Vatican II.

The rules on abstinence from meat were relaxed but not dissolved. Prior to Vatican II, it was a mortal sin to intentionally eat meat on any Friday of the year. After Vatican II, it was modified to permit the substitution of a work of mercy in place of the Friday abstinence, except on Ash Wednesday and all Fridays of Lent, when abstinence from meat was still obligatory for baptized Catholics fourteen years of age or older. Fasting (eating only one full meal for the day with two smaller ones not equaling the larger one if combined and with no snacking between meals) applies only to adult Catholics from the ages of eighteen to fifty-nine on Ash Wednesday and Good Friday.

Vatican II did encourage ecumenical dialogue with other religions. It did not suggest any kind of compromise regarding doctrine, nor did it seek to negotiate union by watering down or diluting church teaching. Dialogue was simply meant to open channels of communications between the leaders and followers of other religions with the leaders and members of the Catholic Church. Working together to protect the sanctity of life, to preserve moral values, to support marriage and the family, to help find ways to reduce poverty, crime, war, violence, hatred, and prejudice were the mutual goals sought by ecumenism. Vatican II did not call for doctrinal or moral compromise just to achieve ecumenical unity or consensus.

Extremists from both the far left (liberal) and far right (conservative) have distorted the message of Vatican II. Ultraconservatives have denied the validity of the

Mass (called the Novus Ordo) and even Holy Orders since the end of the Council. They claim only the Tridentine Mass and priests ordained before 1965 are valid. There are even some ultra-extremists from the far right who deny there has been a valid pope since the death of Pope Pius XII in 1958. They are called "sede vacantists" (meaning "empty chair," "chair" referring to the Chair of Saint Peter, which symbolizes the papacy).

There are also some mainstream Catholics who accept the validity of the Novus Ordo and all the Holy Orders (deacon, priest, and bishop) since Vatican II and who are in full communion with the church and follow Pope Benedict XVI, but who personally prefer the Latin Tridentine Mass. Pope John Paul the Great allowed them to fulfill their spiritual needs since 1980 when Ecclesia Dei allowed every bishop and diocese to provide the Latin Tridentine Mass to anyone who preferred it.

Ultraliberals have, on the other hand, denied doctrines like papal infallibility or have repudiated *Humanae Vitae* (1968), the encyclical of Paul VI which reiterated the condemnation of artificial contraception and abortion. They frequently ignore liturgical rubrics and promote egregious abuses in the Liturgy, from using illicit prayers to breaking Canon Law left and right. Both the ultra-left and ultra-right share one thing—they disobey Rome. Catholics who follow the doctrines, disciplines, teachings, and laws of the universal church are called orthodox (not capitalized), since the word means "correct" teaching. Those opposed to what the official Church teaches or legislates are considered "heterodox," be they left or right.

Question 234. What is World Youth Day?

World Youth Day has origins in the International Jubilee of Youth of 1984 in Rome. Pope John Paul II had opened the Holy Year of Redemption in 1983 to commemorate the 1,950th anniversary of the death of Jesus Christ, which affected the redemption of the human race. He asked the young people of the world to meet him in Rome the following year, and they did, gathering in the Eternal City on Palm Sunday, April 15, 1984.

Three hundred thousand youths from across the globe came to Rome, and joining them was an elderly nun from Calcutta, Blessed Mother Theresa. The following year (1985) was declared International Year of the Youth by the United Nations, so the pope invited the kids back to Rome for another international gathering and three hundred thousand showed up as in the previous year. The actual first time the phrase World Youth Day was coined, however, was in 1985, when John Paul announced that there would be a World Youth Day in Buenos Aires, Argentina, on April 11 and 12, 1987. The year before, on Palm Sunday of 1986, many local dioceses had gatherings for youth and gave Pope John Paul II a one-year breather, so to speak.

1987 was the first official international World Youth Day held outside of Rome, in Argentina. Pope John Paul traveled to Buenos Aires for the event with 900,000 people in attendance. Thus began the tradition of having one international World Youth Day every two to three years for which he would travel to a foreign land, with a smaller local gathering in Rome on the intermittent years to allow the bishops of the world to have their own celebrations as well.

During the few days of World Youth Day, the Pope speaks specifically to the youth; this event is not considered a pilgrimage or a state visit to national leaders. World Youth Day is for young people, and it is always distinct and separate from papal visits to countries.

1989: Santiago de Compostela, Spain; 400,000 attended

1991: Czestochowa, Poland; over 1.5 million attended

1993: Denver, CO, USA; 500,000 attended

1995: Manila, Philippines; 5 million attended

1997: Paris, France; 1.2 million attended

2000: Rome, Italy; 2 million attended

2002: Toronto, Canada (the last WYD for John Paul); 800,000 attended

2005: Cologne, Germany (the first time with Benedict XVI); 1.2 million attended

2007: Scheduled for Sydney, Australia

Chapter 23

THIS AND THAT

This chapter answers an assortment of common questions about Catholicism.

Question 235. What are indulgences?

Most people think the Protestant Reformation began over the selling of indulgences. Unfortunately, some immoral and unscrupulous individuals were selling indulgences, which the Church has always officially considered immoral and sinful (simony) just as the trafficking in Mass stipends (sin of accepting several stipends for one Mass) would be. Nevertheless, despite the abuses committed at the very dawn of the Reformation, the theology of indulgences has never changed nor have indulgences been suppressed since the sixteenth century, even after Vatican II.

An indulgence is *not* a "get out of jail free" card that gives someone *carte blanche* to commit sin and then be forgiven without true sorrow (contrition), firm purpose of amendment, sacramental confession, absolution, and the fulfillment of one's penance. An indulgence does not get any soul out of hell, nor does it prevent you from going to hell if you deserve it. An indulgence is neither a pardon from hell nor an early release from purgatory.

Indulgences are "remission before God of the temporal punishment due to sins whose guilt has already been forgiven, which the faithful Christian who is duly disposed gains under certain prescribed conditions through the action of the Church which, as the minister of redemption, dispenses and applies with authority the treasury of the satisfactions of Christ and the saints" (Catechism #1471).

Every sin has a double consequence. The first is the complete rupture (for a mortal sin) or the partial rupture (for a venial sin) of the spiritual relationship (communion) with God by killing or hurting the life of grace. Eternal punishment of hell is the penalty of unforgiven mortal sin. The second effect is the temporal punishment (purgatory) associated with unforgiven venial sins and already forgiven mortal sins. The reason for this temporal punishment is that even after we express true sorrow (contrition) and obtain absolution and forgiveness, there remains an "attachment" to sin. Those are the pleasant and fond memories we have of our past sins. We may be sorry we did them, but we still have some attachment to them in that we do not despise and hate each and every sin purely because we love God and hate the fact we ever offended Him. Instead, our sorrow is because of the punishment they deserve. Purgatory cleanses our soul so that we can fully appreciate the gravity of sin as God sees it and not just from our standpoint. It is like looking at a virus or bacteria through an electron microscope. Unseen to the naked eye, we may be too casual with ordinary germs. If you could see how ugly and dangerous some of them are with the microscope, then you would take them more seriously. Purgatory is like looking at your sins through a microscope and seeing their ugliness as God sees them.

If the surgeon removes a bullet from your chest, it is like going to confession and having a mortal sin forgiven. It saves the life of your soul. There is still, however, a nasty wound on your chest from the operation which also needs to be healed. Purgatory is nothing more than the removal of stitches and healing of the wound.

Indulgences are spiritual benefits derived from the infinite merits of Christ's Passion and Death on the cross and the superabundant merits of all the sufferings endured by the Virgin Mary and all the Saints by uniting themselves with the Crucified Lord. In other words, Jesus suffered more than He had to, and since He is divine as well as human, every ounce of His suffering has infinite value. Theologians say one drop of blood and one cry from His circumcision as an infant would have been enough to save the human race because He was a Divine Person. Yet, Jesus gave more than one drop. He gave every drop of His blood as He died on the cross. The infinite value of His suffering, and the superabundant value of the suffering of all innocent and holy people throughout the ages combined, leave a vast reservoir of mercy the Church uses through Indulgences. These benefits are applied to the faithful departed who may be in purgatory; their attachments to former sins are "purged" or cleansed away so they can enter heaven spotless. The Church never defined how or when the indulgences help the souls in purgatory, just that they do help. We can also apply them to ourselves to bring about our own detachment from former sins.

Question 236. What are stipends and stole fees? What is simony?

Masses and the Seven Sacraments cannot be sold, nor can the minister charge for celebrating them. That would be the sin of simony. Simony is the sin where someone demands payment for a religious service or tries to sell spiritual benefits, graces, blessings, or sacraments. Stipends are donations given by the faithful to the priest who offers the Mass for a specific intention indicated by the donor, either the repose of the soul of someone deceased (meaning the Mass is offered up that day for the soul of a dead loved one, family member, or friend; the hope is that if their soul is in purgatory, this Mass will help them in some way) or the spiritual welfare of a living person. They are not tips, taxes, fees, or charges since the Mass cannot be bought or sold (otherwise, the sin of simony is committed). Most parish bulletins the daily Mass and times with a specific name. That name is the Mass intention and is determined by the donor of the Mass stipend. The priest offers the Mass specifically for that person, living or deceased.

The practice of making a monetary offering began once the Roman Empire legalized Christianity in 313 AD with the Edict of Milan under Constantine. Clergy were exempt from military conscription and to prevent them from wandering around looking for secular employment to sustain themselves, the people began on their own initiative to make a modest financial gift to the priest in gratitude for celebrating Holy Mass for their intention.

A few abuses immediately compelled the Church to issue strict laws condemning the trafficking in stipends, where a priest would celebrate one Mass but collect several stipends or gifts as if he were going to offer several individual Masses. Every priest is only allowed to accept one stipend per day and per Mass. If he celebrates two or more Masses in one day, he must give the extra stipends to the diocese or to charity. He cannot refuse to celebrate Mass if a person does not offer a stipend or is unable to do so. Parishes can explain, however, that the customary offering is $10 (in the USA). Since priests usually celebrate Mass every day, he may be given thirty stipends for one month.

The diocese knows that every priest receives a stipend for each daily Mass; his regular salary takes that into consideration, and he gets a weekly, biweekly, or monthly wage to live on. Diocesan priests use this total income to pay taxes, buy clothes, make car payments to the bank, pay auto insurance, etc.

Stole fees (*jura stolæ*) are more generous donations or offerings made by the faithful to priests or deacons in appreciation for their kindness. These are usually given at weddings, baptisms, funerals, blessing of homes, etc. and the amount, if any, is at the discretion of the donor. It is forbidden for priests and deacons to demand or request these honoraria, but contemporary custom and convention is that most Catholics realize how small clergy's salaries are, and these "gifts" are very much appreciated. Only religious priests (monks and nuns, as opposed to diocesan clergy) take vows of poverty, where they own nothing and pay no taxes. Diocesan clergy do not take a vow of poverty but are paid a very modest salary. Mass stipends and honoraria for weddings and baptisms help pay incidentals not covered by wages. Diocesan clergy must pay federal, state, local and Social Security taxes, often paying estimated taxes each year. Some dioceses have eliminated all Mass stipends and stole fees (honoraria) by turning all donations and offerings to the parish or the poor box and compensating the clergy with a modest but equitable salary instead.

Question 237. Do all priests take vows? What are they?

Diocesan priests in the Latin church make solemn promises when they are ordained a deacon the year before they are ordained priests. These promises are to live a celibate (unmarried) life, to respect and obey the bishop and his successors, and to be faithful in praying the Divine Office (Liturgy of the Hours or Breviary). When he is ordained a priest, he is again asked to promise celibacy.

Consecrated Religious priests (e.g., Dominicans, Franciscans, Benedictines, Augustinians, Jesuits, Carmelites) do take solemn vows of poverty, chastity, and obedience. These are called the Evangelical Counsels. Religious men and women (brothers and sisters, monks and nuns) take a vow of poverty which means they do not own any personal property. They have no credit card in their name, no bank account, no checking or savings account, and no ATM card. They do not own a car or home. They earn no salary and pay no taxes. Everything they use is owned and shared by the community. If they inherit something or somebody gives them a gift, it does not belong to them individually; instead, it belongs to the religious community they are a part of. The superior of the house (the person elected or appointed to be in charge of the community that lives together under one roof) gives the brothers and sisters money to buy necessities like underwear, toiletries, shoes, socks, medicine, and food. Religious priests who take a vow of poverty do get a very modest monthly allowance ($50-$100) for necessities so they do not have to bother the superior for every little thing.

Diocesan priests do not take the vow of poverty as they typically live alone or with only one other priest in a rectory, whereas religious priests live together in communities as small as five to ten or as large as twenty, fifty, or more. The larger the community, the more shared assets there are; also, those who take the vow of poverty commit to living simple lives.

Diocesan priests live more like their parishioners, paying taxes and insurance, making monthly payments on their cars, paying for the gas and maintenance, and buying clothes and food. This helps them appreciate that their people have financial and economic concerns and worries since they do, too, to some degree. While the residence is provided by the parish, diocesan priests must provide their own transportation and make co-payments for their prescriptions and medical expenses just like the laity. This reality check helps them remember when it comes time to ask the congregation to donate more money each week because they, too, personally know about rising prices and costs of living. Even without a vow of poverty, diocesan priests are asked to live sensibly, modestly, and economically so as not to scandalize the faithful.

Question 238. What is a conclave?

Conclave comes from the Latin *cum clave*, meaning "with key" because the cardinals who elect a new pope are literally locked in the Sistine Chapel at the Vatican until someone is chosen. After the death of a pope, all cardinals under the age of eighty are summoned to Rome. They may elect any baptized male in the world, but they usually choose a cardinal who is already there in the conclave with them. No one is allowed to campaign for himself, and there are no primaries, conventions, or political parties.

While the press and media love to speculate and list possible candidates as *papabile* (Italian for "pope-able"), there is also an old Roman saying which sums the situation up more accurately: "He who enters the conclave as pope, leaves a cardinal." This means that most of the time, it is anyone's guess who the College of Cardinals will elect. No one expected a non-Italian (after 450 years)—and from Poland, no less—when Karol Wojtyla was elected Pope John Paul II in 1978. Even money was on Cardinal Josef Ratzinger when he was elected Pope Benedict XVI in 2005. Half the media thought it would be an Italian, South American, or an African. The other half thought maybe the Germans might have a chance. Sometimes the "favorite" or the best known going in is elected, but often it is the obscure and unknown candidate who is chosen.

A two-thirds majority is required to elect the bishop of Rome, who is simultaneously the pope and Supreme Pastor of the Catholic Church. If after twenty-one ballots no one receives two-thirds of the vote, then whoever gets a simple majority (50 percent plus one) on the twenty-second ballot is elected. The cardinals have a secret ballot, writing down their votes on a piece of paper that is folded and then placed in a large chalice. After the votes are tabulated, if someone gets two-thirds majority, he is asked if he accepts. If he does not or if there is no two-thirds majority, the ballots are burned with wet straw. This makes black smoke, and the chimney is seen by the multitude of faithful crammed into Saint Peter's Piazza. Black smoke means no pope, and the crowd moans, boos, and keeps praying. Whenever there is a two-thirds majority and the selected man accepts, the ballots are burned without straw, generating white smoke, and bells are simultaneously rung so the crowd knows a pope has been chosen.

Then the new pope is asked what name he wants to use. He can use his own baptismal name or keep tradition and pick a new name. After that, they whisk him away, throw on a white cassock, and a cardinal announces from the balcony as they did April 19, 2005: *"Annuntio vobis gaudium magnum: Habemus Papam! Eminentissimum ac reverendissimum Dominum, Dominum Josephum, Sanctæ Romanæ Ecclesiæ Cardinalem Ratzinger, Qui sibi nomen imposuit Benedictum XVI."*

"I announce to you a great joy: We have a Pope! The most eminent and most reverend Lord, Lord Joseph, Cardinal of the Holy Roman Church Ratzinger, Who takes to himself the name of Benedict XVI."

Question 239. What is papal primacy?

Papal primacy is the concept that the bishop of Rome (the pope) is the universal pastor and supreme head of the Catholic Church. He has full, supreme, immediate, and universal jurisdictional authority to govern the church. This means that no bishop, synod, or council of bishops can override his authority. His teaching authority is defined in the doctrine of papal infallibility. His governing authority is contained in papal primacy.

The Eastern Orthodox Church considers the bishop of Rome to have a primacy of honor among the five patriarchs of Jerusalem, Alexandria, Antioch, Constantinople, and Rome. They do not recognize his primacy of jurisdiction, however.

Every bishop in the Catholic Church must be approved by the pope and receive a papal mandate before being ordained and consecrated to the episcopacy (bishopric), and it is the pope who confers on that bishop the authority to govern the diocese to which he has been appointed.

The First Vatican Council defined papal infallibility and papal primacy. *"All the faithful of Christ must believe that the Apostolic See and the Roman Pontiff hold primacy over the whole world, and that the Pontiff of Rome himself is the successor of the blessed Peter, the chief of the apostles, and is the true Vicar of Christ and head of the whole Church and faith, and teacher of all Christians."* (See also Catechism #882.)

The basis for the teachings on papal primacy and papal infallibility are found in Matthew 16:17–19 when Jesus said to Simon, "Blessed are you, Simon bar-Jonah, for flesh and blood has not revealed this to you, but my heavenly Father. And so I say to you, you are Peter, and upon this rock I will build my church, and the gates of hell shall not prevail against it. I will give you the keys to the kingdom of heaven.

Whatever you bind on earth shall be bound in heaven; and whatever you loose on earth shall be loosed in heaven."

Some who dispute papal primacy claim that the original Greek words used by Matthew (*Petros* for Peter and *petra* for rock) show a difference between rock and stone, as if Peter were a small stone and the church was a large rock. Actually, the Greek word for stone is *lithos*. *Petros* is nothing more than *petra* (rock) with a masculine ending. Calling Simon *"petra"* would be like calling John "Joan" or "Johanna." A bunch of fishermen would tease him mercilessly had Jesus given him a name with a feminine ending, something our English language does not have. So despite the feminine ending of Petra, linguistic and biblical scholarship maintains that Simon "Peter" is the rock upon which Christ built his church.

Question 240. What is papal infallibility?

Papal Infallibility is a dogma solemnly defined at the First Vatican Council (1869–1870). Vatican II in *Lumen Gentium* #25, Canon 749 of the 1983 Code of Canon Law and the Catechism #891 explain the doctrine: *"By virtue of his office, the Roman Pontiff possesses infallibility in teaching when as the supreme pastor and teacher of all the Christian faithful, who strengthens his brothers and sisters in the faith, he proclaims by definitive act that a doctrine of faith or morals is to be held."* This charism (gift) of infallibility is exercised only when the Pope issues an *ex cathedra* statement on faith and morals or when he proposes a teaching united with all the bishops of the world.

Infallibility is *not* impeccability (being sinless) and it is *not* inspiration (every word intended and guided by the Holy Spirit). Unlike divine inspiration of scripture, where God directed the sacred authors to write only what He wanted them to write, infallibility merely means there are no moral or doctrinal errors present in the statement. It is true and nothing contradicts what has already been defined as true regarding faith and morals. Papal infallibility means that Catholics believe the pope cannot impose a universal teaching on the faithful which would be false.

It does not mean that every idea or judgment, opinion, or decision of the pope is inspired or always correct. It does not mean the pope cannot personally make mistakes or commit sin, since history has already proved the opposite. Making a mistake is a bad judgment, as to what to say or do, when and how. Infallibility does not affect prudential judgments or even scientific or philosophical knowledge. It merely means that the Holy Spirit guards the Church and the pope in such a way that the pope would be prevented from teaching an error on faith and morals if it were attempted to be imposed upon the universal church.

Whether the pope supported the German or the Italian soccer team in the World Cup has nothing to do with infallibility. His personal opinions on specific military, economic, or political policies are not infallible. Only when he speaks as universal pastor and solemnly defines a moral or doctrinal teaching does extraordinary infallibility occur. Two popes have done that in two thousand years: Pius IX in 1854 when he defined the dogma of the Immaculate Conception and Pius XII in 1950 when he defined the dogma of the Assumption of Mary.

Ordinary papal infallibility is exercised when popes officially teach to the universal Church what has been consistently and perennially taught by previous popes and by bishops around the world united with him. When John Paul II declared in 1994 (*Ordinatio Sacerdotalis*) that women cannot be ordained or receive the sacrament of Holy Orders, that was an infallible teaching but not an *ex cathedra* statement. It is just a technical but precise distinction. Ex cathedra statements are part of the extraordinary papal Magisterium. Since only two of these have ever been made so far, that tells you how extraordinary and rare these are. Ordinary papal Magisterium is more frequent and "ordinary" and, as in the case of *Ordinatio Sacerdotalis*, the content or teaching is infallible but not a specific statement per se. Fallible but official papal teaching does not demand an assent of faith but does require a religious submission of mind and will as explained in *Lumen Gentium* #25 of the Second Vatican Council and in Canon #752 and #892 of the Catechism.

Question 241. What is indefectibility?

Indefectibility is an attribute of the Catholic Church. It means that the Church will endure until the end of time. Nothing can destroy it. It is based on Jesus saying that the gates of hell would not prevail against the Church (Matthew 16:18) and, *"I am with you always even unto the end of time."* (Matthew 28:20)

Though indestructible, the Church has been persecuted through the ages. The Roman Empire persecuted the Church for three hundred years. The Church endured two schisms (Eastern and Western), the Reformation, the German Kulturkampf, Communist oppression, and much more. Even the Borgia and Medici scandals, and the recent clergy sex scandals in the USA, have hurt, but have not destroyed, the Catholic Church. Internal and external opposition have been present from day one, but the Church substantially continues to exist and thrive. With over one billion members around the world, a two-thousand-year-old church speaks for herself.

Indefectibility does not mean, however, that individual members do not need or cannot change or improve themselves. Every pope, bishop, priest, deacon, and layperson is called to do and be better every day of their lives. The Church as a whole is the bride of Christ and is the Mystical Body of Christ. It is in her individual human members that one finds vulnerability, weakness, imperfection, and even sinfulness. The Church as a whole cannot sin, but her members can all the way from the top on down.

The idea of the Church enduring until the end of time does not define the size, either. Saint Ambrose said *ubi Petrus, ibi ecclesia* meaning, "Where there is Peter (the pope), there is the Church." As long as there is a pope, there is a Church.

Question 242. What are the four marks of the Church?

The four marks or characteristics of the Church as listed in the Nicene Creed are One, Holy, Catholic, and Apostolic. Saint Robert Bellarmine (1542–1621) expanded these into fifteen marks, but the Creed still only mentions those four. They denote characteristics of the true Church, that is, the one founded by Christ Himself. Think of them as trademarks that identify the maker of the product.

Unity is the first mark of the Church as expressed in the Creed by the words "I believe in one…Church." When there is unity, there is harmony. The human body is one whole, and the whole is greater than the sum of the parts. We have two lungs, two eyes, five senses, many bones and organs—but it is one whole body. The image and analogy of the body being one yet having many parts with different functions is used by Saint Paul to describe the Church in Romans 12:4–5: "For as in one body we have many parts, and all the parts do not have the same function, so we, though many, are one body in Christ."

The Church has one set of doctrines (Catechism), one unified standard of public worship (Seven Sacraments) and one set of universal rules and regulations (Code of Canon Law). There is one visible head of the Church, the pope, who is simultaneously the bishop of Rome. He is given the title of Vicar of Christ and Successor of Saint Peter, who is considered the first pope of the Church (Matthew 16:18). The Catholic Church in the United States teaches the same doctrines and celebrates the same sacraments as the Catholic Church in Great Britain, Ireland, Italy, Spain, Portugal, Germany, Mexico, Canada, Poland, France, and all over the world. Unity of content of faith (doctrinal and moral teachings), unity of structure (one connected and integrated hierarchy with the pope as supreme head), and unity of worship (the same seven sacraments all over the world) are components of the true Church. This unity does not, however, destroy or oppose diversity. While there is one set of doctrines and discipline, there are many flavors and expressions of faith as we will see in the third mark.

Sanctity, or holiness, is the second mark of the Church as expressed in the words "I believe in one holy...Church." Since the founder is Jesus Christ, and He is the Son of God and the Second Person of the Holy Trinity, and Jesus said He would build His Church (Matthew 16:18), the Church herself must be holy due to her divine origins. The Church is the Mystical Body of Christ (Romans 12:4–5), and she is also the spotless bride (spouse) of Christ (Ephesians 5:25; Revelation or Apocalypse 21:2). Jesus entrusted to the Church the Seven Sacraments, which He Himself instituted. It is through the sacraments that men and women are sanctified and made holy by the divine grace they communicate.

Universality is the second mark of the Church as expressed in the words "I believe in one, holy, Catholic...Church." The diversity of the Church is embodied in the notion that the Church is truly universal (*katholikos* in Greek). This means it is not a national church, like the Church of England or the Church of Scotland. Unlike the Greek Orthodox or the Russian Orthodox Churches, no one nationality or culture exclusively identifies the Church. There is an Eastern (Byzantine) and a Western (Latin or Roman) part of the Catholic Church, yet they all recognize the same leader (the pope) and the same creed (Catechism). Though the head of the Church is the bishop of Rome, he is assisted by cardinals from around the world. Every country has one or more cardinals who advise the pope and who elect a new pope when the old one dies. All of them are also eligible to be elected pope, no matter what their race, language, or nationality. There are several Eastern liturgical traditions in the Church—Ruthenian, Ukrainian, Maronite, Melkite, Coptic, and Ethiopian, to name a few—and in the West there is the *Novus Ordo* of Paul VI (the present day Liturgy in the vernacular since Vatican II) and the Tridentine Mass of Pius V (the old Latin Mass since the Council of Trent). Whether Latin or English, Greek or Old Slavonic, Roman or Eastern, the substantial elements of the Mass (Divine Liturgy) are the same. Bread and wine are considered changed into the real, true, and substantial Body and Blood, Soul and Divinity of Christ by the validly ordained priest saying the exact words of Christ (called the Consecration).

Apostolicity is the fourth mark of the Church as expressed in the words "I believe in one, holy, Catholic and apostolic Church." This term means the religion can trace itself back to the original twelve apostles. Built on the foundation of the apostles (Ephesians 2:20; John 6:70) and continued in their successors, the bishops, the Church exists two millennia later, yet always with a firm connection to its roots. Every bishop who is ordained must be ordained by a bishop who can trace his "lineage of Holy Orders" back to one of the original twelve apostles. This is called Apostolic Succession. Just as Pope Benedict XVI is the 265th successor to Saint Peter, each Catholic bishop is a successor to the apostles. This scrupulous historical connection to the original apostles is not mere nostalgia. Saint Vincent of Lerins (fifth century AD) said it ensured the continuity of faith so that only orthodox teaching would be preserved. Apostolicity ensures that that which is taught everywhere, at all times, in all places (*quod ubique, quod semper, quod ab omnibus*) is sound doctrine.

Saint Augustine (fourth century AD) said, "There are many other things which most properly can keep me in [the Catholic Church's] bosom. The unanimity of peoples and nations keeps me here. Her authority, inaugurated in miracles, nourished by hope, augmented by love, and confirmed by her age, keeps me here. The succession of priests, from the very see of the apostle Peter, to whom the Lord, after his resurrection, gave the charge of feeding his sheep (John 21:15–17), up to the present episcopate, keeps me here. And last, the very name Catholic, which, not without reason, belongs to this Church alone."

Question 243. What does *extra ecclesia nulla salus* mean?

The Catholic Church is for everyone. Founded by Christ, her mission is to save souls and to save as many souls as she can. Sometimes, you may see the term *societas perfecta* in reference to the Catholic Church. It literally means "perfect society." Automatically, some people misinterpret that phrase. It does *not* mean that all or only members of the Catholic Church are perfect or sinless, and it does not mean that only Catholics can go to heaven. What it does mean is that as a society, it perfectly has everything the members need to achieve their goal. A perfect society is not composed of perfect membership; rather, it perfectly and completely provides all that the members need. The fullness of grace (all seven sacraments, not just two) and the fullness of truth (Sacred Tradition *and* Sacred Scripture, not sola scriptura).

Based on this premise that the Catholic Church alone has everything which is needed to satisfy every spiritual need and necessity by having the fullness of grace and the fullness of truth, then it stands to reason the Church is not optional but essential. It was not the apostles who founded the Church; it was Christ who said, "I will build My Church" (Matthew 16:18). He built it upon Peter and the apostles, and their successors continue the work of the Church two thousand years later.

Extra ecclesia nulla salus literally translates, "Outside the church there is no salvation." When taken out of context, it sounds very arrogant, xenophobic, triumphalistic, patronizing, and sectarian. The phrase does *not* mean that only Catholics can go to heaven, nor does it mean that non-Catholics are automatically damned to hell. It does mean that only the Catholic Church can provide what is needed for salvation in that she alone has the fullness of revealed truth, since she embraces both Sacred Scripture (Bible) and Sacred Tradition; religions which profess Scripture alone are limiting themselves to one half of divine revelation. The Catholic Church alone offers the fullness of grace in having all seven sacraments, whereas many Protestant Churches only have two sacraments.

Early in the twentieth century, Father Leonard Feeney, SJ, a Jesuit priest in Boston, taught a radical form of *extra ecclesia nulla salus* which amounted to saying, "If you're not a card-carrying (baptized and registered) Catholic, you're going to hell." His extreme interpretation focused on external membership alone. It also rejected the validity of baptism by blood and baptism by desire which the Catholic Church has always taught are as valid as baptism by water. He was excommunicated in 1949 for his radical beliefs but reconciled before his death in 1978.

There is a proper way to understand this axiom. Anyone and everyone can go to heaven since Jesus Christ died for all, and according to Saint Augustine, God offers every man and woman sufficient grace to be saved. God's grace becomes efficacious only for those who accept and cooperate with it. This universal salvific will of God is taught even by Saint Thomas Aquinas in his *Summa Theologica* III, Q. 68, a. 2, in which he discusses the necessity of baptism for salvation and explains that there is a baptism of desire which suffices for those who, through no fault of their own, are unable to obtain a baptism by water.

Some theologians call it being an anonymous Christian or being an anonymous Catholic Christian if, through no fault of his own, a person does not consciously, deliberately, and willingly reject Christ and the Catholic Church. Invincible ignorance refers to someone who does not know the truth but also does not realize he does not know it. Only someone who knows Christ is the Son of God and then consciously rejects Him, or who knows the Catholic Church is the true Church and consciously rejects it, is held liable for his decision.

The Catechism states:

1258—"Baptism of blood, like the desire for Baptism, brings about the fruits of Baptism without being a sacrament. And in 1260—'Since Christ died for all'…we must hold that the Holy Spirit offers to all the possibility of being made partakers, in a way known to God, of the Paschal mystery.' Every man who is ignorant of the Gospel of Christ and of his Church, but seeks the truth and does the will of God in accordance with his understanding of it, can be saved. It may be supposed that such persons would have desired Baptism explicitly if they had known its necessity."

The Sacred Congregation for the Doctrine of the Faith in the year 2000 said:

#20—"The Church is the 'universal sacrament of salvation' …[but] for those who are not formally and visibly members of the Church, salvation in Christ is accessible by virtue of a grace which, while having a mysterious relationship to the Church, does not make them formally part of the Church, but enlightens them in a way which is accommodated to their spiritual and material situation." [Dominus Iesus]

Does this mean that the Catholic Church is right and the others are wrong? No. It means that the Catholic Church has the fullness of truth (revelation) and the fullness of grace (sacraments), whereas the other churches have some but not all. If there are seven sacraments and a church only offers two, or if divine revelation comes from both Sacred Scripture (Bible) and Sacred Tradition, but a church only teaches from one source, then the members are only getting part of the graces and part of the truth that is available. What they are getting is real, but it is not the totality and fullness of what God offers. Think of it as attending a school where only addition and subtraction are taught. What you learn is true. The school across the street, however, teaches addition and subtraction but also multiplication and division. One place you get some truth, the other, you get all of it. Rather than who's right and who's wrong, the question is who has the most to offer?

Non-Catholic Christians who innocently do not know that the Catholic Church is the true Church will not be penalized for what they do not or cannot know. The late Archbishop Fulton Sheen once said that 98 percent of those who reject the Catholic Church are rejecting what they think the Catholic Church is, not what she truly is. Most people who reject Catholicism reject a distorted concept of Catholicism or an erroneous explanation of her teachings, or base it on the human weaknesses of her individual leaders and members. Many good Protestants, Jews, and other non-Catholics can and do get to heaven by living good moral lives and trying to conform to the will of God; they just do not know what they were missing. Only someone who does know and makes a deliberate choice to reject it is accountable for that decision.

Question 244. What are *Novus Ordo* and Tridentine Masses?

The Tridentine Mass is the Mass from the Council of Trent (1545–1563), hence the name "Tridentine," which was promulgated by Pope Saint Pius V (*Quo Primum*, 1570).

The *Novus Ordo* is the Mass from the Council of Vatican II (1962–1965) which was promulgated by Pope Paul VI (*Novus Ordo*, 1970).

The older Tridentine Mass was divided into two parts, the Mass of the Catechumens and the Mass of the Faithful. The Vatican II Novus Ordo Mass also has two halves, but calls them the Liturgy of Word and the Liturgy of the Eucharist instead.

The Tridentine Mass is celebrated only in Latin, while the Novus Ordo can be celebrated totally in Latin, totally in the vernacular, or with some parts in Latin and the rest in the vernacular.

Both have readings from Sacred Scripture (Bible) for either weekdays or weekends.

Though not mandatory, the customary position for the celebrant is to be facing the people (*versus populum*) during the Liturgy of the Eucharist of the Novus Ordo. The Tridentine Mass mandated that the celebrant offer Mass *ad orientem* (toward the east) or *ad apsidem* (toward the apse or tabernacle) during the Mass of the Faithful.

The Tridentine Mass has extra parts not present in the Novus Ordo, like the prayers at the foot of the altar (*introibo ad altare Dei*), at the offertory (*Suscipe Sancta Trinitas*), the last gospel, and prayers after low Mass (*salve regina* and prayer to Saint Michael). It also had many more signs of the cross for the priest to make and more elaborate rubrics depending on the solemnity of the Mass (high, solemn high, pontifical).

Ecclesia Dei (1988) allowed wider and broader use of the Tridentine Mass for Roman Catholics, who felt it fulfilled their spiritual needs more than the Novus Ordo. Previously, it was rare to find a Tridentine Mass officially sanctioned by the local diocesan bishop after Vatican II, since Pope Paul VI wanted the new Mass to be the standard. The late Archbishop Marcel Lefebvre founded the Society of Saint Pius X in 1970, and they resisted the liturgical changes (to the Mass and the other sacraments) which originated from the Second Vatican Council. When Lefebvre illicitly consecrated bishops without papal mandate, he and those bishops incurred automatic excommunication and were in *de facto* schism. Pope John Paul II issued *Ecclesia Dei*, which also created the Priestly Fraternity of Saint Peter (FSSP) for those former members of the Society of Saint Pius X (SSPX) who wished to return to full communion with Rome. A renegade branch of the Pius X Society is the Pius V Society, which is ultra-traditional. Only religious communities in full communion with Rome, like the Fraternity of Saint Peter, are recognized by the Vatican and local dioceses to licitly celebrate the Tridentine Mass, as well as those Novus Ordo priests who obtain a mandate from their local diocesan bishop.

Byzantine Catholics use the Divine Liturgy of Saint John Chrysostom or the Divine Liturgy of Saint Basil, which is celebrated in Greek, Old Slavonic, Aramaic and vernacular languages.

Question 245. What is a synod?

The word synod which comes from two Greek words *syn* (together) and *hodos* (road) means "a coming together" or "a meeting." A synod is a council of bishops, as in the case of the *Synod of Bishops* created by Pope Paul VI in 1965, which meets periodically at the invitation of the reigning pontiff. Unlike an ecumenical council where every Catholic bishop in the world is invited, a synod is open only to a representation of bishops from each country or national episcopal conference. It has no legislative authority of its own but it advises the pope on current issues and concerns.

The pope sets the agenda, summons, suspends, and dissolves the synod. He can preside himself or appoint a president from the member bishops. There have been twenty-one synods since its creation (1965). Before each begins, a *Lineamenta* (outline) is given to the bishops to set the tone and scope of the upcoming synod. Suggestions from the bishops on possible discussion topics related to the outline are sent to Rome. Once convened, the bishops are given an *Instrumentum laboris* (working copy) outline based on the *Lineamenta* and the suggestions it inspired.

A Metropolitan Archbishop can convene a provincial synod where the bishops from that area gather. For example, the Cardinal Metropolitan of Philadelphia could convene a provincial synod which would entail the Archdiocese of Philadelphia and the suffragan sees of Erie, Pittsburgh, Greensburg, Altoona-Johnstown, Harrisburg, Scranton, and Allentown.

National synods are less common, and the United States has had only three so far. The first three Plenary Councils of Baltimore took place in 1852, 1866, and 1884, and from them came the famous Baltimore Catechism which was the first national catechism for the USA.

A Diocesan Synod is a little different in that there is usually only one bishop, the local Ordinary, or a few if there are auxiliary or retired bishops in the diocese. Most of the synodal participants in a diocesan synod would be representatives of the local clergy, religious, and lay faithful. The diocesan bishop is the only one who has a vote but the very reason he convenes a diocesan synod is to receive counsel and advice from his priests and his lay faithful. The synodal decrees which the bishop approves become diocesan (local) law. They must, of course, be in conformity to the universal canon law of the church and cannot contradict any article of the faith nor can they conflict with the general liturgical laws of the Roman Missal (for the Mass) or Roman Ritual (for the other Sacraments).

Question 246. What is the United States Conference of Catholic Bishops (USCCB)?

The USCCB is the gathering of all the Catholic bishops of the United States from both the Latin (Western Rite) and Byzantine (Eastern Rite) Catholic churches. Each year the group meets twice to discuss topics and issues of concern for the Catholic Church in the nation.

Catholic bishops of the United States formed the National Catholic War Council (NCWC) in 1917 to enable Catholic Americans to contribute funds to provide spiritual care and recreation services to servicemen during World War I. In 1919, Pope Benedict XV urged the hierarchy (the world's bishops) to join him in working for peace and justice, which resulted in the American bishops renaming the organization the National Catholic Welfare Council. Since 1966, after the close of Vatican II, it was known as the National Conference of Catholic Bishops (NCCB) with a sister branch called the United States Catholic Conference (USCC). The name was again changed in 2001 to its current title (USCCB) when the two merged into one entity.

Canon Law is very explicit on the authority of all national episcopal conferences. They are not parallel legislative bodies in the way that the Senate and House of Representatives are. They are not equal or superior to the Holy See which represents the pope and all the departments of the Curia which implement his papal authority of universal jurisdiction. Episcopal conferences are seen as exercises of subsidiarity, which is a principle endorsed by Vatican II that, when possible, work should be done at lower levels by those closer to the scene. Hence, each pastor of a church decides for himself the times of Mass, whereas the diocesan bishop makes regulations on how early Saturday evening Mass can take place and the national conference of bishops decide which holy days are obligatory (pending final approval of Rome).

Sometimes, it helps to see Rome and the Vatican as being like the White House (executive branch), Congress (legislative branch), and Supreme Court (judicial branch) all rolled into one federal authority, with the local diocesan bishop being like the individual states and the local pastor of the parish being like the municipal authority. In this analogy, the USCCB would be akin to a meeting of state governors.

As an assembly of the hierarchy of the United States and the U.S. Virgin Islands, the USCCB can at times exercise authority, but individual member bishops never lose their autonomy to govern their respective dioceses. The decree *Apostolos Suos* issued by Pope John Paul II in 1997 states that episcopal conferences do not possess *per se* doctrinal authority, which is binding and superior to each bishop who comprises them. If doctrinal declarations from a conference are approved unanimously by the bishops, they can be published in the name of the conference itself, and the faithful must adhere to them. Where unanimity is absent or on matters of a liturgical nature, subsequent Vatican approval is necessary.

Question 247. Why do Catholic churches have crucifixes while Protestant churches have crosses?

Crucifixes are crosses which have the corpus (body) of Jesus on them to represent the historical crucifixion of Our Lord. The cross alone, with no body, has been a symbol of Christianity since antiquity. The very instrument of capital punishment and horrible torture by the pagan Roman Empire became a symbol of the loving and forgiving crucified Savior.

Catholics are not the only Christians to use the crucifix in church for public worship or in their homes for personal piety. Eastern Orthodox, Anglican (Episcopalian) and Lutheran Christians also use the crucifix, whereas most Reformed Protestant Christians will only have a cross and never with a corpus. Those who oppose the crucifix consider it a morbid denial of the Resurrection (and some extremists even consider it idolatry), whereas the true intention of those Christian religions which do use it is to remind their followers that Jesus really and actually did die a horrible death to save us from our sins. The Resurrection is not denied, merely the Passion and Death are emphasized, especially near the altar where in Catholic theology, the Mass is considered the unbloody reenactment of Calvary.

The main goal of the crucifix is not to shock or frighten believers, but to remind them of the ultimate price paid for their salvation. Redemption was expensive. Jesus sacrificed His very life and He endured a painful and horrible death just so we could go to heaven. The crucifix brings home the reality that sin caused us to be lost and only the death of the Savior could save us. Celebrating Christian worship on Sunday (rather than on the Sabbath day, Saturday) and calling it the day of the Lord is how Christians honor the Resurrection.

Crosses began to appear in Christian art and worship as soon as the religion was legalized by the Roman Emperor Constantine in 313 AD with his Edict of Milan. The crucifix, however, did not become common and popular until the fifth century AD, when the Roman Empire fell (476 AD). The so-called Dark Ages ushered in by the Barbarian invasions and the Black Death (Bubonic Plague) of the mid-fourteenth century left many in the Middle Ages longing to leave this earth and all its pain and misery. Looking at and meditating on the crucifix, however, helped many in time of trial and tribulation to persevere. The command of Christ in Mark 8:34 to take up our cross and follow Him is poignantly reminded wherever the crucifix is displayed. As Saint Paul says in the sixth chapter of his epistle to the Romans, "Our old self was crucified with Him" and "If we have died with Christ, we believe that we shall also live with him." The crucifix reminds us not only that Christ died, but that we, too, must "die to self"; our ego must perish so that in its place Christ can reign. "I have been crucified with Christ yet I live, no longer I, but Christ lives in me" (Galatians 2:19–20).

When taken in context with what Saint John the Baptist said in the Gospel, "He must increase; I must decrease" (John 3:30), the dying to self is seen by Catholic Christians as a death of the ego—the surrendering of one's own will in order to replace it with God's will. The Crucifix reminds believers of the value of sacrificial love.

Most crucifixes have a sign above the corpus of Christ which reads INRI. That is an abbreviation for the Latin phrase IESVS NAZARENVS REX IVDAEORVM (there was no "U" in ancient Latin, so the "V" is used instead) which translates: JESUS OF NAZARETH KING OF THE JEWS (see John 19:19). Pontius Pilate had ordered this sign posted in Latin, Hebrew, and Greek.

Byzantine Catholic and Eastern Orthodox crucifixes have an extra distinction to them—one short horizontal bar (representing the INRI sign) above the main intersecting one and a lower diagonal one (representing the footrest) below it.

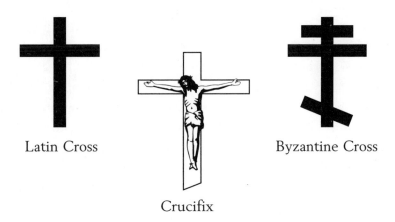

Latin Cross   Byzantine Cross

Crucifix

Question 248. If an Anglican Priest converts to Catholicism, must he be reordained, and why?

In the sixteenth century, Henry VIII, King of England, broke from the Catholic Church when his petition to the pope for an annulment of his marriage to Queen Catherine was denied. He proceeded to marry five times after his legitimate Catholic marriage. He pretended that he was still in the Catholic Church and didn't change the Mass, feasts, or Catholic customs. It was during the reign of his illegitimate daughter, Elizabeth I, that a formal break from Catholicism took place. During her time in power, Thomas Cromwell designed the liturgy in such a way that it would be devoid of any reference to sacrifice which he considered to be a purely Roman invention and a symbol of "popery"—popery being anything which can be associated with or connected to the pope in Rome. Therefore the Holy Sacrifice of the Mass became, in the Book of Common Prayer, a service of Holy Communion.

In addition, the formula for the Rite of Ordination was also tampered with, thereby compromising the validity of the Sacrament of Holy Orders. The Book of Common Prayer and Hymn Book are two tools that unite Anglicanism. In the Church of England, there are many different levels of services known as low, broad, or high. Low services reflect a more evangelical Protestant flavor that is celebrated usually without the service of Holy Communion. Broad services are middle of the road between Protestant and Catholic styles, while high services replicate a more Catholic essence. During the reign of Queen Elizabeth, high service was forbidden because it was too close to Roman Catholicism. It was not until the Oxford Movement in the nineteenth century that liturgical color, vestments, statuary, and things that one usually associates with the Catholic Church came into fashion.

Finally, when England went through civil war, spearheaded by Cromwell in the seventeenth century, any vestige of the Church of England from Henry VIII was completely removed. Cromwell was a Parliamentarian and wanted to rid England of "Crown and Popery." Popery is a derogatory term that denotes anything that looks too Roman Catholic. The episcopacy was completely annihilated. After the Civil War and the restoration of the Crown, the episcopacy was also reestablished. Naturally, candidates were not submitted to the pope for approval. Also, since the Rite of Ordination was changed there existed a complete break from Apostolic Tradition. Accordingly, the Catholic Church deemed Anglican Holy Orders not valid. When an Anglican priest converts to Catholicism, after a period of training and study, he must be ordained in the Catholic Church according to the present Catholic Rite for validity of the Sacrament.

Question 249. How can Catholics consecrate themselves to the Virgin Mary when God says we must love Him with all our heart, all our soul, and our entire mind?

When a Catholic makes an act of consecration to a saint, it is not preempting love of God. Catholics, like any other Christian, only worship God. They honor and respect the saints as perfect examples of living a Christian life. When someone loves other people there is no competition. A child can love both mother and father. Love is limitless. Only hatred is confining.

An Act of Consecration to the Virgin Mary does not take away any love that we have for God. In fact, the more we love God, the more we love those close to Him. The Blessed Virgin Mary is the closest human being to God ever created by Him. In honoring her, we revere her Creator, Almighty God. Prayers, devotions, and acts of consecration are seen as ways of getting closer to God through imitation of the saint being well-regarded.

All devotions, including those to the Blessed Virgin Mary, should lead to Jesus Christ. Jesus Christ is our primary mediator between His Father and us. It is a better knowledge and love of God that we Catholics gain through devotions to the saints, who are His closest friends. In the Act of Consecration to Mary we are asking her to pray with us and for us to her Son.

We look to Mary as a source of inspiration on how to live our lives. Mary was totally obedient to the Word of God. Her fiat, "Thy will be done," is the answer that all Christians should give to the Lord. She lived a life of humility and service. This is the great legacy she leaves for us in order to follow her Son more devoutly. Her life is one of perseverance. Even during the dark trials of her Son's crucifixion, Mary was a pillar of faith—a beacon of hope and comfort to those around her. By modeling our lives after her, we too become closer to her Son.

The Rosary, Litany of Loreto, various novenas to her different titles, wearing the scapular, Miraculous Medal, and praying the Little Office of the Blessed Virgin Mary do not take anything away from Almighty God. Like non-Catholics who ask one another on earth to pray for them to God, Catholics ask the living saints to continue that prayer to God in heaven on our behalf. We most certainly can pray to Jesus directly, but we can also augment our prayer to Jesus with the help of His friends, the saints.

Question 250. What are Byzantine Catholics? What kinds are there?

The true Church of Jesus Christ contains four marks (or characteristics). (See Question #51.) Byzantine Catholics recognize the four marks. There are different rites or liturgical traditions in the Catholic Church. The common term to denote different rites are Eastern or Western, which depends upon the origin of the liturgical tradition. If the rites are in union with Rome then they are a part of the Catholic Church, also known as the Latin Rite, which in the West is by far the largest. There are certain local rites, such as the Ambrosian Rite in Milan and the Mozarabic Rite in Toledo, Spain.

In the East there are many different rites, of which the Byzantine Rite is by far the largest. This rite includes smaller variations such as Albanian, Bulgarian, Byelorussian, Georgian, Greek, Italo-Albanian, Melkite, Hungarian, Russian, Ruthenian, Romanian, Ukrainian, Yugoslav, and Slovak. The Alexandrian Rite includes the Coptic and Abyssinian Rites. The Antiochene Rite includes Chaldean and Syro -Malabarese, Maronite, and Syrian. Finally, there is the Armenian rite descended from the first people to embrace Christianity.

In some cases, the Eastern Rites do have an Orthodox counterpart. The Orthodox broke their ties with the Catholic Church in the twelfth century. Some of the Rites returned to the Catholic Church in the seventeenth century. Pejoratively, they are referred to by the Orthodox Church as Uniates, because these churches sought union with Rome. Since the Second Vatican Council, there has been a return to and respect for the Eastern Rites to be preserved as part of the Universal Church's heritage. Many of the Eastern Churches were "Latinized" and asked by the Council Fathers to return to their liturgical roots.

Question 251. What are litanies?

The word litany is of Greek origin. It is a prayer consisting of a series of supplications and responses said alternately by a leader and a group. Since the Second Vatican Council in 1965, indulgences granted to saying litanies have been reduced to the following: Holy Name, Precious Blood, Saint Joseph, Sacred Heart, Blessed Virgin Mary, and All Saints.

Some litanies come from Sacred Scripture, for example, certain Psalms in the Old Testament. Psalm 135 contains a repeated phrase use in litanies, "for His mercy endures forever." In the Mass, there are various litanies used. For example, in the Penitential Rite, the Lord Have Mercy is sung several times; at the Prayers of the Faithful or General Intercessions, there is a repetition of petitions and responses. Finally, after the Consecration of the Mass "the Lamb of God" is sung at least three times.

Litany of the Saints is the oldest, going back to the fourth century. Recognition of saints, especially martyrs, began early in the liturgical life of the Church. This Litany has been incorporated into the Liturgy of the Church, especially at Baptism and Anointing of the Sick. It is also prayed during the Liturgy, in which the Sacrament of Holy Orders is conferred at the deaconate, presbyterate, and episcopate. At the Easter Vigil Mass, if there is going to be a Baptism, the Litany of Saints is sung. Lastly, at the conclusion of a solemn exposition of the Blessed Sacrament known as Forty Hours Devotion, the Litany of Saints is sung or said.

The Litany of the Holy Name of Jesus is attributed to Saint Bernardine of Siena in the fifteenth century. Litany of the Sacred Heart of Jesus was approved for solemn and public use in the nineteenth century by Pope Leo XIII. Saint Margaret Mary, who received the apparition of the Sacred Heart of Jesus, had much influence on the spread of this devotion. The Litany of Saint Joseph was approved by Pope Saint Pius X in 1909. The Litany of the precious Blood was approved by Blessed Pope John XXIII in 1960.

The Litany of Loreto devoted to the different titles of Mary traces its roots to apostolic times and was formally approved by Pope Sixtus V in the sixteenth century. This litany is often prayed at devotional services in honor of Mary, especially in May, Mary's Month, and October dedicated to Our Lady of the Holy Rosary.

Often it is prayed at the end of the recitation of the Holy Rosary.

Lord have mercy on us. *Lord have mercy on us.*
Christ have mercy on us. *Christ have mercy on us.*
Lord have mercy on us. *Lord have mercy on us.*
Christ, hear us. *Christ, graciously hear us.*
God the Father of Heaven, *have mercy on us.*
God the Son, Redeemer of the world, *have mercy on us.*
God the Holy Ghost, *have mercy on us.*
Holy Trinity, one God, *have mercy on us.*
Holy Mary, *pray for us.*
Holy Mother of God, *pray for us.*
Holy Virgin of virgins, *pray for us.*
Mother of Christ, *pray for us.*
Mother of divine grace, *pray for us.*
Mother most pure, *pray for us.*
Mother most chaste, *pray for us.*
Mother inviolate, *pray for us.*
Mother undefiled, *pray for us.*
Mother most amiable, *pray for us.*
Mother most admirable, *pray for us.*
Mother of good counsel, *pray for us.*
Mother of our Creator, *pray for us.*
Mother of our Redeemer, *pray for us.*
Virgin most prudent, *pray for us.*
Virgin most venerable, *pray for us.*
Virgin most renowned, *pray for us.*
Virgin most powerful, *pray for us.*
Virgin most merciful, *pray for us.*
Virgin most faithful, *pray for us.*
Mirror of justice, *pray for us.*
Seat of wisdom, *pray for us.*
Cause of our joy, *pray for us.*
Spiritual vessel, *pray for us.*
Vessel of honor, *pray for us.*

Singular vessel of devotion, *pray for us.*
Mystical rose, *pray for us.*
Tower of David, *pray for us.*
Tower of ivory, *pray for us.*
House of gold, *pray for us.*
Ark of the covenant, *pray for us.*
Gate of Heaven, *pray for us.*
Morning Star, *pray for us.*
Health of the sick, *pray for us.*
Refuge of sinners, *pray for us.*
Comforter of the afflicted, *pray for us.*
Help of Christians, *pray for us.*
Queen of Angels, *pray for us.*
Queen of Patriarchs, *pray for us.*
Queen of Prophets, *pray for us.*
Queen of Apostles, *pray for us.*
Queen of Martyrs, *pray for us.*
Queen of Confessors, *pray for us.*
Queen of Virgins, *pray for us.*
Queen of all Saints, *pray for us.*
Queen conceived without original sin, *pray for us.*
Queen of the most holy rosary, *pray for us.*
Queen of peace, *pray for us.*
Lamb of God, Who takes away the sins of the world: *Spare us, O Lord.*
Lamb of God, Who takes away the sins of the world: *Graciously hear us, O Lord.*
Lamb of God, Who takes away the sins of the world: *have mercy on us.*
Pray for us, most holy Mother of God, *that we may be made worthy of the promises of Christ.*
Let us pray.
O God, whose only begotten Son, by his life, death, and resurrection has purchased for us the rewards of eternal life, grant, we beseech you, that while meditating of the mysteries of the most holy rosary of the Blessed Virgin Mary, we may imitate what they contain and obtain what they promise, through Christ our Lord. Amen.

Question 252. What are novenas?

The word novena is a derivative of the number nine, which refers to the length of time this prayer would last because of the first novena that was said. Our Lady, along with the apostles, gathered in the upper room after the ascension of the Lord into heaven for nine days of prayer. They did so to prepare for the coming of the Holy Spirit. On the tenth day the Holy Spirit descended (the Solemnity of Pentecost). Pentecost means fifty since it takes place fifty days after Easter.

Novenas can be divided into various categories: to our Lord, our Lady, the saints, and angels. Novenas are usually short prayers that are said consecutively for nine days. However, a novena can be celebrated in a more solemn way. It is customary for the titular saint of the parish to be honored with nine nights of prayer. During these services, prayers to the saint would be said, a priest would expound upon the virtue of the saint, and benediction of the Blessed Sacrament would conclude the devotion. This period of nine nights of prayer is especially popular during the season of Lent, in which Catholics often attend spiritual programs as part of their preparation for Easter.

Novenas can also be perpetual. Instead of nine consecutive nights, they can be prayed every week. The Miraculous Medal Novena is often prayed in Catholic parishes every Monday, either after Mass or with benediction. Saint Catherine Laboure received in 1830 an apparition of Our Lady, in which the Blessed Mother asked Catherine to construct a medal in honor of her Immaculate Conception, with the inscription: O *Mary, conceived without sin, pray for us who have recourse to thee…*

There is also a wonderful devotion to Saint Anthony of Padua, known as the Thirteen Tuesdays in Honor of Saint Anthony. Saint Anthony died on June 13, which is the day that the Church celebrates his entrance into heaven. To prepare for this feast, special prayers, devotions, and litany to Saint Anthony are said for thirteen Tuesdays leading up to June 13.

Another popular novena is the Rosary Novena. For thirty days, certain prayers which accompany the Rosary are said during this special novena. The Rosary Novena can be prayed at any time of the year. Finally, there is the Christmas Novena, thirty days of prayer which is a way of preparing for this Solemnity.

Question 253. Who is the Devil's Advocate?

Technically this term refers to a person who takes the opposing view in any discussion. This person would be employed during the annulment process and would be known as the Defender of the Bond. An annulment consists of a person questioning the validity of the marriage in a Church court known as a tribunal. While the one contesting the validity of the marriage would be assigned an advocate of their own, there is also another person assigned to be the Devil's Advocate or Defender of the Bond. The Defender of the Bond makes sure all precautionary and discretionary data has been researched and completed so that if an annulment is granted there are no mistakes.

In the time prior to the Second Vatican Council, the canonization process also involved a Devil's Advocate. This type of advocate would give reasons why the person up for canonization should not be canonized a saint. If there was very little opposing material, then the candidate would proceed towards canonization. The Devil's Advocate was also known as the Promoter of the Cause or prosecuting attorney. They were authorized to examine virtues and reported miracles of one whose cause for beatification had been opened.

Since the new Code of Canon Law of 1983, the role of Devil's Advocate for canonization has been assimilated into a broader investigation in that the advocate for the saint assumes the responsibilities formerly assigned to the Devil's Advocate. An advocate interviews people who knew the proposed saint, takes testimony, and compiles data on the person. Also, all the letters, books, and articles written by the candidate for sainthood are researched by the advocate. Finally, the people claiming a miracle through the intercession of the saint candidate would have to be investigated. These miracles are not only looked upon by the advocate, but also by medical doctors, psychologists, and clergy. So, there aren't really opposing sides any more, but truth remains the object of all the investigation.

When the pope declares a person to be a saint in a solemn canonization ceremony, he does so infallibly. Papal infallibility is that gift from the Holy Spirit that preserves the pope from error in matters of faith and morals. This is why the investigation process for a candidate for sainthood is such a lengthy and thorough one; there can be no room for doubts. Though "Devil's Advocate" is an archaic term, its function is still very important and used in official canonical processes.

Question 254. Who can become a cardinal, and what do cardinals do?

Cardinals are not a part of the three-fold sacramental character of Holy Orders. In the Sacrament of Ordination, a man is ordained to the deaconate, presbyterate, and episcopate—in other words deacon, priest, or bishop. The term cardinal is an honorary one conferred by the pope, usually to a bishop.

The word cardinal comes from the Latin word *cardo*, which means hinge. Cardinals under the age of eighty years have the great privilege of electing a pope. (See Question 238 on conclaves). Together, the cardinals form a group known as the College of Cardinals or Sacred College, which is an important advisory board to the pope; they have the privileged confidence of the pope. It is in this sense that they are the hinge for the pope to govern the church.

Cardinals have worn red since the time of Pope Innocent IV in 1245. The red symbolizes that they are ready to lay down their life for Christ and His Gospel. They are referred to as Princes of the Church because of their ecclesiastical equivalency to a prince in a secular kingdom. Cardinals can be heads of important archdioceses throughout the world. They are the people in command of important offices in the church, such as congregations and dicasteries. A cardinal may even be the Primate of a country, the archbishop who has authority over a national territory rather than just his own diocese or province. Usually, it is because the Primate's diocese was the first one to be founded in that country, hence it is called the Primatial See (another word for diocese). The Primate may also convoke and preside over national councils.

Most cardinals are also ordained bishops. There are a few that are only priests. Canonically speaking, laymen can also be given the title of cardinal by the pope. There are three levels of cardinals. These levels, however, do not coincide with their ordination, although they use the same names. There are terms like cardinal bishop, cardinal priest, and cardinal deacon, even though they are all ordained to the episcopacy. These are honor levels of distinction, much akin to monsignors. Prothonotary apostolic is the highest monsignor, domestic prelate, the middle, and papal chamberlain is the lowest.

Question 255. What is the Curia?

This is a shared term for the institutions, offices, bodies, and individuals who assist a person in charge in the pastoral and managerial governance. There are two levels, Diocesan and Roman. The diocesan curia is often called the chancery or pastoral offices. Included in these offices are the vicar general, the chancellor, the judicial vicar, and heads of various departments. The curia also contains the archives and finance council.

We read in Canon 469: "The diocesan curia is composed of those institutes and persons who assist the bishop in governing the entire diocese, especially in directing pastoral actions, in providing for the administration of the diocese, and in exercising judicial power." The curia is the principal instrument at the disposal of the bishop for the governance of the diocese. It has the responsibility of permanent watchfulness in matters concerning the diocese.

Every administrative activity in the church has an apostolic content which must receive some juridical framework at the governing level. In other words, so that the diocese can function smoothly, there has to be organization. The church is an institution, like the government, and so it has run accordingly, ensuring that the church will not be hampered in delivering the message of the Gospel and serving the people of Christ. The appointment to the curia is done by the diocesan bishop. All who are admitted to a curial position must promise to fulfill their office faithfully, as determined by Canon Law or the bishop.

At the universal Church level there is a Roman Curia. It functions much like a diocesan curia. This body assists the pope in the governance of the universal Church. There are ten congregations that belong to the Roman Curia: Congregation for Bishops, Congregation for Catholic Education, Congregation for Divine Worship, Congregation for Oriental Churches, Congregation for Religious and Secular Institutes, Congregation for the Causes of Saints, Congregation for the Clergy, Congregation for the Discipline of the Sacraments, Congregation for the Doctrine of the Faith, and Congregation for the Evangelization of People.

Included in the Roman Curia are other agencies, such as the Apostolic Camera, the Prefecture for Economic Affairs of the Holy See, the Administration of the Patrimony of the Holy See, the Prefecture of the Papal Household, and the General Statistics Office of the Church.

Question 256. Where and what are the catacombs?

The term "catacombs" refers to subterranean burial grounds. They can be found almost anywhere; however, the most famous catacombs are located in Rome. They date back to the early Church. Most of the catacombs of Rome are technically located outside the walls of the city on Via Appia Antica, a major road that leads from Rome to the south of Italy. Burial grounds for Christians are an important theological point. First, pagan Romans didn't believe in the afterlife like Christians did. Therefore, when pagans died, they would be cremated, and their remains could be used as amulets, or scattered wherever they wished. Christians definitely believe in the afterlife. The whole idea of suffering and persevering in this Valley of Tears called Earth is possible, because Jesus rose and ascended and prepares a place for us.

In vast contrast to pagans, Christians have great respect for the body. The body, by Baptism, is a temple of the Holy Spirit and therefore even in death the body must be treated with respect. Second, Christians believe in the resurrection of the body. So the earthly remains are buried in anticipation that at the end of the world the body will rise from the dead and be reunited with the soul. Burial grounds became important places for Christians. During the Roman persecution, catacombs were used because they were not in the sight of the enemy. There are many tunnels, and a person could easily escape the threatening hand of the law. Catacombs also became early worship sites. On tombs of martyrs or saints, the Holy Sacrifice of the Mass would often be celebrated. This was done out of respect for the sainted person and also to be close to the saint in order to obtain the same graces of perseverance.

Of the many catacombs in Rome only five are open for tours, and only certain tunnels are open to the public. Most of the tunnels were pillaged and are now empty because of the Barbarian invasions during the fifth century, when the pillagers looked for money and valuables. On the Via Appia, one can visit the catacombs of Domitilla, Saint Sebastian, Callistus, and Saint Agnes. Priscilla is located in the north of Rome and was a part of Villa owned by Priscilla, a wealthy convert to Catholicism. The art of the catacombs is the earliest form of Christian art; the catacomb of Priscilla contains the earliest artistic rendering of Christ. He is pictured as a shepherd carrying a sheep over his back. Catacombs also display many Christian symbols used so that the pagans could not understand—symbols like the Chyro, Alpha and Omega, and dove with a fern.

Question 257. Who are the Swiss Guards and what do they do?

In 1505, Pope Julius II established the Swiss Guards, a distinct body of guards for the pope. Their recruitment is based on the centuries-long agreement between the Holy See and the Catholic civil authorities of Switzerland. They are the official "police" of Vatican City as well as body guards for the pope. Their red, yellow, and blue uniforms were designed by Michelangelo in the sixteenth century and are still used today. The uniform is in the colors of the Medici family, which gave the Church many popes during the Renaissance. They also wear other uniforms and street clothes, and they carry forms of protection more fitting in today's society; nevertheless, anyone visiting Rome will usually encounter the Michelangelo-style guards. They are at every event at which the Pope is present, and they are also stationed throughout the Vatican City which is a separate country from Rome. Since the attempt on Pope John Paul II's life in 1981, Swiss Guards' training has changed to include all aspects of modern protection and security. The guardsmen have completed rugged training in karate, self-defense, judo, and the use of firearms and heavy assault weaponry.

There are 110 guards, plus six officers, and their main responsibility is guarding the apostolic palaces. These soldiers are veterans of the Swiss military and are diplomatic enough to handle all sorts of visitors from cardinals, bishops, and priests, to presidents, kings, and prime ministers. The most famous historical event involving the Swiss Guards was their defense of Pope Clement VII during the sack of Rome in 1527. One hundred and forty-seven Swiss Guards were killed and only forty-two reached safety with the Pope in Castel Sant'Angelo. This castle is located not too far from the Vatican on the Tiber River and is connected to Saint Peters by way of a tunnel. During political upheavals this has proven a successful escape route used by the popes.

The structure of the guards has been modified over the years. Presently, there are seven ranks within the guards. The senior officer holds the rank of colonel. Guardsmen of the lowest ranks are called halberdiers and are not permitted to marry until they reach the rank of corporal. Applicants must also be at least five feet, nine inches in height and have letters of recommendation from past members of the Guard, now returned to Switzerland, a priest, local police and government officials and employers. Papal service is worn as a badge of family honor, and can substitute for compulsory Swiss military service.

Question 258. What are the Stations or Way of the Cross and where did they come from?

Stations of the Cross (also called the *Via Crucis*, Latin for Way of the Cross) are fourteen beautiful meditations about our Lord's journey toward Calvary, which took place on the Jerusalem road called the *Via Dolorosa* (Latin for Way of Sorrow). It winds its way through the markets, businesses, and homes of the city. The stations that form the Way of the Cross mark the various points of Our Lord's Passion. The Stations of the Cross can be biblically traced, though they may not be in chronological order. Also, references are taken from the Old Testament as they prefigure our Lord's Passion. This path taken by Jesus on Good Friday, the day he was crucified and died, is memorialized in many Western Catholic Churches since the time of Saint Francis of Assisi (thirteenth century AD), who is credited with bringing this devotion from the Holy Land to Europe. Normally, seven stations are on one wall of the church and the other seven on the opposite wall. Some shrines have an outdoor Way of the Cross as well as the fourteen stations on the inside walls of the church, chapel, or oratory.

1. Jesus is condemned to death. Luke 23:24–25, *"So Pilate gave sentence that their demand should be granted. He released the man who had been thrown into prison for insurrection and murder, whom they asked for; but Jesus he delivered up to their will."*
2. Jesus takes up His cross. Luke 9:23, *"And He said to all, 'If any man would come after me, let him deny himself and take up his cross daily and follow me.'"*
3. Jesus falls the first time. Isaiah 53:6, *"All we like sheep have gone astray; we have turned every one to his own way; and the Lord has laid on him the iniquity of us all."*
4. Jesus meets His sorrowful mother. John 19:25, *"So the soldiers did this. But standing by the cross of Jesus were His mother, and His mother's sister, Mary the wife of Clopas, and Mary Magdalene."*
5. Simon of Cyrene helps carry the cross. Matthew 27:32, *"As they went out, they came upon a man of Cyrene, Simon by name; this man they compelled to carry his cross."*
6. Veronica wipes the face of Jesus. John 14:9, *"He who has seen me has seen the Father."*
7. Jesus falls a second time. Matthew 11:28, *"Come to me all you who labor and are heavy laden and I will give you rest."*
8. Jesus meets the holy women of Jerusalem. Luke 23:28, *"But Jesus turning to them said, 'Daughters of Jerusalem, do not weep for me, but weep for yourselves and for your children.'"*
9. Jesus falls the third time. Luke 14:11, *"For everyone who exalts himself will be humbled, and he who humbles himself will be exalted."*
10. Jesus is stripped of His garments. John 19:23, *"When the soldiers had crucified Jesus they took His garments and made four parts, one for each soldier; also His tunic. But the tunic was without seam, woven from top to bottom."*
11. Jesus is nailed to the cross. Mark 15:24, *"And they crucified Him, and divided His garments among them, casting lots for them, to decide what each should take."*
12. Jesus dies on the cross. Mark 15:37, *"And Jesus uttered a loud cry, and breathed His last."*
13. Jesus is taken down from the cross. Luke 23:53, *"Then he took it down and*

wrapped it in a linen shroud, and laid him in a rock-hewn tomb, where no one had ever yet been laid."

14. Jesus is placed in the tomb. Matthew 27:60, "And laid it in his own new tomb, which he had hewn in the rock; and he rolled a great stone to the door of the tomb, and departed."

Question 259. What are nuns? Do they live in nunneries? How are they different from other religious women?

The word nun is a technical term for a cloister religious who live in a monastery. (In Shakespeare's *Hamlet,* Act III Scene 1, Hamlet tells Ophelia, "Get thee to a nunnery." The word "nunnery" is an archaic English term for convent or monastery where nuns lived.) Technically, "nun" refers to religious women who take solemn vows, live in a stable manner, and observe the evangelical counsels of poverty, chastity, and obedience. They wear a distinct habit to designate their particular community. Most nuns are cloistered, that is, secluded from the secular world. Anyone visiting a monastery of nuns must speak to the sisters behind the grate or through a turn. A turn is a way of transporting material and messages from the outside to the monastery. The chapel of a monastery is also separated. Behind the grate you can find the women religious; in front of it is the sanctuary where Mass is celebrated and then the congregation. You address a nun as "sister."

Unlike nuns, sisters are women religious who can work among the people and therefore are called active sisters as opposed to contemplative. Some sisters belong to religious orders. Orders were founded before the fourteenth century, and the women in them are in solemn vows that only the pope could dispense. Women religious founded after the fourteenth century are referred to as communities, congregations, or institutes. Women in these religious establishments are not in solemn vows; rather, they take promises. Promises are usually renewed yearly and therefore could be easily dispensed by the superior of the community or the bishop. These women are addressed as sister, and many communities wear distinct habits to signify their specific religious congregation. However, after the Second Vatican Council when women religious were asked to update their specific habits, many dropped them altogether in favor of street clothes. These communities also have distinct apostolates, which are spiritual missions such as helping the poor, caring for the sick, teaching the youth, praying for others, etc.

Question 260. Who are monks and friars?

Just as nuns live in a monastery and live a monastic life, so, too, do monks live in their own monasteries (no coed monasteries) and live a monastic life. Monastic life in the West is based on the style established by Saint Benedict (480–547 AD) in which the emphasis is on *ora et labora* (Latin for "prayer and work"). Monastic life is structured on dividing the day between hours of prayer and hours of work. Monks live in "cells" and take a vow of stability in addition to the vows of poverty, chastity, and obedience. That simply means that the monk is attached to community and that physical place (the monastery) until death.

Technically, friars belong to the mendicant orders which were founded in the thirteenth century. Mendicant orders were not cloistered communities as above; rather, they worked among the people, but lived in strict community and took solemn vows. Two examples of such orders are Franciscans and Dominicans. Saint Francis founded his order in response to an apparition of the Lord in which He instructed him to, "Rebuild My Church." Francis then founded a little band of men that did just that. They brought religion from the monasteries to the people. They traveled from town to town, preaching, teaching, and dispensing the sacraments. Friars would beg for their daily food and pretty much lived hand-to-mouth. Dominicans were founded by Saint Dominic in the thirteenth century. They were formed to preach against certain false teachings (heresies) being disseminated. Dominicans would conduct spiritual missions, retreats, and seminars, and travel from town to town, teaching. They lived a strict community life with vows. In the present day, Franciscans and Dominicans continue to live together in friaries and priories. However, they also staff important colleges and universities throughout the world. They were among the first religious to come to the New World to open institutions of high learning and also to convert Native Americans to Catholicism.

There are also monasteries in which men live a cloister life. Many have their roots in the first type of Western Monastic life, the Benedictines. In the sixth century, Saint Benedict established his rule for monastic living, prayer, study, and work. Presently, Benedictines live in community but are not considered cloistered. Most have external apostolates, such as running schools. Trappists and Cistercians live a more secluded life. They are considered contemplative.

During the Counter Reformation, many new religious communities of men were established, each responding to a specific need or to a charism of its founder. Saint Ignatius founded the Jesuits. Jesuits were considered to be the most successful missionary community in the world and won many souls back to Catholicism in areas where Protestantism had a stronghold. Like the Dominicans, they established centers for higher learning and were some of the best educators in the Catholic Church. Saint John Bosco founded the Salesians in the nineteenth century to help educate poor boys.

Question 261. What does Creed mean?

Creed is a Latin word which means "I believe." The Creed is sort of the mission statement of the Church; it is a formulation of beliefs that are written down, prayed, studied and read, although by no means is it an exhaustive statement of belief. The chief tenets are written down in the Creed. The Creed is based on the Divine Deposit of Faith. The last apostle who received public revelation about God and our plan of salvation was Saint John the Beloved Disciple. When he died, the era of public revelation came to an end. The chief teachings of Christ and the apostles form Sacred Tradition. Out of Sacred Tradition comes the written Word (Scriptures). Sacred Scripture and Sacred Tradition are not in competition; rather, they are complimentary—think of two streams of water coming from the same fountain or source.

The Creed belongs to Sacred Tradition. Over the years it has been added to, not because of any new information, but through a further clarification of theological matters. One of the oldest creeds is the Apostles Creed, a formula of belief in twelve articles. It contains the fundamental doctrines of Christianity. This Creed is a summary of apostolic teachings that were later written down. It is interesting to note that Eastern Christians do not use the Apostles Creed in the Divine Liturgy. In the Western Church, permission has been granted to use the Apostles Creed at Sunday Masses that are centered on children.

The Nicene Creed was a product of the Council of Nicea and the Council of Constantinople of the fourth century. Again, the *doctrines* are from the time of the apostles, but were further delineated by the Council Fathers. The Nicene Creed was composed in response to a specific heresy, Arianism. Arianism denies the divinity of Jesus Christ and therefore is anti-Trinitarian. It became so widespread in the fourth century that two councils had to convene in order to combat these false teachings. At the Council of Nicea, bishops from all over the Roman Empire signed the creed, which affirmed the divinity of Christ and condemned Arianism. Since the fourth century, this Creed is the text for the Profession of Faith and is used at Sunday and Holy Day of Obligation Masses.

Athanasian Creed is one of the approved statements of truths of Faith from the fifth century. Though not written by Saint Athanasius, it articulates and mirrors his teachings. It contains a summary of the Church's teachings on the Blessed Trinity and the Incarnation of Jesus. It differs from the Apostles Creed and the Nicene Creed because it only deals with those two points.

Question 262. What is a Breviary Liturgy of the Hours, or Divine Office?

All three terms—Breviary, Liturgy of the Hours and Divine Office—mean the same thing. Basically, it is a cycle of daily prayer that is celebrated by clerics and religious, and it is part of the public liturgy of the Church, along with the celebration of the Sacraments and Benediction of the Most Blessed Sacrament. It is designed to sanctify the hours of the day. Divine Office connotes sacred duty or opus Dei, the work of God. Since the Second Vatican Council, the laity has been encouraged to pray at least parts of the Divine Office. Many parishes celebrate either Morning or Evening Prayer in Church. It has been traditional since even before the Council to solemnly pray Vespers or Evening Prayer, especially on Sunday evening.

The Catechism of the Catholic Church states in #1175, "The Liturgy of the Hours is intended to become the prayer of the whole People of God. In it Christ Himself 'continues His priestly work through His Church.' His members participate according to their own place in the Church and the circumstances of their lives: priests devoted to the pastoral ministry, because they are called to remain diligent in prayer and the service of the word; religious, by the charism of their consecrated lives; all the faithful as much as possible."

The Liturgy of the Hours is divided up into seven hours or times which are as follows: the Office of Readings, Morning Prayer, Midmorning Prayer, Midday Prayer, Daytime Prayer, Midafternoon Prayer, Evening Prayer, and Night Prayer. There are common elements to the different prayers: introduction, hymn, psalms, reading, responsory, intercessions, Lord's prayer, final prayer, and conclusion. In Morning Prayer, after the responsory, the Canticle of Zechariah is prayed. At Evening Prayer, after the responsory, the Canticle of Mary is prayed, while at Night Prayer the Canticle of Simeon is said.

The Divine Office covers the span of a year. In addition to the psalms and scripture readings it follows the liturgical seasons of the year: Advent-Christmas, Lent-Easter, and Ordinary Time. Throughout the year, saint and martyr days are observed, as well as feasts of Jesus and Mary.

The Little Office of the Blessed Virgin Mary, which was introduced by Saint Peter Damian in the eleventh century, is a shorter version of the Liturgy of the Hours that is traditionally used by many religious communities and members of sodalities.

Question 263. What is an incorruptible saint?

Incorruptibility is a phenomenon in which there is incapacity of the human body to decay. This condition is not dependent upon the manner of burial or the temperature and place of entombment. Tombs or burial chambers that are quite humid, such as the catacombs, often present instances of incorrupt bodies.

In some cases, even when the body has been exhumed and transferred to a church or shrine, the body does not decay—despite the fact that there is no embalming method or any preservation to keep the body intact. Sometimes, the clothing or the wooden casket will have decayed, but not the body. Many of the incorrupt that are saints were found lifelike, flexible, and sweetly scented, even after centuries of lying in the tomb. The Church has confirmed over one hundred men and women displaying this wonder.

Of course, this supernatural marvel is in contrast to artificial means, especially those of the Egyptians, who employed an embalming technique and raised preservation to an art level. Some of the most famous preserved human bodies are what we know as mummies. Interment in warm, dry places such as the deserts of Egypt presented the right condition for the drying process. In addition, when Egyptians performed the process of mummification, they removed all the internal organs. While impressive, these instances of preservation were clearly manmade rather than supernatural incidents.

Saint Cecilia is considered the first to have displayed this supernatural quality. It is interesting to note that incorruptibility is not a phase for sainthood, though it might point to a person's sanctity in life. Saint Cecelia was a martyr who died in 177 AD during one of the Roman persecutions. She was discovered on the floor of her home with her three fingers extended on her right hand and one finger extended on her left. This was her confession of belief in the Blessed Trinity: Three Divine Persons in One God. She was buried in the Catacomb of Saint Callistus. In 822, she was exhumed and her body was transferred to a basilica. The body was found intact and placed below an altar of the church. In 1599, when the Basilica was being restored, the tomb once again was opened, and Saint Cecilia's remains were found in the same position in which she died almost fifteen hundred years earlier.

The list of other great notable saints who have been deemed authentically incorrupt includes:

Agatha, 251
Catherine of Siena, 1380
Francis of Rome, 1440
Bernardino of Siena, 1444
Rita of Cascia, 1457
Catherine of Bolongna, 1463
Catherine of Genoa, 1510
Anthony Zaccaria, 1539
Angela Merici, 1540
John of God, 1550
Francis Xavier, 1552
Stanislaus Kostka, 1568
Theresa of Avila, 1582
Charles Borromeo, 1584
John of the Cross, 1591
Philip Neri, 1595
Mary Magdalen de Pazzi, 1607
Camillus de Lellis, 1614
Rose of Lima, 1617
Francis de Sales, 1622
Jane Frances de Chantal, 1641
Vincent de Paul, 1660
Lucy Filipppini, 1732
Rose Philippine Duchesne, 1852
John Vianney, 1859
Catherine Laboure, 1876
Bernadette Soubirous 1879

It is interesting to note that Rose Duchesne is the only American that has this gift of incorruptibility. Born in France, she was sent by her Religious Order to the United

States. She played a significant role in the development of the Louisiana territory and in the cultivation of the Church in the United States. She established many schools and convents throughout Louisiana and Missouri. She was buried in damp soil, and when she was exhumed to be placed in a chapel, she was in perfect preservation and emanated no foul smell.

Question 264. What are vigils? How can Catholics go to church on Saturday and have it count for Sunday?

Vigils can trace their roots back to Judaism, when the Sabbath is observed from sundown on Friday night to sundown on Saturday night. In the Catholic Church, after the Second Vatican Council, this observance was permitted, especially to those people who could not attend Mass on Sunday morning or on the holy day of obligation. Vigil Masses have become popular and, in many cases, have replaced Sunday attendance. This, of course, is a misunderstanding of the permission. Often people ask when they attend a Saturday afternoon wedding, if this fulfills their Sunday obligation. The answer is no.

Sunday should always take precedence. One should only attend a vigil when it is impossible to attend Mass on Sunday or the holy day. Weddings that are scheduled on Saturdays do not fit in with the other requirements for Mass to be considered a vigil. First the prayers and readings should reflect the Sunday celebration. Second, the time of a wedding is way before 4 p.m. which is considered the appropriate time to begin a vigil. At times, when wedding Masses are celebrated on Sunday, this will fulfill one's Sunday obligation. When planning weekend Mass attendance, Sunday is always the preference. It is the day of the Lord (*dies Domini* in Latin), and the Church extended this time simply so that all would have a chance to attend Holy Mass.

Question 265. What precisely are the rules of fasting and abstinence?

The Gospels speak of a period of seclusion for Jesus in the desert, during which He remained for forty days without eating. It was a time in which Jesus was preparing to embark on His public ministry. Ever since the time of our Lord, fasting and prayer retreats have been looked upon as a great way of discerning career and vocation direction. Fasting also helps to order things in one's life. By fasting, you are able to control the lower passions so that you take only what you need to live and not more.

In the Catholic tradition, fasting has always been a part of our Lenten observance. We learn from the Catechism of the Catholic Church about the fifth precept of the Church in number 2043, "You shall observe the prescribed days of fasting and abstinence. This ensures the times of ascesis (self-discipline) and penance which prepare us for the liturgical feasts; they help us acquire mastery over our instincts and freedom of heart."

The Catechism also explains in number 1438 when one should fast: "The seasons and days of penance in the course of the liturgical year (Lent, and each Friday in memory of the death of the Lord) are intense moments of the Church's penitential practice. These times are particularly appropriate for spiritual exercises, penitential liturgies, and pilgrimages as signs of penance, voluntary self-denial such as fasting and almsgiving, and fraternal sharing (charitable and missionary works).

Each year every diocese issues the common Lenten observance, which instructs the faithful about the days of fast and abstinence. The days of fast and abstinence are Ash Wednesday and Good Friday. All other Fridays of Lent are Days of Abstinence. From the evening Mass of the Lord's Supper on Holy Thursday until the celebration of the Easter Vigil on the evening of Holy Saturday, the Easter Fast should be observed so that, with uplifted and welcoming hearts, we may be ready to celebrate the joys of the Resurrection.

The ancient tradition, intimately connected with the Rites of Holy Week and the Order of Christian Initiation of Adults, is encouraged, especially in those places baptizing catechumens at the Easter Vigil.

The obligation to fast applies only to Catholics between the ages of eighteen and fifty-nine. To fast in the Catholic tradition means to limit oneself to one full meal during the day with no snacks. You are allowed two smaller meals, but only if they are small enough that were you to combine them, they would not equal or surpass the one full meal. The obligation of abstinence affects all Catholics who have reached the age of fourteen. Abstinence in the Catholic tradition means to abstain from flesh meat (beef, pork, poultry, and game—basically, the meat of any warm-blooded animal) and all meat products. Fish and the flesh of all cold-blooded animals, vegetables, and fruit are allowed at any time.

The obligation of fast and abstinence, as a whole, is a serious obligation. While failure to observe any penitential day in itself may not be considered serious, the failure to observe any penitential day at all, or a substantial number of them without good cause, would be considered a grave matter. Those unable to abstain for a valid reason on any given Friday of Lent are asked to perform some other penitential act, or to abstain on another day. Pregnant or nursing mothers, diabetics, anyone needing food with their medication, and those in the military during maneuvers or while in battle, are exempt.

What if you're a vegetarian? Then abstain from one of your favorite vegetables or fruits. You can also eat something you do not like instead of abstaining from something you do like, with permission of your local pastor, should the normal abstinence be difficult or impossible.

Question 266. What does the phrase "offer it up" mean?

The Catholic Church is one big happy family. It includes Church Triumphant (the saints and angels in heaven), Church Suffering (the holy souls in purgatory), and Church Militant (the baptized faithful on earth who keep up the fight of good against evil). As a family we can help each other on our pilgrimage of faith. We do so by performing works of charity, offering up inconveniences and sufferings, praying for one another, and finally, almsgiving.

Praying for one another is not a specifically Catholic custom. All Christians perform this sacred duty. We do so informally through our personal prayers or formally during the Mass, specifically the General Intercessions. Catholics believe this prayer goes beyond the grave. The saints are alive and well in paradise. They are God's closest friends and are enjoying the Beatific Vision. The desire of the saints is for everyone to enjoy this vision. Catholics often call upon the saints to continue their prayers to God in heaven. Catholics will "offer up" their prayers on behalf of other people or for the holy souls in purgatory.

Purgatory is a temporary state. It is not a place. It will come to a close at the end of the world. When a person dies and goes to purgatory, he is guaranteed to go to heaven. The person dies as a friend of God, but is not fully prepared to meet the Lord for all eternity. The person recognizes some imperfections or attachments that must be purged before entering the Pearly Gates. While the person in Purgatory cannot do anything but wait, Church Triumphant and Church Militant can.

On Earth, Masses are regularly celebrated for the departed loved ones, so that the Precious Blood of Jesus at the Holy Sacrifice may be applied to a soul in purgatory. In addition, Catholics may "offer up" their inconveniences or sufferings in order to release a soul to heaven. Any good work that we do is added to the Treasury of Merit won for us by our Blessed Savior on the wood of the cross. We can tap into this treasury and give it to someone in need by performing a penance or work of charity. The next time you miss your bus, are stuck in traffic, or are late for an appointment, don't blow your top—"offer it up" for a holy soul in purgatory.

Question 267. What is a stigmata?

Stigmata is a supernatural occurrence in which a person bears all or some of the wounds of Christ in his own body. It includes areas of the feet, hands, side, and forehead. The wounds appear suddenly and from no external force, like a sharp object. Blood may flow periodically from the wounds. No one is required to believe in stigmata, yet it remains a special sign of a unique relationship with Jesus' passion. There are over 320 cases of stigmatists, and out of this number, sixty have been canonized.

Saint Francis of Assisi is the first and best-known person who spiritually endured the five wounds of Christ. During prayer in 1224, an angel offered him an image of Jesus, crucified, and imprinted upon him the sacred stigmata. Blood regularly flowed from his wounds until his death. When the Church researches to see if an instance of stigmata is authentic, one of the signs is humility. If the person who has the wounds tries to conceal them so that it is not central to his piety, this is one of the signs of authenticity. Saint Francis never boasted about the spiritual phenomena. Other proofs of authenticity include blood flowing from the wounds not from sweat or from hysteria; blood and the pain of the wounds more prevalent on the days or seasons associated with Jesus' passion, like Good Friday; the wounds do not get infected; and the wounds do not need any medical treatment.

Saint Rita of Cassia is another great example. She was a married woman who became a widow and lost her sons to illness. She had always wanted to be a nun. She prayed constantly about it, but no convent would take her. Finally, during the middle of the night, she found herself in the middle of an Augustinian convent in Cassia. When the sisters woke the next morning and saw her, they accepted her presence as a sign from God, and she was allowed to take her vows. Shortly after final vows, she received the wound of the crown of thorns. It bled constantly. Because of its hideousness, Rita was consigned to her room. At that time, the pope called for a Holy Year of Jubilation. Pilgrims traveled to Rome to pray at the basilicas and holy sites. Saint Rita was granted permission to lead the pilgrimage; for that short time the wound ceased. Only when she returned to the convent did the wound reappear.

Saint Pio of Pietralcina is a present-day stigmatist. He died in 1968 and suffered from the five wounds of Christ for forty years. Every time he celebrated Mass, the wounds bled more profusely. In order not to cause attention to himself, he wore gloves.

Question 268. Are angels real?

Angels are heavenly creatures; they are spirits without earthly bodies. There are three levels of angels; in descending order, they are:

1. seraphim, cherubim, and thrones
2. dominations, virtues, powers
3. principalities, archangels, and angels

A reference to seraphim can be found in Isaiah 6:2: "Above him stood the seraphim; each had six wings; with two he covered his face, and with two he covered his feet, and with two he flew." Cherubim are referenced in Genesis 3:24: "He drove out the man; and at the east of the Garden of Eden he placed the cherubim, and flaming sword which turned every way, to guard the way to the tree of life." Thrones are mentioned in Psalm 9:4: "For thou hast maintained my just cause; thou hast sat on the throne giving righteous judgment." Archangels are mentioned in 1 Thessalonians 4:16: "For the Lord himself will descend from heaven with a cry of command, with the archangel's call, and with the sound of the trumpet." The other choirs of angels do not have biblical references; rather, they are mentioned in apocryphal sources or from the Talmud (scriptural commentaries from Jewish rabbis and scholars).

Each angel's name means something. Michael's name means "Who is like God." Raphael's name means "God has healed." Gabriel's name means "the power of God."

Three named Archangels appear in the Sacred Scriptures. Saint Michael is referenced in Daniel 10:13: "The prince of the kingdom of Persia withstood me twenty-one days; but Michael, one of the chief princes came to help me, so I left him there with the prince of the kingdom of Persia." We hear about Saint Gabriel in Luke 1:19: "And the angel answered him, 'I am Gabriel who stands in the presence of God; and I was sent to speak to you and to bring you good news.'" Saint Raphael emerges in Tobit 12:15: "I am Raphael, one of the seven holy angels who present the prayers of the saints and enter into the presence of the glory of the Holy One." (Tobit is one of the seven deuterocanonical books in the Catholic Bible.)

The primary ministry of angels is to give greater honor and glory to God their Creator. The lower choirs also serve in a second ministry. The Catechism of the Council of Trent states in Section IV paragraph 9, "By God's providence angels have been entrusted with the office of guarding the human race and of accompanying every human being in order to preserve him from any serious dangers...our heavenly

Father has placed over each of us an angel under whose protection and vigilance we may be enabled to escape the snares secretly prepared by our enemy, repel the dreadful attacks he makes on us, and under his guiding hand keep to the right road, and thus be secure against all false steps which the wiles of the evil one might cause us to make in order to draw us aside from the path that leads to heaven."

Question 269. Why do Catholics put ashes on their foreheads in Lent, and can anyone else get them?

Ashes for the services of Ash Wednesday are made from burnt palms from the previous Palm Sunday. They are blessed at a Mass on Ash Wednesday and then placed on the forehead of the Catholic attending the service. It is a sacramental, which means it is in close relationship with the Sacraments, but not an actual Sacrament. A sacramental, like a rosary or a blest candle, will remind the Catholic of the presence of God. Ashes remind the Catholic that it is the beginning of Lent. Lent is the season of preparation for the Solemnity of Easter, the Lord's resurrection.

During the season of Lent, Catholics try to get back to the basics and remove the mask they have put up all year that actually takes one away from God and the road to heaven. This is achieved by more fervent prayer, attending a parish mission or novena, frequenting the Sacrament of Penance, doing works of the charity, fasting, and almsgiving. The day before, known in Latin countries as Fat Tuesday (Mardi Gras in New Orleans), there are often celebrations in which people traditionally dress in costume and do not reveal themselves until the stroke of midnight, the beginning of Lent. Again, the theme is that the masks put up a false front from God and neighbor, and Lent is a reminder of one's mortality.

The prayer that is used when putting the ashes on the forehead is, "Remember man thou are dust and unto dust thou shall return." The imposition of ashes, the starkness of the Liturgy, the penitential theme, all relay the theological fact that we are mortals who will die someday and who have an accountability before God for our actions. Ashes remind us that materialism is a passing fancy and will not last forever, so we should concentrate on the eternal things of the spirit and heaven. In the early Church and Middle Ages, there was a formal order of penitence in which the members wore sack cloth and ashes to note their discipline. Ash Wednesday is a reminder of discipline.

In the Book of Genesis 3:19 we read, "In the sweat of your face you shall eat bread till you return to the ground for out of it you were taken; you are dust, and to dust you shall return." This was the punishment for the disobedience of our first parents, Adam and Eve. These words were also commonly used in old English burial services to imply that we were created out of nothing and would return to nothing. This is not to say that our souls don't live on; rather, it reminds us that the world and all of its allurement passes, and we should never forget it.

Question 270. What are Laetare and Gaudete Sundays?

Laetare and *Gaudete* are from the Latin language. *Gaudete* (from the Latin for "rejoice") is celebrated on the Third Sunday of Advent. It is a special day because the preparation for the Solemnity of Christmas is half over. On this day, the vestments, altar cloth, and tabernacle veil are rose-colored instead of the penitential purple. The word *Gaudete* can be found in Philippians 4:4–5, "Rejoice in the Lord always; again I will say, Rejoice. Let all men know your forbearance. The Lord is at hand." This forms the Entrance Antiphon of the Mass.

Laetare Sunday is celebrated on the Fourth Sunday of Lent. It signals that Lent is half over and the Solemnity of Easter will soon arrive, encouraging believers not to lose heart or give up their Lenten commitments. Rose-colored vestments, altar cloths, and tabernacle veil may be employed and flowers can adorn the altar. During Lent, flowers are forbidden in the Sanctuary until Easter except for *Laetare* Sunday. The second reading for the Fourth Sunday of Lent cycle "C" which is from Philippians 4:4–7 is the basis for *Laetare*, which reads "*Laetare Domine semper*" (Rejoice in the Lord always): "Have no anxiety about anything, but in everything by prayer and supplication with thanksgiving let your requests be made known to God. And the peace of God which passes all understanding will keep your hearts and your minds in Christ Jesus."

Question 271. What are ember days and rogation days?

These two liturgical terms belong to the Celebration of Mass before 1969, called the Tridentine Mass or Mass of Saint Pius V. It was revised in minor ways from the Council of Trent (1545–1563) which promulgated this Mass until Pope John XXIII (1958–1963). Pope Paul VI (1963–1978) promulgated the New Mass, which replaced the Tridentine Rite. However, Pope John Paul II commenced permission for this Mass to be celebrated once again throughout the world according to the local ordinary.

The classification of Liturgical Days according to the Tridentine Rite has many different levels of celebration. A Liturgical Day is one which is sanctified by liturgical services: The Holy Sacrifice of the Mass and the Public Prayer of the church, such as the Divine Office. The different kinds of Liturgical Days are as follows.

Sunday: The first day of the week and the most important, liturgically. The yearly cycle of Sundays renews the Life of Christ in all His Mysteries.

Feria: Any day of the week except Sunday. Some ferias possess a special Mass (during Lent and Passion Time); others are assigned the Mass of the preceding Sunday, as indicated in the Missal.

Feasts: A day honoring in a special way the Mysteries of the Lord, the Blessed Mother, the Angels, the Saints, or the Blessed.

Octave: The celebration of the greatest feasts for eight continuous days. Each of these is given a rank, according to its importance: first class, second class, third class, fourth class, or commemoration. This last designation refers to some feasts which do not receive a full liturgical celebration in the Missal and Divine Office, but are treated as feasts being commemorated.

The Missal of 1962, the Tridentine Rite, uses the term Mass of the Seasons; on ferias (liturgical term for any weekday or Saturday) of all classes, the appropriate rubric is given indicating the different Masses that may be said on such days. Ferias of the first class are Ash Wednesday and Days of Holy Week; second class are those from December 17 to 23 and Ember Days of Advent, Lent and September; third class are those from Thursday after Ash Wednesday to Saturday before Palm Sunday, and from the beginning of Advent to December 16. All other weekdays not enumerated above are fourth class.

Ember Days are Wednesdays, Fridays, and Saturdays of four weeks of the year on which fast and abstinence are required. Ember Days occur in Ember Weeks—the week between the third and fourth Sundays of Advent, the week between the first and second Sundays of Lent, the week between Pentecost and Trinity Sunday, and the calendar week after Exaltation of the Holy Cross (September 14). In the Roman tradition Ember Days were associated with farming concerns and included sowing and harvesting festivals. Since 1969 and the New Mass of Pope Paul VI, Ember Days have been replaced with votive Masses for various needs and occasions, and they are not set in the Liturgical Calendar.

Rogation Days are special days of penitential prayer and include Ember Days. In the early church there were two sets of rogation days. The first was commemorated on April 25, the feast of Saint Mark, and the second on the Monday, Tuesday, and Wednesday before Ascension Thursday. Specific rogation days were replaced in the

New Missal of 1969 by periods of prayer for the needs of people of God. The National Conference of Bishops or the local bishop can decide on its usage.

Traditionally Rogation Days commenced in 470 AD when Saint Mamertus, bishop of Vienne in France, introduced processions and the public recitation of the Litanies after the calamities that had afflicted that country. In the time of Pope Leo III in 816 AD, these so-called rogations came to be observed in Rome and were given the name of "Lesser Litanies" to distinguish them from the "Greater Litanies" which had been previously established in Rome by Pope Saint Gregory the Great in 598 AD, for April 25 Feast of Saint Mark. These rogations are earnest prayers to ward off calamities and obtain God's blessings upon crops.

Question 272. What are pilgrimages and why do people go on them?

A pilgrimage, quite simply, is starting in one place and ending in another place for spiritual reasons. Pilgrimages are as old as the Church; Saint James of Compostella in northwest Spain is the oldest continuous destination for a pilgrimage. It is believed that in the Basilica of Saint James the relics of the apostle James are interred and venerated. There are famous routes that go through Spain and France and even to Italy that lead to this site. Today, modern pilgrims trace the roots of their forefathers by walking, biking, or driving these routes. Walking is the most traditional and penitential of methods. All along the pilgrim route are hostels for pilgrims, as well as places to eat and to refresh. At the end of the pilgrimage is the shrine itself. Upon completion of the spiritual act, a plenary indulgence may be received.

Other famous pilgrim destinations are the Four Major Basilicas—Saint Peter, Saint Mary Major, Saint John Lateran, and Saint Paul—outside the Wall in Rome. In addition, a pilgrim may also visit the catacombs and the Chapel of the Holy Stairs. Usually a Catholic would make this pilgrimage during the observance of the Holy Year. Every twenty-five years, the pope proclaims a Holy Year of Grace. With special spiritual practices and prayers, a pilgrim may receive a plenary indulgence. During the Holy Year, when in Rome a pilgrim should go to Saint Peter and enter through the Holy Doors. These doors are open only for the Holy Year and then sealed up by the Pontiff. Special prayers are said as you enter the basilica through these Holy Doors. The next Holy Year will be observed in 2025.

Another famous pilgrim destination is Lourdes, France. It is a site where the Blessed Mother appeared to Saint Bernadette in 1858. Many miraculous cures are made by God at this holy place. Fatima, Portugal is where Mary appeared to three little peasant children in 1917. Every year, the Basilica of Our Lady of Guadalupe in Mexico City is the site of the largest number of pilgrims to visit a Catholic shrine anywhere on earth. This church is where the *tilma* of Saint Juan Diego resides; this peasant cape has an image of Our Lady of Guadalupe (from 1531) miraculously emblazoned on it, without any dye, paint, or human origin. Our Lady of Czestochowa, Krakow, Poland and Our Lady of Knock, Ireland, are just a few of the numerous shrines in the world worth visiting. Finally, the Holy Land (Bethlehem, Jerusalem, Nazareth, Galilee) has been a pilgrim's destination since the early Church. It contains the most sacred places in which our Lord conducted His public ministry.

The Basilica of the National Shrine of the Immaculate Conception in Washington, DC, is also a place of frequent pilgrimage. Located next to Catholic University of America and just a half a block from the Pope John Paul II Cultural Center, the National Shrine is worth a visit by every Catholic in the USA. Each year, the night before the National March for Life, the basilica is filled to capacity with bishops, priests, deacons, nuns, and plenty of laity of all ages, including a huge contingency of youth from across the country. This rally takes place every year on the anniversary of the Supreme Court decision Roe v. Wade in 1973, which legalized abortion. The Basilica of the National Shrine becomes the epicenter of prayer to energize and invigorate the marchers for the next day to have a peaceful, prayerful, and nonviolent protest march to the steps of the Supreme Court.

Another shrine in America worth visiting is the Shrine of the Most Blessed Sacrament in Hanceville, Alabama. It is the place where Mother Angelica and the Poor Clare nuns live in monastic life after moving from their original cramped quarters in Irondale, AL, location of the headquarters of Eternal Word Television Network (EWTN). Sixty miles from the television studios and enormous satellite dishes, the Shrine in Hanceville is almost a replica of any Franciscan shrine found in Italy. An eight-foot monstrance contains the Blessed Sacrament where the sisters, brothers, and laity pray daily.

The Divine Mercy Shrine in Stockbridge, MA; Our Lady of the Snows in Belleville, IL; the Blue Army Shrine in Washington, NJ; National Shrine of Blessed Junipero Serra in Carmel, CA; and the Mother Cabrini Shrine in Golden, CO, are just some of the 135 shrines in the United States where pilgrims often visit.

In every country and every diocese there are usually pilgrimage destinations and holy places known as shrines. These places can be easily accessed and relatively inexpensive to get to; they are highly spiritual centers that should be used by every Catholic.

Question 273. What are bilocation and levitation?

Bilocation is a spiritual occurrence in which a person is in one place at a given time and, at the same moment by a mysterious presence, is in another place a distance away where impartial witnesses hear him speak and see him move in a normal fashion. It is a mystical gift to assist him in serving another person, usually when someone is dying.

Some of the famous saints who have bilocated are:
Saint Alphonse De Liguori, 1787
Saint Gerard Majella, 1755
Saint Paul of the Cross, 1775
Saint Joseph of Cupertino, 1663
Saint Martin De Porres, 1639
Saint Catherine Dei Ricci, 1590
Venerable Mary of Agreda, 1665
Saint Francis of Paola, 1507
Saint Anthony of Padua, 1231
Saint Francis Xavier, 1552
Saint Vincent Pallotti, 1850
Saint John Bosco, 1888
Saint Pio of Pietralcina, 1968

Levitation is another spiritual phenomenon in which a person's body is raised in the air by supernatural means. Usually, the sainted person is experiencing an ecstasy. Ecstasy is an intense spiritual moment, and the holy person is caught up in the powerful mystical instant.

Some of the famous saints who have levitated are:
Saint Theresa of Avila, 1582
Venerable Maria Villani, 1670
Saint Bernardino Realino, 1621
Saint Gerard Majella, 1755

Saint Alphonse De Liguori, 1787
Saint Anthony Mary Claret, 1870
Saint Martin De Porres, 1645
Saint Gemma Galgani, 1903
Saint Paul of the Cross, 1775
Venerable Dominic of Jesus and Mary, 1630
Blessed Thomas of Cori, 1729
Saint Francis of Paola, 1507
Saint Agnese of Montepulciano, 1317
Saint John Joseph of the Cross, 1734
Saint Dominic, 1221
Saint Philip Neri, 1595
Saint John Vianney, 1859
Saint Ignatius of Loyola, 1556
Saint Joseph Cupertino, 1663

Other gifts that the holy person could have would be the odor of sanctity, mystical hearts, miraculous transport, mysteriously provided money, multiplication of food, miraculous protection, lights and rays of love, fire and heat of love, prophecy, invisibility, prior knowledge of the date of their death, stigmata, the gift of tongues, mystical fasts, and mystical knowledge.

Question 274. What are a diocese, archdiocese, and eparchy?

The Catholic Church is divided into different territories and sections. A definite territorial division that has been assigned its own church (that is, a local church) makes up a parish. In the parish, the baptized faithful are guided by a pastor who is charged with attending to their sacramental, spiritual, and doctrinal needs. There are two types of parishes: national and territorial. Territorial parishes are assigned by land divisions, and national parishes by ethnicity. For example, in a city there may be ten Catholic parishes. Out of the ten, five might be national. Anyone in that city can join the ethnic parish, provided they are of that ethnic makeup. Otherwise a person is assigned to a parish in the geographical area in which they live. Today the rules have relaxed a bit, and many national parishes might have different ethnic backgrounds instead of only one. Also, people may join other parishes outside their boundaries provided the pastor permits.

Together parishes make up a diocese. A diocese is also a territorial division, usually defined by counties. Pastors, priests, deacons, diocesan, and clerical religious administrators report to a bishop, who is the head of the diocese. The chancery office is command central for the diocese, and these offices contain the bishop, vicar general, judicial vicar, and all other departments. This office deals with matters pertaining to the clergy and the faithful of the diocese.

An archdiocese is basically a diocese, but of a great city and territory. Usually an archdiocese is also a metropolitan see, in which the archbishop is the "metropolitan" of a district of dioceses. (The term "metropolitan" is used for both the district and the archbishop at the head of it.) A metropolitan has certain distinctions. First, when the dioceses in his metropolitan go to Rome for their "Ad Limina" visit, the metropolitan archbishop has special honors and is the first to see the pope. Second, a metropolitan can oversee a suffragan see if there is a problem. Finally, metropolitan archbishops tend to be elevated to a cardinal. Diocese and archdiocese can have auxiliary bishops assigned to help the ordinary. An eparchy is a diocese for Eastern Catholics. It denotes an ecclesiastical province. The official head of an eparchy is an eparch who is the local ordinary bishop.

All the dioceses and archdioceses of a certain country make up an Episcopal Conference. The Episcopal Conferences sponsor the National Conference of Bishops. As a whole, they decide upon rules and regulations concerning Catholics in their conference, they can make joint statements, and when the Pope leaves matters to be decided regionally, they can act and make decisions with the final approval from the Holy See.

Episcopal Conferences from all over the world make up the Universal Church in which the pope is the head, as Vicar of Christ. The pope is also the head of state. Vatican City is a separate country from Italy. It has its own coins, stamps, police, and government. As head of state, the Pope is the sovereign and has diplomatic immunity. Like other countries, the Vatican has a diplomatic corps all over the world. The official name for an ambassador of the Holy See is an apostolic nuncio.

Question 275. Must people receive both the consecrated bread and the consecrated wine at Holy Communion?

The doctrine of concomitance states that the risen Savior is wholly present under both species (consecrated bread and consecrated wine). Catholics receive the Body, Blood, Soul, and Divinity of the glorified Lord in Holy Communion. The priest separately consecrates the wafers of (wheat) bread and then separately consecrates the chalice of (grape) wine to symbolize the separation of body and blood, so he can sacramentally reenact the sacrifice of Calvary where Jesus shed his blood and was crucified in his body. Yet, it is not dead flesh and blood which is received in Holy Communion, but the risen body and blood of Christ. What was separated in death is united in the resurrection.

Catholic dogma is that *both* the body and blood of Christ are contained in each one—the Sacred Host (consecrated bread) and the Precious Blood (consecrated wine). Hence, if someone only receives the Sacred Host, they are in reality getting both the body and the blood. Otherwise, if it was still separated, He would still be dead. Christ is risen, however, so wherever His body is there is also His blood, and vice versa. Martin Luther and other Protestant Reformers taught that the faithful had to receive both species (forms) of Holy Communion. The Council of Trent in the sixteenth century defined that only the priest had to consume both to complete the sacrifice of the sacrament. The faithful could just receive the Sacred Host and not the Chalice of Precious Blood since in either one is both of them (body and blood of Christ).

People with celiac disease or severe allergies to wheat or gluten can be given only the Precious Blood (consecrated wine), just as alcoholics can take only the Sacred Host. Neither one would be getting half of Jesus. Each one would get the fullness of the Body and Blood, Soul and Divinity of Christ. The appearances of bread and wine remain, but the substances have been miraculously changed by God (through the priest saying the exact words of Christ at the Last Supper, "This is my body" and "This is my blood").

Since the Second Vatican Council (1962–1965) and more recently since the new guidelines in the Roman Missal of 2000, the Church highly encourages Catholics to partake of both sacred species as a more complete sign value (referring to the actions of eating and drinking); however, care must be taken that no one fall into the error of thinking that they must receive both the Sacred Host *and* the Chalice of Precious Blood in order to fully receive the body and blood of Christ. Practical, pastoral, or medical concerns may prevent Holy Communion under the species of consecrated wine, in which case Rome has said that any priest is allowed to give only the host and not offer both host and chalice to all the communicants since in either element, the fullness of Christ resides.

Number 85 of the General Instruction of the Roman Missal reads, "It is most desirable that the faithful, just as the priest himself is bound to do, receive the Lord's body from host consecrated at the same Mass, and that in the instances when it is permitted, they partake of the chalice so that even by means of the signs, Communion will stand out more clearly as a participation in the sacrifice actually being celebrated."

If there are not enough Extraordinary Ministers of Holy Communion to help distribute, however, especially when there is a large crowd, then the priest and deacon (who are the ordinary ministers of Holy Communion) must only give the host. Even though colds and the flu may not be spread through the common cup, it may be wise to dispense with the chalice during such times of illness. The reason for this precaution is that no matter what medical evidence you have to the contrary, most people still think otherwise and will just avoid drinking the Precious Blood during flu season. The alcohol content alone should take care of any potential contagion, but some recent strains of more serious and possibly epidemic level infections have made a lot of people nervous about drinking from the same cup. Ironically, physicians say more germs are transmitted and caught through the hands and handshaking. Rather than having too much leftover Precious Blood (due to a very few communicants receiving from the chalice) at the end of Mass, some priests and parishes just offer it occasionally, once a month or on special feast days, rather than at every Mass. Any leftover consecrated wine must be consumed immediately and cannot be kept in the tabernacle with the consecrated hosts, nor can it be poured down the special drain in the sacristy (called the sacrarium). Discretionary practices should be employed in such times by the main celebrant. In Saint Peter's in Rome and many of the Pontifical Celebrations, due to large numbers, only the host is distributed.

Question 276. What is the difference between an apostle and a disciple?

Technically, a disciple (from the Latin *discipulus*, meaning "one who embraces the teachings of another") is one who is learning from the master. In Christianity, the term refers to any follower of Jesus' teaching. We hear in the Gospel of Matthew 10:1, "And He called to Him His twelve disciples and gave them authority over unclean spirits, to cast them out, and to heal every disease and every infirmity." By the reference to these same twelve men as "apostles" in Matthew 10:2, it is clear that an apostle (from the Greek *apostolos*, meaning "someone who is sent; a messenger") is also a special class of disciple. Some confusion may arise since the Gospels speak of the twelve both as disciples and as apostles, but also refers to seventy disciples distinct from the twelve apostles. Matthew and John were both Evangelists (Gospel Writers) and apostles (two of the twelve), but Mark and Luke, while also Evangelists, were only disciples (part of the seventy).

Apostles refer to the twelve men chosen by Jesus to be His immediate aides. Our Divine Lord instructed them during His public period of three years. After His ascension, the apostles went into the Upper Room with Mary and prayed for nine days for the coming of the Holy Spirit. After Pentecost, when the Holy Sprit descended upon them, they spoke and acted with confidence and assurance in teaching others what the Lord taught them. They became the leaders of the Church with Peter as the head of the apostles. They were ordained to the fullness of the priesthood by Jesus at the Last Supper when He said, "Do this in memory of Me." By this command, they were ordained to continue the perpetual sacrifice of Jesus, but in the liturgical way of the Mass.

Today in the Church, the direct descendants of Peter and the apostles are the pope and the bishops. This is called Apostolic Succession. There has never been a break in this line right down to the 265th pope, Benedict XVI. In Matthew 10: 2–5 we have the twelve apostles' names: "The names of the twelve apostles are these: first, Simon, who is called Peter, and Andrew his brother, James the son of Zebedee, and John his brother; Philip and Bartholomew; Thomas and Matthew the tax collector; James the son of Alphaeus, and Thaddaeus; Simon the Cananean, and Judas Iscariot, who betrayed him."

Since Judas Iscariot eventually committed suicide, there was a need to replace him. Acts 1:26 says, "And they cast lots for them, and the lot fell on Matthias; and he was enrolled with the eleven apostles. Twelve is considered a biblical number. Just as there are twelve tribes of Israel, there are also twelve apostles. The honorary title by way of analogy was given to Mary Magdalene (apostle to the apostles) insofar as she was the first one at the empty tomb on Easter Sunday; she saw the Risen Christ Who instructed her to tell Peter and the other disciples that He had risen. She had no pastoral office, however, and she was not at the Last Supper, either. Only the twelve apostles were there with Jesus.

Question 277. What are altar linens?

Altar linens are the many beautiful sacramentals centering on the Holy Sacrifice of the Mass.

The Sacred Vessels needed for Mass are:

The Chalice: A cup of precious metal (the inside must be gold or gold-plated) that holds the wine consecrated at Mass which becomes the Precious Blood.

The Paten: A small plate of precious metal that holds the Sacred Host.

The Ciborium: A large cup of precious metal, with a cover of the same material, that contains the hosts consecrated for distribution to the faithful in Holy Communion.

The Purificator: A small linen cloth used by the priest to dry his fingers and the chalice when he has washed and purified them after Communion.

The Corporal: The linen cloth spread by the priest on the altar at the beginning of Mass. The chalice, paten, and ciboria rest upon this cloth. All of these things rest upon an altar cloth. There can be many layers of altar cloths, but at least one is used. The top layer, known as the Mensa, must always be white.

A finger towel is used in the Lavabo rite, which follows the offering of the gifts of bread and wine. It symbolizes the priest's sinfulness and the importance of clerical purity at the Holy Sacrifice.

Byzantine antimension is the actual altar in the Eastern Rite Churches. It is a cloth that usually has an imprint of the dead Jesus lying in state. It contains five relics of saints in the four corners and one in the middle. It can be obtained for priests from the Byzantine Eparch. In the Western Rite, the altar is wooden, marble, or some other dignified material such as granite. In it, five relics are placed in a stone or somewhere in the altar itself. This was a requirement until 1969. With the New Mass of Pope Paul VI, relics in altars are optional.

The Pall: A small square of stiffened linen or of cardboard covered with linen, used to cover the chalice.

The Chalice Veil: A cloth covering, of the same color as the Chasuble that conceals the chalice and paten up to the offertory and after Communion.

The Burse: A flat, square container of cloth, the same color as the vestments, in which the corporal is carried to and from the altar. It is placed over the veil on top of the chalice.

Question 278. What are vestments?

The Mass vestments were originally ordinary garments of the ancient Roman world. Although the fashions of dress changed with the passing centuries, at the altar the priest continued to wear the ancient Roman costume of his predecessors. Thus, the priest, vested for Mass, is a wonderful witness to the historical continuity of the

Catholic Church with the early Church of Rome, founded by the Prince of the Apostles. In the order in which the priest puts them on, the Mass vestments are as follows. [These distinctions only apply to clergy of the Latin (Western) church. Byzantine clergy wear similar items with different names, have some additional items, and use different liturgical colors.]

Amice: A square of white linen wrapped around the neck and covering the shoulders. In the Middle Ages, the Amice was worn as a hood to protect the head in cold churches. The Amice symbolizes the "helmet of salvation," such as the virtue of hope that helps the priest to overcome the attacks of Satan. It is usually worn over the cassock (priest's gown) or over his clerical attire.

Alb: A long, white linen garment reaching to the feet. The Alb symbolizes the innocence and purity that should adorn the soul of the priest who ascends the altar. It is worn over the amice unless the alb completely covers the neck and obscures the Roman Collar. Deacons and Priests wear albs.

Cincture: The cord used as a belt to gird the Alb. It symbolizes the virtues of chastity and celibacy required of the priest. The cincture is normally white but is also available in the matching liturgical color of the day to accompany the stole and chasuble.

Stole: Roman magistrates wore long scarves when engaged in their official duties, just as our judges wear court gowns. Whenever a priest celebrates Mass or administers the Sacraments, he wears the stole as a sign that he is occupied with an official priestly duty. When placing the stole about his neck, in vesting for Mass, the priest begs God to give him on the last day the "garment of immortality" that was forfeited by our sinful first parents. It is worn around the neck with the two sides hanging in front of the priest's chest—one on the left and one on the right. Before Vatican II, the Tridentine Mass required the priest to crisscross his stole over his chest, and only a bishop could wear the stole hanging straight. With the Novus Ordo (Vatican II Mass of Pope Paul VI), that requirement no longer applies. Deacons wear the stole diagonally with the top on their left shoulder going down to the waist on their right side.

Chasuble: The outer vestment put on over the others. Originally, this was a very full garment, shaped like a bell and reaching almost to the feet all the way around. Now, they come in several lengths and styles depending on taste and tradition. The Chasuble symbolizes the virtue of charity, and the yoke of unselfish service for the Lord, which the priest assumes at ordination.

Dalmatic: A sleeved outer tunic that came to Rome from Dalmatia, hence the name. It looks like a chasuble but with sleeves. It is worn by the deacon during Mass.

It symbolizes the joy and happiness that are the fruit of dedication to God.

Vestments come in liturgical colors according the season of the Church. (See also Question 279.) They are:

White: The symbol of innocence and triumph. It is used on all feasts of the joyful and glorious mysteries of our Lord's life, such as Christmas and Easter, on the feasts of our Blessed Mother, and on the feasts of angels and saints who were not martyrs. It may also be used in funeral masses.

Red: The color of blood is used on all feasts of our Lord's Cross and Passion, including Palm Sunday and on the feasts of the apostles and all martyrs. Red is also used on Pentecost and in Masses of the Holy Spirit, in memory of the tongues of fire of the First Pentecost.

Purple or Violet: A symbol of penance and reparation. It is used during the penitential seasons of Advent and Lent and at the celebration of the Sacrament of Penance. It may also be used at funeral masses and All Souls Day observances.

Green: The color of budding and living vegetation is the symbol of hope. It is used during seasons outside of Advent-Christmas and Lent-Easter, in what is known as ordinary time.

Rose: This color is permitted in place of purple on the Third Sunday of Advent which is known as *Gaudete* Sunday. It is also used on the Fourth Sunday of Lent which is known as *Laetare* Sunday. The Church tempers the sadness of the penitential seasons with an invitation to rejoice in the goodness of God our Savior.

Gold: Vestments made of gold damask material are permitted in place of white and are usually worn for the Christmas Season, All Saints, Christ the King, and the Feast of the Body and Blood of Christ.

Black: The color of death and mourning. It can be used in funeral masses or commemoration of the dead and on All Souls' Day.

Question 279. What do the different colors of the vestments represent?

We praise God through the five senses. Catholic Churches have always been a feast for the eyes, from the beauty of their architecture to their statuary, paintings, icons, mosaics, frescoes, and stained glass windows. Another example of beauty would be in vestments. Vestments are the liturgical garb that deacons, priests, and bishops wear for Mass or other celebrations. Four principal colors are used in the liturgical vestments which coincide with the seasons in the Church calendar.

First is white, though gold may be used in substitution. White indicates jubilation as well as purity. Some of the feasts that use white are Christmas and Easter. White is used on Christmas because it is the birth of Jesus and the dawn of salvation. On Easter, the white represents the purity and innocence that our Risen Lord gives to our souls through the Sacraments. White is used for any commemoration of feasts of Jesus, Mary, and the Saints who are not martyrs. It is used in celebration of the Sacraments of Baptism, First Holy Communion, Holy Matrimony, and Holy Orders. White is employed in any celebrations involving the Holy Eucharist, such as benediction. In celebration of the Mass of Christian burial, white is worn along with the colors of black and purple. When using white for funerals, you are reminding the faithful of the resurrection of Jesus and our future resurrection.

The second color that is used in the liturgy is green. Green represents ordinary time, which is the liturgical season outside of Advent-Christmas and Lent-Easter. The majority of the year is ordinary, even though saints and martyrs celebrations dot the calendar. Green is the color of life. Christ gives life through the celebration of the Sacrifice of the Mass all year long.

Red is the third color and it is used for the Feast of the Holy Spirit and the Sacrament of Confirmation. Red symbolizes fire; biblically, the Holy Spirit is portrayed as tongues of fire. It is also used for the Passion of Our Lord on Palm Sunday and Good Friday when Christ, the martyr par excellence, shed His blood for the world. Finally, red is used for the commemoration of martyrs. Martyrs shed their blood for Christ; therefore red is a symbol of blood.

Purple is the final color. It is used to convey the meaning of penance and preparation. Advent and Lent are the two seasons during which purple is employed. The priest also wears purple for the Sacraments of Penance and Anointing of the Sick.

Question 280. What is a cassock? What is a biretta?

Outside the Mass there are many vestments and clerical clothing that can be worn by a priest. The cassock is a long black robe that is worn in place of a black suit. In Catholic countries, priests will wear the cassocks in the marketplace, streets, and other secular public areas. In America, the cassock is usually confined to Church property and specifically worn under vestments, or in some sort of official or liturgical duty. There are two styles to a diocesan priest's cassock. First is Roman. Roman style has thirty-three buttons going down the front of the robe signifying the age of our Lord. It may have black piping under the arms to form a holder for a sash. The piping also may outline the sleeves, the button area, and the area around the collar. Priests wear black piping and sashes; monsignors wear purple piping and sashes; bishops wear magenta piping and sashes; cardinals wear red piping and sashes; and the pope wears a white cassock, piping, and sash. These are called choir robes, and would have been worn when priests would congregate in Church for sung prayers. Monsignors who are prelates of honor, prothonotary apostolic, can wear full purple cassock with piping and sashes. Bishops also can wear full magenta cassocks with piping and sashes, and cardinals, full red cassocks with piping and sashes.

In liturgical services outside of Mass a priest wears a surplice over the cassock. This clerical attire can be made of many materials including lace, but is always white. In addition, a stole and cope are worn over the surplice for solemn services outside of Mass, such as benediction, processions, nuptials, baptisms, and burials. A cope is a long cape that matches the material of the stole. It can be in the liturgical colors of the season. However, in the ceremony of benediction, an outer garment, known as a humeral veil, is worn over the cope and must always be white. It is worn for the blessing of the Blessed Sacrament because the congregants are receiving Christ's blessing, not the priest's. At the Holy Sacrifice of the Mass, if a priest is merely preaching and not concelebrating, he may wear a cassock, surplice, and a stole in the color of the season, which signifies his clerical office.

A mozzetta is a short cape that is worn over a prelate's cassock and it is usually designed to be elbow length with a round collar. It is fastened by twelve buttons, signifying the twelve apostles. Usually the color of the mozzetta corresponds to the rank of the prelate. However, the Holy Father may wear velvet and ermine trimmed mozzetta along with a pectoral cross suspended by a cord—red with gold for cardinals and green with gold for bishops.

A biretta is a special square cap of three corners and ridges worn by clerics and is similar in usage to the academic hats (mortarboards) worn in the Middle Ages to distinguish rank. A black biretta with black pom-pom is proper for a priest; a black biretta with a purple pom-pom is for a monsignor; a black biretta with a red pom-pom is for a bishop; a red biretta with no pom-pom is for a cardinal. The pope does not wear a biretta. Four cornered birettas are worn by clerics with a doctoral degree. The zucchetto is worn under the biretta.

Question 281. What do bishops wear and why?

In addition to a cassock, rochet or surplice, mozzetta, and pectoral cross suspended from a green and gold cord, there are many other episcopal accoutrements. First, the crosier is a hook-like staff carried in procession and during the Holy Sacrifice of the Mass. It symbolizes the pastoral care of the people in his diocese. A bishop is the shepherd of the diocese, and like a shepherd who carries a staff to guide his flock, so too does a bishop ceremoniously carry a crosier to lead his flock—the people of god. The earliest known reference of usage is the seventh century. Since the Second Vatican Council, the pope has carried a crosier as a symbol that he is the Chief Shepherd of the Church. Since Pope John Paul II, the pontifical crosier is in shape of a cross.

Zucchettos are small round skullcaps worn by the clergy, specifically prelates in the Catholic Church. The color of the zucchetto corresponds to the office the cleric holds. It had practical purposes back when church buildings were often cold and damp. Clerics were tonsured in the shape of a cross at the crown of the head. When it is cold, the zucchetto warms the head nicely. Today it is used by prelates to complete the clerical attire of cassock, mozzetta, and rochet (which is a white surplice that is worn under the mozzetta along with the pectoral cross). Zucchettos are also worn under the miter when the prelate is dressed for Mass.

A miter is a hat-like object worn on top of a zucchetto on the head of a prelate. It can come in the liturgical colors of the season being celebrated or plain white. It consists of two high, pointed flaps (one in the front, one in the back) that are joined into a headband, and two pieces of material in the shape of a small stole that hangs from the back. Its origins can be traced back to the tenth century and were in full usage by all prelates by the twelfth century. Abbots, though not bishops, function like bishops in their own abbeys that they govern, and therefore have been give the permission to wear a miter. Also, the pope wore a crown known as a tiara to signify his office as Sovereign—not so much in use now; in fact, Pope Paul VI was the last to wear one at his Pontifical Coronation. The tiara has three levels suggesting the three offices of the pope: chief shepherd, sanctifier, and teacher.

A pallium is a circular band of white wool with two hanging pieces that go over the scapular bone of a metropolitan archbishop or the pope. It is decorated with six black crosses. It is worn over the vestments of these prelates at Mass. The pectoral cross is made of precious metal and is often embellished with precious or semi-precious jewels. It is worn over the neck, usually extended on a gold chain worn over the chest (hence the term pectoral) when wearing a black suit jacket or on a chord on a cassock or over Mass vestments. Pectoral crosses are worn by the pope, cardinals, archbishops and bishops, and abbots. Episcopal rings are part of the official dress of prelates including abbots and abbesses and came into usage in the seventh century. A ferraiola is a large silken cloak worn over a cassock. When clergy used to dress in cassocks and attend functions outside the church, the formal attire would often include a ferraiola. Only a prelate may wear a ferraiola made of silk corresponding to his rank. A priest may wear a black cape, but not one made of silk.

Question 282. Why did Saint Christopher get thrown out of the Church?

The Second Vatican Council brought with it a revision in the Church's liturgical calendar. To make room for local saints, some saints that were on the universal calendar, such as Christopher and Philomena, were taken off for a number of reasons; however, they were not demoted. First, one of the functions of a canonized saint is to represent a life worthy of imitation by the faithful. In the instances of Christopher and Philomena, there is not much that is known about their lives.

The relics of Saint Philomena, a third-century martyr, were only discovered in the Catacombs of Priscilla in Rome in 1805. The only thing that is know about her is the fact that she was a virgin and a martyr. This can be proven by two ancient Christian symbols that were used in the Catacombs—a fern for virginity and a vial which contained her blood, poured out for Christ.

Saint Christopher's name means "Christ-bearer" since the legend goes that one day he saw a little boy who wanted to cross the river. Christopher carried the child on his shoulders and proceeded into the water. With each step, the child got heavier and heavier, until Christopher almost collapsed. When they reached the other side of the river, the boy revealed that He was Jesus and He bore the weight of the world on His shoulders, which was why He was so heavy. Though he is believed to have lived in the third century, the lack of documentation for this is what got him bumped off the calendar (but not out of heaven). He remains the patron saint of travelers because of the story of him carrying the child Jesus across the river.

Despite the lack of concrete historical documentation, they are still proclaimed saints. Canonization processes had changed in the last few centuries and have become stricter. However, because of the gift of infallibility in proclamation of saints, they can never be demoted.

With the addition of so many new saints, it is impossible to celebrate every one of them in the Universal Church. Therefore the Church allows local saints to be celebrated in an Episcopal Conference or in the particular religious community that the saint belongs to. Pope John Paul II canonized hundreds of men and women saints, and this new liturgical axiom allows them to be celebrated locally. For a saint to be on the universal calendar, the saint must have universal drawing power, must have been a well-known and strong figure, or there must be historical precedence in celebrating this person's life universally.

The canonization process has become stricter since the Council of Trent in the sixteenth century. There are four stages:

Servant of God: formal process has been open by local ordinary
Venerable: the person has noteworthy characteristics for being considered a saint
Beatification: the person has a miracle attributed to his intercession
Canonization: the last and infallible step reserved for the pope alone

After a lengthy process involving the review of all material written by the blessed, interviewing any known survivors who were in contact with the blessed, and the validation of another miracle brought about by the saints' intercession, the pope can proclaim sainthood in a very beautiful ceremony. However, this saint may only be observed on a local calendar, even though a votive Mass in her honor can be celebrated anywhere. For example, Saint Pio of Pietralcina, Italy, is not on the American calendar, but a votive Mass is celebrated in his honor on his feast day.

Question 283. What is the difference between memorials, feasts, and solemnities?

Memorials are religious commemorations in the liturgical calendar of sainted people. They are remembered by special prayers at Mass and the Divine Office. There are two types of memorials in the present calendar—obligatory, which must be celebrated, and optional, which may be celebrated.

Feasts are special days by which the Church gives honor to God, Jesus, the angels, and saints. They are divided into solemnities and memorials which along with Sundays of the year, Advent-Christmas, Lent-Easter, and ordinary time make up the liturgical year.

Solemnities are the highest rank of feasts. They may or may not be holy days of obligation. The number of holy days of obligation (days on which Catholics are obligated to attend Mass) is determined by the Episcopal Conference. In addition, the

Conference can transfer a holy day to another date or dispense an obligation for that particular year. In the United States the holy days are the Mother of God, Ascension Thursday, Assumption of Mary, All Saints Day, Immaculate Conception, and the Nativity of Our Lord. Certain diocese or provinces (collection of dioceses in a geographical area) have decided to move the Solemnity of the Ascension of our Lord from the fortieth day after Easter to the Sunday following that fortieth day.

Question 284. What is the Roman Martyrology?

A martyrology is a collection of names of martyrs which sometimes includes a short biography or brief history of those who were martyred. Liturgical martyrologies are lists of martyrs read before praying the Divine Office and usually of the saints a particular religious order or community. The Roman Martyrology is the official collection of the martyrs of the Catholic Church. First issued in 1584 by Pope Gregory XIII and then revised by Pope Benedict XIV in 1748, it contains the accounts of the suffering and martyrdom of individual saints. The official Roman martyrology is composed from smaller lists that existed centuries before and also were parts of liturgical calendars. The most famous contribution came from the Hieronymain Martyrology of the seventh century. It contained the martyrology of the Churches of the East, the local martyrology of the Church of Rome, and a general martyrology of Africa. Historical martyrology is another resource; these sources are known for their short histories of saints. The best-known contributor is Bede of the eighth century. Another historical martyrology is *Martyrologium Hieronymianum*, alleged to have been written by Saint Jerome in the fourth century but believed to have actually been written in the sixth century.

Martyrs are as important to us now as they have been to the Church in every age. The blood of the martyrs is the seed of the future Church. In the early Church, especially in Rome, it was common for the faithful to meet on the tomb of a martyr, and a priest would offer the Holy Sacrifice of the Mass. For years, the shape of the tomb became a style of the shape of the altar in churches. Every year, the persecuted faithful in Rome would gather for Mass. This annual gathering became part of the liturgical calendar. In fact, on the universal calendar today, many Roman martyrs are still celebrated. Many of these names are included in the Roman Canon of the Mass. They include John, Stephen, Matthias, Barnabas, Ignatius, Alexander, Marcellinus, Peter, Felicitas, Perpetua, Agatha, Lucy, Agnes, Cecilia, and Anastasia. Veneration of the martyrs' relics also became popular during this time. A first-class relic is part of the bone or tissue. A second-class relic is an article of clothing or some other article used by a saint. Finally, a third-class relic is any object that has touched a first-class relic.

Martyrs are also included in the beautiful Litany of Saints, a prayer said not only in private devotions, but also during the Sacrament of Holy Orders, Baptism, Confirmation, and at the Easter Vigil. Revisions to the Roman Martyrology are reserved for the Roman Curia. Every Catholic is advised to read about the martyrs because knowing one's past can inspire one to be a better Catholic and also give encouragement in the future when facing trials and tribulations.

Question 285. What is an advent wreath? What is a Jesse tree?

Advent wreaths and Jesse trees belong to beautiful customs that have grown outside the Liturgy, but certainly add a flavor to the season.

Historically, the Advent wreath is a Lutheran custom dating back three hundred years ago. However, the custom of using wreaths and greenery dates back to Roman times. During December, the ancient Romans would decorate their homes with greenery for the Feast of the Sun God on December 25. It was a celebration of the return of the sun to the northern hemisphere. Greenery reminded the Romans of vegetation and springtime. Advent wreaths now even adorn our churches for the four weeks of Advent.

Christians, when choosing a day to celebrate the Lord's birth, chose December 25 so that they would not stick out in their society. Remember, they were being persecuted, and Christianity was an underground religion. Christians took the good from other religions and "Christianized" it. The Feast of the Sun God became the Feast of the Son of God and His birthday. Romans celebrated the return of the sun; Christians celebrated Christ who is the Light of the World. Greenery for Christians became a symbol of hope and eternity.

Advent wreaths are made of evergreens and have four candles fastened to them. The colors correspond to the colors of Advent: purple for the first two weeks, rose for the third week (Gaudete Sunday), and then purple for the final week. At home, the candles are usually lit at the evening meal when darkness is all around. The candle represents Christ who is the Light of the World. The wreath itself is an ancient Roman symbol of victory, so the Advent wreath symbolizes the ultimate victory of the Coming of the Lord.

Advent calendars, which originated in Germany, are also used during the season. Colorful scenes are painted on the outside of the calendar with little doors corresponding to the days of Advent. Each day a door is opened revealing a picture, a biblical saying, or even a little chocolate. The sayings or symbols point to the Feast of Christmas. It is customary for little children to perform a good work before they can open the door and receive their little gift.

The Jesse tree is a genealogical tree often displayed in Advent that traces the ancestry of Jesus beginning with Jesse, father of King David. It is usually located in the vestibule of the Church.

Question 286. Who are the Knights of Malta and Knights of the Holy Sepulcher?

Papal Orders are bestowed upon people who have been honored by the Holy Father for service in some way to the Church and / or to the Holy See. This is much like monarchs bestowing knighthood or other different orders, such as the Order of the Garter in England upon worthy subjects. There are quite a few honors in the Catholic Church: the Supreme Order of Christ, the Grand Cross of the Pontifical Order of Saint Gregory the Great, the Order of Christ and the Order of the Golden Spur, the Order of Pope Pius IX, the Order of Saint Sylvester, the Cross Pro-Ecclesia et Pontifice, and the Benemerenti Medal. When Catholics receive these awards from his holiness, they receive the rank of knight.

The Supreme Order of Christ is the highest order of knighthood that the Vatican bestows. This is reserved for Catholic male heads of state and sovereigns and was founded in 1318 AD by the king and queen of Portugal. The Order of the Golden Spur is the second highest honor the Holy See awards. It is awarded by the pope on Catholic and non-Catholic heads of state. The Order of Pope Pius IX is the third of the Vatican orders but the highest to have more than one class and was founded in 1847. There are five classes: Grand Collar, Knight and Dame Grand Cross, Knight and Dame Commander, Knight and Dame.

It is awarded to Catholic laymen at the request of the local ordinary, and is commonly bestowed upon diplomats appointed to the Holy See. The Order of Saint Gregory the Great was instituted in 1831 by Pope Gregory XVI. It was founded with two divisions, military and civil. It has three classes: Grand Cross, Knight and Dame Commander, and Knight and Dame. It is usually bestowed upon people (Catholics or non-Catholics) who serve the Catholic Church or society. The Equestrian Order of Pope Saint Sylvester was established by Pope Gregory XVI in 1841. It too is awarded in three classes: Grand Cross, Knight and Dame Commander, and Knight and Dame.

It is awarded to Catholic and non-Catholic laymen/women who, by their examples in business, the professions, the military, and society, have lived exemplary lives.

The Cross Pro Ecclesia is a papal award founded by Pope Leo XIII in 1888. It is bestowed upon both lay and clerical people who have given service to the Church. The Benemerenti Medal was established by Pope Pius VI in 1791 as an award for military courage in the defense of the Papal States. In 1925, it was updated and is usually given during the Holy Year celebrations or special jubilees given to persons in service to the Church civil, military, lay, and clergy.

The Order of Malta and the Order of the Holy Sepulcher are two other grand honors. Knights of Malta date back to 1070 AD during the time of the Crusades. The Order of Malta is a sovereign power and is recognized as an independent nation-state. The habit of the Order of Malta has remained the same since 1125 AD. It is distinguished by the Maltese cross. The Order of Merit of the Order of Malta is bestowed by the Prince Grand Master. It is usually bestowed to special sovereigns and heads of state. There are three classes of the Order of Merit: the special Civil Class for Gentlemen, the Military Class of Merit, and the Class of Merit for Ladies.

The Equestrian Order of the Holy Sepulcher of Jerusalem can trace its roots to the First Crusade. Unlike the Order of Malta, the Holy Sepulcher is governed by the Church. The head is the pope. Appointed by the pope is a cardinal, who serves for life as the appointed Grand Master. Laymen and clergy may be members of this Order. For clergy they have to be recommended by the local ordinary. Laymen have to be recommended by another member.

The Knights of Columbus is an organization of Catholic men founded by Friar Francis McGiveny in the nineteenth century in order help them financially. Membership is not a papal honor or award. Presently, Friar McGiveny's case is being opened for possible canonization. The Knights of Columbus is one of the largest Catholic fraternal orders in the world. It also maintains one of the largest insurance programs for knights, offering life insurance and retirement plans.

Question 287. What are the Seven Sorrows and Seven Joys of Mary?

The devotion to the Mother of Sorrows (*Mater Dolorosa* in Latin) goes back to antiquity. The Seven Sorrows of the Blessed Mother (Virgin Mary) is a devotion which goes back to the early Middle Ages. The Servite Order (Servants of Mary) promoted it in Monte Senario, Italy, as soon as the community was founded in 1233.

Chaplets (which look like rosaries but have seven sets of seven beads each instead of five sets of ten beads) are used to help Catholics meditate on the seven sorrows Our Lady endured. They begin with the Prophecy of Simeon in the Gospel of Luke when the old man predicted that "a sword shall pierce your heart," and continue with the escape of baby Jesus, Mary, and Joseph fleeing into Egypt to escape the deadly clutches of Herod; they go on to the three days Christ was thought lost at the age of twelve (a mother's nightmare, then and now, not knowing if he was kidnapped, sick, injured, or dead) and continue with Jesus' crucifixion, death, and burial (the worst day for a mother—the burial of her only child).

The Prophecy of Simeon (Luke 2:25–35)
The Flight into Egypt (Matthew 2:13–21)
Jesus is Lost in the Temple for Three Days (Luke 2:41–50)
Jesus meets his sorrowful mother on the way to Calvary (Luke 23: 27–29)
Mary at the foot of the Cross witnesses the Crucifixion and Death of Jesus (John 19:25–30)
The dead body of Jesus is taken down from the Cross and placed in the arms of His sorrowful mother (John 19:39–40)
The burial of Jesus by His sorrowful mother (Luke 23:50–56)

The Seven Joys of the Blessed Mother are also known as the Franciscan Crown or Seraphic Rosary. It is a devotion that recalls seven joyful events in the life of the Blessed Virgin Mary (in contrast to the previous Seven Sorrows). Franciscans in the fifteenth century during the era of Saint Bernardino of Siena (1380–1444) promoted this throughout Italy. Like the rosary, this chaplet has ten Hail Mary's in each set, but like the chaplet of Seven Sorrows, there are seven sets rather than five.

The Annunciation to the Blessed Virgin Mary (Luke 1: 26–33, 38)
The Visitation of the Virgin Mary to her cousin, Saint Elizabeth (Luke 1:39–45)
The Birth of Jesus (Luke 2:6–12)
The Adoration of the Magi (Matthew 2:1–2, 10–11)
Jesus is Found in the Temple (Luke 2:41–50)
The Resurrection of Christ from the grave (Mark 16:1–7)
The Assumption of the Blessed Mother (Virgin Mary) into Heaven, and her Coronation as Queen of Heaven and Earth (Luke 1:48; Revelation 12:1)

Question 288. What is Opus Dei?

Opus Dei is a Personal Prelature in the Catholic Church. Canon 294 of the 1983 Code of Canon Law states that Personal Prelatures "are composed of deacons and priests of the secular clergy. Their purpose is to promote an appropriate distribution of priests, or to carry out special pastoral or missionary enterprises in different regions or for different social groups." Canon 296 says that "lay people can dedicate themselves to the apostolic work of a personal prelature by way of agreements made with the prelature."

A Catholic organization, Opus Dei (Latin for "work of God" or "God's work") was founded by Saint Josemaria Escriva in 1928. Today, there are eighty seven thousand members, 98 percent of whom are laity and only 2 percent of whom are clergy. Of the lay majority, 70 percent are called *supernumeraries*, and they are average and typical married or single Catholic men and women who seek to sanctify their daily work. Only 30 percent are *associates* or *numeraries,* who freely embrace celibacy but do not take vows (evangelical counsels) and are not ordained. Numeraries live in Opus Dei study centers and share their financial resources with the Prelature to support the various apostolates that uphold, spread, and live the Catholic faith. Priests of the Personal Prelature are selected from the lay associates and numeraries to be ordained by the Prelate of Opus Dei. Diocesan or Religious priests cannot incardinate into the Prelature but can become a part of Opus Dei as a *cooperator,* or a member of the sacerdotal society of the holy cross.

Despite the conspiratorial paranoia generated by some fictional books and movies such as *The DaVinci Code,* Opus Dei is not a secret society in the Church; it is not the Vatican equivalent of the CIA or the KGB; and it has no albino assassin waiting for orders to whack someone. The claims that it is a cult are based on distorted facts, preconceived ideas, prejudicial notions, and unsubstantiated complaints from disgruntled former members. The so-called secrecy of Opus Dei is that its members do not brag about or advertise their "work." Since 98 percent are laity and 70 percent are typical husbands and wives, blue- and white-collar workers from all races, nationalities, countries, and cultures, most of their work is what the rest of the world does for a living.

Opus Dei merely helps its members sanctify the world by sanctifying their daily work, be it at the office or factory, shop or store, home, or school. It does not involve proselytism, rather, it is simply doing your regular routine jobs and tasks well, to the best of your ability, with full attention and offering up and consecrating it to God. There is nothing really unique or special or different about Opus Dei spirituality—it's just about being a good, practicing Catholic, at home, at work, at school, and on vacation. Since Saint Joseph and the Virgin Mary spent 90 percent of their lives doing ordinary work (he as a carpenter and husband; she as a homemaker, wife, and mother), and they are considered the holiest people next to Christ Himself, then holiness must not necessarily come only from monasteries, convents, or rectories. If most of the world is called to a vocation of marriage or single life and only a small percentage to priesthood, diaconate, and consecrated religious life, then God must intend that ordinary people become holy in their ordinary lives. Opus Dei is unapologetically loyal to the Magisterium and to the pope and is completely orthodox in its theology and doctrine. What their opponents call "archconservative" is nothing more than fidelity to Holy Mother Church. And no, they do not torture themselves or others.

Question 289. Why do we need a church?

Catholicism believes in the necessity of the church. Church is a word we use for the building where Christians worship, but it is also the assembly of believers, from the Greek word *ekklesia*. So in one sense, the church is where Christians pray and at the same time the church is the actual gathering (congregation, assembly, community) of people, since Jesus said "where two or more are gathered in my name, there shall I be in their midst."

Jesus himself used the word "church" in the Gospel, especially in Matthew 16 when he said to Simon Peter, "I will build my church." Catholics regard the church as being founded by Christ; therefore it is His church. It is not the pope's church, not the bishop's church, and not the priest's church. It is not even the people's church. It is Christ's church.

The main purpose of the church is to continue the work and mission of Christ. Jesus was priest, prophet, and king who sanctified, taught, and governed in his work to redeem and save mankind. His church continues those three-fold missions of sanctifying, teaching, and governing. The church sanctifies by celebrating the seven sacraments instituted by Christ Himself. The church teaches through her magisterium (the official teaching authority of the pope and the bishops in union with him). The church governs and shepherds through the hierarchy, the chain of command from pope down to pastor.

Jesus entrusted the seven sacraments to the church to protect and to faithfully celebrate. It was the church to whom Jesus entrusted divine revelation, both sacred scripture and sacred tradition. While there is an institutional dimension to the church because of its external structure (laws, customs, vocabulary, leadership), the spiritual is primary. The church is often called the primordial sacrament. While not one of the seven sacraments, the church is like a sacrament in that it was founded by Christ and also communicates grace (through the administering of the sacraments).

Saint Paul uses the analogy of a body to describe the church. Jesus is the head; we are the members, like our hands, fingers, toes, feet, eyes, ears, lungs, and heart are members of our physical bodies. Pope Pius XII elaborated further by calling the church the Mystical Body of Christ. A physical body is limited to time and space, but a mystical body stretches from the past through the present toward the future. The Gospel of Matthew describes Christ's Second Coming and the Final Judgment as akin to a shepherd separating sheep from goats. The "sheep" go on the right and enter heaven; the "goats" go to the left and are condemned to hell. But what determines whether one is considered a sheep or a goat? In essence Jesus asks: "When I was hungry, did you give me something to eat? When thirsty, something to drink? Naked, and something to wear? Sick or imprisoned, and visit me? Homeless, and give me shelter?" The message here is that whenever a believer does something good for another person, he does it for Christ, since all the members compose the one mystical body of Christ, the church—the people of God united in baptism. Likewise, if believers neglect anyone's needs, they neglect Christ.

The church on earth is sometimes called the Pilgrim Church or the Church Militant. Pilgrims are people who are on a journey; in the spiritual realm, this means that members of the church are on a journey from this world to the next. The word "militant" in "Church Militant" does not mean the church is hostile to nonmembers; it is not making war between Catholics and Protestants, or Christians and Jews or Muslims. It is militant in that the church is at war with sin and Satan. Racism, bigotry, terrorism, exploitation of women and children, pornography, abortion, euthanasia, sexual licentiousness, lust, greed, anger, and sin in all its forms are the enemies of the church; the weapons to fight this war on sin are truth, grace, mercy, and justice.

The term Church Suffering refers to the members of the church who are dead but in Purgatory, awaiting the glory of heaven. The Church Triumphant is all the saints and angels now in heaven. The Catholic Church therefore sees herself as essential to saving souls since she is the caretaker and guardian of the fullness of grace (all seven sacraments) and the fullness of truth (divine revelation through both sacred scripture and sacred tradition). The church is not just an organization or association. It is an organic community of living beings whom we call the children of God.

Often called Holy Mother Church, the image of mother that comes from the natural realm is mirrored in the supernatural. Our physical mothers gave birth to us; the mother church gives members their second birth by baptism. Our mothers nursed us from their breasts; the mother church feeds the body with the food from heaven, the Holy Eucharist (body and blood of Christ). Our mothers healed us when we were sick; the mother church heals through the sacrament of anointing. Our mothers taught us; mother church teaches through her magisterium. Our mothers disciplined us; the mother church has rules and laws for our benefit. Catholicism sees "church" as being much more than a building or an institution; it is the living, teaching, sanctifying, and shepherding mission of Christ continued through the ages. Membership has its privileges and its obligations.

A final useful analogy is to think of the church as a ship sailing toward the shore of heaven with the pope as captain and the baptized as crew. You can get there swimming alone, but a much easier and better way is to be on board the boat, helping each other.

Question 290. Why is the pope the head of the Church?

The pope is the visible head of the Catholic Church since he is considered the Vicar of Christ. Being Vicar is somewhat like being an ambassador. An ambassador is appointed by the king, president, or prime minister of a nation, to represent the head of state in another country. The pope is ambassador or Vicar of Christ in that he represents Jesus to all the believers on earth. He has been given authority from Christ to act in the name and in the person of Christ.

Catholic theology teaches that Jesus had a three-fold mission: prophetic (to teach), priestly (to sanctify), and kingly (to govern, rule, or shepherd). The Catholic Church continues the same prophetic mission of Christ in her teaching authority (called the magisterium, from the Latin word for teacher, *magister*). She continues the same priestly mission through the Seven Sacraments, and she continues the same kingly mission in her hierarchy (pope, bishops, and pastors).

As Vicar of Christ, the pope possesses full, supreme, immediate, and universal authority to run the Church. This means that he can create or suppress dioceses; appoint or depose bishops; name cardinals; and create, suppress, or interpret church law. He cannot create, change, or eliminate any Divine Law (like the Ten Commandments) or the Natural Moral Law (like the immorality of abortion or euthanasia); however with any human, man-made ecclesiastical (church) laws, he has the last and final word. There is no appeal above the pope's authority, since he is considered the Vicar of Christ on Earth.

In addition to being the Vicar of Christ, the pope is simultaneously the bishop of Rome. The first pope (the first bishop of Rome) was Saint Peter. He was martyred in Rome under the Emperor Nero around 64 AD. If Saint Peter had remained in Jerusalem for his entire life, then the bishop or patriarch of Jerusalem would be pope today. Peter preached and served the Christian community in Rome. His bodily remains are buried directly under the altar of Saint Peter's Basilica in Rome, the Church where the pope most often celebrates Mass. After Peter died, his successor, Linus, took over as bishop of Rome. He was followed by Cletus and Clement and so on. Since Saint Peter, there have been 266 popes, with Pope Benedict XVI being the current one (which also makes him the 265th successor of Saint Peter).

Jesus said, *"Blessed are you, Simon bar-Jonah. For flesh and blood has not revealed this to you, but my heavenly Father. And so I say to you, you are Peter, and upon this rock I will build my church, and the gates of the netherworld shall not prevail against it. I will give you the keys to the kingdom of heaven. Whatever you bind on earth shall be bound in heaven; and whatever you loose on earth shall be loosed in heaven"* (Matthew 16:18–19). What we cannot see in the English version is better seen in the Greek since the name "Peter" in Greek is *Petros,* and the Greek word for "rock" is *petra.* Peter, therefore, means "rock."

Catholics interpret Matthew 16 to mean that Saint Peter and his successors (the popes) have full authority to teach (papal infallibility), to govern (papal primacy), and to preside over all acts of sacred liturgy. Each of these successors to Peter acquired these powers the moment he became pope.

When the Roman Empire's three-hundred-year persecution of Christians was brought to an end with the Edict of Milan in 313 by Constantine, the bishop of Rome became a prominent figure. He and the patriarchs of Jerusalem, Antioch, Alexandria, and Constantinople, were given highest honors among their peers. When the Western empire fell to the Barbarians at the sack of Rome in 476 AD, only the church remained intact. Roman law, government, and culture collapsed, yet it was the bishop of Rome who retained respect, honor, and authority even after the Latin Emperor abdicated. Pope Leo (I) the Great convinced the fierce and ferocious Attila the Hun not to sack Rome in 452, and he did so without any army or weapons whatsoever. This is a clear indication of the respect and authority accorded to the bishop of Rome at that time.

The popes increased in power and prestige over time as more and more Barbarians invaded Europe, settled down, and began to form their own kingdoms and principalities. The patriarch (bishop) of Constantinople, on the other hand, while prominent and important, never got more powerful than his contemporary the Eastern Byzantine Emperor, since the Emperor kept the throne until well into the fifteenth century, when Emperor Constantine was deposed by the Ottoman Muslim Turks in 1453. When Pope Leo III crowned Charlemagne the first Holy Roman Emperor in 800 AD, it furthered the political prestige and influence of the papacy since many subsequent popes reminded emperors and kings that their temporal (or secular) authority was contingent on the religious authority to anoint those emperors and kings as monarchs. Excommunicated rulers were not owed any allegiance or obedience by their subordinates, hence, many secular rulers in Western Europe had no choice but to respect the position of the pope.

After the Papal States (those areas over which the pope was secular and temporal ruler) were captured and assumed into the new Italian nation under King Victor Emmanuel in 1870, the pope ceased to be a significant temporal power. Even after the Lateran Treaty of 1929, by which the Vatican City was recognized as a sovereign, independent nation (the smallest country in the world), the spiritual authority of the pope never diminished in the Catholic Church.

The First Vatican Council (1869–1870) defined the dogma of papal infallibility, but the Second Vatican Council (1962–1965) also taught that the teaching authority of the pope, even when noninfallible, required religious submission of intellect and will by the faithful (*Lumen Gentium* #25; CIC #749-750; CCC #891-892).

Question 291. Why do popes change their names?

Popes have changed their names to honor one of their predecessors or to take a Christian name if they were not born with one. It is an unwritten custom which does not have to be followed. No pope is required to change his name anymore than someone who is about to be confirmed has to take a different name for the sacrament. Traditionally, however, since most Catholics are baptized as infants, they have no choice in their first name (or baptismal name). When a person is confirmed, she can (and often does) choose another name for confirmation, usually taken from a saint whom she hopes to emulate and model her life upon. Popes can keep their baptismal or birth name, as did Saint Peter (the first pope) and all the popes who followed through to Pope Boniface II (the fifty-fifth pope) who reigned from

530–532 AD. The fifty-sixth pope was the first pope to change his name. His given name was "Mercury" from a pagan Roman god, and upon becoming pope he took the name "John" and became Pope John II (rather than Pope Mercury). No one told him he had to do it. He merely did it of his own free will. The next ninety-plus popes retained their baptismal names until 1009 AD, when Sergius IV started the custom of every pope taking a new name, regardless of what his birth or baptismal name was.

The current pope, Pope Benedict XVI, was born Joseph Ratzinger; before him, John Paul II was born Karol Wojtyla; John Paul I was Albino Luciani; Paul VI was Giovanni Montini; John XXIII was Angelo Roncalli; Pius XII was Eugenio Pacelli.

There is no rule which prohibits any name, but custom and respect for the first pope has dissuaded bishops of Rome from taking the name Peter. There are superstitious rumors and private revelations which the Church has never endorsed nor approved that claim the last pope before the end of the world will take the name Peter (hence, he would be Pope Peter II). Catholics must keep in mind, however, that if a newly elected pope were to take that name, it would necessarily not mean the end was near, since "we know not the day nor the hour."

Question 292. Can popes be impeached or retire?

A pope is elected for life unless he willingly and freely chooses to retire or resign (abdicate) his position. No one can force him to do so, however, since no other bishop, cardinal, or even ecumenical council has more authority than him. If he is sick and incapacitated, there is no "vice pope" to fill in or take over should the current pope die or resign. Sadly, there have been several bad popes in history, yet their immoral behavior was never promoted or deemed acceptable by the Church. As bad and as evil as some of these scoundrels were (members of the Borgia and Medici families, for example), committing sins of fornication, adultery, murder, theft, greed, and violence, not one of them ever tried to eliminate one of the commandments nor did any of them attempt to convince the faithful that their personal sinfulness was something to imitate. They may have had few or no scruples, yet they never taught as official doctrine a repeal of any of the moral laws of God. Some had their enemies poisoned; some had illegitimate children. None ever taught that what they did was okay.

Of the 266 popes in history, despite these bad popes, three times as many have been named saints, and the rest are considered reasonable and decent fellows. When a bad pope appears, there is only one remedy: prayer. Catholics must pray that the man repents from his evil and turns back to being good or pray that the good Lord takes him from this earth.

Pastors and bishops are asked to resign when they turn seventy-five, and cardinals are ineligible to vote in conclaves after they turn eighty. There is no such retirement age for a pope. His mission is for life, even when the latter years are filled with illness and suffering, as in the case of Pope John Paul the Great who shepherded the church to his dying breath.

Question 293. What happens when the pope dies?

There used to be a small silver mallet that was ceremonially tapped three times on the forehead of the dead pope while his baptismal name was called out, to make sure he was dead and not asleep. Today, the papal physician declares to the senior ranking cardinal when the pontiff is medically dead. In turn, this cardinal notifies all the eligible cardinals in the world (less than eighty years of age) and tells the world that the pope is dead. The actual funeral and burial of the pope take place four to six days after his death. This is followed by a nine-day period of mourning (called the *novemdiales*, Latin for "nine days"). The papal conclave to select a successor normally takes place fifteen days after the death of the pope, but it may be extended to a maximum of twenty days in order to permit other cardinals to arrive in the Vatican City.

Conclave is a word that comes from the Latin (*cum* + *clave* = with + key) since they literally lock the doors of the Sistine Chapel until the cardinals elect a new pope. There are no primaries, no campaigns, no debates. The cardinals can vote for anyone they choose. Ninety-nine percent of the time, they choose another cardinal, since they know each other to a degree; however, theoretically, any bishop, priest, deacon, or layman can be elected.

A two-thirds majority of the ballots cast are needed to elect a new bishop of Rome and pope of the Catholic Church. All votes are secret and if no one is elected, wet straw is mixed with the paper ballots and they are burned so the smoke which can be seen outside by the crowds gathered in Saint Peter's Piazza appears black in color, to signify that there is no pope yet. If a two-thirds majority is given to one man, then that cardinal is asked if he accepts. If he does, he is asked what name he will go by (like John Paul II or Benedict XVI) and the ballots are burned without wet straw so that the smoke seen outside by the crowds is white, meaning, "we have a new pope." Bells are rung to let the people know for sure.

Two votes take place each day, and if there is no one with two-thirds majority by the twenty-second ballot, then whoever receives a simple majority (50 percent plus one) wins. Once the winner accepts and chooses a name, the announcement is made on the balcony of Saint Peter's: *Annuntio vobis gaudium magnum: Habemus Papam!* ("I announce to you with great joy: we have a pope!")

If the cardinals elect a man who is not a bishop, then before being installed as pope, he must be ordained and consecrated a bishop, since the pope is always simultaneously the bishop of Rome. If a layman, he would need to be ordained a deacon, a priest, and then a bishop before being installed as pope. Traditionally, the triple tiara (triple crown) was used for centuries to "crown" popes, and the ceremony was called a papal coronation until recently when John Paul I declined to be crowned as did his next two successors, John Paul II and Benedict XVI. They preferred to have the *pallium* put on them, which is a stole-like band of lamb's wool that symbolizes the rank of metropolitan. Future popes, however, can certainly restore the practice of coronation, since the pope is the one who makes the rules. The reason for a triple crown dates back to the Middle Ages. In the days of the Holy Roman Empire, a single-level crown was worn by kings, and a double crown was worn by the emperor. The pope acquired a triple crown to signify his autonomy from secular control and his superior spiritual authority over the secular world. The crown also symbolized that in the papacy there was one person who embodied the legislative, the executive, and the judicial branches of power.

Question 294. What is the hierarchy of Catholic clergy?

The Sacrament of Holy Orders consists of deacons, priests, and bishops. The diaconate is the first level of Holy Orders whereby a man is ordained a deacon. The second level is the priesthood, and the third is the episcopate, where a priest is ordained a bishop. To become a bishop, a man must have previously been ordained as a priest, and to become a priest, a man must have previously been ordained as a deacon. Not all deacons become priests, however, just as not all priests become bishops.

While these three levels of Orders exist within the Church, there are more designations and subdivisions which are not part of Holy Orders per se in that they are not derived from the Sacrament. The hierarchy of the Catholic Church uses the ordained ministry since Canon Law stipulates only someone in Holy Orders (called a cleric, whether a deacon, priest, or bishop) can exercise governance in the Church. The clergy have the right, the duty, and the obligation to govern the Church while the laity are empowered to govern the secular world, especially in terms of government. Clergy are now prohibited from holding public office since that is the proper arena of laity. Likewise, only clergy (ordained deacons, priests, or bishops) can be named as pastors of parishes since the role involves ecclesiastical governance, which is the proper arena of clergy.

At the lowest level of the hierarchy are the deacons (permanent and transitional) and the parochial vicars (priests who help the pastor). Newly ordained priests (formerly called curates, assistant pastors, or associate pastors) are first assigned to a parish with the title of parochial vicar. The parochial vicar, along with any deacons assigned in that parish, provides assistance to the pastor by helping teach religion class, visiting the sick and bringing them Holy Communion, baptizing infants, preparing couples for marriage, performing the marriage ritual, conducting wake services and burial rites for the deceased, celebrating Benediction of the Blessed Sacrament, and preaching the homily at Mass.

The pastor is the priest assigned by the local bishop to care for the entire parish. He determines the time of the Masses, assigns the parochial vicar and deacon their duties, and signs the checks. Pastors have ordinary jurisdiction, which means they can baptize and marry any Catholic who lives in the territory of the parish. A parish is usually a geographical area comprised of several neighborhoods. An exception would be an ethnic or national parish; for example, an African American, Italian, or Polish parish where the language or culture is what defines membership rather than zip code.

Most parish pastors are diocesan priests and some are also titled Monsignor, an honor given by the pope for personal recognition. The parish pastor, whether a Monsignor or just a priest, is the one responsible for the spiritual and temporal welfare of the parish. Canon Law provides for the assistance of parochial vicars, deacons, and a parish council and a finance committee (both of which have no deliberative authority, but are consultative, giving advice and counsel to the pastor).

Several parishes in an area are usually designated as a deanery, and the dean is the priest given the responsibility of reporting and communicating matters of concern between the parishes and pastors of the deanery and the local bishop. The dean has no authority over the local pastors, but if one of them is derelict in his duties, the dean is to report this to the bishop and can then inform the pastor of the bishop's response.

Once Christianity became legal in the Roman Empire in 313 AD, the Church embraced the Roman system of law and imperial order to help govern a growing and soon-to-be worldwide religion. Hence, the designation of local pastors and parishes, deans and deaneries, bishops and dioceses, and so on often resembles the Roman model of the provincial delineation of authority.

All the deans of a diocese meet regularly with the local Bishop, who is considered the pastor of the diocese. A diocese is a geographical area, like a deanery, except that the borders are determined by the Vatican. Each bishop defines the area of deaneries and parishes since they fall within the boundaries of his jurisdiction.

Bishops are appointed by the pope and have authority over all the parishes, parochial schools, and associations (hospitals, nursing homes, and so on) that lie within their territory. The pope can send him a personal helper called an auxiliary bishop who can ordain and confirm but who has no power to govern outside of what he is specifically entrusted with by the local bishop. Bishops also have a vicar general and chancellor to help in the daily business of the diocese. There are also the College of Deans, the Board of Consulters, the Presbyteral Council, the Personnel Board, and the Finance Board which offer advice and counsel but have no deliberative authority of their own.

Several dioceses in a geographical region also comprise what is called a province, and that is led by the metropolitan archbishop of the nearest archdiocese. Like the dean, who keeps an eye on the parishes in his deanery and reports any problems to the bishop, the metropolitan does not directly interfere with the regular business of the local bishops, but does intervene if one misbehaves, in which case the matter is reported to Rome. Every five years, the bishops of the same province go to Rome for the ad limina visit, which is an official meeting with the pope and each local bishop to explain how things are going. The bishops of a country or nation assemble once or twice a year in an episcopal conference to discuss areas of concern, to network with each other, and occasionally to issue some guidelines for their people; in the USA, this is the USCCB (United States Conference of Catholic Bishops).

Every nation has a personal representative of the pope who acts as the papal ambassador to that country, and his residence is the equivalent of a foreign embassy. Countries that do not have diplomatic relations with Vatican City have apostolic delegates that represent the pope to the head of state and to the local bishops of that country. Where there is diplomatic recognition (via treaty or concordat), the papal ambassador is called the apostolic nuncio, and his embassy is called the nunciature. In addition to his diplomatic role with the national government, the nuncio also gathers names from which the pope selects bishops for that nation. He also reports any serious problems which need to be made known to the Holy Father.

The Vatican has various cardinals who help administrate the global and universal church. The curia and all the preceding elements of the hierarchy help in the governance of the Catholic Church. (See Questions #254 and #255 for more on cardinals and the curia.)

Question 295. Is the Church a monarchy or a democracy?

It is neither. The Catholic Church is not a democracy nor a republic since it was not founded by human beings like secular nations are. It was founded by Jesus Christ, who personally entrusted the fullness of His authority to Saint Peter and his successors. Christ also commissioned the apostles to help govern the local churches. Their successors, the bishops, work in union with and in obedience to the successor of Saint Peter, the pope (bishop of Rome).

Lay parishioners do not elect their leaders (pastors) as they would in a democracy, and priests do not choose their bishops. The authority of the Church comes from God, who entrusted it to the Hierarchy of the Church (the pope and bishops). The Church is not a monarchy, either, because the pope does not name his successor. The College of Cardinals elects the new pope. The Catholic Church is unique in that other religions are governed by synods (councils of bishops), boards, or committees. Catholicism, however, depends on the Petrine ministry (the papacy) in conjunction with the local bishops and the parish priests to effectively serve the spiritual needs of God's people.

Question 296. Why does the pope wear white?

Popes have not always worn white. Until Pope Saint Pius V (1566–1572), the bishops of Rome wore Cardinal robes of scarlet red, but to distinguish themselves from the other Cardinals, their robes had white ermine trim. Pius V had been a Dominican friar before he was elevated to cardinal, and Dominicans wear all-white habits. When he became pope, Pius V retained his white wardrobe and modified it for his new assignment as pope. Since that time, all popes have worn an all-white cassock with white zucchetto (skullcap). Had Pius been a Franciscan friar instead of a Dominican, his brown habit would have resulted in the popes wearing a brown cassock. (Cardinals, by the way, wear scarlet red to represent their willingness to die for the pope.)

Question 297. What is ecumenism?

Ecumenism is the effort of the Church to build bridges of dialogue between other religions and itself. It is not a plan to establish a single, lowest-common-denominator religion where doctrines and disciplines are diluted and compromised so that anyone and everyone can fit in. Ecumenism acknowledges the historical realities of mistakes and abuses made by individuals within the church and the disunity which now exists, especially among the numerous Christian denominations. (See Questions #211 and #232 for more on how these divisions and denominations arose.)

Catholic ecumenism does not try to impose unity, nor does it pretend complete unity exists. Ecumenical work seeks to heal old wounds of division, but not by altering doctrine. It seeks cooperation and mutual respect wherever possible. Charitable works of mercy have been jointly done by Catholic charities and Lutheran social services, for example. Thanksgiving prayer services have been held across America where Protestants, Catholics, Jews, Muslims, and others gather and express gratitude for the blessings God has sent to our nation.

Ecumenism seeks to avoid name-calling, and rather than presenting doctrines in an either-or context, tries to show that Catholicism firmly believes she has the fullness of truth and grace, but that other churches also have some truth and some grace. So, it is no longer "We're right, and you're wrong;" rather, it is "We have the full and complete story." Since the Eastern Orthodox Church has valid sacraments, the efforts of reunifying them with the Latin Roman Catholic Church were a high priority to Pope John Paul the Great and now to Pope Benedict XVI as well. Union with Protestants is more problematic due to the enormous and significant differences of doctrine, discipline, and worship. Yet popes and councils have never stopped making efforts to work together as fellow Christians to feed the poor, minister to the sick, and work for peace.

Question 298. How can the Church be a "perfect society" when its members are sinners?

The phrase "perfect society" (*societas perfecta* in Latin) that is sometimes used to describe the Catholic Church is not meant to identify Catholics as if they were perfect. It does not even mean that Catholics are somehow better than anyone else, since they're not. All men and women are equal in terms of their human dignity, worth, and value in the eyes of God and the Church.

"Perfect" in this context does not refer to moral perfection. When an organization, association, or group provides everything the members need, it is considered a perfect society. Similarly, since the Church, founded by Christ Himself, has all seven sacraments (the fullness of grace), the totality of Divine Revelation as found in both sacred tradition and sacred scripture (fullness of truth), she perfectly provides for all the spiritual needs of all her members; they do not need to go to any other institution to have their spiritual needs met.

The federal government only provides for some of our temporal needs, so it cannot be called a perfect society. We need state and local governments in addition to federal. Even though a shopping mall may have every kind of store, restaurant, and bank available, it is not "perfect" since we need more than just clothes, food, and things. We also need schools for education and hospitals for healing. The Church, however, has everything each member needs for his spiritual life and health. The teaching authority (magisterium), the sacraments and divine worship (liturgy), and the hierarchical structure give those who belong to the Church exactly and completely what they need, namely grace and truth.

Obviously, the leaders of the Church (from popes to pastors) have never been nor ever will be perfect or sinless. The members (from laity to clergy and religious) are not perfect, either. Yet the Church perfectly provides what her members need—maybe not what they want, but what they need. This is the only correct interpretation of the phrase "perfect society."

Question 299. Do pets go to heaven?

Only man (male and female) has an immortal soul, and only man is made in the image and likeness of God. When Jesus Christ, the Second Person of the Holy Trinity, became man, thus divinity and humanity were united, and men and women were redeemed and saved. When a human dies, only their body dies; their immortal soul continues to exist. Particular judgment happens immediately and the soul goes to heaven, purgatory, or hell.

We do know that only angels and human beings can go to heaven, since only angels and man have immortal souls. Animals have souls, but not immortal ones. Animals were not made in the image and likeness of God, and Jesus Christ is not their Lord and Savior. Does this mean that those in heaven will never see Sylvester the cat or Spot the dog ever again? No; the Church has never taught nor decided what happens at the end of time. (For more on heaven and resurrection, see Questions #51 and #52.)

While not by dogma, doctrine, or even official teaching, most theologians speculate that after resurrection of all the dead, the just and righteous souls in heaven will have their glorified bodies reunited with their immortal souls, and God will also allow us to enjoy our former pets as we will also enjoy good food, music, and all that is good that God created.

Only the damned in hell, who will also have their bodies reunited to their immortal souls, will be deprived of any pleasure or happiness. They will get bad food, smell rotten odors, hear horrible noise, and feel painful cold and heat. Their beloved pets will not join them (but the nasty neighbor's dog just might).

Question 300. Are Catholics Christian?

Yes, Catholics are Christian, as are Protestants and Eastern Orthodox Christians. A Christian is someone who professes the belief that Jesus Christ is the Son of God and that He is Lord and Savior of mankind. Christians believe in the divinity of Christ and in His humanity (that Jesus is God and Man). They also believe in the doctrine of the Holy Trinity—that there is only One God, yet that one God is also three Persons (Father, Son, and Holy Spirit). Catholics also believe, as do all Christians, that the Bible (sacred scripture) is the inspired, inerrant written Word of God.

Some non-Catholic Christians accuse Catholics of not being Christian because they misinterpret some Catholic teaching or practice and judge it to be contradictory to Christian belief. For example, Catholics do not worship Mary, but are accused of it often. (For more on this, see Question #39.)

Catholicism does not see itself as another variety of Christianity as many Protestant denominations see themselves. Catholics are not better, smarter, holier, or more fun than Protestants, Orthodox, Jews, or Muslims. Catholicism as a religion does see herself as having and providing more for her members, and the Church believes she can give all that her members need for their spiritual life.

Index

About the Authors

Rev. Fr. John Trigilio, Jr., PhD, ThD, a native of Erie, Pennsylvania, is pastor of Our Lady of Good Counsel (Marysville, Pennsylvania) and St. Bernadette Catholic Churches (Duncannon, Pennsylvania). He attended St. Mark High School Seminary and College Seminary, Gannon University, Holy Apostles Seminary, and Mary Immaculate Seminary and earned a Bachelor of Arts (BA), Master of Divinity (MDiv), Doctor of Philosophy (PhD) in Mediaeval Philosophy, and Doctor of Theology (ThD) in Biblical Studies. Father Trigilio was ordained a priest for the Diocese of Harrisburg (Pennsylvania) in 1988 and is the current President of the Confraternity of Catholic Clergy. He also cohosts two weekly television and radio series on the Eternal Word Television Network (EWTN): *Web of Faith* and *Crash Course in Catholicism*. He also serves as a theological consultant and online spiritual advisor for EWTN. He's been listed in *Who's Who in America* in 1993 and *Who's Who in Religion* in 1999 and is a member of the Fellowship of Catholic Scholars and former member of the Canon Law Society of America, and is a Fourth Degree Knight of Columbus and a Cooperator in Opus Dei.

Rev. Fr. Kenneth D. Brighenti, PhD, a native of New Britain, Connecticut, is pastor of Saint Ann Catholic Church (Raritan, New Jersey). He attended Holy Apostles Seminary, Mary Immaculate Seminary, and Seton Hall University and Seminary and earned a Bachelor of Arts (BA), Master of Divinity (MDiv), and Doctor of Philosophy (PhD) in Theology. Father Brighenti was ordained a priest for the Diocese of Metuchen (New Jersey) in 1988 and served as a U.S. Naval Reserve Chaplain for ten years. He is the Managing Editor of *Sapientia* magazine, a member of the Board of Directors for the Confraternity of Catholic Clergy, and a Third Degree Knight of Columbus. Fr. Brighenti cohosts the weekly TV and radio series on EWTN called *Crash Course in Catholicism* with Fr. Trigilio and both of them have coauthored the following books: *Catholicism for Dummies* (2003); *The Everything Bible Book* (2004); *Women in the Bible for Dummies* (2005); *John Paul II for Dummies* (2006); *101 Things Everyone Should Know About the Bible* (2006); *Frauengestalten in Der Bibel Fur Dummies* (2006, German); *Katholizismus Fur Dummies* (2006, German); *Le Catholicisme pour les Nuls* (2006, French); and *Katholicisme voor Dummies* (2006, Dutch).